W0246797

PENGUIN MODERN CLASSICS
MY NAME IS RADHA

Saadat Hasan Manto, the most widely read and the most controversial short-story writer in Urdu, was born on 11 May 1912 at Samrala in Punjab's Ludhiana district. In a literary, journalistic, radio scripting and film-writing career spread over more than two decades, he produced twenty-two collections of short stories, one novel, five collections of radio plays, three collections of essays, two collections of personal sketches and many scripts for films. He was tried for obscenity half a dozen times, thrice before and thrice after Independence. Some of Manto's greatest work was produced in the last seven years of his life, a time of great financial and emotional hardship for him. He died several months short of his forty-third birthday, in January 1955, in Lahore.

Muhammad Umar Memon is professor emeritus of Urdu literature and Islamic studies at the University of Wisconsin-Madison. He is a critic, short-story writer, translator and editor of the *Annual of Urdu Studies*. He has translated the best of Urdu writers. His most recent translation is *Collected Stories*, a selection of stories by Naiyer Masud.

MY NAME IS RADHA

RADHA

THE ESSENTIAL MANTO

TRANSLATED FROM THE URDU BY

MUHAMMAD UMAR MEMON

PENGUIN BOOKS

An imprint of Penguin Random House

PENGUIN BOOKS

USA | Canada | UK | Ireland | Australia
New Zealand | India | South Africa | China | Singapore

Penguin Books is part of the Penguin Random House group of companies
whose addresses can be found at global.penguinrandomhouse.com

Published by Penguin Random House India Pvt. Ltd
4th Floor, Capital Tower 1, MG Road,
Gurugram 122 002, Haryana, India

Penguin
Random House
India

First published in Penguin Modern Classics by Penguin Books India 2015
This edition published 2016

Introduction, selection and translation © Muhammad Umar Memon 2015

All rights reserved

10 9 8 7 6 5 4 3 2

This is a work of fiction. Names, characters, places and incidents are
either the product of the author's imagination or are used fictitiously,
and any resemblance to any actual person, living or dead, events or
locales is entirely coincidental.

ISBN 9780143426806

Typeset in MinionPro by Manipal Digital Systems, Manipal

Printed at Repro India Limited

This book is sold subject to the condition that it shall not, by way of trade
or otherwise, be lent, resold, hired out, or otherwise circulated without the
publisher's prior consent in any form of binding or cover other than that in
which it is published and without a similar condition including this
condition being imposed on the subsequent purchaser.

www.penguin.co.in

MIX
Paper from
responsible sources
FSC® C047271

This is a legitimate digitally printed version of the book and therefore might not
have certain extra finishing on the cover.

Contents

Contents

Preamble

> Any literary work that aspires to the condition of art must forget
> politics, religion, and, ultimately, morals. Otherwise it will be
> a pamphlet, a sermon, or a morality play.
>
> —GUILLERMO CABRERA INFANTE

By common consensus of most Urdu critics and readers of fiction,
Saadat Hasan Manto (1912–55) is unquestionably the pre-eminent
Urdu short story writer of the first half of the previous century. And
even now the popularity of this iconic writer has not waned. He is avidly
read and admired across the South Asian subcontinent and is also well
known overseas, thanks to the many translations of his choicest work
into English and other European languages. A prolific writer and, in his
early years, a translator and journalist, he managed to produce in his
short life of only forty-three years an enormous literary corpus, mostly
short stories, but also plays and works of non-fiction, collected in five
fat tomes of roughly a thousand pages each—an amazing testimony to
the astonishing range of the author's thematic reach!

Born in Ludhiana in British India, Manto started work as a member
of the editorial staff of *Masāwāt*, an Urdu daily published from his
native Ludhiana. In 1936 he moved to Bombay to work as a scriptwriter
for films before moving on to Delhi in 1941. Here, he joined the Urdu
Service of All India Radio and wrote radio plays. The following year
saw him back in Bombay, where he resumed his earlier work for the
film industry.

With the political situation in Bombay deteriorating rapidly in the aftermath of Partition, and communal rioting having erupted across the country, Manto felt constrained to leave for Pakistan in 1948. The move does not appear to have been motivated by ideological reasons. In Bombay, Manto had enjoyed relative prosperity and at times even abundance. In Pakistan he was reduced to living in financial straits, made worse by his chronic dependence on alcohol, which led to cirrhosis of the liver that eventually claimed his life.

Manto's short fiction offers a wealth of thematic diversity. However, he is chiefly—perhaps even exclusively—remembered as a writer on Partition and prostitutes. The present selection seeks to correct this reductionist impression of a writer who is concerned more with the unique substance of his characters than with social problems and political events as the mainstay of his creative work. No surprise if he has titled some of his major stories with their protagonists' names. This book, therefore, presents an assortment of the author's fictional and non-fictional writing as well as three pieces by two Urdu critics. The presence of the latter may seem unconventional, if not entirely out of place, in a book that purports to be a selection of his short stories.

A translator's choice is determined no doubt by his preferences, biases and idiosyncrasies; mine being no exception. Some of Manto's best-known stories are here followed by a few that are less often talked about. They have been chosen to give, hopefully, a more rounded and balanced view of the author's creative work, its delightful diversity and its underlying assumptions.

In the non-fictional pieces the author speaks directly about himself, his literary milieu and, in some, he clarifies, among other things, his position regarding the alleged 'obscenity' in his work—a charge frequently hurled at him by the Progressives and one that landed him, by his own admission, in the courts of law, both during British India and, later, in Pakistan, five times. The pieces also give us some idea, in a style daubed with pain and occasional humour, about the man Manto was, about his uneasy relationship with the Progressive establishment, and his immense reluctance and pain at leaving Bombay, the city he loved.

Included here are two pieces by critic Muhammad Hasan Askari (1919–78), 'Communal Riots and Our Literature', and 'Marginotions', which he contributed as a preface to Manto's collection of Partition vignettes *Siyāh Hāshiye* (Black Margins). Partition? Yes, but only as a convenient classificatory term. In essence they are little stories of individuals who each work in unexpected ways when flung in the midst of a harrowing event.

Askari's pieces are important for two reasons: (a) they critically examine the tenor of much of Urdu fictional writing inspired by Partition and show its inherent conceptual fallacies and weaknesses resulting from limiting the event to merely one of its offshoots, namely, the communal rioting and its toll in human lives and property, without any regard for its effect on both the perpetrator and the victim of oppression which, he argues, cannot by itself constitute a valid subject of literature; and (b) the uniqueness of Manto in dealing with it in purely human terms, in the actions of the oppressor and the oppressed, with a neutrality few among his contemporaries writing on the subject could rival.

The last piece, 'Recounting Irregular Verbs and Counting She-Goats', is presented as a defence of Manto against the charge of 'obscenity'.

Over the years a thick layer of interpretive fog has slowly accumulated around Manto's work. It has quite obscured the notion of (a) literary autonomy and self-sufficiency, and (b) the primary allegiance of a writer to his calling. Social scientists and historians and, now, even experts of psychoanalysis have jumped into a terrain whose natural custodians appear to have, by and large, lowered their guards and abdicated their responsibility. To a degree it was perhaps inevitable. Where Premchand, importantly, finalized as a dialectical necessity the short story's impending break with the cloying romanticism in which such writers as Sajjad Haidar Yildirim, Niaz Fatehpuri and Laam Ahmad had plunged it, he also saddled it with a reformist purpose, later embraced in earnest by the Indian Progressive Writers. Manto, by temperament, and even more by the demands of his calling, simply could not accept any social, political, or religious purpose as the primary concern of his writing. But challenged so often as he was by his detractors and just as often put into the dock for the charge of obscenity, he felt compelled to vindicate himself by repeated attempts to explain the underlying

assumptions of his art. This never allowed the discourse to rise above
the narrow confines of literature as socio-politically determined. An
impression was created that his writing did have a sleazy or noble
purpose, but purpose all the same, which he managed to obfuscate by
eloquent casuistry.

In his delightful little book *Letters to a Young Novelist*, Mario Vargas
Llosa describes the writer as someone afflicted with a 'tapeworm'. His
own life—why, even his own will—is forfeit to this creature; whatever
he does is for the sake of this grisly monster, and he feeds off of himself
for his themes, like the mythical 'catoblepas'. So writing is a calling
and one writes from an inexorable inner compulsion, unlike the
'graphomaniacs' Milan Kundera has deplored. The compulsion arises
from what some might call the wayward desire to see a different world
in place of the real, with its inherited values and mores and certainties
that admit to no contradiction in human action and stifle questioning.

One understands the world through the prism of one's own
imagination, which only brings forth outcroppings of subliminal
desires rehabilitated or transplanted in imaginative geography. For
most Manto critics, the writer and the world are the only two terms
of the equation—the substantial agency of human imagination that
mediates between the two is routinely thrown overboard.

Strangely, though, Manto's stories do easily lend themselves to
such easy distortion because of their deceptive proximity to workaday
life (and yet the external reality of the surface is often subverted in the
subterranean landscape of his work so subtly that it provokes doubt and
ambiguity in what was taken as a straightforward matter). No one asks,
not even the critic: Why write stories if all you want is to substantiate
reality as it is? Is that what stories are meant to do? Or are they supposed
to mount an exploration into the existential situation of the character
(and discover, in Kundera's words, what the novel—read fiction—alone
can discover)? Is fiction not expected to create parallel worlds? Or, at
the very least, scramble the elements of existing reality and conjure
them back to life in dizzying combinations whose entire geometry is
drawn from a playful imagination delightfully irreverent to the rules of
conventional values and modes of thinking?

It is easy to interpret a story through reference to something outside
of itself (say, a political or social event), but far more difficult to analyse
it through an exploration of its particular mode of being, its possibility

and promise—indeed its poetics. Literary critics are a sad lot; not only is their work necessarily derivative and posterior to creation, it must also formulate its criteria of success and failure from the fictional work under consideration. Few Urdu critics have tried to delve deeper into the elusive poetics of Manto's creative world. Instead, most have attempted to analyse his stories by recourse to criteria that are organically at odds with the nature of fiction. Political events are not the measure of the success or failure of a work of art, but rather, whether or how well the work has lived up to its latent promise.

Manto may well have written 'Toba Tek Singh' following his brief stint in an asylum. Though doubtful, he may even have intended it to be read as 'a scathing indictment' of Partition. (I rather think Manto was quite taken with the character he had created and wanted to follow along with him on his existential odyssey, ready to be surprised by his every reality-defying move.) But should we read it as such? After all, paraphrasing Kundera, it is not the business of fiction to write the history of a society; it is very much its business to write the history of the individual. That Stalinism is criminal is evident to everyone, he says in 'The Making of a Writer', you do not have to yell it in the form of the novel. And judgement ('indictment') has no place in his calling. At day's end, what remains looming on the horizon is the larger-than-life image of the protagonist, Partition having shrunk back into the distance. In a paradoxical way, it is Bishan Singh who retroactively makes history meaningful, indeed inevitable, with an insight that quite escapes the historical narratives of the apocalyptic event, and not the other way around. History merely provides the occasion to discover some hitherto unknown aspect of human existence, some truth about the character. That is, precisely, what fiction does.

As for explaining away the work of a writer by relating it back to his biography, characters are seldom the mirror-image of the writer's persona. Even when they appear to bear strong resemblance to certain individuals around us, they remain entirely composite—something Manto has expressed himself:

Literature isn't a portrayal of an individual's own life. When a person sets out to write, he doesn't record the daily account of his domestic affairs, nor does he mention his personal joys and sorrows, or his illness and health. It's entirely likely that the tears in his pen-portraits belong to his afflicted sister; the smiles come from you, and the laughter from some down-and-out manual worker. To weigh them against one's own tears, smiles and laughter is a grievous error. Every creative piece seeks to convey a particular mood, a particular effect and a specific purpose. If that mood, effect and purpose remain unappreciated, the piece will be nothing more than a lifeless object.[*]

If Sahae, Mozel, Babu Gopinath, Toba Tek Singh, Radha, Janki or Saugandhi impinge upon our consciousness with indomitable force, it is precisely because, in the balance of his major works, Manto saw none of them as a typical representative of their social or religious group or as one shaped by its determinants. (Was Mozel a representative of the Jewish community of Bombay and her character shaped by its values?) More often, he saw each one in deathly opposition to the certainty of inherited values. Which, at any rate, is the business of fiction. If his characters behave contrary to conventional logic, it is because they act in consonance with fictional logic and 'a law that is stronger than the laws of reason and the world'. Only in the hospitality of fictional spaces can polarities coexist without one trying to eliminate the other. Manto's genius lay in recognizing these characters as discrete entities, and history, or social and religious determinants, as merely the backdrop against which each of them, in his or her own eccentric way, stumbled through their particular existential trek.

To read 'Mozel' as a story about Partition would be to ignore the simultaneous presence of the many contradictory forces and paradoxes in her complex personality. Partition did not give birth to Mozel or shape her behaviour; it only furnished Manto with the occasion to explore and subsequently reveal a truth about the eponymous character. Any traumatic event would have worked just as easily for such exploration and activated her inherent tendencies that only surface, unexpectedly, towards the end of the story.

Manto knew too well that most humans live and breathe in the obscuring haze of contradictory impulses and that certainties—the arbiter of human behaviour so predisposed to doling out reward and punishment—are the prerogative only of ideologues, whether religious or political. Fiction can ill afford certainties, and judgement on their

---

[*] Saadat Hasan Manto, 'Kasautī', in Saverā, No. 3 (n.d.), p. 61.

basis even less. Take, for instance, Sahae: 'A staunch Hindu, who worked the most abominable profession, and yet his soul—it couldn't have been more radiant.'* He was a pimp in Bombay who ran a brothel and dreamed of making thirty thousand rupees so that he could return to his native Benares and open a fabric shop. Religious devoutness here exists in perfect symbiosis with the demands of a 'filthy' profession. It is a meeting of opposites. In real life, a devout man would not come anywhere near a whorehouse, much less run it, though in the same life most people would display an amazing motley of contradictory impulses. Sahae will remain forever suspect to conventional morality. We may side with this morality but we cannot deny his behaviour as a possibility of being, even if it exists only in the liminal spaces of the imagination, even if we only admit to its nebulous existence grudgingly.

Can one call Esther's transformation towards the end of Sándor Márai's novel *Esther's Inheritance*† even remotely logical? Robbed and duped by the same swindler, 'that piece of garbage', all her life, she is still willing to sign her last possession over to Lajos. She does not believe a word of what he is saying, yet she finds that his statement—'there is a law that is stronger than the laws of reason and the world' (p. 143)—contains a substantial core of truth. In the real world, even if this ambiguous truth does not change anything, its potential existence cannot be barred from our consciousness. Many of Manto's characters, too, display such logical but entirely human contradictions.

Life is not the Straight Path leading to heaven for a writer. It is, rather, a trek riddled with potholes and detours and mind-boggling surprises, leading eventually to an infinite, mirror-encrusted maze of giddying, colliding images. The coffin has been lowered into the freshly dug grave for burial, the mourners stand around in a semicircle, the priest is only halfway through intoning his eulogy for the dearly departed when a 'neurotic gust of wind' lifts the hat off Papa Clevis's head and drops it at the edge of the grave. Eventually it will tumble into the grave, but for now Clevis, hesitating between should he or shouldn't he pick it up, lets his gaze crawl along the erratic course of the bobbing hat. The attention of everyone in the small band of mourners has wavered. No

---

* 'Sahae', in Saadat Hasan Manto, *Mantorāmā* (Lahore: Sang-e-Meel Publications, 1990), p. 24.

† Translated from the Hungarian by George Szirtes (New York: Alfred A. Knopf, 2008).

one is listening to the eulogy any more; instead their eyes are riveted on the comic drama unfolding before them. The funeral loses its gravitas and laughter is born.*

Such utter disregard for decorum, such hilarity in the most solemn moment of grief and loss—only a writer can think of such contrary situations because he is not beholden to the rules of conventional decorum. He cannot be tamed by the tyranny of conventional behaviour or some social, political or jingoistic agenda. Literature, as Manto says, is

> an ornament, and just as pretty jewelry isn't always unalloyed gold, neither is a beautiful piece of writing pure reality. To rub it over and over again on the touchstone like a nugget of gold is the height of tastelessness . . . [It] is either literature or it is the worst kind of offense . . . an outrageous monstrosity.†

And to those who censured him for immorality and obscenity, instead of delving into the tortuous by-lanes of his art, his unequivocal answer would be: 'By all means, call me names. I don't find that offensive—swearing isn't unnatural—but at least do it with finesse so your mouth doesn't begin to stink and my sense of decency isn't injured.'‡

Lamentably, too often Manto has been drafted into the service of one social or political issue or another. The greater part of the critical commentary on his writing has mainly focused on prostitutes (a social phenomenon) and Partition (a political event).

Of course the remnants of the Progressives and a fair bunch of those too eager to deny fiction its radical autonomy would likely rush to declare—teary-eyed, I might add—'Hatak' (Spurned) as yet another story about the debasement of women. They would go for the nearest truncheon, in the absence of a cleaver, to bash the head of a society intent on sending its womenfolk to eke out a living by selling their charms and the physical repository of those charms. They would not fail to stick

---

* This scene occurs in Milan Kundera's *The Book of Laughter and Forgetting*, translated from the Czech by Michael Henry Heim (Harmondsworth, Middlesex, England: Penguin Books, 1981), pp. 219ff.

† 'Kasautī', p. 60.

‡ Ibid.

a feather in Manto's cap for exposing this crass injustice, the sordid underbelly of society. And they would also dig up a motive for his doing this: infinite compassion for the downtrodden, disenfranchised female of the South Asian subcontinent.

To speculate on why a woman chooses to sell her body is the business of sociologists, to judge the morality of such a choice is the business of the custodians of morality. Is it also the business of fiction? Was it Manto's business? No, the business of fiction is to see what she makes of this life, independently of the circumstances that brought her to this choice.

In his non-fictional piece 'Iṣmat-Farōshī',* (selling of virtue: prostitution)—an impassioned defence of women who practise the world's oldest profession—Manto goes into great detail arguing vigorously for prostitution's similarity to every other profession, and hence, deserving of respect. We do not look down on a typist, or even a sweeper woman, why should we ride roughshod over a bawd? All three do what they do in order to earn a living. In other words, a prostitute does not forfeit her right to be an individual by the choice of her profession. We must go past her profession to see her human possibility.

In 'Spurned', Manto leaves the protagonist's reasons for selling her flesh entirely opaque, or rather, creatively vague, as any good writer would. He is not interested in telling us why she opted to become a *fille de joie*. Was it a forced or bad marriage? Had her husband ditched her and, thus disgraced, she could not return to her parental home? Was she abducted and raped? (This is precisely what happened to many Hindu women during Partition. Many interviews with such women in Ritu Menon's *Borders and Boundaries: How Women Experienced the Partition of India* attest to the fact that, after being repatriated to India, these women chose to live and die in an ashram rather than return to their ancestral homes and bring ill-repute to their families.) Or was it domestic abuse or sexual violence? Dire poverty? What? In a devilish vein, one might also posit that she turned tricks simply because she loved sex, though this possibility should quickly be ruled out because the story does not offer any compelling grounds for such an assumption. In fact, Saugandhi's 'mind considered sexual intimacy patently absurd', and yet

---

* In Saadat Hasan Manto, *Manto ke Mazāmīn* (Lahore: Idāra-e Adabiyāt-e Nau, 1966), pp. 155–72.

'Every limb of her body yearned to be worked over, to exhaustion, until fatigue had settled in and eased her into a state of delightful sleep.' No, Manto does not give us a clue. He refrains because it is not important for him or for us to know. On the other hand, he forecloses any possibility of our being tempted, or being rash enough, to ask by deftly slipping a tiny detail into the narrative: 'Of course, she didn't look quite as fresh and vibrant as she did five years ago when she lived with her parents, unencumbered by any cares whatsoever.'

So there was a time, not so long ago, when Saugandhi lived a carefree life with her parents. Between that time and selling her body in a seamy neighbourhood of Bombay there lies a dark abyss into which Manto does not delve, nor does he invite us to look. Whatever happened in the intervening period is anyone's guess, but any reason that might be suggested will have absolutely no bearing on the story or its protagonist. Manto, rather, wants us to know what happened this particular night when she was spurned and rejected by a pot-bellied seth who came along in his fancy car, pointed the beam of his flashlight at her, and sounded his disapproval with a cryptic 'Oh no!' Manto wants us to know how she dealt with this gut-wrenching denial of her being, this denial of who she was, by initiating a veritable ontology of selfhood.

A man feels the need for a woman, runs to the nearest brothel and finds himself one. End of story. Manto would not be doing that, would he? And if he were, what is the point of the story. No, he wants to deal with Saugandhi as a woman, yes, a woman very much her own, not simply some type that can be enlisted for a dramatic dressing down of society. What society is like is for us to decide, independently of whether it has any critical role to play in the story at hand. Manto wants to deal with Saugandhi as an individual—a *fille de nuit*, yes, but unlike any of her sisters in the profession. In her unexpected reaction lies the falsity of any overt or covert notion of an agenda to take society to task.

As it is, the greater number of Manto prostitutes really do not behave as one might expect them to. In the end, they vehemently resist categorization into a particular type. Many if not all—such as Siraj and Shakuntala—jealously guard their virginity by not letting any 'passengers' (Manto's favourite word for a prostitute's client) ride their train. And they all seem to crave love and suffer from its absence in their desolate lives. Siraj had willingly eloped with her lover, who ran away during the night leaving her asleep in the hotel. This clouded her entire existence. Only after she had exacted her vengeance—turning the tables on her fickle lover by spending a whole night with him and then abandoning him in like manner, throwing her burqa over him while he slept at that—could she recover. Society plays little, if any, part in this drama, or in the story 'Shārdā.' Sharda gives herself physically to Nazir in a manner he had never experienced before, but she is unwilling to enter the profession or allow her sister to enter it. When she leaves Nazir, who does not believe in love, she does so with a dignity few 'respectable' women could rival. Zeenat, the Kashmiri *kabutri* in 'Babu Gopinath', eventually settles down with the respectable Hyderabadi landowner Ghulam Ali. And Kanta opens the door for her pimp Khushia while she is stark naked. Khushia does not like this show of immodesty. 'You could have let me know you were bathing. I would have come back another time.' She smiles and throws every ounce of his male pride into a tumultuous vortex with her answer, 'When you said it was Khushia, I thought, "What's the harm. It's just our Khushia. Let him come in."'

And Navab of 'Behind the Reeds', as the narrator tells us, 'wasn't averse to her profession'. When her mother, or 'whoever she was', introduces her to her first man, the terribly simple and naive girl thinks that this is how young women 'were initiated into their youth'. She gets 'accustomed to her prostitute's existence' and believes that her life's ultimate purpose lay in sleeping with men, and she quite liked the expensive silks and jewellery they brought as gifts. There is no trace of regret in her acceptance of this life. But 'she was every bit an indecent young woman—which is how our noble and chaste ladies are wont to look upon her and her ilk—but truth be told, she didn't realize even for a moment that she was living a life of sin'.

If we look at these women as individuals, all the talk about society's role in reducing them to a life of ignominy and want loses much of its force. Manto doesn't use 'Spurned' as an occasion to spill his guts against society's treatment of 'fallen' women. (Nor do these women themselves indulge in this exercise.) He is far removed from handing out judgements. In fact, he would not even use the word 'fallen' to describe these women because of its judgemental overtones. Rather, he is using the story as an occasion to discover some truth about the person that Saugandhi is. And in doing so, he shrewdly guards his role as a narrator, never once surrendering his neutrality and objectivity. This is in contrast to a story such as 'Nannhī ki Nānī' (Tiny's Granny), where Ismat Chughtai has smothered the individuality of the granny and turned her into a veritable mouthpiece for the author to vent her righteous anger against society. Manto never allows his narrator to transform into an interventionist, not even when the narrator bears his own name, which happens quite often in his stories. At several points in the short story 'Sirāj', Manto purposely alerts us to the fact that as a writer-narrator he has no right to inject his own reactions and thoughts into the story. For instance, 'This was more than enough detail for me. How I reacted to it is my concern, not something I should tell you, not as a short story writer anyway.' And, 'I would rather not talk about the backstory my mind had woven for Siraj, [...].' What lingers in our minds after we are done reading 'Shārdā' is her immense grace and dignity, not how good she was at sex, but her love for Nazir. Giving herself so tenderly, so fully was a consequence of that love, not the result of some pathology of eroticism or promiscuity.

It is about time that we discarded the myth about Manto tacitly following some Progressive–Socialist–Reformist agenda in his fiction; if anything, he was following his own agenda as a writer true to his calling.

I believe it should be evident by now that at the time of writing, a writer's loyalty rests only with himself and his work, not with his society, country and his nation, which is not to deny his role as a citizen. Long ago Muhammad Hasan Askari, perhaps the single most perceptive early critic of Manto, had underscored this role in his article 'Communal Riots and Our Literature'[*] by graphically setting it apart from Manto's role as a writer. He gives the example of some French writers who had, during the tumultuous period of the Second World War, started to produce a series of underground books with the title *Les Éditions de Minuit*. They were given a major literary award after France became free but declined to accept it. Everything they had written, they said, was simply to serve the nation. It was not literature, nor had they written it as literature.

The fashionable, entirely unwarranted and uncritical classification of Manto's corpus by social scientists and historians into stories about (a) Partition and (b) prostitutes ignores the primary function of literature. As Askari comments:

[*] 'Fasādāt aur Hamārā Adab', in his *Insān aur Ādmī* (Aligarh: Educational Book Depot, 1976), pp. 139–49.

Actually, literature is indifferent to who is behaving like an oppressor and who is not. [. . .] Its business is to observe the internal and external behaviour of the oppressor and the oppressed during commission of oppression. Insofar as literature is concerned the external act of oppression and its equally external complements are meaningless. [. . .] These stories are not about communal riots (*fasādāt*). They are about human beings.[*]

Could one call Elie Wiesel's *Night* a novella about the Holocaust? Is it not rather about the little Jewish boy, the elect of God, who had, as François Mauriac puts it, 'lived only for God and had been reared on the Talmud, aspiring to initiation into the cabbala, dedicated to the Eternal'[†]— the boy who was condemned to witness the horror of the death of God in the depths of his soul and subsequently did not bow to Him?

The unwarranted preoccupation with society at the expense of the individual has, in my opinion, done grave injustice to Manto as a writer—injustice in the sense that socio-political analyses rarely rise above reductionist interpretations of works of literary art. What I have tried to do in my selection is to steer clear of such external determinants and see them as stories about particular individuals. This is reflected, I hope, in the way I have grouped the stories, and even more in the way Manto himself has chosen to title some of his major stories after the names of their protagonists (Radha, Janki, Siraj, Mummy, Khushia, etc.). I have tried to dispel, as best as I can, the notion that the only legacy Manto has left us is his pathological obsession with prostitutes and Partition and join those who wish to restore to his stories the dignity of a world created with love, immense imagination and humanity.

Manto's major stories, and recently some minor ones, have been translated so often that yet another translation would perhaps seem unwarranted. Initially I was hesitant to undertake this project. Would it be possible to transport into the target language in a readable way,

---

[*] Muhammad Hasan Askari, 'Hāshiya-ārā'ī', in Saadat Hasan Manto, *Mantonumā* (Lahore: Sang-e-Meel Publications, 1991), p. 748.

[†] See his Foreword, in Elie Wiesel, *Night* (New York: Avon Books, 1958), p. 7.

without making too many compromises, the particular ambience of some of his stories and their cultural specificity? Would I be able to tone down, suppress, add or subtract, rearrange content or rewrite simply as a concession to the sensitivities of the English reader? And I also did not think that it would be right to clutter a book of short stories with cultural notes in order to make a story properly glow and resonate for the reader. Some Manto characters breathe in a fictionally recreated cultural space of the Punjab. The swear words they use stubbornly resist translation and whatever may be found by way of their English equivalents sounds not just unnatural but grotesque. Take, for instance, 'santokh sar ke kachhve', 'Oaye Bābā Tal ke karāh parshād' or 'Oaye khinzīr ke jhatke' in 'The Last Salute'. Or the pun on the word 'kār' (car) and the compound 'kār-sāz' in 'Babu Gopinath', which does not mean 'car-maker' but rather one, usually God, who is able to find a way, put things right, or make something unexpectedly come true for you. I have therefore left them in the original. If I were to translate the sentence 'He heard her clear her throat and then start to sing the ghazal by Ghalib which begins with the line 'Nukta-chīñ hai gham-e dil . . .' ('Kingdom's End') as 'He heard her clear her throat, then in a very soft, low voice she sang him a song,' wouldn't the omission of this inconspicuous little detail about Ghalib and especially about the particular ghazal result in the loss of the allusion that has a bearing on the story? This verse of Ghalib indirectly suggests a lot about the state of the woman's mind and her emotions because in her culture women are not supposed to be so open and direct about their feelings for men. The generic word 'song' fails to summon up this complexity for the reader. It also suppresses another fact: Manto's enduring fascination with Ghalib, whose poetry he often quotes in his stories and his non-fiction pieces. Maybe all this is less important for the reader. For me it was not. I decided to bite the bullet. But, of course, I might have done a better job. I have tried to remain as close to the original as I possibly could. As for my failures, which are many, I beg the reader's indulgence.

Besides stories and non-fiction, Manto also wrote radio plays and at least one stage play, Is Manjhdār Mein (In This Maelstrom), for which he chose the subtitle 'A Melodrama'.

It is puzzling why Manto called it a 'melodrama', which it is not for a number of reasons. Eric Bentley, after rehabilitating 'tears' (which only reflect our anxiety not to appear vulnerable in this modern age) as a perfectly natural phenomenon and part of the human condition, defines the main ingredients of melodrama as *pity, fear of villain* and *exaggerated* or *elevated language*.* While there may be some *pity* for the central character Amjad—though pity alone does not, indeed should not, qualify a work as melodrama—there is no fear of the villain. The villain is just not there, let alone being superhuman or diabolic. Though melodramatic vision is paranoid[†] one does not have to be persecuted by a real flesh-and-blood villain; even the landscape can sometimes oppress and persecute. Manto's landscape, though, is invested with breathtaking beauty. More importantly, this beauty is not presented as axiomatic. It derives dialectically from the generally positive manner in which the characters react and respond to it. Then again, while a typical melodrama rarely moves beyond pity and fear, *In This Maelstrom* is not defined by this attribute. Although we do feel a certain sense of pity for Amjad, we feel greater sympathy for his wife Saeeda and wish for her beauty and youth, now hopelessly wasting away, to blossom.

The characters, too, are not the stock characters of a melodrama. Neither cast according to the 'Progressive' formula, nor defined by bourgeois *moeurs*, they vibrate with a life all their own. They are imbued with remarkable individuality and amazing independence of will, and reveal a complex psychology in their thoughts, feelings and actions. Thus Amjad, who has picked Saeeda from among countless other women to be his wife, knows that his choice amounts to no more than the impulse to pick up the finest thing in the market. As for loving her—that, he freely admits to the maid Asghari, he does not. Still this does not stop him from wondering: 'I can't understand why I want to keep her shackled in chains whose every link is as uncertain as my life.' Well aware of the illicit love between his wife and younger brother, he appears to be strangely free of the slightest trace of jealousy, so unlike, one might almost say, most men.

I do not agree with Mumtaz Shirin's contention that Saeeda is less a character than a 'symbol of beauty'.[‡] Surely she is an aesthetic

---

* In his *The Life of the Drama* (New York: Atheneum, 1979), pp. 195–218.

† Ibid., p. 202.

‡ See her 'Manto ki Fannī Takmīl', in her *Me'yār* (Lahore: Nayā Idāra, 1963), p. 277.

attribute, but she is also much more. She is both attractive and aware of her tremendous attraction for men. Nothing so extraordinary perhaps. However, where she parts company with a stereotypical young South Asian Muslim woman is when she 'unabashedly', though not without disarming directness and honesty, mentions to Asghari the desires raging inside her, and catalogues her frustrations. She says:

> I'm young. I'm beautiful . . . numberless desires surge inside me. For seventeen long years I've nurtured them with the nectar of my dreams. How can I stifle them? [. . .] Call me weak . . . cowardly . . . immoral. [. . .] I confess before you that I cannot ravage the garden of my youth, where the vein of every leaf and flower throbs with the hot blood of my unfulfilled desires . . .

And Asghari, the maid: her frequent caustic jibes at the crippled Amjad, in spite of knowing the extremely brittle state of his mind; her scathing, abrasive wit; and, above all, her hesitation in accepting Amjad's love even though she is in love with him herself—all these raise her above the meek and obsequious world of a South Asian domestic to the plane of a fairly complex personality.

Although Majeed is not fully developed as a character, in coveting the wife of his own brother he, too, appears to be refreshingly less typical.

Melodrama is often characterized by its use of an exaggerated—a heightened, lyrical—form of language. A declamatory, excessively rhetorical style of speech is no doubt noticeable in a couple of long-winding speeches by Amjad addressed to Saeeda at the mid-point in the play and to Asghari at the end, and in a single piece where Saeeda addresses Asghari. But in these instances the elevated language appears called for by event and situation, which it dialectically supports and enhances. It does not appear tired, crude or otherwise logically non sequitur. Moreover, 'Intensity of feeling', as Bentley says, 'justifies formal exaggeration in art' (p. 204). A brief sequence of emotionally charged utterances would be inadequate ground to place the work in the category of melodrama, or sob-stuff.

Finally, one thing is sure: We certainly do not get a 'good cry' or a good laugh out of the play. What we do get instead is the calm of a sobering moment in which our temporarily frozen senses—because of two suicides at the end—gradually thaw out to a sense of beauty and blossoming optimism towards life's continuity and renewal which is far in excess of our initial shock at the twin suicides. We come to accept, almost as a necessity, the suicides as the price life must pay to remain ongoing and whole. Thus the very subject of the play argues forcefully against its being a melodrama.

Manto, of course, is not interested in celebrating promiscuity per se, here as elsewhere. He, therefore, neither jeers at the invalid husband for the loss of his sexual prowess, nor, on the other hand, helps initiate the lovers in the ways of pleasure. By avoiding any explicit or implicit reference to actual sexual contact—though not to the fact of sexual attraction—between the lovers, he seems to give us a clue to his deeper purpose, which is to transcend the confining circumstances of self-indulgent sensual love itself and give it a creative, complementary role integral to the wider scheme of things.

Except for a few pieces, the balance of Manto's work presented here is taken from his collected works published in five volumes by Sang-e-Meel Publications of Lahore (1990–95 and 2004). Where this is not the case, the source has been cited in the footnote with the piece in question.

Generally, non-Urdu words (personal names, titles, etc.) have been spelled according to common sense and South Asian custom. Diacritics have been used sparingly in the Preamble and the three article towards the end of the book.

This book of translation owes a great deal to R. Sivapriya of Penguin. Her constant encouragement helped me overcome my initial hesitation to undertake yet another translation of Manto's stories. I would like to thank Moazzam Sheikh, who collaborated on our translation of the short story 'Barren', and my former students Wayne R. Husted and M. Azam Dadi for their collaboration in translating the play *In This Maelstrom* well over three decades ago. I would also like to thank Jane A. Shum for going over the manuscript and offering valuable suggestions for improvement. Shatarupa Ghoshal has a special claim to my deepest gratitude for her most careful editing of the manuscript and I acknowledge it with the greatest pleasure.

Muhammad Umar Memon
5 January 2015

My Name Is Radha

I am talking about a time when there was absolutely no hint of war anywhere. It happened eight, maybe nine, years ago, when, quite unlike today, madness had method and tumultuous events followed a predictable course. Today—well, tumultuous events occur without rhyme or reason and throw everything upside down.

I was then employed in a film company at a monthly salary of forty rupees. Life was chugging along smoothly. I would show up at the studio at ten, feed the villain Niaz Muhammad's two cats two paise worth of milk, write banal dialogues for a banal film, joke around for a while with the Bengali actress, 'the nightingale of Bengal' as she was called in those days, fawn over Dada Gora, the greatest director of his time, and return home.

Like I said, life was chugging along smoothly with the usual ups and downs. The proprietor of the studio, Hurmuzji Framji, a whimsical man of Iranian origin with big fat ruddy cheeks, was head over heels in love with a middle-aged Khoja woman. Feeling up the breasts of every newly arrived girl was his habitual pastime. There was this Calcutta whore, a Musalman, who was carrying on with her director, sound recordist and storywriter all at the same time. Carrying on meant that the tender affections of all three would remain reserved only for her.

The shooting of *Ban ki Sundri* was in progress. Every day, after feeding the villain Niaz Muhammad's cats the two paise worth of milk—God only knows what kind of impression he expected to create on the studio-wallahs by keeping them—I would write dialogues for the film in some unfamiliar language. I knew absolutely nothing about the film's story or its plot because I was merely a munshi—a pencil-pusher—in those days and didn't pull much weight. My work only involved writing on a sheet of paper in mutilated Urdu whatever I was ordered to and what the director could understand, and hand it over. Anyway, the shooting of *Ban ki Sundri* was under way. Rumour was rife that Hurmuzji Framji was bringing an entirely new face from God knows where for the part of the vamp, while Raj Kishore had been assigned the role of the hero.

Raj Kishore, a native of Rawalpindi, was a handsome and healthy young man. It was widely believed that his body was very manly and had a graceful shape. I thought about his body often. It was certainly athletic and well proportioned, but I found nothing else appealing in it. Maybe that was because I myself am frightfully gangly, look more dead than alive and, besides, am given to wonder rather too much about my kind of people.

I didn't hate him; I've rarely hated anyone in my life. Let's just say that I didn't much care for the man. The reason will reveal itself as you go along.

I absolutely loved his pure Rawalpindi accent, his language, his manner of speaking. Only in the Rawalpindi dialect of Punjabi can you find the sweetest, most endearing cadence. It has a strange kind of rugged femininity, at once sweet and mellow. Should a Rawalpindi woman talk to you, it would feel like having mango juice dribbled into your mouth. But I'm not talking about mangoes; I'm talking about Raj Kishore, whom I liked much less than that heavenly fruit.

As I mentioned, Raj Kishore was a good- and healthy-looking young man. Well, had the matter ended there, I'd have had no cause to grumble. What was worse was that he was also overly conscious of his physique and good looks. And this I could scarcely stomach.

Being healthy is a good thing, but to inflict one's health on others like a disease is something else again. Well, Raj Kishore suffered from this disease. He never lost an opportunity to flaunt his health and his well-proportioned and shapely limbs before those less healthy than he was.

Doubtless, I'm a frail and chronically ill man. One of my lungs can hardly pump enough oxygen into my body. But as God is my witness, I have never ever put my weakness on display, although I know that one can exploit one's frailty as much as one's strength. But I believe one should not do that.

To me, true beauty is the kind that you quietly admire in your heart, not broadcast with your tongue. I consider such beauty an affliction that hits you with the impact of a rock. All the beauties that a young man should have, Raj Kishore had them. But, regrettably, he also had the nasty habit of exhibiting them in the crudest fashion, such as by flexing his arm muscles while talking to you; or worse yet, praising them unabashedly himself. Or, in the midst of a discussion on some serious issue, such as swaraj, unbuttoning his khadi kurta and measuring the unusually wide span of his chest.

Ah, yes, khadi—it reminds me: Raj Kishore was a staunch Congressite. Maybe that's why he wore khadi. But the thought that he didn't love his country as much as he loved himself never ceased to peck at my heart.

The majority of people thought that my opinion of the man was grossly unjust. This was because, whether in or out of the studio, everyone admired him for his beauty, his thoughts, his simplicity, and his language with its perfect Rawalpindi accent, which I also loved.

Unlike most other actors, he didn't keep to himself. You were sure to find him in any and all Congress rallies, as well as literary gatherings. Regardless of how busy his life was, he always found time to share in the joy and sorrow of his neighbours, even those with whom he had only a nodding acquaintance.

Every film producer regarded him highly on account of his celebrity and his spotless character. And not just them, even the public knew all too well that Raj Kishore's life was free of scandal. It's not easy to be part of the film world and remain squeaky clean. That Raj Kishore was a successful hero further jacked up his stature in everyone's eyes.

I spent part of my evenings at Shamlal's paan shop in Nagpara. Here, people often gossiped about actors and actresses, none of whom was free of some scandal or other. Not so with Raj Kishore. Whenever his name cropped up in a conversation, Shamlal asserted proudly, 'Manto Sahib, Raj Bhai is the only actor who's not easy on his zipper.'

I didn't know why Shamlal had started calling him 'Raj Bhai', nor was I too surprised by it because every little thing Raj Bhai did soon became public knowledge as a veritable achievement. How much he made, how much he gave to his father every month, or donated to orphanages, or spent on himself—people knew these details as if they had been singed into their memories.

One day Shamlal told me that Raj Bhai was exceptionally nice to his stepmother. When times were hard and he had no source of income, both his father and his father's new wife had put him through all manner of hardship. But remarkably, Raj Bhai never shirked from his duty and welcomed them all with open arms. Now his father and his stepmother sat majestically on their canopied bed and ruled the roost. And Raj Bhai went every morning to touch his stepmother's feet and joined his hands before his father, ready to carry out immediately any order the old man might give him.

Please don't mind if I say that every time I came across such overblown praise for the man, I couldn't help but feel uneasy. I don't know why. God forbid, I didn't hate him, as I've said before. He had never given me cause to despise him. Then again, at a time when we munshi-folk counted for nothing, worthy neither of respect nor importance, Raj Bhai would talk to me for hours. So, while I can't say why, the thought that all of this was only so much posturing, that his life was an absolute sham, never failed to flash in some dark corner of my mind. The problem was, no one shared my opinion. So while everyone else worshipped him like a god, I stewed in my own juice.

He was married, had four children, was a model husband, an exemplary father. Turn up whatever corner of his life you wish, you wouldn't find anything even vaguely dubious or dark. That's all fine, but this idea—it never failed to rattle my brain.

I swear, I cursed myself several times for harbouring doubts about the man. 'You're rotten. Why do you needlessly mistrust a man whom the whole world considers good, and about whom you yourself don't have any complaint? What's wrong if he never tires of looking at his well-proportioned body? You'd likely do the same if you had a body like his.'

Still, I could never bring myself to look at him with the eyes of others. This often drove me to argue with him during our conversations. If something he said didn't sit right with me, I went all out against him. But after every such altercation, I would see only a smile on his lips and feel an indescribably bitter taste sloshing around in my throat, which pissed me off even more.

Without a doubt, his life wasn't stained by any scandal. He had no relations, innocent or otherwise, with any woman except his wife. I also admit that he called every female actor his sister, and they, in turn, called him brother. But my heart always questioned my mind: Why establish this relationship in the first place? A sister–brother relationship is one thing, but calling a woman your sister, that too so demonstratively, like putting up a sign that says 'Road Closed' or 'No Pissing Allowed', is quite another.

If you're not intending to establish a sexual relationship with a woman, why announce it in public? If even the thought of a woman besides your wife can't enter your heart, why bother to advertise the fact? Since I couldn't resolve this, and other similar issues, a strange perplexity gripped me.

Anyway—

The shooting of *Ban ki Sundri* was progressing. The studio was bustling with activity. A slew of extras, both men and women, showed up every day and we had a nice time indulging in light-hearted banter with them.

One day, the make-up master, whom we called Ustad, walked into the villain Niaz Muhammad's room with the news that the new girl who had been signed up for the role of the vamp had arrived, so filming was expected to start very soon.

We were having a round of tea at the time. We warmed up at once, partly from the tea and partly from the news. The arrival of a new girl in the studio was always a pleasant event, so we all quickly exited the room to have a look at this new creature.

We finally saw her when Hurmuzji Framji came out of his office, took two paans out of drummer Isa's silver box, stuffed them inside his humongous cheeks, and headed for the billiard room.

All I could see of her was her dark, brownish complexion as she quickly shook hands with the seth and rode away in the studio car. A bit later Niaz Muhammad told me that she had rather puffy lips. Perhaps he was only able to see her lips. Ustad, who hadn't glimpsed even that much, remarked, shaking his head with an air of disapproval, '*Onh, kandum!*' No good! The girl didn't come to the studio for the next four or five days. On the fifth day—or was it the sixth?—as I was coming out of Gulab's restaurant after taking my tea, I suddenly bumped into her.

I tend to look at a woman surreptitiously. If she appears in front of me suddenly, I'm unable to see anything of her. Since this girl had materialized so unexpectedly, I couldn't get a good enough look at her to form an opinion of her appearance, although I did see her feet; they were squeezed into a pair of new-style sandals.

The path from the lab to the studio was topped with gravel that had numerous pretty round stones sticking out. This made walking in her open sandals rather difficult for her, as they kept slipping on the round stones again and again.

After this encounter Miss Neelam and I gradually became friends. The studio personnel didn't know it, but our relations were quite informal. Her real name was Radha. Once I asked her why she had changed her beautiful name and she replied, 'Oh, no particular reason,' then added a minute later, 'it's too beautiful to be used in films.'

You might think that Radha was a religious kind of woman. Not at all. She couldn't care less about religion and its trappings. But just as I inscribe '786', the numerical value of 'bismillah', on top of the first sheet of paper before writing a new story, she also just happened to love the name Radha dearly. Since it was her wish that we not call her Radha, henceforth I will only call her Neelam.

Neelam was the offspring of a Benares prostitute. And it was with a Banarasi accent and cadence that she spoke. It sounded very sweet to the ear. She always called me Sadiq, though my name is Saadat. 'Neelam,' I once said to her, 'you can just as easily call me Saadat. I know you can. So why don't you? For the life of me, I can't understand it.'

A faint smile appeared on her dark, thin lips. 'Once I've made a mistake, I stick to it.'

I think very few people were aware that the person everyone in the studio considered just an ordinary actress happened to possess a unique personality. She didn't have the shallowness, the baseness of other run-of-the-mill actresses. Her gravitas, which everyone at work saw through his own lens and misinterpreted, was her loveliest attribute, entirely endearing.

This gravitas, this charming sturdiness served as the most becoming make-up on the clear, smooth surface of her darkish complexion, though it cannot be denied that it had packed the corners of her thin lips with the unnamed bitterness of sorrow—a quality, let's accept it, that set her apart from other women.

I have never ceased to wonder, then or now, why they picked her for the role of the vamp in *Ban ki Sundri*. She wasn't even nominally foxy or sharp. When she appeared on the set wearing a skimpy choli to play her part for the first time, I was terribly shocked. She could immediately guess people's reactions, so the minute she saw my expression she explained, 'Director Sahib ordered me to appear in this outfit because I'm not playing the part of a respectable woman. You know what I told him, "If this is an outfit, I'm willing to walk with you naked."'

'So what did Director Sahib say?'

Again a faint smile appeared on her thin lips. 'He immediately started imagining me naked . . . How silly can these people get! What need was there to tax his poor imagination once he had seen me in this wispy outfit.'

This should suffice by way of Neelam's introduction for an intelligent reader. Let me now proceed with the events which I must record to finish this story.

In Bombay the monsoon starts in June and continues till the middle of September. The first couple of months the rain comes down so hard that it's impossible to work in the studio. The shooting of *Ban ki Sundri* had started towards the end of April. We were just about finishing the third set when the first rains broke on us. Only one small scene that had no dialogues remained, so we kept shooting. Once that ended, we were at a loose end for months.

This provided many opportunities for people to spend time together. I spent nearly the whole time sitting in Gulab's restaurant, sipping cup after cup of tea. Whoever walked in was dripping wet, or almost. All the flies outside had swarmed in. The atmosphere became unbearably filthy. A cleaning rag lying on one chair, an onion-chopping knife on another. Gulab Sahib standing nearby, churning out his Bombay Urdu with his disease-rotted teeth: '*Tum udhar jaane ko nahin sakta*' (You can't go there), '*Ham udhar se ja ke aata*' (I'll go there and come back), '*Bohat lafra hoga . . . han . . . bara vanda ho ja'ienga*' (It will create a big mess . . . yes . . . it will result in a big loss).

Everyone came to this restaurant, with its corrugated tin roof, everyone except Seth Hurmuzji Framji, his brother-in-law Edalji, and all the heroines. Niaz Muhammad was obliged to come here twice because of his pets Chunni and Munni. Raj Kishore showed up once a day. The minute he crossed the threshold with his tall, athletic body, everyone's eyes suddenly lit up, but not mine. The young male extras immediately got up to offer Raj Bhai their seats. Once he sat down, everyone crowded around him like so many moths. After that, you heard only two types of things: the extras praising Raj Bhai's marvellous acting in old films, or Raj Bhai regurgitating the ancient history of how he dropped out of school and, later, out of college to join the film world. Since I had memorized all of this by now, I would greet him when he entered and get out of the place.

One day, after the rains had stopped, Niaz Muhammad's cats scared the daylights out of Hurmuzji Framji's German shepherd, who ran to Gulab's tea joint with his tail tucked between his legs. As he was running in, I saw Neelam and Raj Kishore talking on the round platform under the *maulsiri* tree. Raj Kishore was standing and, as usual, nodding his head, which meant that as far as he was concerned he was making interesting conversation. I don't remember now when or how he'd been introduced to Neelam, but she'd known him well even before she joined films. And if I remember correctly, she had casually praised his good-looking, well-proportioned body once or twice.

I came out of Gulab's restaurant and had just made it to the eves of the recording studio when I saw Raj Kishore take down his khadi bag from his broad shoulder with a jerk and pull out a fat notebook. I immediately knew that it was his diary.

After finishing the day's work and receiving his stepmother's blessings, he was in the habit of writing in his diary before he went to bed. Even though he loved Punjabi dearly, he wrote the diary in an English that was vaguely reminiscent of the delicate style of Tagore in some places, and Gandhi's political manner in others. It also reflected a significant influence of Shakespearean drama. But I never did see any sincerity in anything he wrote. Should you ever come across this diary, you'll know all there is to know about ten, maybe fifteen years of his life. How much money he donated, how many poor he fed, the meetings he participated in, which outfits he wore and which he discarded . . . and if my guess is right, you'll also spot my name on some page beside the figure 35, the amount I once borrowed from him and haven't returned to this day since I figured he'd never note that it had been returned.

Anyway, he was reading some pages of his diary out loud for Neelam's benefit. Even though I was quite some distance from them, I surmised from the way his lips moved that he was praising the Lord in the style of Shakespeare.

Neelam sat quietly on the round cement platform under the maulsiri. From her elegantly serious face, it was apparent that Raj Kishore's words were making no impression on her. She was looking, rather, at his protruding chest. His shirt was open and his dark black hair looked ravishing on his fair chest.

Everything looked washed and immaculately clean in the studio, even Niaz Muhammad's cats, who normally looked revoltingly filthy. Both of them were lying on the bench opposite me, cleaning their faces with their soft velvety paws. Neelam wore a spotless white georgette sari with a matching blouse of white linen, creating a subdued and pleasant contrast against the darkish skin of her slender arms.

For a moment I wondered, 'Why is she looking so different?'

Suddenly our eyes collided and I found the answer in her distracted glance. She'd fallen in love.

She gestured to me to come over. For a while we talked about this and that. After Raj Kishore left, she asked me, 'Will you come along with me today?'

We arrived at her house at six in the evening. She tossed her bag on the sofa as soon as we entered and said without looking at me, 'It's not what you're thinking.'

I understood her meaning. So I asked, 'How do you know what I was thinking?'

The same muted but mysterious smile appeared on her lips again.

'Because we had both thought the same thing . . . Maybe you didn't think about it later, but after much deliberation I've concluded that we were both wrong.'

'What if I say we were both right?'

'Then we are both stupid,' she said, plopping down on the sofa.

In no time at all the sombre look on her face deepened. 'How can that be, Sadiq? I'm not a naive young girl who doesn't know what's inside her heart. How old do you think I am?'

'Twenty-two.'

'Absolutely right. But what you don't know is that I already knew what love was when I was only ten years old. Forget knowing what love is, I was actually *in* love. By God I was. I was seized by a murderous love clear up to the age of sixteen. How can I ever love anyone now? Not a chance.'

She looked at my frozen expression and said nervously. 'I know you'll never accept it, no you won't, not even if I bare my heart to you.

Don't I know you well enough? But by God, may I die if I lie to you . . . my heart is incapable of loving anyone any more. However, I can at least say this much . . .' She hesitated.

I kept quiet as she had already drifted into deep thought. Perhaps she was trying to articulate what that 'this much' was.

Soon the same fleeting smile that had a way of adding a touch of knowing mischief crossed her lips again. She sprang up from the sofa and began saying, 'But at least I can say that it's not love. I'm positive. Whether it is some other affliction . . . I can't say. Sadiq, I want to believe it.'

'You mean you want to make yourself believe it?'

That blew her fuse. 'You're very mean . . . One must never abandon good form when saying something . . . Why do I have to make you believe me anyway . . . It's me I'm trying to convince. The trouble is, I'm finding that hard to do. Can't you help me?'

She sat down beside me, toying with her little finger, and asked, 'What's your opinion of Raj Kishore? I mean, what is it in him that you think I have a thing for.' She let go of the finger and started playing with her fingers one by one, distractedly. 'I don't like the things he says, I don't like his acting, I don't like his diary . . . God knows what nonsense he was spewing out.'

Cranky, she got up from the sofa. 'Don't know what's happening to me. I just want a big commotion . . . a big noise, like cats going at one another . . . clouds of smoke spilling forth . . . I'd be drenched in sweat . . .' Then she suddenly turned towards me and asked, 'Sadiq, what do you think, what kind of woman am I?'

I smiled and answered, 'I've never understood either cats or women.'

'Why is that?'

I thought for a moment and said, 'A cat used to live in our house. Once a year she was seized by bouts of terrible whining . . . and then a tomcat would suddenly appear out of nowhere and the two would go at it with more ferocity than you ever saw, leaving both of them bruised, battered and bleeding. But soon after, our auntie cat would become the mother of four kittens.'

She looked as though some disagreeable taste had flooded her mouth. 'Sheesh, what a dirty mind you have!' Then, after chewing a cardamom to improve the taste in her mouth, she said, 'I hate kids. Anyway, let's just drop it.'

She opened her paan box and started preparing one for me with her slim, delicate fingers. With tiny spoons she dug into small, narrow cups

containing lime and catechu pastes and, with finesse, applied them to a
paan leaf already stripped of its central vein. She folded the leaf into a cone
and offered it to me. 'Sadiq, what do you think?' she asked absent-mindedly.

'About what?'

Chopping a piece of roasted betel nut into smaller bits with her
sarota, she replied, 'About this silliness that has started for no sane
reason at all. If it's not silliness, what else could it be? I mean I'm totally
confused. Tearing at myself, mending myself. God only knows what
lies ahead if this stupidity is allowed to continue. You don't know, I'm
a formidable woman.'

'Formidable—whatever do you mean?'

The same mysterious, almost imperceptible smile flitted across her
face. 'You're awfully shameless. You know everything, yet you insist on
poking me with these soft needles to make me blurt it out myself.'

The whites of her eyes turned a shade of pink.

'I'm a very hot-tempered woman—is that so difficult to understand?'
She suddenly sprang to her feet. 'Go now. I want to take a bath.'

I left.

For quite a while after that she didn't mention Raj Kishore to me.
Still, we somehow knew one another's thoughts. I knew what was going
through her mind and she, mine. This silent exchange went on for a
few days.

One day Kirpalani, who was directing *Ban ki Sundri*, was watching
the heroine rehearse her song. All of us had piled into the music room.
Neelam was ensconced in a chair and was slowly tapping her feet,
keeping time to the music. It was a pedestrian song, but the melody was
quite good. When the rehearsal ended, in walked Raj Kishore with his
khadi shoulder bag. One by one he greeted director Kirpalani, music
director Ghosh, and sound recordist P.N. Mogha in English. He joined
his hands and said namaskar to Miss Eidan Bai and then informed her,
'Sister Eidan, yesterday I saw you in Crawford Market. I was buying
oranges for *aap ki bhabhi.** when I spotted your car . . .' As he turned his
head, his eyes fell on Neelam who sat buried in a low chair by the piano.
His hands rose spontaneously to say namaskar to her, but the moment
she saw him she catapulted out of her chair and warned him, 'Raj Sahib,
please don't call me "sister".'

---

* For your sister-in-law, i.e. Raj Kishore's wife.

She said it with such measured gravity that everyone in the music room was dazed for a moment. An embarrassed Raj Kishore could only mutter a feeble 'Why?'

She didn't answer and stomped out.

Three days later when I went to Shamlal's paan shop at about three in the afternoon, people were still gossiping about this incident. 'Saali, her own intentions must be dirty,' Shamlal was asserting proudly. 'Why else would a woman mind Raj Bhai calling her sister? But mark my words—she won't get what she's after. Raj Bhai doesn't go easy on his zipper.'

This Raj Bhai's zipper was getting on my nerves. I didn't say anything to Shamlal. I just sat down and quietly listened to his and his customers' chatter, laced with exaggeration and next to nothing of substance.

Everyone at the studio knew what happened in the music room. Actually, for the third day running this was the only topic one heard being discussed: Why did Miss Neelam suddenly forbid Raj Kishore from calling her 'sister'? While I didn't hear anything directly from Raj Kishore about the matter, it reached me through one of his friends that he had made interesting comments about the incident in his diary and prayed to God to keep Miss Neelam's heart and mind chaste. Nothing notable happened for a few days after the incident.

Neelam had grown more sedate than before, and Raj Kishore's shirt remained open all the time, the dark black hair on his muscled white chest poking out.

Since it hadn't rained for a couple of days and the paint on the fourth set of *Ban ki Sundri* had dried, director Kirpalani put up a notice saying that shooting would start shortly. The scene to be shot was between Neelam and Raj Kishore. I had written the dialogues, so I knew he would kiss her hand during their conversation. There was no compelling reason for a kiss in the scene, but as per the formula, it had been thrown in merely to excite the public, just as women were made to appear on screen in clothing that titillated the senses.

I was present when filming started. My heart was throbbing. I was wondering how the two would react. The very thought of it sent a tingling sensation through my body. The scene ended and nothing happened. Electric lamps came on and went off after every dialogue with tiring monotony, and the calls of 'Start' and 'Cut' rose and subsided.

Around dusk, at the climax of the scene, Raj Kishore grabbed Neelam's hand romantically, but turned his back to the camera and kissed his own hand instead before releasing hers.

I was expecting her to pull her hand away and smack his face so loudly that it would burst the eardrums of P.N. Mogha in the sound studio. But on the contrary, I found a melting smile on her thin lips, entirely bereft of even the slightest trace of wounded feelings.

I was terribly disappointed, but I didn't mention it to Neelam. When a couple of days had passed and she too hadn't said anything about it, I imagined that she probably hadn't realized the significance of that kiss; rather I should say, the thought of it hadn't even crossed her sensitive mind. The only reason could be that in those moments she was listening to words of love pouring out of the mouth of someone who was otherwise used to calling women his sisters.

But why had he kissed his own hand? Was he getting even with her? Was he trying to humiliate her? A spate of such questions crowded my mind without yielding a satisfactory answer.

On the fourth day, when I went, as usual, to Shamlal's, he complained, 'Manto Sahib, you never tell us anything about your company. Is it because you don't want to or because you don't know anything? Do you know what Raj Bhai did?'

Then he began telling the story in his own style: 'There was this scene in *Ban ki Sundri* in which Director Sahib ordered Raj Bhai to kiss Miss Neelam on the lips. But Sahib, Raj Bhai is one thing, and that saali, that whore, is quite another entirely. No comparison. Raj Bhai blurted out right away, "No, Sahib, not a chance. I won't ever do such a thing. I have my own wife. How will I ever touch her chaste lips after kissing this foul woman?" Well, sir, Director Sahib had to change the scene right away and Raj Bhai was told, all right, don't kiss her lips, just kiss her hand. But Raj Bhai is no greenhorn whom you can take for a ride. No sir! When the time came, he kissed his own hand instead so deftly that everyone thought he had kissed that saali's.'

I didn't mention this to Neelam. She was totally unaware of the whole thing, so why make her unhappy.

Malaria is rampant in Bombay. I remember neither the month nor the date, except that it was raining hard when they were putting up the fifth set of *Ban ki Sundri*. Neelam suddenly came down with a high fever. Since there was no work for me at the studio, I would sit by her side for hours and look after her. Malaria had added a strangely melancholic pallor to the brownish hue of her face. A glimpse of some obscure vulnerability could be seen in the indescribable bitterness that never left her eyes and the corners of her thin lips.

The quinine shots affected her hearing so much that she had to raise her voice when she spoke, perhaps thinking that I too was hard of hearing.

One day, after her fever broke and she was lying in bed thanking Eidan Bai in a feeble voice for inquiring after her, a car honked in the street below. I noticed that the noise sent a shiver through Neelam's body.

Minutes later the room's heavy teakwood door opened and Raj Kishore appeared in his white khadi shirt and tight pyjamas, with his old-fashioned wife in tow. He greeted Eidan Bai by addressing her as 'Sister Eidan', shook hands with me and, after introducing his wife—very much an ordinary-looking housewife but with prominent features— sat down on Neelam's bed. For a few moments he stared vacantly into space, smiling, and then looked at Neelam. For the first time I spotted the traces of some obscure feeling in his limpid eyes. I hadn't yet been fully surprised when he started out in his playful manner. 'I have been meaning to come and inquire after you for some time, but this blasted car, the engine gave out on me. The garage took ten days to fix it. I just got it back today. I immediately said to Shanti (he pointed at his wife), "Get up, right now, let's go . . . someone else will take care of the kitchen work. Luckily, today is also the festival of Raksha Bandhan. We'll both inquire after sister Neelam and have her tie the rakhi on my wrist."' He promptly took a silken *gajra* out of the pocket of his khadi shirt. The pallor on Neelam's face became slightly more pronounced.

Raj Kishore was purposely avoiding Neelam's eyes. 'But no,' he said to Eidan Bai instead, 'not like this. It's a joyous festival. Sister Neelam shouldn't tie the rakhi when she's feeling indisposed . . . Shanti, get up and put some lipstick on her.'

'Where's the make-up box?'

It was lying on the mantelpiece. Raj Kishore took a few giant strides and brought it over. Neelam remained silent . . . her thin lips tightened, as if she was finding it hard to hold back from screaming.

Neelam didn't resist when Shanti, like a dutiful wife, tried to put some make-up on her. Eidan Bai propped her up, supporting her listless body like a corpse. Shanti began applying a coat of lipstick rather awkwardly. Neelam looked at me and smiled. And in that smile I could feel the resonance of a stifled scream.

I thought . . . no, I was positive that something was about to happen . . . Neelam's tightly pressed lips would explode and, like mountain streams that break through the most formidable dykes under the onslaught of punishing rains, she would release a torrential deluge of dammed emotions that would topple us and carry us to God knows what unknown depths in their fury. Strangely, she remained silent, absolutely silent, only the melancholy pallor of her face tried to hide behind the vaporous redness of powder. She remained as inert as a graven image. Her make-up done, she said to Raj Kishore in a strangely firm manner, 'Please give me the rakhi, I will tie it on your wrist now.'

Within seconds the tasselled silken rakhi was on his wrist and Neelam, whose hands should have trembled, was knotting the cord with steely calm. During all this, I once again caught a glimpse of some obscure emotion floating in Raj Kishore's limpid eyes before it quickly dissolved in a laugh.

According to custom, he gave Neelam a gift of money in an envelope. She thanked him and tucked the envelope under her pillow.

After they left and Neelam and I were alone, she cast a desolate glance at me and lay down quietly, resting her head on the pillow. Raj Kishore had forgotten to take his bag; it was still on the bed. When she saw it, she pushed it aside with her foot. I sat by her side browsing through the newspaper for nearly two hours. When she didn't say anything, I left without asking her permission.

Three days later, as I was shaving inside my nine-rupees-a-month *kholi* in Nagpara, and listening to the vituperations of Mrs Fernandez who lived next door, someone barged in. I turned around to look. It was Neelam.

For a moment I thought it was someone else . . . the deep red lipstick smeared across her lips somehow gave the impression of a mouth that had been left unwiped after spitting blood . . . her hair terribly mussed up, her white sari practically in tatters, several buttons on the front of her blouse torn open, revealing scratches on her light-almond-coloured breasts.

I was so dazed looking at her in this condition that I couldn't even ask what had happened or how she had found the address to my kholi.

The first thing I did was shut the door. After I pulled up a chair and sat down across from her, she opened her lipstick-coated lips to say, 'I came straight here.'

'From where?' I asked, softly.

'From my place . . . and I've come to tell you that *that* silliness has now ended.'

'How?'

'I knew he would return when I was quite alone. So he came . . . to reclaim his bag.' The same mysterious smile curved her thin lips, now utterly disfigured by lipstick. 'He came to pick up his bag . . . I said to him, "Come, it's in the other room." Perhaps my tone sounded different, because he tensed a little . . . "Don't be nervous," I said. In the other room, I didn't return his bag. I sat down at the dressing table and started putting on make-up.'

She stopped, picked up the glass sitting on my broken table, quickly emptied it, wiped her mouth with the corner of her sari, and resumed. 'I kept applying make-up for a whole hour. I smeared my lips with as much lipstick as I could and rubbed on as much rouge on my cheeks as I could, while he stood in a corner, watching my face in the mirror. When I had turned myself into a veritable witch, I walked over to the door on firm feet and bolted it.'

'And then?'

When I looked at her for the answer, she seemed totally changed. Her lips seemed different now that they'd been wiped; her tone sounded about as muted as a piece of red-hot iron being pounded with a hammer.

At the moment she didn't look at all like the witch she had no doubt resembled after painting herself with all that make-up.

She didn't answer right away. She got up from my charpoy, installed herself on top of the table, and said, 'I gnawed at him . . . stuck to him like a wild cat. He scratched my face, I clawed at his. We wrestled for quite a while . . . oh, he was so strong . . . but . . . as I once told you, I'm a formidable woman. The weakness brought on by the malaria just vanished. My body was on fire . . . my eyes were shooting sparks . . . my bones were becoming rigid. I grabbed him and sprang on him like a furious cat . . . I don't know why . . . I have no idea why I tangled with him so thoughtlessly. Neither of us said anything that anyone might understand . . . I kept screaming, and he kept saying, "Yes, yes" . . . I tore off pieces of his white khadi kurta with my fingers . . . He yanked out clumps of my hair right from their roots . . . He used his utmost force, but I was determined to win at all costs. This left us totally exhausted. He was lying on the rug like a corpse and I was gasping so hard, I felt my heart would give out any moment. In spite of my breathless state I still managed to tear his kurta to shreds. As soon as I saw his broad chest I realized the essence of that silliness . . . the silliness that both of us had wondered about but neither of us could make any sense of . . .'

She got up quickly, jerked her dishevelled hair over one shoulder and continued, 'Sadiq . . . the bastard, he really has an exquisite body . . . I don't know what came over me. I suddenly lowered myself over him and started biting him. He cringed with pain. But when I stuck my bleeding lips to his and kissed him passionately, he suddenly cooled off like a sated woman . . . I got up . . . And in a flash I felt hatred for the man surge up in me. I peered down at him intently . . . the red of my blood and lipstick had traced hideous patterns on his broad chest . . . I glanced around my room and suddenly everything seemed like a sham. Afraid that I might suffocate, I quickly opened the door and came straight to you.'

She fell silent, as silent as a corpse. I was frightened. I touched her arm dangling from the edge of the bed . . . it was as hot as fire.

I called her name loudly several times, but she didn't answer. Finally, when I screamed, 'Neelam!' in sheer terror, she started.

As she was leaving she only said, 'My name is Radha!'

Scorned

Drained from the day's gruelling work, Saugandhi had fallen asleep almost as soon as she hit the bed. Minutes ago, the city's sanitary inspector—she called him 'Seth'—had gone home to his wife, dead drunk, after a prolonged session of stormy sex which had left even her bones aching. He would have stayed for the night but for the regard he had for his wife who loved him dearly.

The money that she had received from the inspector for her services was still stuffed in her tight-fitting bra, now stained with the man's drool. Every so often the silver coins clinked a bit with the rise and fall of her breathing, the sound blending with the irregular rhythm of her heart. It was as if the molten silver of the coins was dripping into her bloodstream. Her chest was on fire, partly from the half-bottle of brandy the inspector had brought along and partly from the raw country liquor they had downed with plain water when the soda ran out.

She was lying face down on the large teakwood bed, her bare arms splayed out like the bow-shaped rib of a kite that has come loose from its dew-drenched paper. The grainy flesh visible in her right armpit had acquired a bluish tint from frequent shaving and looked like a graft from the skin of a freshly plucked chicken.

It was a small room. Miscellaneous objects were strewn about. A mangy dog was stretched out under the bed on a heap of shrivelled, weather-beaten chappals, snarling at some invisible object in his sleep. The mange had left the severely affected areas of his body so totally hairless that a person might think a folded rag being used as a doormat had been left on the floor.

A small shelf on the wall held an assortment of make-up: rouge, lipstick, face powder, combs and metallic hairpins that she probably used to keep her chignon in place. In a birdcage hanging from a hook near the rack slept her parrot, its head tucked inside its feathers. Bits of unripe guava and rotting orange peel lay inside the cage, their putrid smell attracting a hovering swarm of mosquitoes and minuscule fruit flies. A wickerwork chair, its backrest grimy from overuse, stood near the bed. To its right was an elegant three-legged tea table supporting a portable His Master's Voice gramophone draped with a decaying black cloth. Rusted gramophone needles were scattered not just on the table but all over the dingy room. Four framed photographs of some individuals hung on the wall directly above the table.

Slightly to one side of the photographs, near the entrance, hung a brightly coloured portrait of Ganeshji, adorned with strings of faded flowers. The picture was likely some fabric brand label that had been removed from the bolt and stuck into a frame. A lamp and a cup filled with oil sat on a small, greasy rack near Ganeshji's picture, along with a smattering of curled-up ash that had fallen from incense sticks. In the stagnant atmosphere of the room, the flame in the lamp burned as perfectly straight as the tilak mark on someone's forehead. Saugandhi habitually touched her day's first earnings against this image of Ganeshji and then against her own forehead before tucking them inside her bra; regardless of how many banknotes she stuffed there, they remained safe in the hospitable space between her ample, protruding breasts—safe, that is, until Madho showed up from Puna, taking a day or two off from his job. Then she would be forced to stash some of the money inside the hole she had dug under one of her bedposts just for such a situation. It was Ramlal who had let Saugandhi in on this trick for keeping her money safe. Hearing how Madho came over from Puna now and then and played around with her infuriated Ramlal so much that he let her have it one day: 'Since when have you made that son-of-a-bitch your lover? Some affair you've got there! That bum! Doesn't have to spend even a paisa of his own money, but ends up having a good time with you all the same. And to top it all off, he even swindles you out of some of your own money . . . Why, don't I know every last weakness of you girls? After all, I've been in this business for seven years.'

Ramlal, who worked as a pimp in different quarters of Bombay for some one hundred and twenty girls who could be had for anywhere from ten to a hundred rupees, went on to give Saugandhi a piece of his mind. 'Stupid woman, don't fritter away your money. You just watch, one day he'll snatch the very clothes off your body. I'm telling you, he *will*—that damned lover of your goddam mother! Listen to me; dig a hole under one of the bedposts and stash all your earnings in it. When he shows up, say: "By your life, Madho, I haven't seen even a paisa since morning. Come on, send for a cup of tea and some Aflatoon biscuits from the café downstairs. I'm so ravenously hungry and starved that my stomach is rumbling." Understand! These are critical times, my dear. The damned Congress has slapped this accursed ban on alcohol and ruined our business. You, at least, get something to drink, one way or another. Do you know how I feel when I see an empty bottle in your room and the smell of booze wafts up my nostrils—by God, I feel like migrating inside your skin.'

Saugandhi was particularly fond of her breasts. One time Jamuna had advised her: 'Keep those watermelons of yours in good shape. Use a bra and they'll stay firm.'

Saugandhi laughed and said, 'Jamuna, you think everyone is like you. People come and ride roughshod all over your body for a measly ten rupees a pass and you think this is what happens to everyone else. Let anyone so much as touch me in places I don't want them to and . . . Which reminds me to tell you about yesterday. Ramlal brought this guy, a Punjabi, at two in the morning. We settled on thirty rupees for the night. Anyway, when we slipped into bed I turned off the light. Would you believe it, the guy panicked! Did you hear me? All his swagger, that macho bravado—it vanished in the dark, just like that! He took such a fright. I said, "Get on with it, man, why are you wasting time. It's nearly three and it will be daybreak soon." "*Roshni*," he begged, "roshni, please." "Roshni," I said, "what's that?" "The light! The light! Please turn on the light." His choking voice made me laugh. "No, I'm not going to," I said, and pinched his fleshy thigh. He jumped up and immediately switched on the light. I quickly pulled the sheet over my body and said, "Aren't you ashamed of yourself, lout?" When he climbed back into bed I got up and turned the light off once more with a quick movement of my hand. He began to feel nervous all over again. I swear by your life, Jamuna, the night was totally out of this world! So enjoyable—now dark, now light, off again, on again. As soon as the rumble of the first tram was heard, he hurriedly slipped on his pants and took off. The son-of-a-bitch must have made the thirty rupees playing the stock market. He just threw them away without getting anything for them . . . You really are terribly naive, Jamuna. But me, I know a lot of tricks for dealing with them.'

The fact is, Saugandhi did know many tricks and even shared them freely with her friends in the profession. 'If the fellow turns out to be a gentleman, not given to talking much, play tricks with him and keep talking endlessly. Tease him, tickle him, and play with him. If he has a beard, run your fingers through it, pulling out a hair or two now and then. If he has a big fat belly, pat it. Never ever give him a moment to do what he wants. But these quiet types—they're the worst. They'll crush your bones if they have their way.'

Saugandhi wasn't quite as clever as she let on. She had very few clients. Being overly sentimental, she allowed all her wiles to slip from her mind and straight down into her belly, which having once given birth to a child was now lined with stretch marks. When she first saw those marks, she thought her mangy dog had clawed her there. Every time a bitch passed by him indifferently, he traced similar lines in the dust, as if to hide his smallness, his sense of shame at being ignored so heartlessly.

For the most part Saugandhi lived inside her own mind. Still, when someone spoke to her with kindness, or said just a gentle word, she melted on the spot and let it work its magic throughout her body. Although her mind considered sexual intimacy patently absurd, every other part of her body longed for it. Every limb yearned to be worked over, to exhaustion, until fatigue settled in and eased her into a state of delightful sleep—the wondrous sleep that comes after the body has been crushed, the torpor that follows when the body has been roughed up badly, when every limb aches and the joints loosen and relax, and a sleepy languor takes over. At times you feel you're very much there and then you're not, and sometimes in this middling state of being and non-being you feel as if you're suspended very high in the air, with nothing around you—above, below, to the right or left—but air. Even the sensation of choking in this air has a pleasure all its own.

Even as a little girl, when Saugandhi hid in her mother's big trunk during a game of hide-and-seek, she had felt the same suffocating pleasure when her heartbeat quickened from the lack of oxygen in the closed space and the fear of being caught.

She desperately wanted to spend her whole life hiding inside a trunk just like that one, with her seekers going round and round looking for her; she wanted them to find her sometimes, so that she might try to find them in turn. Wasn't this life she'd been living the past five years like a game of hide-and-seek, after all? Sometimes she sought someone out, sometimes someone searched for her. This is how her life bumped along. She was happy, because she had to be. Every night there was a man by her side in her large teakwood bed and Saugandhi, who knew umpteen tricks to thwart their attempts to get fresh with her, who had firmly resolved not to succumb to their unreasonable demands, and would treat them with a forbidding coldness, was always swept away by her emotions and remained only a woman craving love.

Every evening her companion, someone new or a regular, would profess, 'Saugandhi, I love you,' and she, knowing only too well that he was lying, would melt away, believing he truly did love her. Love—could any word be sweeter! The desire to melt it and rub it all over her body until it penetrated every pore overwhelmed her. Or, if not that, then perhaps if she could somehow crawl completely inside it and lower the lid, as though it were some sort of box. Sometimes, when the desire to love and be loved became dire, she felt like gathering the man lying beside her into her lap and rock him to sleep, singing lullabies.

Her ability to love was so profound that she could love and remain true to any man who visited her. Wasn't she, after all, harbouring her love to this day for the four men whose pictures hung on the wall facing her! The feeling of being a good woman—indeed a *very* good woman— never left her. Why, oh why, were men so bereft of goodness? Once, contemplating herself in the mirror, the words 'Saugandhi, the world hasn't treated you well' involuntarily escaped from her lips.

The past five years, every night and day of them, were inextricably woven into every fibre of her being. And even though she hadn't been quite as happy during this time as she had wished to be, she nonetheless longed for her days to continue along the same course. Why lust after money—after all she wasn't planning to become rich. Her going rate was ten rupees, out of which Ramlal took two and a half as his commission. The balance was quite adequate for her needs. In fact, when Madho came down from Puna—'to storm her', as Ramlal put it—she had saved enough to even offer him ten or fifteen rupees by way of tribute. Tribute for what? Let's just say she had special feelings for him. Ramlal was absolutely right. The man had something about him that Saugandhi fell for. No point hiding it. Might as well let it out. During their first encounter Madho had told her flat out: 'Have some shame! You're wrangling over your price? Don't you know what you're dickering over and what it is I've come for? For heaven's sake! A mere ten rupees, out of which Ramlal takes a quarter. That leaves seven and a half, doesn't it? And for this measly sum you promise to give me what you have no power to give, and I come to take what I really can't take. I need a woman. But do you need a man, right now, this minute? For me, any woman would do. How about you, do you fancy me? Nothing tangible binds us together . . . nothing except these ten rupees, out of which a quarter will go as commission and the rest you'll spend as you will. You hear their jingle, so do I. Your mind is on one thing, mine on another. Why not talk about something totally different: like you need me and I need you. Look, I'm a havildar in Puna. I'll visit you once a month, for, say, three or four days. Give up this business. I'll pay your expenses. Well now, how much rent must you dish out for this kholi?'

Madho had said quite a few other things as well. They affected her so deeply that for a moment she thought she was already a havildar's wife. After talking for a while, Madho brought some order into the things that were scattered around her room, and then tore up the smutty pictures she had on the wall above her bed without waiting for her permission. 'Well, Saugandhi,' he said, 'I can't allow these here . . . and,' he added, 'this water pot, look how grimy it is. And these rags . . . my God, they smell awful. Come on, throw them out! And why have you ruined your hair? And . . . and . . . and . . .'

After jabbering for three hours the two started feeling quite close. Saugandhi began to feel as though she had already known the havildar for some years now. No one had minded the presence of smelly rags, the grimy water pot, or the smutty pictures in the room before, nor had anyone ever made her think that she too had a place of her own that she could turn into a home. Men came and went without noticing even the grime and filth of the bed. No one had ever said, 'Saugandhi, your nose looks quite red today. You aren't coming down with a cold, are you? Okay, I'll go get some medicine for you.' How awfully considerate Madho was! Whatever he said was absolutely right. Hadn't he given her a piece of his mind without mincing words! The thought that she needed Madho began to take hold. So they hitched together.

Madho came over from Puna once a month. Before leaving he never failed to warn her, 'Look, Saugandhi, if you ever go back to turning tricks again, we'll have to break up, and if I ever catch you with another man here, I'll drag you by your hair and throw you out . . . and yes, I'll send you this month's expenses by postal money order as soon as I get back. So now, what's the rent for this kholi?'

Madho never sent her any money from Puna, nor did Saugandhi stop turning tricks. Both knew well enough how things were. But she never turned on Madho, never said, 'What's this harping about money all the time! When have you ever given me even a chipped pie?' Nor did Madho ever ask, 'So where do you get all this stuff from when I never give you anything?' Liars—both. Living a sham. And yet Saugandhi was happy. If you can't afford real gold jewellery, you settle for fake.

At that moment a bone-tired Saugandhi was fast asleep. The electric bulb overhead, which she had forgotten to turn off, was shining right above her closed eyes drowned in heavy sleep.

Someone knocked at the door. Who could it be at two in the morning? The sound of the knock filtered faintly into her ears like a distant hum. When the knock came again, insistent, more urgent, she woke up with a start. The two different kinds of liquor she had downed last evening and the bits of fish still caught between her teeth had produced a sticky, acidic saliva in her mouth. Rubbing her eyes groggily, she wiped the foul-smelling gob off her lips with the edge of her dhoti. She was the only one in the bed. She leaned over and peeked underneath only to find her dog sleeping with his head resting on the weather-beaten chappals, snarling as usual at something invisible. The parrot, too, was asleep with its head tucked into its feathers.

When someone rapped on the door again, Saugandhi forced herself out of bed. She had a splitting headache. She filled a mug with water from the pot, rinsed her mouth, filled the mug again and hurriedly gulped down the water. She opened the door just a crack and asked, 'Is that you, Ramlal?'

Tired from repeatedly banging on the door, Ramlal exclaimed with visible annoyance, 'Did a snake bite you or something? I've been knocking now for over an hour. Where the hell were you?' Lowering his voice, he added, 'You haven't got anyone inside, have you?'

When she told him there wasn't anyone inside, he raised his voice again and asked, 'So why wouldn't you open the door? This is the limit.

By God, you sleep like a log. If it takes two hours to fix up each one of you with a customer, I might just as well say goodbye to my business. Now don't stand there gawking at me. Take off this dhoti and put on a sari, the one with the floral print, and put some powder on your face. Then come with me. A seth is waiting for you outside in his car. Come on, hurry up!'

Saugandhi plunked down in the armchair while Ramlal walked over to the mirror and started combing his hair.

She reached towards the tea table, picked up the jar of balm and said as she unscrewed the cap, 'Ramlal, I don't feel well today.'

He put the comb back on the shelf, turned to her and said, 'Oh, I see . . . You should have said something earlier.'

Saugandhi rubbed the balm on her forehead and along her temples. To let him know that it wasn't what he was thinking, she explained, 'Now don't get any wrong ideas, Ramlal. It's just that I had a bit too much to drink.'

Ramlal's mouth began watering. 'If there's any left, let me have a drop! I haven't tasted any for ages.'

She put the jar back on the tea table and said, 'If I had saved any, I wouldn't be having this infernal headache. Look, why don't you bring the guy in.'

'No, there's no way he would come here. He's a respectable man, a "gentleman". As it is, he was feeling quite nervous about parking the car outside in the street. Change your clothes and come with me out to the corner. Everything will be all right.'

It was only a seven-and-a-half-rupee deal. Under normal circumstances, Saugandhi would never have accepted it when she had such a terrible headache, but she desperately needed money. The husband of her next-door neighbour, a Madrasi woman, had been run over by a car and died. She needed to return to her hometown with her young daughter, but she had no money and was languishing here, feeling utterly despondent. Just the other day Saugandhi had comforted her by saying, 'Sister, don't you worry. My man is due to arrive from Puna any day now. I'll ask him for some money and arrange for your travel.' That Madho would descend from Puna was certain, but the money was something else again. Saugandhi would have to arrange for it herself. So she got up and was ready to go in five minutes flat, her floral sari draped perfectly, and face powdered

and rouged. She drank another mug of cold water and set off with
Ramlal.

The street, quite a bit wider than the ones in small towns, was
perfectly still. A feeble glow filtered through the gas streetlamps whose
shades had been partially blackened out because of the war. In this
muted light she could make out the dim silhouette of a car parked at the
very end of the street.

The sight of the dark shadow of the black car at this late hour on
a night filled with mysteries gave Saugandhi the inescapable feeling
that her headache had seeped out and permeated the atmosphere. The
air even had a fetid taste, as if saturated with the stench of brandy and
country liquor.

Ramlal went on ahead and spoke to the man inside the car. When
Saugandhi caught up with him, he moved to one aside and said, 'Here
she is . . . a very fine piece . . . She's joined the business only a few days
ago.' And then, addressing Saugandhi, 'Come a bit closer, Saugandhi.
Show yourself to Sethji. He'd like to see you.'

Twisting a corner of her sari around her finger, she came forward
and stood near the window. The seth turned the torch straight on her
face and her drowsy eyes were dazzled momentarily. The light went
dead with a click at the same time as an 'Oh no!' escaped from the seth's
lips. At once the engine sputtered and the car sped away.

It was gone before Saugandhi had time to think. The intense light
from the torch was still lodged in her eyes. She hadn't even seen the
seth's face properly. What had happened? What was the meaning of
that 'Oh no!' which was still ringing in her ears? Yes, what? . . .

'He didn't like you,' she heard her pimp say. 'Okay, I should move
along. Two hours wasted.'

When she heard this, Saugandhi's legs, arms, hands, indeed her
entire body was overcome by the violent urge to spring into action.
Where was that car? That damned seth? He didn't like her—is that what
the 'Oh no!' meant? A curse word rose from the pit of her stomach but
stopped at the tip of her tongue. Whom would she aim it at? The car
had already taken off, its tail lights fading before her in the gathering
darkness of the bazaar. It felt as though the 'Oh no!' was driving deeper
into her breast like the red-hot bit of an auger. She felt like screaming
her lungs out: 'O Seth, stop, wait just a minute.' But the seth, God curse
him, was long gone.

She stood in the desolate bazaar alone. Her floral sari, worn only on special occasions, was fluttering in the gentle breeze of the late night hour. Suddenly, she found she detested it and the velvety rustle it made with every fibre of her being. The desire to shred it to bits seized her; its every flutter seemed to mimic that unforgiving 'Oh no!' She had dabbed her cheeks with powder and painted her lips red. All this to look desirable—the very thought evoked feelings of shame and she began to perspire from a surge of regret. She made up a slew of excuses to shake off that crushing feeling of humiliation: 'I didn't do it to show myself off to that potbelly. I always use make-up. Why, everyone does. But . . . but at two in the morning? And Ramlal the pimp, this bazaar, that car . . . and the glare of the torch . . .' The thought of it made her head swirl and an infinity of bright spots began to stream past her as far as her eyes could see. The snarl of the car's engine was audible in every gust of wind.

Because of the perspiration, the make-up over the balm on her forehead started to run and her forehead felt like someone else's, not her own. When a puff of air brushed over it, she felt as though someone had pasted a patch of cerotin there. The racking headache was still there, though a plethora of noisy thoughts had subdued it temporarily. Many times she tried to help the headache rise above the surface of her thoughts but failed. She desperately wished for her body—her head, her legs, her stomach, her arms, everywhere—to ache all over, so severely that she would be aware only of the pain and oblivious of everything else. Suddenly something happened to her heart in the midst of her thoughts. Was it pain? Her heart contracted for a moment and then relaxed. What was that? Curses! It was that same 'Oh no!' causing her heart to contract and expand by turns.

She had just started to walk back home when her feet froze. 'Does Ramlal think the man didn't like my looks?' she wondered. 'Well no. He didn't say anything about my looks. All he said was, "He didn't like you." And even if he didn't like my looks, so what? I also don't like the looks of many men. The guy, the one who came on the night of the new moon, what a grotesque face he had! Didn't I turn my nose up at him in disgust? Didn't I find him revolting when he got into bed with me? Didn't I feel like throwing up? That may well be, Saugandhi, but at least you didn't turn him away, or spurn him. But the seth, who came riding in his fancy car, he flat out spat in your face: "Oh no!" What else could that "Oh no!" have meant? Except, huh, A muskrat rubbing jasmine oil in its smelly head!—as the saying goes—or My, my, such high hopes with a face like this! "Oh, Ramlal, is this the girl you were praising to high heaven?—This girl . . . for a full ten rupees! Why not a donkey . . .'"

She was deeply immersed in her thoughts while ferocious flames were leaping from her big toe to the top of her head. By turns she felt angry with herself and then Ramlal, who had caused her so much misery at two in the morning. The next moment she felt that neither of them deserved any blame; instead, her thoughts focused on the seth. And with that, her eyes, ears, arms and legs, in fact every inch of her body instinctively turned around trying to find him somewhere. The desire to see the earlier scene play out again, just once, gripped her: she moves slowly towards the car, a hand pulls out the torch and points the beam at her, she hears that 'Oh no!' again and, straight away, she pounces on him like a wild cat and starts scratching his face mercilessly with her fingernails, grown long according to the current fashion. She should yank him out of the car by his hair, pummel him with her fists and . . . break into sobs, exhausted.

The thought of crying surfaced only because a few big fat teardrops had collected in her eyes from an excess of fury and despondency. All of a sudden she confronted her eyes: Why are you weeping? Why are you shedding these tears? The answer floated for a few moments in the droplets hesitating on the edge of her lashes. For the longest time Saugandhi kept looking through the liquid screen of her tears off into the space where the seth's car had vanished.

Thump-thump-thump . . . What was this sound? Where was it coming from? With a start, she scanned the whole area. She couldn't see anyone around her anywhere. Ah, it was the sound of her own heart, which she had taken for the sputter of a car's engine. What was the matter with her heart—running so smoothly and then suddenly this thump-thump-thump? Like a needle stuck on a worn-out record that keeps regurgitating the single word 'stars . . . stars . . .' at the end of the line 'I spent the night counting stars'.

The sky was filled with stars. She looked at them and exclaimed, 'How pretty they look!' She wanted to think about something else, but as soon as she uttered the word 'pretty' a new thought leapt into her mind: 'Yes, sure, the stars are pretty. But you're not. You're ugly. Hideously ugly! Have you forgotten that you were spurned just now?'

Saugandhi, you're not ugly! And with this thought every one of the countless images of herself that she had contemplated in front of the mirror over the last five years flitted before her eyes. Of course, she didn't look quite as fresh and vibrant as she had five years ago when she lived with her parents, unencumbered by any cares whatsoever. But she hadn't exactly become ugly either. She looked like any other woman who always attracted the amorous glances of the men who passed her by. She had all the essential qualities that she thought anyone wanting to spend a few nights with a woman would want to see in her. She was young. She had a shapely figure. When her eyes sometimes fell on her thighs while bathing, she admired their round firmness. She was affable and genial. Hardly any man had come away from her place feeling dissatisfied in these five years. She was friendly and full of compassion. Last Christmas, when she was living in Golpetha, a young man had spent the night with her. In the morning he went into the other room to put on his jacket and found his wallet missing. The poor boy was terribly upset. (Saugandhi's maid had swiped it.) He had come from Hyderabad to vacation in Bombay. Now he had no money to pay for the return trip. Saugandhi had taken pity on the lad and returned his ten rupees to him.

'What's wrong with me?' she asked every single object that was in front of her: the dimmed gas lamps, the iron lamp posts, the square cobblestones of the sidewalk, and the dislodged gravel from the road. She looked at each of them in turn and then raised her eyes to the sky hanging low overhead. But none returned an answer.

The answer was there inside of her. There was nothing wrong with her, and she knew that. She was, in fact, good. Yet she wanted to hear someone praise her. Have someone, anyone, put his hand on her shoulder right now and just say, 'Who says you're bad, Saugandhi? If anyone calls you bad, they must be bad themselves.' All of this wasn't even necessary. Just 'Saugandhi, you're very good!' would have sufficed.

Why did she want someone to praise her, she wondered. She hadn't ever needed to hear this so desperately before—so desperately indeed that today she had even looked at inanimate objects with such solicitous intensity as though hoping to extract from them a confirmation of her goodness. Why was every atom of her being pining to become a 'mother'? Why was she preparing herself to gather everything on earth into her lap like a mother? And why did she want to wrap herself around the lamp post up ahead, to rest her warm cheek on its frosty surface and take away its chill?

For a moment she felt as though the dim light of the gas lamp, the metal lamp post, the square cobblestones of the sidewalk, in fact everything around her in the still night, was looking at her compassionately. The sky overhead, now a dark grey sheet with numerous holes, seemed to understand her, just as she seemed to understand the meaning of the blinking stars. But why this tension that was churning her inside? Why did she feel like the weather just before the rains? She wanted every pore of her body to burst open and let out whatever was boiling inside. But how could that happen? How?

She was now standing by the red letter box at the end of the street. A strong gust of wind shook the metal flap hanging like a tongue in an open mouth. The ensuing rattle made her look automatically in the direction the car had sped away, but she couldn't see anything there. How desperately she yearned for the car to approach her once again and . . . and . . .

'To hell with it! What do I care! No point making my life miserable! Let's go home and take a long, restful nap. Nothing will be gained by engaging in this kind of thinking. Get moving, Saugandhi, go home and have a mug of cold water, rub on a dab of balm, and doze off. You'll have a good sleep, absolutely first rate. Everything will be all right. To hell with the seth and his car . . .'

Suddenly she felt light. It was as if she had just emerged from a dip in the refreshingly cool waters of a pond. It was the same lightness she always felt after puja. It caused her steps to falter a few times as she started walking home.

As she was nearing her place, the entire episode shot through her heart like an obdurate pain and spread over her whole being. Her steps began to feel heavy once again and the memory of how a man had sent for her, slapped her with the beam of his torch, and insulted her in the middle of the bazaar a short time ago came back to haunt her and made her feel absolutely miserable. The very thought made her feel as if someone was poking at her ribs with his hard fingers, as though she were a sheep or a goat and he wanted to check whether the animal had any flesh at all. 'That seth, may God . . .' Saugandhi thought of cursing him, but stopped short. What would be the point? She would have enjoyed it far more if he had been standing in front of her and she could curse every single part of his being, from top to bottom, using such foul, abrasive language that he would be writhing in agony for the rest of his life. She would have torn her clothes and stood in front of him stark naked, saying, 'This is what you came for, didn't you? Here, take it! Take it for free! But whatever I am, whatever lies hidden inside me, you can't buy it, no one can buy it—not you, not your father, not anyone—not for all the money in the world!'

Ever-changing methods of exacting revenge were insinuating themselves into Saugandhi's mind. If only she could come face to face with that seth again . . . she would do this to him . . . no, not this, but that . . . avenge herself like this . . . no, like that. But realizing such an encounter was next to impossible, she contented herself with a single invective, a small one, which she wished would stick to the lout's nose like a pesky fly, never to leave it for as long as he lived.

Absorbed in this back and forth with her inner self, she had climbed up to her second-floor kholi. She took out the key from her bra and reached to unlock the door. The key turned in the empty air. There was no padlock on the door. She gave the door panels a gentle push and heard them creak softly. Someone unlatched the door from the inside. The panels yawned open and she stepped in.

Madho laughed through his moustache. Closing the door after Saugandhi he said, 'Good, you finally took my advice. An early morning walk is good for your health. If you keep it up, you'll be cured of your sluggishness. And the back pains that you keep complaining about all the time, they'll disappear too. Guess you must have walked up to the Victoria Gardens, right?'

Saugandhi didn't answer, nor did Madho show any desire to press on. When he talked, it never required her participation. They talked only because they thought they had to.

Madho plunked down into the wickerwork chair; its backrest had a big grimy stain left by his heavily oiled hair. He crossed his legs and started stroking his moustache.

Saugandhi took a seat on the bed and said, 'I was expecting you today.'

Madho lost his bearing. 'Expecting me?' he said. 'How in the world did you know I was coming today?'

Her tightly pressed lips parted a little and a wan smile appeared. 'I dreamt about you tonight. When I woke up, you weren't there. So I told myself, "Let's go somewhere for a stroll." And . . .'

'And I showed up,' said Madho, beside himself with delight. 'So, after all, the sages have said it: Caring hearts reach out for each other. When did you have this dream?'

'At about four,' she replied.

Madho got out of the chair, walked over to the bed and sat down next to her. 'And you know what? I saw you in my dream at around two, in a floral sari, exactly like the one you have on, standing before me, holding, yes, a bag full of money. You put the bag in my lap and said, "Madho, why do you worry? Here, take it. After all my money is your money." Would you believe it, Saugandhi, I swear by your life, I got up right away, bought my ticket and headed your way. Oh, what can I tell you? I'm in a terrible mess. Somebody has lodged a court case against me for no reason at all. If only I had twenty rupees to bribe the inspector with, I could perhaps buy my way out. You aren't tired, are you? Come, lie down, I'll massage your feet. Surely a person feels tired when they're not used to taking walks. Here, extend your feet towards me.'

Saugandhi lay down, supporting her head on her folded forearms like a pillow and, in a tone that wasn't her own, said, 'Madho, who is this rogue suing you? They won't put you in prison, will they? Just tell me if that might happen . . . What are twenty or thirty rupees? Fifty, even a hundred to warm the hands of the police in such a predicament is worth it. One can make millions as long as one's life is saved! Enough! You can stop now. I'm really not that tired. Stop massaging and tell me everything. My heart has been thumping violently ever since I heard the word "case". When do you have to go back?'

Madho smelled liquor on Saugandhi's breath. He thought the time was right and blurted out, 'By the afternoon train . . . I'll have to. If by evening I don't unload fifty or hundred on the sub-inspector of police . . . No need to give him more, I think fifty will be plenty to do the job.'

'Fifty it is!' Saugandhi said calmly, rising slowly from the bed and proceeding quietly towards the wall with the four photographs. The third from the left was Madho's. He was sitting on a chair in front of a curtain with a large floral print. His arms were stretched out along his thighs and he was holding a rosebud in one hand. Two fat books sat on a tea table nearby. He was so overwhelmed by the thought of being photographed that everything about him was spilling out and screaming: 'I'm having my picture taken! I'm having my picture taken!'

In the photo he was glaring at the camera so intently it seemed as if he was in the throes of some incredible ordeal at the time.

All of a sudden Saugandhi broke into peals of laughter. It was so sharp and pointed that Madho couldn't help feeling needles poking deep into his flesh. He got up from the bed and walked over to Saugandhi. 'Whose picture is making you laugh like this?'

She pointed at the first photograph on the left. 'His, the city's sanitary inspector. Just look at his stupid face. He says a rani fell in love with him. A rani—huh! Not with a face like that!'

As she said it she pulled the frame off the wall with such force that even the nail came out and with it a fair chunk of the plaster.

Madho had still not quite gotten over his initial surprise when Saugandhi threw the frame out of the window. It fell down two floors and crashed noisily on to the pavement. 'When the sweeper woman Rani comes to collect the trash in the morning,' Saugandhi said through the splintering echo of the glass, 'she'll pick up my raja too.'

Once again, a burst of the same sharp, pointed laughter began to spew from her lips, as though she was sharpening a knife blade on it.

Madho smiled. And then he laughed too, 'Hee-hee-hee . . .' but with considerable difficulty.

Saugandhi plucked the second frame off the wall and flung that out of the window as well. 'What's this saala doing here? No ugly faces are allowed! Isn't that right, Madho?'

Once again Madho smiled, and then snickered, but with no less difficulty than the time before.

With one hand Saugandhi grabbed the frame that held the photo of some guy flaunting a turban. She stretched out her other hand towards Madho's frame while he stood there cringing, as if her hand was coming towards him instead. In a split second, the frame with his photo was off the wall and in her hand, nail and all.

Saugandhi let out a booming laugh, exclaimed 'huh', and tossed both frames out of the window. When they crashed on the pavement two floors below, Madho felt as though something had exploded into pieces inside him. With tremendous difficulty he laughed and said only, 'You did well; I didn't like it either.'

'Oh, you didn't like it either?' she said, edging closer to him. 'But what I would like to know is this: Is there anything about you that someone could like? Your big fat nose, like a pakora? This hairy

forehead? These puffy nostrils? These twisted ears? Your awful breath?
Your filthy body? You didn't like your photo? How could you, since it
hid all your faults? Can't be helped, for such are the times: If you conceal
your faults, you're damned.'

Madho stepped backwards, until he was flat against the wall. Then,
injecting some firmness into his voice, he blurted, 'Looks as though
you're back to turning tricks. I'm telling you for the last time . . .'

Saugandhi interrupted him and finished the rest in his own style:
'If you ever go back to turning tricks, it will be over between us, and if
I ever catch you with another man here, I'll drag you by your hair and
throw you out . . . And yes, I'll send you this month's expenses by postal
money order as soon as I get back. Now, what's the rent for this kholi?'

Madho's head began to spin.

Saugandhi kept going: 'I'll tell you . . . fifteen rupees a month for
the kholi and ten a night for the use of my body, of which, as you
already know, my pimp takes away one quarter. As for the remaining
seven and a half, I had promised to give what I have no power to
give, and you had come to take what you can't take. What was there
between us? Nothing! Nothing at all, except these ten rupees. So we
decided to do something else—something that would make us need
each other. Until now it was ten rupees that jingled between us, now
it's fifty. You can hear their jingle, and so can I . . . What have you
done to your hair, anyway?'

With a quick movement of her finger, Saugandhi flipped the cap off
Madho's head. He was pissed off. 'Saugandhi!' he said sternly.

But she yanked Madho's handkerchief out of his pocket, sniffed it,
and tossed it on the floor. 'This filthy rag . . . how awfully smelly it is.
Throw it out! Come on . . .'

'Saugandhi!' Madho yelled.

'Saugandhi *ke bachche*!' she yelled back, even more sharply. 'Why
have you come here in the first place? Why? Does your mother who'll
dish out fifty rupees to you live here? Or are you some strapping
young man who's stolen my heart? You pig, you wretch. Look at you,
ordering me around! Am I under your thumb or something? Moocher,
what do you think you are? A thief, a pickpocket—what? Why have
you come here at this hour? Should I call the police? Whether you
have a court case against you in Puna or not, I'll definitely drag you
into one here!'

Intimidated, Madho could only mumble, 'Saugandhi, what's come over you?'

'Who are you to ask, you stinking bastard? Get out of here, or else . . .'

Her screams made her mangy dog, sleeping with his head resting on her weather-beaten chappals, wake up with a start. He got on his feet, raised his snout and began barking, eliciting a bout of hysterical laughter from Saugandhi. Madho was petrified.

When he bent over and reached for his cap, Saugandhi thundered, 'Don't you dare touch that . . . Leave it there and get out. As soon as you're back in Puna, I'll send it to you by *postal money order*.'

With another cackle, she plopped down into the wickerwork chair. With his ferocious barks, her mangy dog sent Madho scurrying out of the room and down the stairs. When the dog returned, wagging his stumpy tail, and sat at her feet flapping his ears, Saugandhi was startled. She felt a terrifying stillness around her, a stillness she had never experienced before. A strange emptiness engulfed everything, and she couldn't help thinking of a train standing all alone in its metal shed after disgorging every last one of its passengers. This feeling of emptiness which had suddenly arisen weighed heavily on her. She made repeated attempts to fill the void but failed. She was trying to stuff her brain with countless thoughts all at once, but it was like a sieve. As fast as she filled it, everything filtered out.

She sat in the chair for the longest time. When she couldn't find anything to distract her mind with even after a long and desperate search, she picked up her mangy dog, put him down beside her in the spacious teakwood bed, and went to sleep.

Janki

Just as the racing season was getting under way in Puna, Aziz wrote from Peshawar: 'I'm sending Janki, an acquaintance of mine. Do find her work in some film company in Puna or Bombay. You're well connected in the film world. Hope it won't be too much of a bother for you.'

The timing wasn't the problem; the problem was that I had never done anything of the kind before. Usually the men who took women to film companies were ones who sought to live off their earnings. So, obviously, the proposition made me quite uneasy. Then I thought, I really shouldn't disappoint him. He and I had known each other for a long time and he was sending her with such confidence in me. Besides, the thought that the doors of any film company would be open for a young woman reassured me to some degree. Why fret, she would find a job in some film company or other without my help anyway.

Four days later she arrived. She had travelled a long distance, from Peshawar to Bombay and then on to Puna. After the train came to a halt, I started down from one end and began looking for her, someone I'd never seen before. I had passed only a few carriages when a woman got out of a second-class compartment with my photograph in her hand. Standing with her back towards me, she rose up on her toes and started looking for me in the crowd. I came closer to her and said, 'Perhaps I'm the one you're looking for.'

She turned around. 'Oh, you.' She looked at my photo and said quite casually, 'Saadat Sahib, it was such a long journey. At Bombay, after I got off of the Frontier Mail, the atrocious wait for this train drained everything out of me. I really am totally worn out.'

'Your luggage?' I asked.

'I'll bring it out,' she said. Stepping back into the carriage, she brought out two suitcases and a bedroll.

I hailed a coolie.

Outside the station she said, 'I'll stay in a hotel.'

I got her a room in the hotel right across the road from the station. She needed to take a bath, change and get some rest, so I gave her my address, asked her to come to see me at ten in the morning, and left.

At half-past ten the following day she arrived at my place in Prabhat Nagar; I was staying in a friend's small, newly built flat. Janki had got delayed because it took her quite a while to find the place. My friend was out. I'd woken up late as I was working on my film script well into the night. After my bath, I was having tea when, all of a sudden, she walked in.

Despite the fatigue of the trip, she had appeared quite sprightly on the platform and, later, at the hotel. Now, though, as she stepped into the room where I sat in my pyjamas and undershirt, she looked terribly haggard and in bad shape.

She had been bubbling with life on the platform; not so when she came to see me in Flat No. 11, Prabhat Nagar. It seemed as though she'd either just donated a pint of blood or had an abortion.

As I mentioned, I was staying at my friend's to finish my script. There was no one else in the flat, except for an idiotic servant. The house was quite desolate, and Majeed was the kind of servant whose presence only heightened the sense of desolation.

I poured out some tea in a cup and offered it to Janki. 'You must have had your breakfast at the hotel,' I said. 'All the same, have some tea.'

She bit her lips nervously, picked up the teacup and started sipping from it, all the while shaking her right leg. Her quivering lips gave the impression that she wanted to say something to me but was feeling hesitant for some reason. Maybe some traveller at the hotel had tried to get fresh with her, I thought.

'You didn't have any problems at the hotel, did you?' I asked.

'Oh no. None.'

Her brief answer left nothing to go on so I kept quiet. But after we had finished tea, I thought I should say something. 'How is Aziz Sahib?'

She returned the cup to the teapoy without answering and quickly got up. 'Manto Sahib, do you know a good doctor?' she said hurriedly.

'Not in Puna, I don't.'

'Oh!'

'Why, are you sick or something?' I asked.

'Yes.'

She sat back down in a chair.

'What's the problem?'

Her full lips, which contracted automatically, or perhaps wittingly, when she smiled, opened. She tried to say something but couldn't. She got up again, picked up my cigarette tin, took one out and lit it, and said, 'Please forgive me, I smoke.'

Only later did I discover that she didn't just smoke; she smoked with a zest and gusto usually seen only in men. She held the cigarette between her fingers like they did, took deep long drags like they did, and blew the smoke out of some seventy-five cigarettes in a day.

'Why don't you say what's wrong?'

Annoyed, she stomped her foot petulantly, like a young girl.

'Hai Allah! How can I tell you . . .' She smiled, the arch of her curved lips revealing a line of exceptionally clean and sparkling white teeth. She sat down again and, making every effort not to let her tremulous eyes look straight into mine, said, 'It's like this: I'm late by fifteen days and I'm afraid that . . .'

At first, I didn't get her drift. But when she stopped abruptly, I had a vague feeling that I knew what she was alluding to.

'Well, such a thing often happens.'

She took a deep drag, blew out the smoke forcefully like men, and said, 'No. This time it feels different. I'm afraid I am pregnant.'

'Oh!'

She took a final drag of the cigarette and crushed it in the saucer. 'And if that's what's happened, I've got a big problem. Something like this happened in Peshawar once. But fortunately Aziz Sahib got me such potent medicine from a hakim friend of his that it aborted in no time at all.'

'Don't you like kids?' I asked.

She smiled. 'I do . . . but the hassle of raising them.'

'You do know that killing unborn babies is a crime, don't you?'

She quickly sobered up . . . and then said in a tone full of amazement, 'Aziz Sahib said the same thing. But really, Saadat Sahib, why is it a crime? After all, it's a personal matter. Besides, those who make laws, they must know how painful an abortion can be. Crime, huh!'

I couldn't help laughing. 'You really are a strange woman, Janki.'

She also laughed. 'Aziz Sahib says so too.'

In the midst of her laughter tears appeared in her eyes. I've noticed that when sincere people laugh, their eyes invariably well up. She took out a handkerchief from her bag, wiped her tears, and asked with a child's innocence, 'Tell me, Saadat Sahib, do you find what I say interesting?'

'Very,' I said.

'That's a lie!'

'And what's your proof?'

She lit up again. 'Oh, maybe it is so. All I know is that I'm a little dumb-headed. I eat a lot, chatter a lot, laugh a lot. You can see for yourself how badly my stomach has puffed up from eating too much. Aziz Sahib keeps admonishing me not to overeat, but I never listen. The thing is, Saadat Sahib, if I eat less, I feel as if there's something I wanted to tell someone but forgot.'

She started to laugh again. I joined her. It was strange, this laugh of hers. It sounded like the tinkling of ankle bells.

Just as she was about to resume talking about abortions, the friend with whom I was staying returned. I introduced Janki and said that she wanted to work in films. My friend took her to his studio. He was confident that the director for whom he worked as a secretary would select her for a particular role in his new film.

I tried to find work for her in all the film studios in Puna and pulled whatever strings I could. She was voice-tested in one place, camera-tested in another, and in a third they assessed her in different outfits, but nothing worked out. She was already quite upset about missing her period, and the week she had to spend in vain in the cheerless, depressing atmosphere of different film studios made things even worse. On top of that, the twenty green quinine pills she was popping every day to abort were making her even more sluggish. How Aziz Sahib was faring in her absence back in Peshawar was yet another cause of her constant worries. She had fired off a wire immediately after arriving in Puna and a letter a day thereafter, urging in each that he not neglect his health and take his medicine regularly.

What illness Aziz Sahib suffered from, I don't know; nonetheless, I did gather from Janki that he loved her and immediately did whatever she asked him to do. Many times his wife quarrelled with him about being lax in taking his medicine, but when Janki made the same request, he didn't so much as make a peep.

At first I thought her concern for Aziz Sahib was just for show. Slowly, though, her unpretentious talk convinced me that she really did care for him a lot. Whenever he wrote to her, tears would gather in her eyes while she read his letter.

Our repeated trips to film companies produced no result. And then one day she became overjoyed to learn that her fears were unfounded. Surely she had missed her period, but pregnant she was not.

Twenty days had passed since her arrival in Puna. During this time she had continued sending Aziz letter after letter. He also wrote pretty lengthy love letters to her. In one he suggested that if no job was forthcoming in Puna, I should try in Bombay. It was teeming with studios. It was a reasonable suggestion. However, as I was far too busy writing the script at the moment, it was difficult for me to accompany her there, so I phoned my friend Saeed who was playing the part of the hero in a film. By chance, he wasn't at the studio, but Narain was. When Narain found out that I was on the phone, he took the call, shouting loudly, 'Hello, Manto . . . Narain speaking. Tell me, what do you want? Saeed isn't here. He's sitting at home . . . settling accounts with Razia.'

'Whatever do you mean?' I asked.

'They had a fight. Razia is carrying on with someone else.'

'But settling accounts with Razia . . . what accounts?'

'Yaar, this Saeed, he's terribly mean. He's asking her to return all the clothes he ever bought for her.'

'Look, a friend of mine from Peshawar has sent a woman here. She's eager to work in films.'

Janki was standing close by. I realized I hadn't explained myself properly, and was about to correct myself when Narain's loud voice crashed against my ears. 'Woman, wow! From Peshawar? Wow again! *Khu*, send her, send her double quick. I too am a Pathan . . . a Pathan from Qusur.'

'Don't talk nonsense. Listen, I'm sending her to Bombay tomorrow, aboard the Deccan Queen. You or Saeed should pick her up at the station. Deccan Queen, remember.'

'But how will we recognize her?' I heard him ask.

'She'll recognize you. But do try to find work for her.'

'You're going to Bombay tomorrow on the Deccan Queen,' I told Janki. 'I'll show you Saeed's and Narain's photos. Both of them are tall, stout and handsome. You'll have no problem spotting them.'

I took out the album and showed her their pictures. She looked at both for a long time, though I noticed she looked at Saeed's more closely. She put the album aside and, making a faltering attempt to look straight into my eyes, asked, 'What kind of men are they?'

'What do you mean?'

'I mean what kind of men are they? . . . Most men in films tend to be quite nasty, I've heard.'

I detected a trace of probing in her grave tone.

'That, of course, is true. Why would anyone want good men working in films?'

'Why not?'

'There are two types of people in this world: those who grasp the extent of their pain from their own suffering, and those who grasp it by looking at the suffering of others. Tell me, which of the two do you think truly feels the real pain of suffering and its agony?'

After some reflection she answered, 'Why, those who have suffered themselves.'

'Exactly,' I said. 'Those who've been through real suffering can portray it best in films. Only a man who has floundered in love knows what heartbreak is. A woman who spreads out the rug and prays five times a day, who thinks love is as unlawful as eating the flesh of a pig, how can she profess love to a man in front of a camera?'

She reflected again for a bit. 'So you mean a woman should know about everything before entering films?'

'Not necessarily. She can also learn after she's begun.'

Janki paid no heed to all this and repeated her earlier question, 'So what kind of men are Saeed Sahib and Narain Sahib?'

'You want me to describe them in detail?'

'What do you mean by "in detail"?'

'Basically just which one will be better for you.'

She didn't like what I said.

'What kind of talk is that?'

'The kind you wanted.'

'Drop it.' She smiled. 'I won't ask you about anything any more.'

'But if you were to, I would recommend Narain.'

'Why?'

'Because he's a much better person than Saeed.'

I think so even now. Saeed is a poet, a terribly heartless poet. He won't slaughter a chicken with a knife; he'll wring its neck, pluck its feathers and then make broth out of it. He'll drink the broth, chew on the bones, then sit in a corner comfortably and write a poem about the chicken's demise, with tears in his eyes.

When he drinks, he never really gets drunk. This is something that annoys me a lot. It kills the very purpose of drinking. In the morning, he takes all the time in the world to wake up. The servant serves him tea in bed. If Saeed finds some rum on the bedside table left over from the previous night, he'll dump it into his tea and drink the mixture one mouthful at a time, as if he has absolutely no sense of taste.

If a sore appears on his body and begins to fester, he pays no attention to it, none at all, not even if puss starts to ooze out and the sore threatens to morph into a dangerous abscess. He won't deign to visit the doctor. If you try to say something, his only answer will be, 'Maladies often become a permanent part of the body. When this wound doesn't trouble me, why bother treating it?' Meanwhile, he'll look at the wound as if he's chanced upon a beautiful line of poetry.

He'll never understand film acting because he's nearly bereft of all delicate feelings. I saw him once in a film that became quite popular because of the songs sung by the heroine. At one point in the story he was scripted to hold her hand and profess his love to her. I swear, he grabbed her hand as if he was grabbing a dog's foot. How often have I told him, 'Put the thought of acting out of your mind. You're a darn good poet. Stay home and write poems.' But will he listen? He's obsessed with being an actor no matter what.

Narain now, I like him a lot. I also find the rules he's devised for working in a studio quite appealing.

1. One should never marry during his acting career. If he must marry, he should give up acting right away and open a dairy shop instead. If he's been a good actor, he'll make good money.
2. The minute an actress addresses you as 'bhai' or 'bhaiya', immediately whisper in her ear, 'What size is your bra?'

3. If you've gone gaga over an actress, don't waste your time pussyfooting around. Meet her in private and tell her flat out, 'I too have a tongue in my mouth.' If she doesn't believe it, stick out your whole tongue at her.
4. Should you be so lucky as to bag an actress, don't ever take even a penny from her earnings, even though that is kosher for her husband and brothers.
5. Make absolutely sure no child of yours is born to her, but she's free to bear your child after swaraj.
6. Remember, even an actor has to face Judgement Day. So don't even try to pretty up your record with a comb and razor; instead, use some crude method for it, such as doing a good deed every now and then.
7. Pay the greatest regard to the Pathan watchman at the studio. Greet him first thing in the morning when you come in. You'll reap a reward if you do, in the next world if not in this, for there aren't going to be any film companies in that other world.
8. Never become addicted to liquor and actresses. Who knows, the Congress may put a ban on both of them one day!
9. A Muslim or a Hindu can be a businessman, but an actor cannot be a Hindu actor or a Muslim actor.
10. Don't lie.

He has inscribed all of these under 'Narain's Ten Commandments' in his diary. They give a good idea of what kind of man he is. People say he doesn't abide by them himself, but that's not true.

Although Janki hadn't asked, I shared with her my thoughts about the two men. I told her plainly that if she made it into the film world, she would need the support of one man or the other. And Narain, in my view, would prove to be a good friend.

She heard me out and left for Bombay. When she returned the next day she was overjoyed. Apparently, Narain had signed her up with his studio for a whole year at a monthly salary of five hundred rupees. We talked for quite a while about how she got the job. After listening to her, I asked, 'You met both Saeed and Narain, right? Who liked you more?'

The hint of a smile appeared on her lips. Again with her hesitant eyes she looked at me and said, 'Saeed Sahib,' and then suddenly she became serious. 'Saadat Sahib, why did you praise Narain to high heaven?'

'Why? What happened?'

'He's so awful! In the evening when they both sat down to drink, I happened to address Narain as 'bhaiya' and he quickly bent over and whispered into my ear, "What size is your bra?" Bhagwan knows this burned me up, from my head right down to my very toes. What kind of lewd man is he?'

Her forehead started to perspire. I let out a resounding laugh.

'Why are you laughing?' she screamed.

'Oh, at his silliness,' I said and stopped laughing.

After fulminating against Narain for a while, she started talking about Aziz in a tone full of concern. For days now there hadn't been a letter from him. All kinds of misgivings were crowding her brain: Has he caught a head cold again? Some bike accident? He rides so recklessly. Maybe he's on his way to Puna because, when he was sending her off, he'd told her that he would sneak up to see her one of these days.

Reciting her concerns calmed her frayed nerves a little and she launched into praises of Aziz. He takes good care of his kids at home. He puts them through an exercise routine every morning, bathes them, and takes them to school. His wife is so gauche, so lacking in social graces that he has to show proper courtesies to relatives himself. When Janki came down with typhoid once, he looked after her continually for twenty days like a dutiful nurse. And so on and so forth.

The next day, after thanking me in appropriately warm words, she left for Bombay where the gates of a bright new life had been flung open to embrace her.

It took me another two months to finish my film script. I collected my payment and proceeded to Bombay where I was to receive another contract. At about five in the morning, I arrived in Andheri where Saeed and Narain were sharing a bungalow that was not much to speak of. I walked on to the veranda and found the front door locked. 'Perhaps they're sleeping,' I thought. 'Best not to bother them.' There was a back door which was often left open for the servants. I entered through it. The kitchen and adjacent dining room were, as usual, terribly untidy and grimy. The room across from them was reserved for guests. I opened the door and went in. There were two beds. Saeed and someone were sleeping together in one of them, covered with a quilt.

I was feeling very sleepy and didn't bother to change. I stretched out on the other bed and threw the blanket lying at the foot of the mattress over my legs. I was about to fall asleep when a bangle-clad forearm shot up from behind Saeed and reached towards the chair standing nearby, on which hung a white muslin shalwar.

I sat up with a start, only to see Janki in bed with Saeed. I picked up the shalwar and tossed it to her.

I went to Narain's room and woke him up. He'd been out on a film shoot until two in the morning. I felt sorry for waking the poor man up, but found him quite eager to chat, though not on any particular subject. My sudden appearance had apparently provoked him into talking a bit of nonsense with me so we indulged in such talk till nine o'clock. The subject of Janki cropped up several times during our gossip session.

When I told him about the bra incident, he laughed his head off, and mentioned, 'The juiciest part is yet to come: When I stuck my mouth to her ear and whispered, "What size is your bra?" she told me straight away, "Twenty-four." Sometime later, she suddenly realized the strangeness of my question and started cursing me. She's just like a little girl. Whenever we run into each other, she quickly pulls her dupatta over her breast. But, Manto, let me tell you, she's really a very faithful woman.'

'Just how do you know that?' I asked.

'How?' He smiled. 'A woman who gives the size of her bra to a total stranger could never dupe anyone.'

Strange logic, that! But Narain bent over backwards to convince me that Janki was, in fact, a very sincere woman. 'Manto,' he said, 'you have no idea how devoted she is to Saeed. It's no picnic looking after someone as indifferent as him. I see how well she's acquitting herself of this difficult but self-imposed responsibility. She's not just a woman, she's also a diligent and honest ayah. She spends a good half an hour every morning waking that donkey up. She makes him brush his teeth, helps him dress, feeds him breakfast, and, at night, when he goes to bed after a shot of rum, she closes the door and settles in beside him. If she runs into someone at the studio, she only talks about Saeed. "Saeed Sahib is such a nice man. Saeed Sahib sings so well. Saeed Sahib has put on weight. Saeed Sahib's pullover is ready. I've sent for a pair of Potohari sandals from Peshawar for Saeed Sahib. Saeed Sahib has a slight headache, I'm going to get some Aspro for him. Saeed Sahib wrote a *she'r* for me today." But whenever she bumps into me, she invariably frowns remembering the incident about the bra.'

I stayed with Saeed and Narain for nearly ten days, but Saeed didn't once talk to me about Janki, perhaps because their affair had become an old story by that time. But Janki and I talked quite a bit. She was very happy with Saeed, though she complained a lot about his devil-may-care attitude. 'Saadat Sahib,' she would say, 'he doesn't give a damn about his health. He's so careless. He's always immersed in his own thoughts and pays no attention to anything. What! You're laughing? Would you believe it, I even have to ask him every day whether or not he's been to the toilet.'

Everything Narain had told me about Janki was absolutely correct. I always found her fretting over Saeed. During my ten-day stay at Andheri, I found Janki's selfless dedication to Saeed very impressive, but I also kept thinking about Aziz. 'Janki had worried about him no less.' I wondered, 'Has she entirely forgotten him now that she's met Saeed?'

Had I stayed longer, I would certainly have asked Janki about it. However, I got into an argument over something with the owner of the film company that wanted to negotiate a contract with me, and to ease my anxiety I immediately took off for Puna. Barely two days passed before I received Aziz's telegram—he was in Bombay, on his way to Puna. Six hours later he was with me.

And early the next morning Janki was knocking at the door.

Aziz and Janki met, but they didn't show the ardour or the impatience of lovers meeting after a long separation—perhaps because my relations with Aziz had been quite formal and reserved right from the start of our friendship and they didn't want to appear impetuous in my presence.

Aziz thought that he might stay in a hotel. However, the friend with whom I was staying was in Kolhapur on an outdoor shooting assignment so I let Aziz and Janki stay with me. The flat had three rooms; Janki and Aziz could sleep in separate rooms. I suppose I ought to have put both in one room, but I couldn't. I wasn't that informal with Aziz. Besides, at no point had he ever even vaguely hinted at his affair with Janki.

In the evening, the two of them went out to see a movie. I stayed home as I wanted to get started on a new film script. I was awake until two in the morning and then fell asleep. I'd already given the spare key to Aziz, so there was no reason to worry about letting them in.

Regardless of how late I work, I always wake up once between three-thirty and four o'clock to have a drink of water. Out of habit, I woke up that night too. It just so happened that Aziz was occupying the room in which I had set up my bed, and where my water pitcher was kept.

I would never have bothered Aziz had I not been so awfully thirsty. My throat was completely parched from the large amount of whisky I had guzzled. I knocked. Some time elapsed before the door opened. Rubbing her dopey eyes, Janki said, 'Saeed Sahib!' But when she saw me, a soft 'Oh' escaped from her lips.

Inside Aziz was sleeping on the bed. I smiled spontaneously. Janki smiled too, her lips twisted to one side. I picked up the pitcher and left.

I woke up in the morning to a smoke cloud in my room. I rushed to the kitchen, only to find Janki burning piles of paper to heat water for Aziz's bath. Tears, from the smoke, were streaming down her cheeks. When she saw me, she smiled and blew into the brazier. 'Aziz Sahib catches a cold if he takes a cold bath,' she explained. 'He was sick the whole month I wasn't in Peshawar to look after him. And why wouldn't he be sick! He'd stopped taking his medicine! Did you notice how much weight he's lost?'

After his bath Aziz went out to take care of some business and Janki asked me to send a telegram to Saeed. 'I really should have informed him yesterday, right after I arrived here. Oh, what a terrible mistake! He must be worried sick.'

She had me write out the text. She informed him of her safe arrival in Puna, but she seemed more concerned about how he was doing and whether he was taking his shots regularly.

Four days went by, during which Janki sent Saeed five telegrams. He didn't write back. As she made plans to return to Bombay, suddenly, towards evening, Aziz came down with something. Janki asked me to send Saeed another telegram. She spent the whole night ministering to Aziz. It was just an ordinary fever, but Janki was exceedingly worried. I think there was also a measure of anxiety over Saeed's silence. 'I'm convinced,' she said, 'Saeed Sahib is ill, otherwise he would surely have written back.'

On the fifth day, Saeed's telegram arrived in the evening. Aziz was present at the time. 'I'm very sick,' Saeed had written and instructed her to 'return forthwith'. Just before the telegram arrived, Janki was laughing her head off over something I'd said, but the minute she heard

about Saeed's illness she fell silent. Aziz took her silence very badly and
when he addressed her, I could sense the bitterness in his tone. I got up
and went out.

When I returned in the evening I found the two sitting apart as
though they'd had a prolonged quarrel. There were dried tear stains on
Janki's cheeks. After some small talk, she picked up her handbag and
said to Aziz, 'I'm going, but I'll return soon,' and then to me, 'Saadat
Sahib, please watch over him; his fever still hasn't broken.'

I accompanied her to the station, bought her a ticket on the black
market and left after seating her in her carriage.

Back at the flat, Aziz had a light fever. We talked a long time,
without any mention of Janki.

Three days later, around five-thirty in the morning, I heard the
sound of someone opening the front door. Janki entered. She was asking
Aziz in convoluted words about his health and whether he had taken his
medicine regularly while she was away. I didn't hear what Aziz said, but
half an hour later, just as my eyes were closing under the onslaught of
sleep, I heard the muted sound of Aziz's angry voice. I couldn't make
out anything clearly except that he was giving her a piece of his mind.

At ten, he took a cold bath, leaving the water Janki had heated for
him untouched. When I reported this to her, tears welled up in her eyes.

After the bath, Aziz got dressed and went out. Janki stayed in bed.
About three in the afternoon I approached her, only to find that she was
running a very high temperature. I went out to get a doctor and saw that
Aziz was having his stuff loaded on to a tonga.

'Where are you headed?' I asked.

He shook my hand and said, 'Bombay. God willing, we'll meet
again.'

He hopped on to the carriage and left before I could tell him about
Janki's raging fever.

The doctor examined her carefully and diagnosed bronchitis.
If proper care were not taken, it was likely that it would turn into
pneumonia. He wrote out a prescription and walked out. Janki asked
me about Aziz. My first thought was to suppress the information, but
there was no point in hiding it. I told her he had left. She was shocked.
She buried her head in the pillow and cried for a long time.

The next morning, her fever had gone down one degree and she
was feeling slightly better when Saeed's telegram arrived from Bombay,

around eleven. In very harsh words he reproached her, 'Remember, you didn't keep your promise.'

I tried as hard as I could but wasn't able to stop her from leaving at once. She boarded the Puna Express in her precarious condition and left.

Five or six days later, Narain sent me a telegram. 'An urgent matter has come up; come at once.'

I thought he had negotiated a contract for me with some producer. This was not the case. When I reached Bombay, he told me that Janki's condition was very grave. Her bronchitis had in fact turned into pneumonia. And that, after arriving in Bombay, she had fallen while attempting to board a moving train bound for Andheri and hurt both of her thighs badly.

Janki bore her bodily pain bravely, but when she came to Andheri and Saeed pointed to her baggage and said, 'Please leave,' her spirit broke. Narain told me, 'Saeed's cold words left her stunned for a moment. I'm sure she must have thought of throwing herself under a train and dying. Saadat, regardless of what you may say about Saeed, his conduct with women is atrocious, downright unmanly. The poor thing! She was running a high fever and she'd fallen from a moving train, all of that just to get to this donkey as soon as possible. But he couldn't care less! He repeated "Please leave!" without even a wisp of emotion, so coldly, just like a line of newsprint spilling out of a linotype machine. It hurt me a lot. I got up and left. When I returned in the evening, Janki was nowhere; Saeed was sitting on the bed writing a poem with a glass of rum in front of him. I didn't say a word to him and went to my room. The next day I found out at the studio that Janki was lying critically ill at the house of one of the girls who work as extras. I talked to the owner of the studio and had her admitted to a hospital. She's been there since yesterday. Tell me what else I can do. She hates me, so I can't visit her. You go and check on her condition.'

I went to the hospital. The first thing she asked was how Aziz and Saeed were doing. I must say, I was deeply touched by her concern for the two even after how shabbily they had treated her.

Her condition was critical. The doctors told me that she had inflammation in both lungs and her life was in danger. What floored me, though, was that Janki was weathering her condition with fortitude.

When I returned to the studio and looked for Narain, I was told that he had been gone since morning. In the evening, when he came back, he showed me three small vials, their mouths tightly sealed with rubber caps, and asked, 'Know what these are?'

'No. They look like some kind of shots.'

He smiled. 'Yes, shots. Penicillin shots.'

I was astounded. Penicillin, in those days, was being produced in very small quantities in America and England, and all of it was earmarked strictly for military hospitals. 'Penicillin is a rare commodity. How did you get hold of it?' I asked.

He smiled and said, 'When I was a boy I was quite the expert at breaking into our family safe to steal money. Well, I did that again today. I sneaked into the military hospital and swiped these three vials from the refrigerator. Let's move Janki to a hotel. Come on, hurry up.'

I took a taxi to the hospital and brought her to the hotel where Narain had already booked two rooms.

In an exceedingly feeble voice, she asked over and over again why I had brought her here, and every time I replied that she would know soon. When she did learn, that is, when Narain entered the room with a syringe in hand, she turned her face away in dismay and said to me, 'Saadat Sahib, tell him to go away.'

Narain smiled. 'Darling, spit out your anger. Your life is at stake.'

Janki became furious. In spite of her weak condition, she sat up in the bed and said, 'Saadat Sahib, either you throw this bastard out or I'm leaving.'

Narain pressed her back on the bed and said smiling, 'This bastard won't budge without giving you the shot. I'm warning you, don't even try to resist.'

He gave the syringe to me, grabbed her arm with one hand, rubbed her upper arm with a cotton ball doused in alcohol, handed the cotton to me, took the syringe and plunged the needle into the muscle. She screamed, but the penicillin had entered her body.

As soon as Narain released her arm, she began to cry. He paid no attention, cleaned the injection site with the cotton ball, and went into the other room.

The first shot was administered at nine in the evening. The second was due in three hours. Narain warned me that if it was delayed by even half an hour, the penicillin's effect would wear off entirely. So he stayed awake. At eleven he got the stove going, sterilized the needle in boiling water, and filled the syringe with the next dose.

Janki's eyes were shut, her breathing raspy. Narain rubbed an alcohol-soaked wad of cotton on her other arm and jabbed the needle. A shrill cry escaped from her lips. Narain pulled the needle out, rubbed the cotton over the spot on her arm, and said, 'We'll give her the third dose at three o'clock.'

I have no idea when he gave her the third or even the fourth injection. When I awoke I heard the hissing sound of the burning stove and Narain asking the attendant for some ice. He had to keep the penicillin chilled.

At nine in the morning, we entered her room to give her the fifth shot and found her lying in bed with her eyes open. She scowled at Narain with hatred in her eyes, but said nothing. Narain smiled. 'How are you feeling, my dear?'

Janki remained quiet.

Narain stood close to her and said, 'These shots I'm jabbing into your arm are not love shots. They're meant to cure your pneumonia. I swiped them from the military hospital . . . Come on, lie on your stomach and slide your shalwar down your bottom a bit. Have you ever taken an injection there?'

He poked a spot on her derrière with his finger. Naked hate, tinged with awe, surfaced in Janki's eyes.

When she turned over, Narain said, 'Shabash!' and before she could resist, he pulled down her shalwar and ordered me, 'Come on, rub some alcohol here!'

She started to thrash her legs every which way. 'Don't,' Narain shouted, 'I'm giving you a shot, one way or another.'

The fifth injection was given successfully. Fifteen more remained, to be administered every three hours. The whole course required forty-five hours.

Five injections later, Janki's condition still hadn't shown any signs of improvement. But Narain believed in the miraculous potency of penicillin. He was absolutely sure that she would walk out of here fully cured. We talked a long time about this drug.

Around eleven Narain's servant walked in with a telegram for me. It was from a film company in Puna. They had asked me to rush over. I had to leave.

I returned to Bombay on the company's business about ten or fifteen days later. After finishing my work I went to Andheri. Saeed told me that Narain was still holed up in the hotel. Since the hotel was quite far away in the city, I spent the night in Andheri.

I reached the hotel the next morning around eight and found Narain's door ajar. I entered but found the room empty. I pushed on the door to the other room. Something flashed before my eyes. The moment she saw me, Janki slipped under the quilt. Narain was sprawled out next to her. Seeing me leave, he shouted, 'Come, Manto, come in. I always forget to latch the door. Come, yaar, sit down in this chair, but first hand Janki's shalwar to her, will you?'

Mozel

For the first time in four years, Trilochan was looking up at the night sky, and only because anxiety was gnawing at his heart. He had gone up to the terrace at Advani Chambers to clear his mind in the fresh air.

The cloudless sky stretched out like a sprawling canopy over the whole of Bombay. The city lights, dotting the landscape as far as Trilochan could see, appeared like so many fallen stars caught in a maze of tall buildings, glimmering like fireflies in the darkness.

It was an entirely novel experience for him to be out under the open sky at night. He had an overwhelming feeling that he'd been cooped up inside his flat for the last four years, and deprived of one of nature's great bounties. It must have been around three in the morning. A light, cool breeze was blowing around him, unlike the usual mechanical breeze of the electric fan, which always felt uncomfortably thick and heavy. When he woke up in the morning it was never without the feeling that his body had been thrashed all night long. Now, as every fibre of his being joyously soaked in the fresh morning air, he felt delightfully revived. He had climbed up to the terrace in a feverishly agitated state, but within half an hour it had subsided enough for him to think clearly.

Kirpal Kaur and her entire family lived in a mohalla teeming with Muslim fanatics. Several houses had been torched and many lives lost already. He might have brought them out to safety, but a curfew was on and there was no telling how long it would last—forty-eight hours perhaps. There were Muslims of the awfully dangerous kind everywhere. And to make matters worse, news of Sikhs making short work of Muslims and subjecting them to all manner of atrocities were filtering in from the Punjab. Trilochan felt totally helpless. Any Muslim hand could easily grab Kirpal Kaur's arm and send her to her death.

Kirpal's mother was blind and her father disabled. She did have a brother, but Niranjan had been living in the Devlali area for some time now, supervising a construction contract he had recently taken on.

Trilochan found Niranjan's attitude thoroughly annoying. He read the newspaper regularly and had warned Niranjan a week or so ago about the speed and ferocity with which riots were erupting everywhere. He'd told him quite plainly, 'Forget about the contract for now. These are treacherous times. And even if you stay with your family, it would still be better if you brought them over to my house. I know it isn't large enough, but in these days of such uncertainty . . . well, we'll manage somehow.'

But would Niranjan listen! He just stroked his bushy moustache and smiled. 'Yaar, you're worrying your head over nothing. Riots . . . I've seen many such riots here. This is Bombay, not any old place like Amritsar or Lahore. How long since you moved here? Four years, right? Well, I've been living here for twelve.'

God knows what Niranjan took Bombay for. Probably a city where, even if riots did break out, they would die down on their own, as if it possessed some magical power to quell them, or was perhaps a fairy-tale castle impervious to calamity. But in the fresh morning air Trilochan could see clearly that the mohalla wasn't quite as safe as all that. In fact, he wouldn't be the least bit surprised if he read in the newspaper one of these days that Kirpal and her family had been murdered.

He didn't much care about her blind mother or her disabled father. As far as he was concerned, it would be fine if she was saved and they were killed, and even better still if her brother was also killed for then there would be nothing standing in his way. Niranjan, especially, was proving to be the biggest hurdle, a *khingar*, a veritable brick wall in his path. When he and Kirpal Kaur talked, he referred to her brother as 'Khingar Singh' instead of his real name 'Niranjan Singh.'

The morning breeze was stirring gently around him. His head, now bereft of his kes, felt the refreshing coolness. But his mind, that was something else entirely—countless misgivings were colliding there.

Kirpal Kaur had come into his life only recently. Unlike her brother Khingar Singh, who was a burly young man, she was extremely delicate and nimble. Despite growing up in a village and experiencing its pastoral way of life, she displayed none of the coarse masculinity usually found in Sikh girls from rural areas who are accustomed to hard, physical labour. Her features were still evolving and her tiny breasts still needed many more layers of fat to fill out. Her complexion was fair and her body was as smooth as mercerized cotton. She was also very shy.

Although Trilochan was from the same village, he hadn't spent much time there. After finishing his primary education in the village school, he had left for the city to study in high school and, afterwards, college, and kind of just stayed on there. He returned to the village on many occasions but he never heard of anyone called Kirpal Kaur at any point, perhaps because he was always in a big rush to return to the city.

His college days were long gone. Easily ten years separated the terrace at Advani Chambers from college. During that period, Trilochan's life was filled with unusual experiences: Burma, Singapore, Hong Kong and, finally, Bombay, where he'd been living for the past four years.

Tonight was the first time he'd looked up at the sky and found the sight agreeable: countless little lamps glimmering in the grey canopy overhead and a light, cool refreshing breeze.

While thinking about Kirpal Kaur his thoughts drifted off to Mozel, the Jewish girl who rented a flat in Advani Chambers. Trilochan had fallen deeply in love with her—'up to his knees', as the Sikhs would say. He'd never experienced such crazy love before in all his thirty-five years.

He had bumped into Mozel on the very first day he moved into a second-floor flat in the building, which he'd acquired with the help of a Christian friend of his. His first impression was that she was a mad woman, dangerously mad. She wore her brown hair short and quite dishevelled, and a thick coat of lipstick that was dried up, cracking here and there on her lips, reminding him of a clot of blood. Her lips were not as thick as they appeared. It was the thick, reddish-brown lipstick that made them look beefy. A long tunic hung loosely on her body, its open collar exposing a generous expanse of her bulging breasts with their web of thin, blue veins. Her bare arms were covered with a layer of fine fuzz that gave the impression that she'd just emerged from a beauty parlour with wispy clippings of hair still sticking to her.

Trilochan's flat was right across from hers with only a narrow
corridor in between. Just as he approached his door, Mozel came
barging out of hers. The noise of her wooden clogs stopped him. She
gaped at him from under her unruly hair and tittered, which threw
him off balance. He quickly pulled the key out of his pocket and turned
towards his door, but just then one of her clogs slipped on the glossy
cement floor and her whole body collided with him.

When he attempted to collect himself, he found her sprawled on
top of him with her long loose tunic pushed all the way up and her
bare, stout legs on either side of him. He tried to rise, but got even more
entangled with her, as if he was a blanket covering her body.

Gasping, he apologized to her profusely. She straightened her
dress and smiled. 'These clogs—they're atrocious,' she said as she
slipped her big toe and the one next to it into the clog and strode
down the hallway.

Trilochan had thought it would be hard to befriend her, but within
a short period she herself was drawn to him. She was a very headstrong
woman, however, and didn't show him much regard. She made him
take her out to dinner, buy her drinks, take her to movies, and spent
whole days with him splashing on the beach at Juhu, but when he tried
to go further than just hugging and kissing, she told him to lay off so
sternly that all of his fervent desires just crumbled.

He'd never been in love before. Whether in Lahore, Burma or
Singapore, whenever he had needed a woman he just picked one up
and paid for her services. Not even in his dreams had he ever imagined
that he would fall 'up to the knees' in love with a wilful Jewish girl soon
after arriving in Bombay. She treated him with the utmost indifference
and lack of civility. If he invited her for a movie, she would immediately
spring to her feet and get ready, but the minute they were seated, she
would let her eyes wander. If she spotted an acquaintance, she would
wave at him vigorously and, without excusing herself, get up and go sit
with the other fellow.

It was no different in restaurants. He would order special dishes for
her, but the instant she saw an old friend, she would get up abruptly,
abandon her meal and go over to sit by his side, leaving Trilochan to
fume by himself.

Her indifference really got to him at times. If he grumbled about it,
she would stop seeing him for days, complaining now of a headache,

now about her stomach, which Trilochan well knew was solid steel and impervious to any kind of ailment.

The next time they met she told him, 'You're a Sikh. How would you understand anything delicate!'

'What's delicate about your old lovers?' Trilochan fired back in a rage.

Standing with arms akimbo and feet apart, she retorted, 'Why do you keep taunting me? Yes, they are my lovers and I do love them dearly. If that bugs you, so be it. I couldn't care less.'

'Well then, how can we carry on like this?' he said, attempting to reason with her.

She burst out laughing. 'You really *are* a Sikh—no doubt about it! And an idiot to boot. Whoever said anything about carrying on with me? If that's what you're looking for, go back to your village and find some Sikhni to marry. If you want to hang out with me, this is how it will be.'

In the end Trilochan always capitulated. He couldn't help it. Mozel had become his greatest weakness. He wanted to be around her at any cost. She often humiliated him, sometimes even in front of ill-bred 'Kristan'* boys, but he resolutely suffered all the belittlement because of his heart.

When belittled and humiliated thus, it is revenge that one seeks, but not so Trilochan. He had firmly closed his mind's eye and plugged his ears. He not only liked her, he was, as he often described his obsession to his friends, 'up to his knees' in love. All he could do now was submerge the rest of him in the bog and be done with it.

He steadfastly endured this wretched state of affairs for two years. Finally one day, when Mozel seemed to be in a good mood, he gathered her in his arms and asked, 'Mozel, don't you love me?'

She pulled away from his tight embrace, sat down in a chair and started staring vacuously at the hem of her tunic. After some time she raised her large Jewish eyes, batted her thick eyelashes and said, 'Me love a Sikh? No way.'

It was as if someone had shoved red-hot coals inside Trilochan's turban. His entire body sizzled with rage. 'Mozel, you always make fun of me,' he blurted out. 'But it's my love that you deride.'

* Christian.

Mozel quickly got up from the chair, toyed with her short brown hair seductively and said, 'If you shave off your beard and let down your hair, I promise many young men will come on to you. You're quite handsome, really.'

Trilochan felt as if more burning coals had been shoved into his kes. He took a few steps towards Mozel, dragged her into his arms and pasted his moustachioed lips on her mouth.

She pushed him away. 'Phew!' she said. 'Don't bother! I already brushed my teeth this morning.'

'Mozel!' Trilochan screamed.

She withdrew a small mirror from her bag and started examining her lips where the thick layer of lipstick had cracked. 'By God, you don't know how to use your bristles properly. They're perfect for brushing my navy-blue skirt; just a bit of petrol is needed along with them.'

Trilochan's anger had risen to the point where it lost all its vehemence. He calmly sat down on the couch. Mozel sat beside him and started to unravel his beard, removing the hairpins one by one and holding them between her teeth.

He really was handsome. Before hair appeared on his face, people had often mistaken him for a beautiful young girl. But this shag of hair had obscured his fine features. And he was aware of it. Being a dutiful young man who held his religion in high regard, he loathed the idea of eliminating any of the things that were an outward expression of his faith.

'What are you doing?' he asked, after Mozel had completely undone his beard and left it to hang down over his chest.

She smiled despite the pins clenched in her teeth and said, 'Your hair is too soft. I was wrong to think it could brush my skirt clean. Triloch, give your hair to me. I'll make myself an exquisite woven handbag.'

Trilochan was furious. 'Have I ever made fun of your religion?' he asked in dead seriousness. 'Why then do you mock mine? It's not nice to ridicule a person's religious feelings. I would never have tolerated it, but I've looked the other way because I love you. I love you very much. Don't you know that?'

She stopped playing with his beard. 'I know,' she muttered.

'So?' he asked, deftly folding his hair and pulling the pins out of her mouth. 'You know perfectly well that my love isn't some kind of claptrap. I want to marry you.'

She got up, shaking her hair softly. 'I know,' she said, and looked intently at the picture hanging on the wall. 'In fact, I've nearly made up my mind to marry you.'

'Do you mean it?' He jumped up with elation.

Her reddish-brown lips parted in a broad smile and her strong white teeth glimmered for an instant. 'I do—I really do!'

His beard only half folded, he embraced her passionately and asked, 'When . . . when?'

Mozel pulled away and announced, 'When you get rid of this mop of hair.'

'I will, tomorrow,' he said without thinking. He was so overcome that he would have agreed to anything.

Mozel began to tap-dance. 'Rubbish, Triloch! You don't have the spunk!'

This had driven every single thought of religion flying out of his mind. 'You'll see.'

'So I will,' she said, darting towards him and kissing him on his moustache. Then with another 'Phew!' she breezed out.

It would be useless to recount here what all went through his mind that night and the torment Trilochan suffered. The next day he went to a barber in the Fort area and had him cut off his hair and shave off his beard. Trilochan kept his eyes tightly closed and let it happen. After it was over he opened his eyes and contemplated his face in the mirror for the longest time—even the most beautiful woman in Bombay would have found this face irresistible.

Trilochan was now feeling the same eerie chill he had felt when he stepped out of the barbershop. He quickened his steps across the terrace that was crowded with a network of water tanks and pipes. He wanted to avoid the rest of the story but it proved impossible.

He remained in his flat the whole day. The next day he sent his servant with a note for Mozel saying that he wasn't feeling well. She came to see him. The sight of his head without its shag of hair threw her off for a moment. Then she exclaimed, 'My darling Triloch!' and began hugging him and painting his whole face a deep red with her kisses.

She ran her hand over his smooth cheeks, combed her fingers through his hair, now trimmed short in the English style, and kept exclaiming loudly in Arabic. She shouted so much that her nose began to run. When she realized it, she just lifted the hem of her skirt and wiped her nose. Trilochan blushed. He quickly lowered her skirt and admonished her, 'You should at least wear something underneath.'

Mozel only smiled and said, 'It bothers me. Makes me feel cooped up, strangely. It's fine this way.'

Trilochan remembered their first encounter, when the two had collided in the hallway and their bodies had become entangled in a strange way. He smiled and took her in his arms. 'We'll marry tomorrow!'

'Yes, tomorrow,' she agreed, caressing his smooth chin with the back of her hand.

They chose Puna for the wedding. Since it would be a civil marriage conducted before the court, a fortnight's notice was required. So Puna seemed quite feasible. Not only was it close, Trilochan also had some friends there. According to the plan, they would leave the next day.

Mozel worked as a salesgirl in one of the Fort area stores. She had asked him to meet her at a taxi stand not far from her workplace. Trilochan arrived at the appointed time and waited a whole hour and a half, but she never came. The next day he heard that she had left for an indefinite stay in Devlali with an old friend who had just bought a new car.

How Trilochan bore his agony is a fairly long story. Briefly, he inured himself to this calamity and eventually got over it. Not long afterwards he met Kirpal Kaur and fell for her. It didn't take him long to realize that Mozel was a heartless coquette who kept hopping from tree to tree like a bird. The thought that he had been saved from making the terrible mistake of marrying her eased his heart a little. But there were times when the memory of her returned like an old pain. He liked her even though she didn't much care about people's feelings. He couldn't resist wondering now and then about what she might be up to in Devlali with this other man who had bought himself a new car. Was she still with him or had she ditched him for yet another man? Given his knowledge of her true character, Trilochan couldn't bear the thought of her being with any man other than himself.

He'd spent a fortune on her, quite willingly though. Most of the time Mozel wasn't hard to please. She frequently went for the cheap stuff. Once, he wanted to buy her a fairly expensive pair of gold earrings, but she was so taken by the sight of some cheap, gaudy ones in the same store that she begged him to buy those instead.

He still hadn't quite figured her out. What substance was she made of—really? She let him kiss her for hours, spread himself all over her like a blanket, but never anything beyond that. 'You're a Sikh—I hate you!' she would say playfully.

He knew she didn't mean it. Had she really hated him, she wouldn't have spent so much time with him. Her impatience wouldn't have allowed her to put up with him for two full years and would have settled the matter in two minutes flat instead. She didn't like to wear undergarments because they bothered her. He often tried to knock some sense into her about the necessity for them, to instil some regard for propriety, even tried to appeal to her sense of modesty, but she refused to budge.

Whenever he brought up 'modesty' and 'propriety' it always raised her hackles. 'Modesty—what's that? Just close your eyes if you care so much for it. Name one piece of clothing that can hide a person's nakedness or that your eyes can't see through. Spare me such nonsense. You're Sikh—I know you guys wear some silly shorts under your pants. They are also part of your religious trappings, like your beard and long hair. You should be ashamed of yourself—a grown man who still believes his religion resides in his underpants.'

At first, this sort of talk greatly infuriated him, but later, after he thought about it, he didn't feel quite so sure about it himself. Perhaps what she said wasn't completely preposterous after all. In the end, after getting rid of his hair and beard, he was convinced that he'd been carrying this excess baggage all along for no sane reason at all.

Trilochan stopped near a water tank. He uttered the coarsest swear word he could think of for Mozel and put her out of his mind. The life of the virginal Kirpal Kaur whom he loved very much was in danger at that moment. Her mohalla had become the haunt of militant Muslims and had seen a few incidents already. The problem was that it had been placed under a forty-eight-hour curfew, but if these chawl Muslims got it into their heads, they wouldn't be deterred by a curfew. They could easily dispatch Kirpal Kaur and her parents without anyone so much as catching a whiff of it.

Plagued by such thoughts, Trilochan sat down on a section of the huge pipeline. His kes had grown back some already and, he hoped, would reach its former length within a year. His beard was also growing fast, though he didn't want it to get too bushy. This barber in the Fort area, he trimmed it so deftly that it didn't appear as though it had been touched.

He ran his fingers through his long soft hair and sighed. Just as he was thinking of getting up, the jarring clip-clop of wooden clogs struck his eardrums. Who could that be—he wondered? Quite a few Jewish women lived in the building and they all wore clogs indoors. The sound kept getting closer. Suddenly he saw Mozel. She was clad in the familiar long, loose Jewish tunic and yawning loudly near another water tank, so loudly indeed that for a moment he thought the air around her might shatter.

He stood up, wondering where she had materialized from so suddenly and what she was doing here at this hour.

She yawned again. Trilochan felt as if his bones were about to crack from the sound.

Her large breasts heaved inside her baggy tunic. Several flat, round bluish-black veins swirled before Trilochan's eyes. He coughed loudly. Mozel turned around and saw him. Her reaction was pretty mild. Dragging her clogs, she walked up to him and gawked at his diminutive beard.

'Oh, you've become a Sikh again, Triloch?'

His beard began to irk him.

She took a step forward, rubbed the back of her hand against his chin and smiled. 'Perfect, I can clean my navy blue skirt now,' she said. 'Too bad, I seem to have left it in Devlali.'

Trilochan remained silent.

She pinched his arm and said, 'Why don't you say something, Sardar Sahib?'

He didn't wish to repeat his earlier mistakes. Still, he looked closely at Mozel's face in the faint light of the morning. It didn't show any noticeable change, except that she looked a bit thin. 'Have you been ill?' he asked.

'No.' She shook her head slightly.

'But you look a little frail.'

'I'm dieting.' She plopped down on the pipe and started to tap the terrace floor with her clogs. 'So you're . . . you're becoming a Sikh again?'

'Yes, I am,' Trilochan said, rather audaciously.

'Congratulations!' She removed one of her clogs and started tapping it on the pipe. 'Are you in love with some other girl?'

'Yes,' he replied softly.

'Good for you. Someone from this building?'

'No.'

'That's too bad,' she said, slipping the clogs over her toes and standing. 'One should always think of one's neighbours first.'

He remained silent. Mozel touched his beard with all five fingers and asked, 'Growing this at the girl's behest?'

He was feeling quite unnerved, as if the hair in his beard had become tangled while being combed. 'No,' he said sharply.

Her lipstick looked like a piece of shrivelled meat on her mouth. When she smiled an image of the village butcher in his shop—where jhatka meat was sold—slashing a massive chunk of meat in two with a quick movement of his knife floated in his mind.

She laughed. 'I swear I'll marry you if you shave off this beard.'

Trilochan felt like telling Mozel to go to hell. He was in love with a chaste, pure-hearted girl from his village and would marry only her. What was Mozel compared to her? Just a lewd, promiscuous woman, ugly, rude and insensitive. But he wasn't mean, so he only said, 'Mozel, I've made up my mind to marry this girl from my village. She's a very simple, religious girl. I'm growing back my hair for her sake.'

Although Mozel wasn't someone who thought long and hard about anything, she did think for a moment. After a while, swivelling around in a half circle on the heels of her clogs, she said, 'How on earth do you expect her to marry you if she's so observant of her religion? Wouldn't she know you once had your hair cut?'

'She doesn't know about that yet. I started growing my beard soon after you took off for Devlali . . . to get back at you. I met Kirpal Kaur shortly afterward. But I wrap my turban so cleverly that maybe only one in a hundred people would guess that underneath it my kes is clipped. And in any case, it won't be long now before it grows back to its former length.' He started combing his fingers through his soft hair.

She pulled up her tunic and started scratching her fleshy white thigh. 'That's wonderful . . . Damn these mosquitoes, they've even invaded here. Look, how badly it bit me.'

Trilochan looked away. Mozel bent down, moistened her fingertip with a dab of saliva, pressed it over the tiny red spot and then, letting her tunic drop back down, stood up again and asked, 'So when is the wedding?'

'Can't say . . . nothing is definite,' he replied and became pensive.

After a brief silence, sensing his anxiety, she asked in a serious tone, 'Triloch, is something wrong?'

He desperately needed someone, even Mozel, to empathize with him, to appreciate his predicament. He told her everything.

'You're a complete moron.' She let out a laugh. 'Go and get her. It's not that difficult.'

'Difficult! You don't seem to understand the precariousness of this situation . . . of any situation for that matter. You're a devil-may-care sort of person—precisely why we couldn't hit it off together, something that I'll regret for the rest of my days.'

She banged the pipe forcefully with her clog in dismay. 'To hell with your regret. Idiot, you should be thinking about how to get your— what's her name?—out to safety. Instead, here you are, moaning about our affair. We would never have made it. You're a silly fool . . . a coward . . . I want a man, a fearless man. But there's no time for idle talk. Come on, let's go and get her.'

She grabbed his arm.

A befuddled Trilochan asked, 'Where to?'

'Where she is—where else? I know every last brick of that mohalla. Come on, let's get going.'

'But listen . . . there's a curfew.'

'Not for Mozel . . . Now come on.'

She dragged him towards the door that led to the stairs. She opened it and was about to go down when she stopped and looked at his beard.

'What's the matter?' he asked.

'This . . . your beard,' she said. 'Well, okay. It isn't too long. If you walk bareheaded, no one will take you for a Sikh.'

'Bareheaded?' He was a bit fazed. 'I'm not going there bareheaded.'

'Why?' she asked, naively.

'You don't understand,' he said, pushing a lock of hair to the back of his head. 'It isn't right for me to go there without my turban.'

'Why not?'

'Try to understand. She's never seen me bareheaded. She thinks I have kes; I don't want her to know my secret.'

'You really are a nut, a first-rate nut. You stupid ass.' She stomped her clog on the threshold of the door. 'It's a question of her life—what's her name, this Kaur you love?'

'Mozel, she's a religious kind of person.' Trilochan tried to impress it upon her. 'If she saw me without my turban, she would start hating me.'

Mozel was pissed off. 'To hell with your love. Tell me, are all Sikhs as stupid as you? Her life is in danger, and what do we have here: you, dead set on wearing your turban and maybe even those underpants that look like shorts.'

'I wear those all the time,' he said.

'Good for you. But now, do some thinking. She lives in a neighbourhood which is crawling with *miyan bhai*s,* each more ferocious than the other. If you walked in with your turban on, they would make mincemeat out of you in no time.'

He gave a quick answer, 'I don't care. If I go there with you, it will be in my turban. I can't risk my love.'

Mozel became irritated; her body quivered with anger, so much so that her breasts shook inside the bodice of her tunic. 'You ass, where will your love be when you're not here, your—what's that dumdum's name—when she's not there, her family isn't there? By God, you *are* a Sikh. A first-rate idiot Sikh. No doubt about it.'

That was the last straw. 'Shut up!' he screamed.

She burst into laughter and flung her fuzz-covered arms around his neck. Turning a bit she said, 'All right, darling, as you wish. Go, don your pagri. I'll wait for you downstairs in the bazaar.'

She started to go down but Trilochan stopped her. 'Aren't you going to change your clothes?'

She shook her head. 'This will work fine.'

And she went down clip-clopping in her clogs. He could hear them all the way down to the lowest steps of the stairs. He gathered his hair at the back of his head and went to his flat to quickly change his clothes. The turban was already furled so he fixed it on his head neatly, locked the door behind him and went downstairs.

He found Mozel standing on the pavement, her feet wide apart, smoking a cigarette, just like a man. When he neared her, she filled her mouth with the smoke and released it on his face mischievously.

'You're really very mean,' he blurted out in anger.

* Muslims.

'That's nothing new.' She smiled. 'Haven't I heard that many times before? She looked at his turban. 'Nice job! It does give the impression that you have kes.'

The bazaar was deathly still; there was not a soul anywhere. The only sound was the breeze, which blew softly as if it too was afraid of the curfew. The lights were on, but they gave off a sickly glow. Usually trams started running by this hour and one could see a lot of activity with people moving about in the street. But now it seemed as though no one had ever walked here nor ever would.

Mozel walked ahead of him, her clogs clicking on the pavement, shattering the pervading silence with their sharp noise. Trilochan damned her silently for not putting on something better than these godforsaken clogs. He felt like telling her to get rid of them and walk barefoot, but he knew she would never listen to him. Better not stir up a fuss.

He was deathly afraid—even the slightest rustle of a leaf made his heart skip a beat. She, on the other hand, walked along fearlessly, leisurely blowing smoke as if she was taking the air along a garden promenade.

As the two of them approached an intersection, a policeman hailed them, 'Hey, you—where are you going?'

Trilochan cringed, but she walked over to the cop, fluffed up her hair a little, and said, 'Oh, it's you! Don't you recognize me . . . Mozel.' Then pointing to an alley, 'That way. My sister lives there. She's ill. I'm taking the doctor to see her.'

The cop was still struggling to recognize her when she pulled out a pack of cigarettes from God knows where. 'Here, have a cigarette.'

The cop took one. 'Light?' She held out the cigarette still smouldering between her lips.

The cop took a long drag on his cigarette. She winked at him with her right eye and at Trilochan with her left and then clip-clopped towards the alley leading to Kirpal Kaur's mohalla.

Trilochan was silent. He could sense the strange joy Mozel was feeling in defying the curfew. She had always liked to play dangerously. Every time they visited the Juhu beach, she would fight her way through the humongous waves, swimming quite far into the sea, and leaving him petrified with the fear that she might drown. When she returned her body was always full of cuts and bruises, but she didn't seem to care.

Every now and then Trilochan looked around furtively, afraid that some knife-swinging fellow might materialize from somewhere. Mozel halted. When he caught up with her, she tried to reason with him. 'Triloch dear, don't panic. If you do, something awful will surely happen. Believe me, I know.'

He kept quiet.

A few steps into the alley leading up to Kirpal Kaur's mohalla, Mozel stopped abruptly. Up ahead a Marwari's shop was being pillaged piece by piece. She studied the situation for a second and said calmly, 'It's all right. Let's keep going.'

They started moving. Suddenly a man with a big platter on his head bumped into Trilochan, knocking the platter to the ground. He looked at Trilochan closely. That he was a Sikh was written all over him. The man quickly reached for the knife tucked into his waistband, but Mozel came tripping over as if dead drunk and pushed him away. 'Hey, are you crazy? Killing your own brother? I'm going to marry this man.' She then turned to Trilochan, 'Karim, pick up the platter and put it back on his head.'

The man quickly withdrew his hand from his waistband, looked lustily at Mozel and touched her boobs with his elbow. 'Go on, saali, have fun!' He moved on, balancing the platter on his head.

'Bastard, what an atrocious thing to do,' Trilochan mumbled in disgust.

She touched her breasts. 'Atrocious—not at all. It works. Let's go!'

She started walking briskly. Trilochan tried to keep pace. They came to the end of the alley and entered Kirpal Kaur's mohalla.

'Which street?' she asked.

'The third. That building on the corner,' he said in a hushed voice.

She turned in that direction. Despite being densely populated, the whole area was enveloped in an eerie silence; not even the sound of a child crying could be heard anywhere.

When they came closer, they saw signs of some surreptitious movement. A man darted out of one building and ran into another. Minutes later, three men came out of one building, looked around and dashed into the next. Mozel stopped short. She gestured to Trilochan to get into the cover of the darkness and whispered, 'Triloch, dear, take off your turban.'

'Never!' he answered resolutely. 'I won't, no matter what.'

She was annoyed. 'As you wish. But don't you see what's going on?'

Something awful and very mysterious was indeed going on and both of them could sense it. When two men emerged from the building on the right with gunnysacks on their backs, Mozel's whole body shuddered for a moment. Something resembling a viscous fluid was dripping from the gunnysacks. Mozel chewed her lips nervously. Perhaps she was thinking of some plan. When the two men disappeared at the end of the street she turned to Trilochan. 'Look, here's what we'll do: I'll run to the corner building and you come after me, fast, like you're chasing me. Got it? But all this has to be done in a split second.'

Without waiting for his answer, she took off towards the building, her clogs clip-clopping noisily on the cobblestones. Trilochan ran after her, fast. Within a few seconds they were inside the building, at the foot of the stairs. Trilochan was out of breath, but she seemed fine. 'Which floor?' she asked.

'Second,' he replied, wetting his parched lips.

'Come on, let's go.' She started to climb up the stairs. Trilochan followed her. The steps were stained with big splotches of blood and gore. He blanched.

Trilochan walked part way down the corridor on the second floor until he came to a door. He knocked softly while Mozel stood some distance away, by the staircase.

He tapped on the door again, stuck his face up to it and called, 'Maha Singhji! Maha Singhji!'

'Who is it?' someone asked in a feeble voice.

'It's Trilochan.'

Slowly the door opened. Trilochan beckoned to Mozel and they went inside. Mozel saw a wisp of a girl standing to the side, petrified, and only had a few moments to look at her closely. The girl had delicate features and a beautifully crafted nose, now red from a cold. Mozel hugged the girl to her enormous bosom and wiped her own runny nose with the hem of her loose-fitting tunic.

Trilochan's face flushed.

'Don't be afraid,' she said to the girl lovingly. 'Trilochan has come to take you out of here.'

Kirpal Kaur disengaged herself from Mozel's arms and looked at Trilochan with frightened eyes.

'Please ask Sardar Sahib to get ready fast, and your mother too . . . quickly.'

Just then screams and the sound of scuffles erupted on the floor above them.

'They got him!' A muffled scream escaped from Kirpal Kaur's throat.

'Who?' Trilochan asked.

Before Kirpal Kaur could answer, Mozel grabbed her arm and pushed her into a corner. 'Good, they got him. Now take off these clothes.'

Kirpal Kaur barely had time to react before Mozel quickly stripped her of her shirt. A terrified Kirpal Kaur tried to cover her nakedness with her arms. Trilochan turned his face away. Mozel removed her loose tunic and slipped it over Kirpal Kaur's body. Now she herself was stark naked. Quickly loosening the waist cord, she pulled the girl's shalwar down and ordered Trilochan, 'Go! Get her out of here . . . Wait . . .' She hurriedly untied the girl's hair, and said, 'Now go, get out of here as fast as you can, both of you!'

'Come on,' Trilochan gestured to the girl. Halfway to the door he suddenly stopped, turned around, and looked back at the stark-naked Mozel. The soft fuzz on her arms was standing upright in the cold.

'Why don't you leave?' she shrieked, obviously irritated.

'What about her parents?' he said, softly.

'They can go to hell. You take her and get out of here!'

'And you?'

'I'm coming.'

All of a sudden the stairs rang out with the sound of hastily descending feet. Several men banged on the door so violently it seemed they would knock it down.

Kirpal Kaur's blind mother and handicapped father were moaning in the other room.

Mozel reflected for a moment, jerked her hair slightly, and said to Trilochan, 'Listen, I can only think of one thing now: I'm going to open the door.'

Kirpal Kaur stifled a scream in her dry throat. 'The door!'

'I'll open the door and run up the stairs. You follow me. These people will forget everything and come after us . . .'

'And then?' he asked.

'This will give your, what's her name, a chance to escape. No one will bother her in this tunic.'

Trilochan quickly explained the situation to Kirpal Kaur.

Mozel raised a frightening scream, threw open the door and rushed out, tripping over the men outside who had no time to react and made way for her. She righted herself and ran up the stairs, with Trilochan close on her heels.

Mozel was climbing the stairs blindly, still in her clogs. The men who'd been trying to break down the door ran after the two of them. Suddenly her foot slipped and she tumbled down the stairs all the way to the stone landing, her body knocking against the steps and the wrought-iron balustrade.

Trilochan rushed down the stairs only to find her lying there, blood oozing out of her nose, mouth, even her ears. The men who had stormed the door quickly gathered around. Someone asked what happened. They were looking silently at her fair-skinned, naked body covered with bruises.

Trilochan shook her arm and called out, 'Mozel! Mozel!'

She opened her large Jewish eyes, now blood red, and smiled.

Trilochan quickly removed his turban, undid it, and spread it out over her naked body. She smiled again and winked at him. Spewing tiny red bubbles from her mouth, she said, 'Go . . . see whether my underwear is still there . . . I mean . . .'

Trilochan got her drift, but he didn't want to leave her. Which angered her. 'Damn it, you're a Sikh after all. Go and see.'

He rose and went to Kirpal Kaur's flat. Through her dimmed eyes Mozel looked at the men gathered around her and said, 'He's a miyan bhai . . . so crazy that I always call him a Sikh . . .'

Meanwhile, Trilochan returned. He let her know with his eyes that Kirpal Kaur had made her escape. She sighed in relief, but more blood bubbled out of her mouth from the effort. 'Damn it,' she said, wiping it on her arm. Then she said to Trilochan, 'All right, darling, bye-bye!'

He wanted to say something, but choked on his words.

Mozel pushed his turban cloth off her body. 'Take this with you . . . this scrap of your religion,' she said, as her arm fell limp over her plump, round breasts.

The Black Shalwar

Before moving to Delhi she had lived in Ambala Cantonment where she'd had several goras among her clients. Through them she had learned to speak a smattering of English, which she didn't use in ordinary conversation. When her business failed to pick up in Delhi, she said to her neighbour Tamancha Jan one day, 'This *lef*—very bad.' Meaning, this is a bad life, you can't even earn enough to make ends meet.

She'd done quite well for herself in Ambala. The cantonment goras came to her drunk. She would be done with eight or ten of them in three or four hours and make twenty to thirty rupees. They treated her much better than her own countrymen did. True, they spoke in a language Sultana couldn't understand, but this ignorance only worked to her advantage. If they tried to bargain for a lower rate, she just shook her head uncomprehendingly and said, 'Sahib, I don't understand what you're saying.' And if they tried to get fresh with her, she broke into a round of profanities in her own language. When they gawked at her nonplussed, she'd say to them, 'Sahib, you're a bloody fool, a bastard . . . understand?' She didn't utter these words brusquely, but in a tone full of affection and geniality. The goras would laugh, and when they laughed they did look like bloody fools to her.

Here in Delhi, though, not a single gora had visited her since her arrival. She had now been here for three months, in this city of Hindustan where, she had heard, the Big Lord Sahib lived, who customarily spent his summers in Simla. So far only six people had visited her, only six— that is, two a month—and she could swear by God she had made a total of eighteen and a half rupees from them. None of them wanted to pay more than three rupees. Sultana had quoted her rate as ten rupees to five of them but, strangely, every one of them said, 'Not more than three.' God knows why they thought she was worth only three rupees. So when the sixth one came along, she herself said, 'Look, I charge three rupees for each *taim*. I won't accept anything less. Stay or leave.' There was no haggling; he stayed. When they went into the other room and he started taking off his coat, Sultana said, 'And a rupee for milk.' He didn't give her one rupee though; instead, he took out a shiny eight anna bit with the head of the new king from his pocket and offered it to her. She took it quietly, thinking, 'At least it's better than nothing.'

Eighteen and a half rupees in three months! Just the rent for her *kotha*, which her landlord referred to by the English word 'flat', was twenty a month. This flat had a toilet with an overhead chain. When the chain was pulled, water gushed out noisily and carried all the waste to an underground drain. Initially, the noise of the torrential water had scared the daylights out of her. On her first day in the flat when she had gone to the toilet, her back was hurting badly. As she was getting up from the toilet seat she grabbed the chain for support. The sight of the chain had made her think that since the flats were built especially for important people, the chains were provided for their convenience. But the instant she grabbed the chain to rise, she heard a clanking sound and suddenly water was released with such force that she shrieked, frightened out of her wits.

Khuda Bakhsh was in the other room busy with his photographic material and pouring hydroquinone into a bottle. When he heard Sultana scream, he stepped out of the room and asked her, 'What's the matter? Was that you screaming?'

'Is this a toilet or what?' she replied, her heart pounding with fright. 'What's this chain hanging down like the ones in a train carriage? My back was aching, so I took hold of it for support. The instant I grabbed it there was this horrible explosion . . .'

Khuda Bakhsh laughed uproariously. He explained, 'It's a new-style toilet. When you pull the chain, it sends the filth to an underground sewer.'

How Khuda Bakhsh and Sultana got hitched together is a long story. He hailed from Rawalpindi. After passing his Intermediate he learned to drive lorries. For four years he ran a lorry between Rawalpindi and Kashmir. In Kashmir he had an affair with a woman, whom he persuaded to abscond with him. They went to Lahore where, since he couldn't find work, he set her up as a prostitute. This went on for two or three years until the woman ran away with another man. When Khuda Bakhsh found out that she was in Ambala, he went looking for her. There he met Sultana, who liked him, and so they decided to band together.

Her business picked up after Khuda Bakhsh got together with her. A superstitious woman, she attributed her success to Khuda Bakhsh's presence. She took him to be someone blessed by God. This faith jacked up his stature in her eyes.

Khuda Bakhsh was a hard-working man who didn't like to lie around and while away his time. He struck up a friendship with a photographer who took photos with a Mint camera outside the railway station. He learned photography from him and, later, took sixty rupees from Sultana and bought his own camera. Gradually he acquired a background screen, bought two chairs and equipment for developing film and set up his own business. The business boomed. Shortly thereafter he established himself in Ambala Cantonment where he photographed goras and, within a month, came to know several of them rather well. So he moved Sultana to the cantonment area too and many goras became her regular clients through him.

Sultana bought herself a pair of earrings, had eight gold bangles made, each weighing five and a half *tola*s, and also collected an assortment of some fifteen fine saris. The house also got some furniture.

In short, she was quite well off in Ambala Cantonment. Then, suddenly, God knows how, Khuda Bakhsh got it into his head to move to Delhi. How could she refuse? After all he was a godsend, her lucky break. She gladly agreed to go with him. In fact, she even thought her business would prosper further in such a large city where the Big Lord Sahib lived and which a friend of hers had praised to high heaven. Besides, the shrine of Hazrat Nizamuddin Auliya, for which she felt a special reverence, was also in Delhi. She quickly sold her heavier household goods and came to the city with Khuda Bakhsh, who rented this place for twenty rupees a month and both settled in.

It was a row of newly built lookalike units running along the road. The municipal committee had assigned this area of the city to prostitutes to stop them from setting up businesses all over the city. The ground floor had two shops and the upper, a pair of flats. Because all units looked alike, at first Sultana had a lot of difficulty finding her flat. This became easier when the laundry shop on the lower level put up a sign 'Clothes Washed Here' which she used as a landmark. And this was only one of the signs that worked as a marker for her. There were others. For instance, her friend Hira Bai, who sometimes sang on the radio, lived above the place where 'Coal-Shop' was inscribed in large letters. The shop announcing 'Excellent Food for Gentlemen' was right below Mukhtar's flat and Anwari, another friend, lived above the small factory that made broad tapes for bed meshing. She was in the employ of its owner who needed to keep an eye on the work at night and stayed with her.

During the first month, in which she remained idle, Sultana consoled herself with the thought that a newly launched business usually didn't pull in customers right away. But anxiety swept over her when not a single customer turned up in two months. She asked Khuda Bakhsh, 'What do you think, Khuda Bakhsh? We've been here for two whole months and no one has come along. I know business is slow these days, but it can't be so slow that no one will come our way at all.'

The matter had been weighing no less heavily on Khuda Bakhsh, but he'd kept quiet. But now that Sultana had brought it up he said, 'I've been thinking about it myself for some time now. The only thing that comes to mind is that people are so preoccupied with other things because of the war that they can hardly think of anything else. Or perhaps—'

His sentence was interrupted by the sound of someone coming up the stairs and their attention became fixed entirely on the sound of approaching feet. Shortly, there was a knock on the door. Khuda Bakhsh darted to open it. A man entered. This was her first customer and they settled for three rupees. Later, she had five more, that is, six in all in a month and a total of eighteen and a half rupees.

Every month, twenty alone went for the flat's rent. Utilities were extra. Add to it all the other household expenses: food, drink, clothes, medicines. And no income. Eighteen and a half rupees in three months could hardly be called any kind of income. Sultana really became distraught with worry. The eight bangles she'd had made in Ambala were all eaten up one by one. When it was time to sell the last one she said to Khuda Bakhsh, 'Listen to me, let's go back to Ambala. This place is a bummer. Maybe it has something, but not for us. It hasn't been kind to us. You were doing quite well there. Come on, let's go back. We'll consider our losses a sacrifice. Go, sell this bangle; meanwhile, I'll start packing and getting everything ready. We'll leave by the evening train.'

He took the bangle and said, 'No, my darling, we're not going anywhere. We'll stay right here and make it work. You'll see, all these bangles will come flying back to you. Have faith in God. He knows how to help. He will find a way for us!'

Sultana said nothing. The last bangle too was sold. The sight of her bare wrists saddened her. But what could she do? They had to fill their stomachs somehow.

When five months went by and her earnings remained less than even a quarter of their expenses, her anxiety mounted. Meanwhile, Khuda Bakhsh had also started to stay away from home the whole day, which was yet another source of her grief. It was true that a few of her friends lived in the neighbourhood and she could while away the time with them, but she didn't feel comfortable hanging out with them for hours every day. Gradually she stopped visiting with them altogether. She stayed in her empty house all day long, crushing betel nut or mending her old clothes. Sometimes she went out on to the balcony, stood against the railing, and watched the moving and stationary engines in the railway yard across the street for hours.

A warehouse stretched from one corner to the other on that side of the street. To the right, huge bales and piles of different goods lay under a metal roof. To the left was an open space with innumerable intersecting railway tracks. Whenever the iron tracks flashed in the sun, Sultana's eyes fell on her hands where the protruding blue veins looked very much like those tracks. Engines and carriages were moving all the time in the open space, this way and that, creating a veritable din with their chug-chug and clatter. On the days when Sultana woke up early in the morning and went out to the balcony, a strange sight greeted her: engines in the misty dawn spewing out thick smoke that climbed slowly towards the murky sky like plump, beefy men. Clouds of steam rose noisily from the tracks and quickly dissolved in the air. Now and then the sight of a shunted carriage left to run on its own along a track reminded her of herself: She too had been pushed out to run on her own along the track of her life. Others simply changed the switches and she kept moving forward—to God knew where; one day, when the momentum had slowly spent itself, she would come to a halt, at some place unknown to her.

She would peer for hours at the criss-crossing tracks and the engines standing or gliding along them, her mind ceaselessly assaulted by all kinds of thoughts. In Ambala Cantonment, too, her house had been close to the railway station, but she had never looked at these things in such a way there. It was different now. This network of tracks, the steam and smoke rising from them here and there—all this seemed to her like an immense brothel; a profusion of trains being pulled this way or that by big, fat engines. Sometimes the engines looked like those seths who'd visited her in Ambala from time to time. And sometimes when she saw a solitary engine passing slowly by a row of carriages, her mind conjured up the image of a man looking up at the balconies as he passed through the prostitutes' quarters.

Sultana was sure that such thoughts would drive her mad some day, so when they started to assault her mind regularly she stopped going to the balcony.

She pleaded with Khuda Bakhsh repeatedly, 'For God's sake have some pity on me. Stay at home. I languish here all day like a sick person.' But each time Khuda Bakhsh calmed her down, saying, 'My love, I go out to earn something. God willing, our hard days will soon come to an end.'

A full five months passed but neither Sultana's nor Khuda Bakhsh's hard days came to an end. The month of Muharram was fast approaching. Sultana had no money to buy herself the customary black outfit. Mukhtar had a snazzy Lady Hamilton shirt with black georgette sleeves made for herself and, to go with it, she already had a black satin shalwar which glistened like kajal. Anwari had bought a fine georgette sari. She'd told Sultana that she would wear it over a white bosky petticoat because this was all the rage. She had also bought dainty sandals of black velvet to match her sari. When Sultana saw all this finery the thought that she had no means to buy such clothes to celebrate Muharram deeply saddened her.

She returned home feeling despondent. It was as though a tumour had sprouted inside her. The house was empty. Khuda Bakhsh was out as usual. She stretched out on the dhurrie and put a bolster under her head. She lay there for quite a while, until her neck began to feel stiff because of the height of the bolster. She got up and went out on to the balcony to expel her agonizing thoughts.

She saw several carriages standing on the tracks but not a single engine. It was evening. The street had been hosed down to keep the dust from rising. Men who furtively glanced at the balconies and then quietly headed home had begun to appear in the bazaar. One of them looked up at Sultana. She smiled at him but quickly forgot about him because an engine had suddenly materialized on the tracks across from her. She looked at it intently and the idea that the engine too was wearing black slowly formed in her mind. To rid herself of this strange thought she turned her gaze to the street and saw the same man who had stared at her lustily standing by an oxcart. She beckoned to him. He looked around him and then, with a subtle gesture, asked her the way to her flat. She let him know. The man waited a little as if thinking and then briskly came up the stairs.

Sultana seated him on the dhurrie. To start the conversation she asked, 'Why were you afraid to come up?'

'What makes you think I was afraid?' he said, smiling. 'What was there to be afraid of?'

'Because you hesitated, took some time to think before coming up.'

The man smiled again and said, 'You're mistaken. Actually, I was looking at the flat above yours. A woman there was sticking her tongue out at a man. I found it amusing. When the balcony lit up with a green light, I stayed on a bit longer. I like green light. It's very soothing to the eyes.' He let his gaze wander all over the room and then got up.

'You're leaving?' Sultana asked.

'No. I want to look at your house. Come on, show me all the rooms.'

One by one she showed him the three rooms. He checked them out without saying a word. When they returned to the room where they had been sitting earlier, he said, 'My name is Shankar.'

For the first time she looked at the man closely. He was of medium height and had rather ordinary features, except for unusually bright, clear eyes that occasionally gleamed with a strange brilliance. His body was firm and compact, and his hair was greying around the temples. He had on grey woollen pants and a white shirt with an upturned collar.

Shankar sat on the dhurrie as though Sultana, not he, was the client. This annoyed her a bit, so she asked, 'Yes . . . what can I do for you?'

Now he lay down and said, 'What can you do for me? Rather, what can *I* do for you? After all you're the one who summoned me.'

When Sultana didn't reply, he sat up again. 'Oh, I see,' he said. 'All right, now listen to me. Whatever it is that you were thinking is wrong. I'm not one of those who come up here, pay and leave. I have my fee too, like doctors. Whenever I'm sent for, I expect to be paid.'

Although this threw her off balance she couldn't keep from laughing.

'What do you do?' she asked.

'I do what you all do,' he replied.

'I . . . I . . . I don't do anything.'

'And neither do I.'

'This makes no sense,' she said in a huff. 'Surely, you must do something.'

'And so must you,' he said with perfect equanimity.

'I waste my time.'

'So do I.'

'Well then, let's waste it together.'

'Fine with me. But remember, I don't pay for wasting time.'

'Come to your senses. This isn't a charity house.'

'And I'm not a volunteer either.'

Sultana paused and then asked, 'Who are these "volunteers"?'

'*Ulloo ke patthe!*'[*]

'Well, I'm not a "volunteer".'

'But that guy, that Khuda Bakhsh who lives with you, he certainly is.'

'Why?'

'Because for days he's been visiting a fakir, hoping he will turn his fortunes around when the man can't even change his own fortunes.' Shankar laughed.

'You're a Hindu,' Sultana shot back, 'that's why you make fun of our holy men.'

Shankar smiled. 'The question of Hindu or Muslim doesn't arise in a place such as this. If the most accomplished pandits or maulvis were to come here, they would all behave like perfect gentlemen.'

'God knows what nonsense you're talking about. Tell me plainly, will you stay or leave?'

---

[*] Idiots!

'I'll stay, but only on the condition I told you.'

Sultana got up and said, 'In that case, you'd better be on your way.'

Shankar leisurely got up, thrust both of his hands into his pockets and said on his way out, 'Now and then I pass by this bazaar. Call me whenever you need me. I'm a very useful man.'

Shankar departed and Sultana, forgetting all about the black clothes, kept thinking about him for a long time. His banter had appreciably lightened her heart. Had he visited her in Ambala, she would likely have viewed him in a different light. She might even have thrown him out. But here, in her current depressed state of mind, she liked his chatter.

When Khuda Bakhsh returned in the evening, she asked, 'Where have you been all day?'

Looking bone-tired, Khuda Bakhsh said, 'I had gone to the Old Fort. A holy man is staying there for a few days. I visit him every day in the hope that he might help turn our luck around.'

'Has he said anything to you?'

'No, so far he hasn't. He hasn't turned his attention to me, but I'm serving him with my whole heart and soul. It won't be in vain. With God's grace our good days will come. Of that I'm sure.'

Preoccupied with the thought of celebrating Muharram, Sultana said in a doleful voice, 'You disappear for the whole day every day, while I stay here, cooped up in a cage, unable to go anywhere. Muharram is upon us. Has it occurred to you that I need black mourning clothes. We haven't got a pie in the house. One by one, all the bangles were sold. Just tell me how we're going to manage. How long are you going to run after fakirs? It seems to me that God has withdrawn His grace from us here. I say, go back to your old business—it will at least bring in something.'

He lay down on the dhurrie and said, 'To restart I'd need a little bit of cash, wouldn't I? For God's sake, don't talk of such painful things. I can't bear them any more. I made a terrible mistake in leaving Ambala, yes. But whatever happens happens by God's will . . . and for our own good. Who knows, after suffering a while longer we . . .'

Sultana cut him short. 'For God's sake, do something! Steal. Rob. But get me a shalwar's length of fabric. I already have a white bosky shirt; I'll have it dyed. And the white cotton dupatta which you gave me at Diwali can also be dyed along with the shirt. I only lack a shalwar, which you must get me one way or another. Look, you must swear by my life that you'll get it for me, or you'll see me dead.'

Khuda Bakhsh quickly sat up. 'You keep insisting, but it isn't fair. Where am I going to get it from? I don't have a penny even for my opium.'

'I don't care. Do whatever you must, but bring me four and a half yards of black satin.'

'So pray. Pray that God may send you two or three customers tonight.'

'But you're not going to lift a finger—is that it? If you tried you could easily make enough to buy the fabric. Satin sold at twelve, at most fourteen annas a yard before the war. Now it's gone up to a rupee and a quarter. How much money does one need for four and a half yards?'

'All right, if you must insist, I'll think of some way.' He got up. 'But for now, put it out of your mind. Let me get some food from the restaurant.'

Food arrived. They ate without enjoyment and went to bed. At daybreak Khuda Bakhsh again set off to see the fakir at the Old Fort. Sultana was left alone. She lingered in bed, lolled around some, slept some, and then she got up and wandered around the rooms for a while. After the midday meal she took out her white cotton dupatta and bosky shirt and brought them over to the laundryman downstairs to be dyed black. The laundry shop both washed and dyed clothes.

She returned home and browsed through some film magazines that featured stories and songs from films she had seen, and dozed off at some point. When she woke up she could tell that it was already four o'clock as the sun was now abreast of the drain in the railway yard. After her bath she threw a woollen shawl around herself and sauntered out on to the balcony. She lingered there for a good hour. Evening had set in, lights were beginning to come on, and the first signs of life could be seen moving about in the street below. There was a nip in the air, but she didn't find it unpleasant. She had been watching the traffic of cars and tongas for some time when she suddenly caught sight of Shankar. As he came directly underneath her flat, he raised his head and smiled at Sultana. She spontaneously called him up with a gesture of her hand.

When he entered, she found herself at a loss for words. She had called him up on an impulse, without thinking. Shankar was completely at ease, as if he was in his own home and, just as he did on his previous visit, stretched out on the dhurrie, supporting his head on the bolster. Realizing that Sultana hadn't spoken a word for a long time he said, 'You can call me a hundred times, and send me back just as easily a hundred times . . . it doesn't bother me—never.'

She was at her wits' end and didn't know what to do. 'No, no, sit down,' she said. 'Who's asking you to leave?'

Shankar smiled. 'So you accept my conditions?'

'What conditions?' she said, laughing. 'You aren't entering into a formal marriage contract with me, are you?'

'Contracts . . . marriage? Neither you nor I will ever get married. These conventions aren't for the likes of us so drop this nonsense and talk about something real.'

'Well then, what would you like me to talk about?'

'You're a woman. Say something to amuse my heart for a while. There's more to life than just business.'

By now Sultana had started to look favourably at the man. 'Tell me plainly,' she said, 'what do you want from me?'

'Why, the same thing the others want.' He sat up.

'So there's no difference between you and them?'

'Between you and me, none, zero; but there's a world of difference between them and me. There are things that one should never ask about, they should just be sensed.'

After thinking a while about the underlying meaning of his words, Sultana said, 'I think I understand.'

'So what do you say?' he asked.

'All right, you win. But I'm sure no one has ever accepted such a proposition.'

'You're wrong. You don't have to go very far. In this very neighbourhood you'll find many absolutely simple-minded women who would find it very difficult to believe that a woman could ever accept the kind of debasement you go through without even feeling its sting. But regardless of whether they accept it or not, women like you abound . . . you're Sultana, aren't you?'

'Yes, Sultana.'

He stood up and laughed. 'And I'm Shankar. These names, they make no sense. Come on, let's go to the other room.'

When they returned to the room with the dhurrie, they were both laughing, God knows why or about what.

Just as he was about to leave, Sultana asked, 'Shankar, will you do something for me?'

'First tell me what it is.'

She felt a bit embarrassed. 'I'm afraid you might think I'm trying to extract my payment. But . . .'

'Yes, yes, don't stop.'

She summoned up the courage to say, 'The thing is, Muharram is coming and I don't have enough money for a black shalwar. You've already heard from me about all our woes. I gave my shirt and dupatta to be dyed just this morning.'

Shankar heard her and said, 'So you want me to give you money for a black shalwar?'

She quickly replied, 'No, I don't mean quite that. But, if possible, could you get me a black shalwar?'

Shankar smiled. 'When did I ever have any money in my pocket? If I do occasionally, call it pure luck. Anyway, I'll try. You'll get your shalwar on the first day of Muharram. Happy now?'

He glanced at Sultana's earrings and said, 'Can you give me those earrings?'

'What will you do with them,' she asked, laughing. 'They're pretty ordinary silver earrings . . . worth five rupees at the most.'

'I'm asking for the earrings, not their price. Will you?'

'You can have them.' She removed the earrings and handed them over to Shankar, only to regret it later, but by then Shankar was long gone.

She absolutely didn't believe that Shankar would keep his word. But eight days later, on the first of Muharram, she heard a knock at the door at nine in the morning. She opened the door. Shankar was standing in front of her. He handed her something wrapped in a newspaper and said, 'It's a black satin shalwar. Have a look at it. It might be a bit long on you. I have to go now.'

He just handed over the packet and left without saying anything more. His pants looked crumpled and his hair was pretty messy, as though he'd just gotten up and headed straight to her flat.

Sultana undid the wrapping. It was a black satin shalwar, exactly like the one she'd seen at Mukhtar's. She felt overjoyed. The regret she'd felt over her earrings and the 'transaction' with Shankar evaporated into thin air. He had lived up to his promise and she'd got her shalwar.

At noon she collected her shirt and dupatta, now dyed black, from the laundry. After she'd changed into her black outfit she heard someone rapping on the door. She opened it. Mukhtar walked in. She saw the three-piece ensemble on Sultana and said, 'The shirt and dupatta both look dyed, but the shalwar is new. When did you have it made?'

'The tailor delivered it just this morning.' As she said this, her glance fell on Mukhtar's earrings. 'When did you get these?' she asked.

'Just today.'

And then neither could say anything for a while.

Siraj

Dhondo stood leaning against the lamp post outside the Irani teahouse near the park across from the Nagpara Police Station. He came there regularly, normally around sundown, and conducted his business until four in the morning.

No one knew his real name, but everyone called him Dhondo— quite an appropriate appellation considering that his business was procuring suitable girls for his clients, depending on their tastes and dispositions.

He'd been in this business for nearly ten years. Thousands of girls of every colour, religion and disposition had passed through his hands during this time.

And this spot had been his hangout from the day he began this business: across from the Nagpara Police Station, right in front of the park, outside the Irani teahouse, leaning against the lamp post. The lamp post had become his trademark, and to me it was Dhondo himself. Whenever I happened to pass by and my glance fell on this lamp post where countless people had wiped their fingers, leaving lime and catechu stains, I would suddenly feel as though Dhondo was standing there, chewing his paan wrapped around shards of roasted betel nut.

The lamp post was quite tall and so was Dhondo. A network of power lines extended outward from the top: one line running all the way to the next lamp post before getting lost in that post's maze of similar lines; another went to an adjacent building; still another to a shop. That the reach of this lamp post extended quite far and, along with its mates', spread over the entire city was beyond question.

The telephone administration had attached a box-shaped terminal to this lamp post. Now and then it was used to check the condition of the telephone wires. I often thought of Dhondo as a similar box, attached to the lamp post to help maintain the sexual health of people. He knew all the seths living in the area who needed their sexual wires, loose or taut, restored to perfect working condition from time to time, or all the time.

He also knew all the girls in the profession, the smallest attribute of their bodies, their temperaments, and who would be best suited for a particular client at a particular time—all the girls, that is, except Siraj. He hadn't been able to get a handle on her so far, or delve down to her depths.

He often told me, 'Saali, she's gone cuckoo. I just can't make her out, Manto Sahib. What kind of girl is she? Now this, now that—refuses to make up her mind. One minute she's fire, next minute water. She'll be laughing her head off one moment, then suddenly break into sobs the next. She can't get along with anyone, saali! Very bitchy. Fights with every "passenger". I've told her repeatedly, "Look, get your head examined, or else go back to where you came from. You have no clothes on your body, nothing to fill your stomach. Fighting won't work, dearie." But does she listen, the pighead!'

I'd seen Siraj a couple of times. She looked skinny, but rather beautiful. Her eyes were much too large for her oval face, looming menacingly, as if bent on extracting from everyone an admission of her superiority. I was quite disconcerted when I first saw her on Clare Road. The desire to ask those eyes to step aside so that I could look at the real Siraj stirred in me, but they didn't budge, though I'm sure they understood my meaning.

She had a slight but compact frame, like a goblet filled beyond capacity with watered-down spirits that thrashed and spilled out from the pressure.

I say 'watered-down spirits' because she had the bitter taste of strong liquors, but it seemed as if some crook had added water to increase the volume. Whatever amount of femininity she had was still there, not an atom less. Her irritation oozed out of her thick hair, pointy nose, tightly pressed lips and her fingers, which reminded me of the sharpened pencils of draughtsmen. It gave me the impression that she was perpetually cross with everything and everyone: Dhondo, the lamp post against which he always leaned, the clients he propositioned for her, and even the exceptionally big eyes that dominated her entire face. But most especially she was angry at her sharp-pointed draughtsmen's pencils because they had failed to draw the map of her life the way she wanted it to be.

These, at any rate, are the impressions of a short story writer who can ascribe to the softest of moles the rigidity of a black stone. Dhondo, of course, had his own views. He said to me one day: 'Manto Sahib, saali got me into trouble again. Fortunately, the recompense for some good deed I may have once done came in handy and I was saved. Thanks to your blessings, all the officers of the Nagpara Police Station are soft on me, otherwise I'd have been in the slammer yesterday. She raised such hell, *baap re baap!*'

'What happened?' I asked.

'The same thing that always happens. I cursed my seven generations up and down. I said to myself, "Bastard, why do you keep finding clients for her? Is she your mother or your sister that you're so concerned about her? Why?" Manto Sahib, I'm at my wits' end.'

We were sitting in the Irani teahouse. Dhondo poured his coffee–tea mixture into the saucer and started slurping it.

'Why?' I asked.

He threw his head back, saying, 'Don't know why. I wish I did. Maybe this daily misery would end then.' All of a sudden he turned his cup upside down on the saucer and said, 'Did you know, she's still a virgin!'

Believe me, that unsettled me for a moment. 'Virgin—how so?'

'I swear by your life.'

'No, Dhondo, that can't be,' I said as though I wanted to edit my earlier comment.

He didn't appreciate my doubting his word. 'I'm not lying to you, Manto Sahib. One hundred per cent virgin. You can bet on it.'

'How can that be,' was all I was able to say.

'Why not?' he demanded with conviction. 'A girl like Siraj can keep her virginity intact all her life, even in this profession. She won't let anyone touch her. I don't know her full history, but I do know this: She's a Punjaban. She worked with a madam on Lamington Road for two or three months. The madam threw her out; she had quarrelled with every passenger. The madam had other girls, ten, maybe twenty, but Manto Sahib, how long can one just keep feeding someone. The madam threw her out; she had nothing but the clothes she was wearing. Then she went to another madam on Faras Road. There too she remained as much of a nutcase as ever. She bit one passenger. She only lasted a couple of months. A real fireball! Who'd want to cool her down? Then—so help me God!—she hung out at a hotel in Khetwadi, where she raised the same hell all over again. The manager got fed up and packed her off. What can I say, Manto Sahib! She doesn't care about food or drink. Her clothes are infested with lice, head unwashed for months. Loves to smoke joints when she can lay her hands on any. And stand in front of some restaurant, listening to film songs on the radio.'

This was more than enough detail for me. How I reacted to it is my concern, not something I should tell you, not as a short story writer anyway.

Just to keep the conversation rolling, I asked, 'It doesn't look as though she's interested in this business; why don't you send her back home to Punjab? I'll give you her train fare.'

Dhondo was put off by my offer. 'Manto Sahib, train fare isn't the problem. Do you think I can't pay for it myself?'

'So why don't you?' I tried to poke around.

He was quiet for a while. Then he removed the cigarette tucked behind his ear, lit it, and, expelling twin jets of smoke from his nostrils, said only, 'I don't want her to go.'

I had the uncanny feeling that I was finally on to something. 'Are you in love with her?' I asked.

This had a strange effect on him. 'What kind of talk is that, Manto Sahib?' He touched both his ears, and said, 'I swear by the Qur'an, I wouldn't even dream of such a filthy thought. I just . . .' he hesitated, 'just . . . kind of like her.'

'Why?'

I guess I had asked him the right question for Dhondo also gave the right answer: 'Because . . . because she isn't like other girls. They *crave* money! What wouldn't they do to grab it—those bitches! But this one, she's something else. When I bring her out to a passenger, she gives the impression that she's willing, so the deal is struck and she hops into the taxi or the victoria. Now, Manto Sahib, the passenger is out to have a good time, he wants some action, it's why he's spending so much money after all. So he tries to feel her with his hand, or just touch her. And that's when all hell breaks loose. She creates a ruckus and resorts to fisticuffs. Now, if the man is a gentleman, he takes to his heels, but if he's drunk or a rake, a storm erupts. Every time something like this happens I'm dragged into it and put on the spot. I have to return the money and get on my knees to calm down the enraged client. All for the sake of Siraj, I swear by the Qur'an . . . and, Manto Sahib, that saali has wrecked my business, it's down by half—honestly.'

I would rather not talk about the backstory my mind had woven for Siraj, except to say that it didn't match whatever Dhondo had told me about her.

The thought that I could meet her without Dhondo's knowledge crossed my mind one day. She lived near Byculla Railway Station in an atrociously dingy area surrounded by great piles of garbage and refuse. The corporation had put up numerous metal housing units for the poor there. I don't want to discuss the plush high-rise buildings that loomed just a short distance away from this slimy filth; they have nothing to do with this story. Where is there a world bereft of highs and lows?

Dhondo had once told me about her place. I went there, doing my best not to let my respectable appearance stand out in this ramshackle milieu, but here, of course, it is not I who am the subject.

Anyway, I went there. A she-goat was tethered outside her shack. It bleated the moment it saw me. An old hag came out tapping her walking stick, looking like a witch who had stepped straight out of some moth-eaten pages of ancient *dastaan*s. I was about to turn back when I spotted two inordinately large eyes behind the tattered gunnysack curtain hanging over the entrance, gaping as wide as the holes in the curtain. And then I saw Siraj's oval face. Anger at those eyes that had so brazenly appropriated most of that face swelled inside me. She saw me. God only knows what she was doing inside the shack. Whatever it was, she stopped and came out immediately. 'What brings you here?' she asked, ignoring the old crone.

'I wanted to see you.' I gave a brief answer.

'Come in,' she said, with equal brevity.

'No, you come with me.'

'It will be ten rupees,' the dastaanesque old witch said in a brusque, businesslike manner.

I pulled out a ten-rupee note from my wallet and gave it to the old hag. 'Come,' I said to Siraj.

The penetrating intensity of her unusually large eyes subsided just a little for me to look into hers unhindered for the briefest moment. I again concluded that she was beautiful. A shrivelled, embalmed beauty, preserved and buried for centuries in an underground vault. For a moment I felt I was in Egypt, digging up ancient tombs. I don't want to go into greater detail.

Siraj and I went to a restaurant. She sat across from me in her filthy clothes, her eyes crowding her oval face, and not just her face but her entire being, so mercilessly that I couldn't discern even an atom of her being.

I had already handed over the ten rupees the old hag had quoted to me. I now gave Siraj forty more. I wanted her to quarrel with me, just as she did with the others, with the same vehemence. That's why I didn't say anything that might have seemed loving or sincere in the least. I was also apprehensive about her big eyes—big enough to see not just me but the whole world around me as well.

She was absolutely silent. To touch her in a provocative manner required that I feel aroused not just in my body but also in my thoughts, so I downed four pegs of whisky and groped her like any old passenger. She didn't resist. Then I did something totally atrocious, which I thought would be the spark needed to ignite the explosives collecting inside of her for ages. Instead—I noticed with not a little amazement— she became much calmer. She got up and, assessing me with her large eyes, said, 'Get me a joint.'

'Have some liquor instead.'

'No. I want pot.'

I ordered a joint. She took a drag in the peculiar manner of seasoned users and looked at me, her eyes having relinquished their relentless possession of her face, though not ungrudgingly. Her face now took on the desolation of an overrun kingdom, a land laid to waste. Its every feature merely traced a line of utter bleakness, of stark despair. What was this desolation . . . and why? Often it is the inhabited settlements that cause their own ruination. Was she a habitation that had been stifled in its growth by some invader, leaving its walls, barely a metre high, in ruins?

I was extremely muddled, but I don't want to drag you into this confusion. What I was thinking and what conclusion I drew is not your business.

Whether or not Siraj was a virgin was not something I wanted to know. But in the curling smoke of the joint I did observe a gleam in her blank, melancholy eyes which even I can't adequately describe.

I wanted her to talk to me, but she had no interest. I wanted her to argue and squabble with me; here too she disappointed me.

Finally I took her back to her place.

Dhondo was quite offended when he found out about my secret meeting with Siraj. Both his friendly and business feelings were adversely affected. He didn't let me explain myself and said only, 'Manto Sahib, I didn't expect this from you.' He spoke his mind, stepped away from his lamp-post anchor, and left.

Strangely, I didn't see him at his haunt at his regular time the next evening, which made me think he might be sick. But he didn't show up the following day either.

A week went by. I passed this spot every morning and evening. The sight of the lamp post never failed to remind me of Dhondo. I even went to that unspeakably squalid slum near Byculla Station to find out if Siraj was still there, but I only found the crumbly old witch. 'She left,' she said when I asked her about Siraj. Then, evoking sexual desires that had lain dormant for aeons in her toothless smile, she added, 'There are others . . . Shall I send for someone?'

'What does this mean—both of them gone?' I wondered. 'And that too in the wake of my secret meeting?' While I wasn't at all concerned about my secret meeting—here again I don't wish to reveal my thoughts—I was quite amazed at their simultaneous disappearance. Nothing like what passes for 'love' existed between the two. Dhondo was above such things. He had a wife and children whom he loved dearly. Then what was behind their disappearance?

I thought it likely that Dhondo had suddenly decided it would be best for Siraj to return to her native Punjab. He might have been undecided about it earlier, but then he must have quickly made up his mind.

A whole month passed.

One evening, unexpectedly, I spotted Dhondo glued to the same lamp post. This gave me the unavoidable feeling that the electricity, which had been out for quite a while, had suddenly been restored and had brought the lamp post back to life, the telephone box too. The networks of lines above the post, running every which way, seemed to be whispering among themselves. He looked at me and smiled as I passed by.

We were sitting in the Irani teahouse now. I didn't ask him anything. He ordered the usual coffee–tea blend for himself, a plain tea

for me, and squirmed in his seat a while before settling down in a way
that suggested he was about to tell me something very serious. But he
only said, 'So tell me, Manto Sahib, how's it going?'

'What's there to tell, Dhondo, it just plods along.'

He smiled. 'Absolutely right! It plods along . . . and will plod along.
But this silly "plodding along" is strange. And if you ask me, just about
everything in this world is strange.'

'You're right, Dhondo.'

The tea arrived. As was his habit, he poured some in his saucer and
said, 'Manto Sahib, she told me everything. She said, "That seth friend
of yours—he's cuckoo in his head."'

I laughed. 'What made her say that?'

'She said, "He took me to a restaurant . . . gave me so much money
. . . but he had nothing of the usual seths in him."'

I felt embarrassed at my callowness. 'Couldn't be helped. The whole
thing was so weird.'

Dhondo laughed his head off. 'Don't I know it! Please forgive me
for having lost my cool that day.' His voice inadvertently took on a
shade of informality. 'But that story is over now.'

'What story?'

'That saali . . . Siraj . . . her story, who else's?'

'What happened?' I asked.

Dhondo started twittering: 'When she came back after meeting you
that day, she told me, "I have forty rupees. Come, take me to Lahore." I
said, "Saali, what devil has gotten into your head all of a sudden?" She
said, "No, Dhondo, let's go. I beg you." As you know, Manto Sahib, it's
not in me to turn her down, because I kind of like her. So I said, "Fine,
let's go." We bought tickets and boarded the train. At Lahore, we stayed
in a hotel. She asked me to get her a burqa so I did. She donned it and
started roaming around the streets and alleys all over the city. After a
few days, I told myself, "Well, Dhondo, that's something! She was crazy
and now you've gone bananas too. No sane person would have come
with her to the end of the world."

'Then, one day, she suddenly asked the coachman to pull the tonga
over. She pointed at a man and told me, "Dhondo, go get him. I'm going
back to the hotel. You bring him there." I lost my wits, Manto Sahib. I
got down from the tonga and she took off. There I was, following that
man. By the grace of God and your blessings, I kind of guessed what

kind of man he was. I exchanged a few words with him and found out that he was the kind that are on the lookout for fun and action, no doubt about it. I told him, "I've got a choice piece from Bombay, what do you say?" He said, "Take me to her right away." I said, "No, first show me the dough." He pulled out a whole wad of notes. I said to myself, "Dhondo, my man, yes, you're in business here too." What puzzled me, though, was why Siraj had singled him out in all of Lahore. "Well," I said to myself, "here goes." I hired a tonga, took him straight to the hotel and informed Siraj. She said, "Wait for a while." We waited for some time, and then I took the man inside. By the way, he was quite good-looking. The minute he saw Siraj he reared up like a horse, but she grabbed him.'

Dhondo paused. He finished his coffee–tea mix, stone cold by now, in one big gulp and lit a biri.

'So Siraj grabbed him,' I prompted.

'Yes, she did, that saala,' he said in a loud voice. 'She told him, "Let me see where you'll escape to now. You made me leave my home—what for? I loved you. You said that you loved me too. But when I eloped with you, leaving behind my home and my parents, leaving Amritsar, we stayed here in this very hotel and you disappeared during the night. You left me all alone. Why did you bring me here? Why did you make me run away? I was ready for everything, but you didn't care a fig about me. You took off. Come on, it's me who's calling you now. My love is still fresh. Come on . . ." Manto Sahib, she draped herself around him. That saala started shedding big fat tears. He begged for her forgiveness, saying, "I made a terrible mistake. I panicked. I'll never leave you again." He kept swearing to God that he would never do such a thing again. God knows what else he kept babbling! Siraj gave me a sign and I left the room. Next morning as I was sleeping on a cot outside, Siraj woke me up. "Well, Dhondo, let's go," she said, "Go where?" I asked. "Back to Bombay," she answered. "And where is that saala?" I asked. She said, "He's sleeping. I've put my burqa on top of him."'

Just as Dhondo was ordering another cup of coffee mixed with tea, Siraj came in, her fair, oval face fresh and blossoming, her great big eyes looking like two lowered railway signals.

Sharda

Nazir went to buy a bottle of whisky from the black market. There was a cigarette stall near the entrance to the pier, just before the main post office, where he always got Scotch at a reasonable price. He paid thirty-five rupees and took a bottle wrapped in paper. Must have been around eleven in the morning. Although he usually started drinking after sundown, the weather was so gorgeous that he'd thought he might get started now and keep going well into the evening.

Bottle in hand, he set out for home in an exuberant mood. He decided to catch a taxi at the Bori Bunder stand, leisurely sip a bit of the Scotch during the ride and arrive home pleasantly inebriated. If his wife made a fuss, he would simply say, 'Just look at the weather—isn't it heavenly?' and then recite a few lines of insipid poetry, 'The clouds won't let the angels in; / all sins will be counted as good deeds today.' Of course, she would nag him for a while, but eventually she would calm down and, perhaps, at his request, get busy making parathas filled with ground meat.

He had only taken a few steps away from the stall when a man greeted him. Given his weak memory, Nazir failed to recognize him but he pretended otherwise and said courteously, 'Where have you been all these days? Haven't seen you in ages.'

The man smiled. 'Sir, I'm always right here; it's you who have made yourself scarce.'

Nazir still couldn't place him. 'Well, I'm here now.'

'In that case, come with me.'

Nazir was in a very buoyant mood. He said, 'All right, let's go.'

Spotting the bottle tucked under Nazir's arm, the man said with a knowing smile, 'You seem to have everything else with you.'

'He's got to be a pimp,' Nazir suddenly realized. 'What's your name?' he asked.

'Karim. Don't tell me you forgot.'

It all came back to Nazir. Before he got married, a certain Karim used to procure nice girls for him. He was an exceptionally honest pimp. Nazir looked at him closely and saw a familiar face. The events of a not-so-long-ago past floated in his memory. 'Sorry, yaar, I didn't recognize you,' he apologized. 'It's been nearly six years since we last met, wouldn't you say?'

'I think so.'

'You used to do your business at the corner of Grant Road.'

'I've moved,' Karim said with burgeoning pride as he lit his biri, 'thanks to your good wishes. Now I work from a hotel.'

'Excellent!' Nazir congratulated him. 'You've done well for yourself.'

'Altogether I have ten girls,' Karim said with even greater pride, 'and one of them is brand new.'

'Oh, you guys! You always say that,' Nazir teased him.

But Karim took it badly. 'I swear by the Qur'an, I've never lied in my entire life. May I eat a pig's flesh if this girl isn't a novice.' He then dropped his voice and whispered conspiratorially, 'She had her first *passenger* just eight days ago—I'll be damned if I lie.'

'Was she a virgin?'

'Absolutely. That passenger had to shell out two hundred rupees.'

Nazir poked Karim in the ribs. 'I see you're already at it, I mean fixing the price.'

Karim felt offended. 'By the Qur'an, may he who bargains with you become a swine. Please come with me. Pay whatever you will. I'll accept it gladly. Karim has a lot to thank you for.'

Nazir had four hundred and fifty rupees on him. The weather was exceptional, and his mood no less exuberant. He travelled six years back in time, inebriated already without even having a drop. 'Why not, yaar, let's live it up. But first, let's get another bottle.'

'How much did you pay for this one?' Karim inquired.

'Thirty-five.'

'Brand?'

'Johnnie Walker.'

'I'll get you one for thirty,' Karim said, patting his chest.

'Don't let me stand in your way, be my guest—here.' Nazir took out three ten-rupee notes and handed them to Karim. 'After you've taken me to her, the first thing you should do is get the bottle. Remember, I don't like to drink alone.'

'And, perhaps you remember, I never drink more than a peg and a half,' Karim said smiling.

Yes—Nazir recalled—six years ago, Karim had always drunk only a peg and a half. The memory made him smile. 'Have two today.'

'No, sir, not a drop more.'

Karim stopped near a dismal building with a shabby sign in one corner announcing Marina Hotel. It was a beautiful name, but the building was filthy, with a rickety, crumbling staircase. A bunch of Pathan moneylenders in baggy shalwars lounged on cots near the entrance. The ground floor seemed to have been appropriated by Christians; a slew of native sailors lived on the second floor; and the third had been taken over by the hotel's owner for his personal use. Karim had a corner room on the fourth floor, where several girls sat huddled together like chickens cooped up in their pen.

He sent for the key from the owner and opened the door to a spacious but ill-proportioned room. It had a steel-frame cot, a chair and a tea table. The room was exposed on three sides, that is, it had a profusion of windows, most of them with the glass broken. If nothing else, at least it boasted an airy environment.

After cleaning the filthy armchair with a filthier rag, Karim invited Nazir to take a seat. 'But let me tell you upfront,' he said, 'the room will cost you ten rupees.'

Nazir examined the room closely and said, 'Yaar, isn't ten a bit steep.'

'It is, I agree, but can't be helped. The hotel owner, saala, he's one hell of a money-sucker. He won't take a penny less. And Nazir Sahib, what's money to someone out on a binge, after all.'

Nazir thought a bit. 'You couldn't be more right. Shall I pay for it in advance?' he asked.

'No, that won't be necessary. First have a look at the girl,' he said as he went out.

He returned in a bit with an exceedingly shy girl in tow—a plain sort of Hindu girl of about fourteen in a white dhoti, not exactly a beauty queen but endearingly simple and naive all the same.

'Sit down,' Karim told her. 'This gentleman is a friend of mine. He's one of our own.'

The girl perched herself on the cot with her eyes lowered. Karim left the room saying, 'Make sure you're satisfied. I'll fetch some glasses and soda.'

Nazir got up from the chair and sat down next to the girl. She cringed and pulled away. Nazir asked, exactly the way he used to six years ago, 'What's your name?'

She didn't reply. Nazir edged closer to her, took her hand and asked again, 'What's your name, madam?'

The girl pulled her hand free and said, 'Shakuntala.'

Nazir recalled the Shakuntala with whom Raja Dushyanta had fallen in love. 'And I'm Dushyanta,' he said. Nazir, in a pleasant mood, seemed hell bent on having a good time. The girl heard him and smiled. Meanwhile, Karim returned and presented four bottles of soda dotted with condensation. 'I remembered that you like Roger's soda. They're chilled.'

Nazir was delighted. 'Man, you're something else again!' Then he asked the girl, 'Madam, would you like to have some?'

She didn't respond. Instead, Karim answered, 'Nazir Sahib, she doesn't drink. It's only been eight days since she came here.'

Nazir felt a bit let down. 'That's no good,' he said.

Karim opened the whisky and poured out a shot for Nazir. Then he winked at him and said, 'Well, see if you can bring her round.'

Nazir emptied the glass in one gulp. Karim had only half a peg. The liquor affected him immediately. 'You like the girl, don't you?' he asked, swaying a little from the rapid inebriation.

Nazir thought about it but couldn't say whether he did or didn't. He looked intently at Shakuntala. He might have liked her if she hadn't had that name. The Shakuntala whom Raja Dushyanta had seen during his hunt and instantly fallen in love with was very beautiful, or so the books said. They described her as lovelier than the sun and moon, with the eyes of a gazelle. Nazir looked at his Shakuntala one more time. Her eyes weren't bad, though not exactly like a gazelle's, but they were her own eyes, large and dark. He didn't deliberate further and said, 'Fine, yaar. How much?'

Karim poured himself another half peg and said, 'A hundred.'

Nazir was no longer thinking. 'Okay, a hundred it is.'

His drink finished, Karim left the room. Nazir got up and closed the door. When he plopped down beside Shakuntala, she became nervous. And when he tried to kiss her, she sprang up with a start. He found this very unpleasant, but attempted it again. He grabbed her by the arm, made her sit next to him and forcibly kissed her. The whole thing was proceeding in the worst possible way. At least the effect of the whisky was superb; he had downed six pegs by now. Soon, though, he began to feel quite disappointed that all this expense would be a waste since this Shakuntala had turned out to be totally raw and knew next to nothing about the protocol of this trade. It was as if he had been condemned to swim with a rank amateur. At last he lost interest. He opened the door and called out for Karim, who sat cooped up in the grubby den with his girls.

Karim scurried over. 'What's the matter, Nazir Sahib?'

'Nothing, yaar,' Nazir said in desperation. 'It won't work.'

'Why?'

'She doesn't seem to know what's involved.'

Karim took Shakuntala aside and reasoned with her at length, but failed to get through to her. Adjusting her dhoti, she scuttled out of the room, blushing all over. 'I'll bring her right back,' Karim said.

'Don't bother,' Nazir stopped him. 'Bring me some other girl.' Then, suddenly, he changed his mind. 'Go and buy another bottle with the money I gave you and bring however many girls you have around here—except Shakuntala. I mean, all the ones who drink. Today, I'll just sit with them and drink. Nothing else.'

Karim, who understood Nazir well enough, sent in four girls. Nazir looked at them cursorily. He'd made up his mind to just drink in their company so he sent for more glasses and started drinking with them. In the afternoon he had lunch brought over from the hotel and chattered with them until six in the evening. Meaningless jabber, but it seemed to revive his spirits; the vexation Shakuntala had caused him was more than redeemed.

Half a bottle of whisky still remained, so he took it home. A fortnight later the weather was again heavenly and Nazir was overcome by the desire to drink all day long. Instead of buying his liquor at the cigarette stall, he decided to get it for less through Karim, and went to his haunt. Luckily Karim was there. The minute Karim saw him he said in a hushed voice, 'Nazir Sahib, Shakuntala's elder sister is here. She arrived by the morning train. A tough cookie, I must say, but I'm sure you will be able to tame her.'

Nazir hardly took time to think it over. 'Let's see,' he said to himself. 'Come on, yaar, get some whisky first,' he told Karim, giving him thirty rupees.

Karim took the bills and said, 'Okay, I'll get it. You go into the room and have a seat.'

Nazir had only ten rupees left. All the same, he had the room opened and sat down on the chair. He had decided that he would take the bottle of whisky, briefly look at Shakuntala's sister and then be on his way, tipping Karim two rupees for his trouble.

In the abundantly airy room, seated on the terribly grimy chair, Nazir lit a cigarette and lifted his legs up on to the bed. Shortly afterwards he heard the sound of footsteps. Karim entered and whispered into Nazir's ear, 'She'll be here in a second. But mind you, you'll have to tackle her yourself.'

Karim left the room, and five minutes later a girl resembling Shakuntala and, like her, draped in a white dhoti entered with a frown on her face. She raised her hand to her head and, with utter indifference, said 'Aadaab' and sat down on the bed. Nazir felt as though she'd come looking for a fight. Recalling his style from six years ago he addressed her courteously, 'You're Shakuntala's sister?'

'Yes,' she replied in a sharp, angry tone.

Nazir was quiet for some time, intently observing this girl who was perhaps three years older than Shakuntala. She didn't like it, and was, in fact, miffed at being checked out so blatantly. 'What is it, do you want to tell me something?' she asked, swinging one leg back and forth in agitation. The same smile that was his wont six years ago appeared on his lips. 'Madam, why be so angry?'

'Why wouldn't I be angry? This Karim, your friend, kidnapped my sister from Jaipur. Don't you think that's reason enough for my blood to boil? I hear she was also offered to you.'

Nothing like this had ever happened before. After some thought Nazir said to the girl in all earnestness, 'The minute I saw Shakuntala I knew she wasn't my type. She's very raw and inexperienced. I don't prefer such girls. You might not want to hear this, but the fact is I'm much more drawn to women who know how to make a man happy.'

The girl didn't say anything.

'Your name?' he asked.

'Sharda,' she replied tersely.

'Where are you from?'

'Jaipur.' Her tone was still sharp with anger.

Nazir smiled. 'Look,' he began, 'you have no right to be angry with me. If Karim has offended you, you should punish him. I haven't done anything wrong.'

He got up, gathered the girl in his arms and kissed her on the lips. Before she could say anything, he addressed her: '*This*, of course, is my offence. I plead guilty and am ready for my punishment.'

Myriad expressions flitted across her face. She spat on the floor a few times. For a moment it seemed as if she was about to unload a volley of curses, but she didn't. She sprang up from the bed and sat back down just as quickly.

'So, have you decided on the penalty?' Nazir was tempted to ask.

Just as she was about to open her mouth, the cry of a child sounded from the chicken coop. The girl got up again but Nazir stopped her. 'Where are you going?'

Suddenly she was a mother. 'Munni is crying for milk,' she said and left the room.

Nazir tried to think about her but his mind got muddled. Meanwhile, Karim returned with a bottle of whisky and some soda. He poured soda for Nazir, finished pouring his own drink, and asked him slyly, 'Were you able to strike up a conversation with Sharda? I thought you would have brought her round by now.'

'Boy, oh boy, she's got one hell of a temper,' Nazir answered with a smile.

'That she does. She arrived just this morning and already she's made my life a living hell. Do try to break her down. Shakuntala came with me of her own will because her father had abandoned her mother. Just like Sharda's husband, who took off for God knows where soon after they got married. She lives with her daughter at her mother's place now. Please try to persuade her.'

'Persuade her . . . Whatever do you mean?'

'You know.' Karim winked at him. 'Saali, will she listen to me! No, sir. From the moment she set her foot in here she's been railing me up and down.'

Meanwhile, Sharda came in lugging her one-year-old and glowered at Karim testily. He hastily downed his half peg and went out.

Munni had apparently caught a bad cold; her nose was running profusely. Nazir called Karim and gave him five rupees, saying, 'Go buy some Vicks.'

'What's that?' Karim inquired.

'Cold medicine,' Nazir said and wrote out the name on a scrap of paper. 'You can get it from just about any store.'

'Okay.'

After Karim was gone Nazir turned his attention to Munni. He loved children and although Munni wasn't a pretty girl, Nazir found her quite charming. He took her in his arms and cuddled her. Sharda was having a hard time putting her to sleep. Nazir caressed her head gently with his fingers until she dozed off. 'Looks as though I'm her mother,' he said to Sharda, who smiled and asked him to give the child back to her so she could lay her down on the bed in the other room.

By the time she returned all traces of anger had disappeared from her face. Nazir sat down close to her. After a brief silence, he asked, 'Would you allow me to be your husband?' and embraced her without waiting for her reply. She didn't resist.

'Madam, please answer.'

She remained silent. Nazir got up and swallowed a peg. Sharda contorted her face. 'I hate this stuff,' she said.

He poured some whisky in a glass, threw in some soda, and sat down by her side. 'Why do you hate it?' he asked.

'I just do,' she said briefly.

'But you won't, from this day forward. Here.' He offered the glass to her.

'I won't touch it, not in a million years.'

'And I say you'll not refuse, absolutely not.'

Sharda took the glass and let her gaze linger on it a while. Utterly helpless, she looked at Nazir and then, pinching her nose, swallowed the whole glassful in one big gulp. She felt as if she was about to throw up but managed to keep it down somehow. Wiping her tears with the edge of her dhoti, she said, 'This is the first and last time . . . But why did I take it in the first place?'

He kissed her moist lips. 'Don't even try to find the answer,' he said. He walked over to the door and fastened it.

It was seven in the evening when he unlatched it. As soon as Karim
came in, Sharda left the room with her head bowed. Karim looked
ecstatic. 'Man, oh man, I can't believe it! Was it a miracle or what? I
won't ask for a hundred. Just give me fifty.'

Nazir was well satisfied with Sharda, indeed so pleased that he'd
already forgotten all the other women he'd had before. She was the
perfect fulfilment of every sexual desire he'd ever had.

'I'll pay tomorrow,' he said to Karim. 'The rent too. After the thirty
I gave you for the whisky, I only have ten left.'

'No problem. That you tamed Sharda is compensation enough for
me. Believe me, *huzoor*, she was getting on my nerves. But now she
can't admonish Shakuntala.'

Karim left. Sharda came in with Munni in her arms. Nazir gave her
five rupees, but she declined. Nazir smiled. 'What's this, am I not her
father? Why are you refusing?'

Sharda very quietly took the money. Whereas earlier she had
seemed quite talkative, now she was unusually quiet and reticent. He
took Munni in his arms, kissed her. As he was leaving, he said, 'Well
then, Sharda, I have to go now. If not tomorrow, I'll come the day after.'

Nazir showed up the very next day. Sharda had slaked his sexual
appetite so well, and returned his passion with such an unalloyed spirit
of giving that he was completely swept away. He paid Karim the amount
due, had him bring a bottle, and sat down with Sharda. He asked her to
join him in drinking, but she said, 'I told you that was the first and last
time.'

Nazir continued drinking alone. From eleven in the morning till
seven in the evening he remained closeted with Sharda. He returned
home feeling extremely sated, even more than the day before. Despite
her very plain looks and unusual reticence, Sharda had completely
overwhelmed his sensual appetites. Time after time he wondered, 'What
kind of woman is she? Never before in my life have I seen a woman so
undemonstrative yet so sensuous.'

He started visiting her every second day. She had no interest in
money, nor did she ever mention it to him. Nazir paid sixty rupees
to Karim, who paid ten for the room and deducted seventeen as his
commission. But Sharda never mentioned it to Nazir.

Two months went by. Nazir had practically exhausted his budget.
He also noticed that his association with Sharda was beginning to affect

his marital life. Every time he slept with his wife, he felt that something
was missing. He wanted Sharda in her place. This wasn't a good thing.
Being conscious of the impropriety, he desperately wished that his
affair with Sharda would somehow end. Eventually, he himself brought
up the matter with her. 'Sharda,' he said, 'I'm a married man. All my
savings are gone. I don't know what to do. I don't want to give you up,
but at the same time I never want to come here again.'

Sharda was quiet for some time after he spoke. Then she broke her
silence. 'Whatever money I've saved, you can have it. Just let me keep
enough for the train fare back to Jaipur for me and Shakuntala.'

He kissed her and said, 'Don't be silly. You don't seem to get my
meaning. If I can't see you any more it's because I've run out of money.
I was wondering how I might continue to see you despite that.'

She didn't say anything. When he came to the hotel the next day
after borrowing money from a friend, Karim told him Sharda was all set
to leave for Jaipur. When Nazir sent for her, she didn't come. Instead
she gave Karim a wad of banknotes for him with the message, 'Please,
accept this and write down your address for me.'

Nazir gave his address to Karim, but returned the money. Sharda
came with Munni in her arms. She greeted him with 'Aadaab' and then
told him, 'I'm returning to Jaipur this evening.'

'But why?'

Her answer was brief: 'I don't know.' Then she left.

Nazir asked Karim to send her back, but she didn't come. Nazir left
with the strange feeling that his body had gone completely cold; she had
abandoned him without really answering his question.

She had gone away. She really had. Karim was terribly upset. He
complained, 'Nazir Sahib, why did you let her go?'

'Friend, I'm not some seth loaded with money,' he replied. 'How
could I possibly spend fifty rupees every other day, plus another ten for
the room, thirty for a bottle, and a little extra as well. I've drifted into
bankruptcy. By God, I'm in debt.'

Karim was quiet.

'I couldn't help it . . . I couldn't have gone on like this.'

'Nazir Sahib, she loved you.'

Nazir knew nothing about love. He only knew that Sharda was
generous in giving of herself physically. She was the perfect answer to his
sensual needs. Beyond that he knew next to nothing about her, except

that she had once mentioned in passing that her husband had been a sucker for pleasure. He had left her because she couldn't conceive for two years, but Munni came along within nine months of their parting. She so resembled her father.

Sharda had taken Shakuntala along. She wanted her sister to get married and live a respectable life. She was very fond of her. Karim had tried hard to get Shakuntala started in the oldest profession. There was no dearth of 'passengers' willing to pay two hundred rupees for a night, but Sharda wouldn't allow it and would start quarrelling with Karim. And when Karim taunted her, saying, 'What exactly do you think you're doing?' she would shout back, 'If you weren't in the middle, I wouldn't do it! I would never let Nazir Sahib spend a penny.'

Once, she had asked Nazir for his photograph so he had brought one from home and given it to her. She had taken it with her to Jaipur. She had never spoken to him about her love for him. Whenever he was in bed with her, she remained totally silent. Nazir would try to provoke her into speaking but to no avail. He only knew that she never held back in giving herself to him physically. At least in that she was sincerity personified.

Nazir felt a sense of relief at Sharda's departure. She had gravely affected his relationship with his wife. If she had stayed much longer, chances were that he would have become entirely indifferent to his wife. However, as time passed, Nazir slowly reverted to his old life and the memory of Sharda's touch gradually began to fade from his body.

One day, exactly a fortnight after Sharda left, Nazir was at home busy doing some office work. His wife, who usually collected and opened the morning mail, brought an envelope over to him saying, 'Can't tell whether this is in Hindi or Gujarati.'

Nazir looked at the letter and put it aside in the tray, unable to make out the language. A short while later his wife called her younger sister Naima. As soon as Naima appeared she handed her the letter. 'Perhaps you can read it; you know both Hindi and Gujarati. What does it say?'

Naima glanced at it and said, 'It's Hindi,' and started to read: 'Jaipur . . . Dear Nazir Sahib . . .' She stopped. Nazir started. Naima read another line, 'Aadaab. You must have forgotten me. But ever since I've come back here, I've been thinking of you . . .' Naima blushed and quickly turned the page over. 'It is from some Sharda,' she said.

Nazir rose quickly, snatched the letter from Naima's hand, and said to his wife, 'God knows who it is. I'm going out. I'll have it read and transcribed into Urdu.' Without letting his wife say anything, he left the house. He went to a friend and had him rewrite the same letter in Hindi on identical paper and with ink of the same colour, keeping the opening sentences intact but altering the rest of the contents so that it read to the effect that Sharda had met him at Bombay Central and was delighted to have met such an illustrious artist, and so on.

That evening, he gave the new letter to his wife and read out the Urdu translation. When she asked who this Sharda was, he said, 'A while back I went to the station to see off a friend who knew this girl called Sharda. She was standing on the platform. My friend introduced us. She is a painter too.'

The matter ended there. But the very next day he got another letter from her, which he subjected to the same treatment. He immediately sent a telegram to Sharda advising her to stop sending letters and wait for his new address. At the post office he instructed the mailman for his area to hold back any mail from Jaipur and keep it with him. He would come every morning and collect it himself. He received three more letters in this manner. Afterwards Sharda wrote to him in care of a friend of his.

Sharda, never much of a talker, wrote very long letters. While she had never admitted her love to his face, her letters overflowed with her feelings—the same reproaches and complaints, the same pain of separation that is the staple of love letters. Nazir, though, didn't feel love for her, the kind of love found in romantic stories and novels, and didn't know what to write to her. He commissioned a friend to do this job. His friend would write out a letter in Hindi and read it to him, and he would invariably say, 'Yes.'

Sharda was dying to come to Bombay but didn't want to stay at Karim's. Nazir couldn't put her up in a house since houses were scarce and hard to find. He thought about sending her to a hotel but hesitated lest this should let out their secret. He had his friend write to her to wait a while longer.

Just then communal rioting erupted throughout the country. A strange panic and confusion seized people in the days just prior to Partition. Nazir's wife wanted to move to Lahore. 'I'll stay there for a while,' she told him. 'If conditions get better, I'll come back, otherwise you come over there too.'

He kept her from going for a few days, but when her brother got ready to leave for Lahore both she and her younger sister went along with him. Nazir was left alone. He mentioned casually to Sharda in his next missive that he was all by himself. She telegrammed to say that she was coming. It seemed from the message that she had already left Jaipur. Nazir found himself in a terrible fix, although his body was feeling a blossoming sense of anticipation. He was thirsting for her body and her genuine devotion. He yearned for the days when he had clung to her for hours, from eleven in the morning to seven in the evening to be precise. There was no question of spending money now, or of Karim's involvement, or even of the rent for the room. He thought, 'I'll take my servant into my confidence and everything will be fine. A few rupees will be enough to shut his mouth. He won't breathe a word if my wife does decide to come back.'

He went to the station the next day. The Frontier Mail arrived but, despite a long search, he couldn't find Sharda. Maybe something held her up, he concluded, and she'll probably send another telegram.

The next day he left for the office as usual by the morning train. When the train pulled into the Mahalakshmi station, where he usually got off, he spotted Sharda on the platform and cried out loudly, 'Sharda! Sharda!'

A startled Sharda looked at him. 'Nazir Sahib.'

'What—you here?'

She complained, 'You didn't come to meet me so I decided to go to your office. There they told me that you weren't in yet so I was waiting for you here on the platform.'

He thought for a bit and then said to her, 'Stay here. I'll go to office, arrange a few days off and come right back.'

He sat her down on a bench and hurried off to his office. He wrote out an application to be absent for a few days, handed it to the office boy, and took Sharda home. Neither spoke a word on the way, but their bodies were communicating perfectly, drawing ever closer to each other.

'You'd better bathe,' he said to Sharda after reaching home. 'Meanwhile, I'll have some breakfast prepared for you.'

While she was bathing, he told the servant that a friend's wife was visiting him; he should quickly prepare breakfast. He then took a bottle from the cabinet, poured a double shot, added some water and gulped it down.

He wanted to make love to her in the same spirit as in the hotel.

Sharda emerged from her bath and started on the breakfast. As she ate, she talked to him about a hundred different things. Nazir noticed a change in her. She had been quite taciturn and had preferred silence most of the time, but now she couldn't resist using every opportunity to impress upon him how madly she was in love with him.

'What is this "love"?' Nazir wondered. 'Wouldn't it be nice if she never mentioned it? Frankly, I liked her silence better. It communicated a hell of a lot more. God knows what's gotten into her now. When she talks, it seems as if she's reading out loud from her letters.'

After she was done eating, Nazir mixed a drink and offered it to her. She refused. When he pressed her, she pinched her nose and drank it just to please him. She grimaced and rinsed her mouth. Nazir felt a twinge of regret. 'Why did she drink it? It would have been infinitely nicer if she had turned it down in spite of his insistence.' He didn't exercise his mind about it further. He sent the servant away on an errand, bolted the door, and lay down with her on the bed.

'You wrote, when will those days come again,' she started. 'Well, they've come—and not just the days, but the nights as well. Back then there weren't any nights, only days—those dirty, filthy days at the hotel. Here, everything is so bright, so immaculate. No more paying rent for the hotel room, or tolerating the presence of pesky Karim. Here, it's just the two of us, our own masters.'

She told him how badly she'd suffered during their separation, how she survived that agonizing period—the same garbage found in romantic books. Complaints and reproaches, sighs, sleepless nights spent counting stars.

Nazir downed another peg and thought: 'Who would ever count stars. There are so many, how can anyone possibly count them? Absolute nonsense. Rubbish.'

He gathered her in his arms and held her close. The bed was clean, Sharda was clean, he himself was clean, even the atmosphere in the room was clean. Why then were his senses failing to evoke the same sensations he'd felt with her on that steel bed in the dingy hotel room?

Maybe he hadn't really had enough to drink—he thought. He got up, poured another peg, swallowed it in one mouthful and lay down beside Sharda again. Immediately, she resumed her litany of separation, the same complaints and reproaches. Feeling fed up, Nazir's body worked itself into a state of suspended numbness. A nagging thought crossed his mind: Sharda's body had lost its consuming passion, so much so that it blunted his own desire and became useless, no longer able to ignite his passion. Even so, he lay next to her a long time.

When he finally got out of bed he felt a violent desire to grab a taxi and go home to his wife. But he quickly realized that he was, in fact, home and his wife was in Lahore, which rankled him. Insanely, he wished his home were the hotel.

Sharda's body was still as physically hospitable as before, but the vibes were no longer the same. There was no haggling over price, no giving with one hand and taking with the other, and there was no hotel filth either. The ambience created by all these things was conspicuously absent. Nazir was in his own home, in the bed where his simple-minded wife slept with him. Ever since this nagging thought took hold of his subconscious he had felt quite conflicted. Sometimes he thought the whisky wasn't potent enough, sometimes that Sharda hadn't shown him proper regard, and sometimes that it would have worked out if she had just chosen to keep her mouth shut. Then he thought about the fact that she was seeing him after a long and painful separation; the poor thing needed some time to vent her feelings after all. She would become normal in a day or two, like her old self.

A fortnight passed but Sharda still didn't give him the feeling that she was the same girl he'd carried on with in the hotel. Her baby daughter was in Jaipur. Back then she was with Sharda at the hotel, and Nazir would have medicine sent for to treat her head cold, her boils or her throat. None of this was there any more. She was alone now. Nazir had always thought of Sharda and Munni as one.

Once he had embraced Sharda rather tightly and the pressure had caused a few drops of milk to ooze out of her swollen breasts on to his hairy chest. It had given him a pleasurable sensation. How wonderful to be a mother! And this milk!—he'd thought. Men are the poorer for their inadequacy: They eat and drink and produce nothing, whereas women take nourishment and sustain others through it. What a sublime experience to be able to nourish someone, especially your own child!

Now Munni wasn't there with Sharda. The poor woman was incomplete. And so were her breasts. They no longer had much milk in them—that white elixir of life. Now she didn't protest if he pressed her tightly to his chest. She wasn't the old Sharda any more, though, in fact, she was every bit the same, perhaps even more than the Sharda he had known. With separation, her sensual ardour had grown keener, and now she also loved him with her soul. Still Nazir felt she had lost her earlier allure or whatever it was.

Such was his conclusion after a fortnight of being close to her continually. Well, fifteen days of absence from the office was long enough. He resumed his work, leaving for the office in the morning and returning home in the evening. Sharda took to serving him like a devoted wife. She bought some wool and knitted him a sweater, made sure he had enough soda for his drinks when he came home, and kept plenty of ice in the thermos. In the morning she laid out his shaving kit on the table and warmed up some water. After he was finished, she cleaned away the shaving paraphernalia and busied herself with housework. She swept the floors herself.

Nazir couldn't take this any more.

Until then they had been sleeping together. Now he started sleeping alone on the pretext that he needed to do some thinking. Sharda moved to the other bed. But this only added to his turmoil. While she slept soundly, he lay awake wondering what this was all about. This Sharda—why was she here? Yes, he had spent a few quite marvellous days with her at Karim's hotel, but why had she stuck to him? What was all this leading to? Where would it end? Love and all that—pure nonsense! It was just a minor thing, and even that was no longer there. It was time she returned to Jaipur.

Not long afterwards Nazir was seized by the thought that he was committing a sin. Of course, he had sinned at Karim's hotel, and umpteen times even before his marriage. But at that time he wasn't conscious of sinning. Now, increasingly, he felt as though he was cheating on his wife, his simple-minded wife whom he had lied to so often about Sharda's letters. Sharda seemed even less attractive to him now. He started treating her coldly, but she was never ungracious to him, never complained to him about his coldness, thinking that, after all, artists tended to be quite moody.

A whole month had slipped away since she had arrived in Bombay to be with him. When Nazir counted the days he felt troubled. 'Can't believe this woman has been living here for a whole month. What a rotten egg I am . . . writing a letter to my wife every day like a faithful husband! As if all I care about in the world is her . . . as if life is hell without her. Could there be a greater impostor than me? Deceiving her there and Sharda here. Why can't I tell this woman plainly, "Look, woman, I no longer feel the same way about you?" But do I really no longer feel the same way, or is she no longer the same Sharda?'

He thought and thought but the answer eluded him. His mind was in a shambles. He had even started to reflect on morality. Guilt over betraying his wife haunted him night and day, and as the days rolled past it became more pronounced. He began to hate himself. 'I'm scum. Why has this woman become my second wife? When did I ever need her? Why has she stuck to me so? Why did I allow her to come here?' Because she'd written to him—that's why. 'But it was sent when I could no longer stop her. She was already on her way.'

Then his mind would strike out on a different line of thinking: Whatever Sharda does . . . it's all make-believe, a sham. She wants this charade to drive a wedge between my wife and me. Reasoning like this alienated him further from Sharda, and his attitude worsened. But this only made Sharda gentler and even more submissive. She went to great lengths to ensure his comfort and ease, and that behaviour irritated him even more. Now he began to hate her.

By chance one day he had no money on him. It had slipped his mind to go and withdraw some from the bank. He arrived at the office quite late because he wasn't feeling well. When he was leaving, Sharda had said something to him and he had yelled back: 'Shut your trap! I'm all right. I forgot to get cash from the bank and I haven't got any money for cigarettes.'

He got a tin of Gold Flakes from the cigarette stall near his office. Although he hated this brand, it was the only one he was able to get on credit. He smoked two or three willy-nilly. That evening at home he saw a tin of his favourite brand on the tea table. At first he thought it was just an empty tin, or that maybe it had just a couple of cigarettes. When he opened it, it was full. He asked Sharda, 'Where did this come from?'

She smiled. 'It was sitting in the cupboard.'

He must have opened it at some point, left it there and then forgot about it, he decided. The next day another full tin was sitting on the tea table. When he asked Sharda, she repeated, again with a smile, the same answer as the day before.

'Nonsense,' he snapped angrily. 'I don't appreciate such antics. I can buy my own, thank you. I'm not a beggar who needs you to buy his cigarettes every day.'

'I took the liberty because I know you sometimes forget,' she said tenderly, lovingly.

For no reason at all Nazir blurted out furiously, 'Well, of course, I'm absent-minded! But I don't like such boldness.'

'I apologize.' Sharda's tone grew infinitely softer.

Sharda was hardly to blame, Nazir thought for a moment; perhaps he should step forward and kiss her for caring. But the next instant the thought that he was betraying his wife overpowered him, so he said to her with all the hate he could pack into his voice, 'Hold your tongue. I think I'll send you back first thing tomorrow. In the morning I'll give you whatever money you need.'

Sharda remained quiet. She slept with him that night, caressing and hugging him with all the tenderness of her being the whole time. It irritated him, but he didn't let her know.

In the morning he found a variety of tasty dishes for breakfast. Still he didn't say a word to Sharda. Immediately after breakfast he left for the bank, saying only, 'I'm going to the bank. I'll be right back.'

The branch where Nazir had his account was close by. He withdrew two hundred rupees and hurried home. He planned to give it all to Sharda, buy her train ticket and pack her off. When he arrived the servant informed him that she had already left.

'Where did she go?' Nazir inquired.

'She didn't say. She left with her trunk and bedding.'

Nazir entered his room and found a tin of his favourite cigarettes on the tea table. It was full.

Babu Gopinath

I believe I met Babu Gopinath in 1940. Back then I was the editor of a Bombay weekly. One day when I was busy writing the lead, Abdur Rahim 'Sando' stormed into my office, followed by a puny little fellow. Sando greeted me in his typically shrill manner and then introduced his companion, 'Manto Sahib, please meet Babu Gopinath.'

I got up and shook hands with him. As usual, Sando rattled off a list of overblown compliments: 'Babu Gopinath, you're shaking hands with India's number one writer. Here he writes, there *dharan takhta*. A master of establishing *kuntinutely* among people and things. So Manto Sahib, what was that joke you unleashed the other day? "Miss Khurshid bought a car; verily, God is a great carmaker." Now, Babu Gopinath, wouldn't you say this is right *aynti ki paynti po*?'

Abdur Rahim Sando had quite the way of talking. *Dharan takhta*, *kuntinutely* and *aynti ki paynti po* were phrases he'd coined himself and would slip into conversation quite naturally.

After introducing me, he turned to Babu Gopinath, who appeared to be quite overwhelmed. 'And this is Babu Gopinath, the home-wrecker—his home, of course—come to Bombay from Lahore, fooling around all the way, a Kashmiri kabutri in tow.'

Babu Gopinath smiled faintly.

Thinking he hadn't done justice to the introduction, Sando added, 'World's number one gullible fool, if ever there was one. People butter him up and cheat him out of his money. I squeeze two boxes of Polson's butter out of him every day just by talking. He's a very *antiphilogistine* type of person, Manto Sahib. Do come to his flat this evening.'

111

Babu Gopinath, whose mind seemed to be elsewhere, started and said, 'Yes, yes, Manto Sahib, you must come.' Then he asked Sando, 'Does Manto Sahib enjoy . . . You know . . .?'

Sando exploded into laughter. 'Are you kidding? He enjoys everything, not just that! Manto Sahib, you must come this evening. I've started drinking too, because it's free.'

Sando gave me the address. I arrived there at about six as promised. It was a neat and tidy three-room flat boasting brand new furniture. Apart from Sando and Babu Gopinath, two other men and two women were in the living room. Sando introduced them to me.

One of the men was Ghaffar Sain, the perfect image of a Punjabi peasant. He was clad in a sarong and had a string of large beads around his neck. 'Babu Gopinath's legal adviser. You know what I mean?' said Sando, introducing the man. 'Any lunatic with a runny nose and a drooling mouth becomes a man of God in Punjab. This one's also a man of God, or is getting there. He tagged along with Babu Gopinath from Lahore because he had no hope of ever finding another sucker in that land. Now he guzzles Scotch, smokes Craven A cigarettes and prays for Babu Gopinath's well-being.'

Throughout this introduction Ghaffar Sain kept smiling.

The other man, tall and athletic with a pockmarked face, was called Ghulam Ali. Sando introduced him as: 'My acolyte. He's following precisely in the footsteps of his guru. The unmarried daughter of a well-known Lahore prostitute went bonkers over him. She brought all kinds of *kuntiniutlian* into motion to trap him, but he said, "Do or die, I'm not about to drop my pants." He ran into Babu Gopinath at some shrine and has stuck to him ever since. He gets his meals and a tin of Craven A every day.'

Ghulam Ali also kept smiling through this parsing of his person.

There was also a fair-skinned, rosy-cheeked Kashmiri kabutri in the room. As soon as we walked in I concluded that she was the same Kashmiri kabutri Sando had alluded to in the office. A neat-looking young woman with short hair that gave the impression of just having been cut though it actually hadn't been. Her eyes were clear and gleaming. Her features betrayed a coltishness and a lack of worldly experience. Sando introduced her thus: 'Zeenat Begum, or Zeeno for short, as Babu Sahib calls her lovingly. This apple, plucked from Kashmir, was brought to Lahore by a seasoned madam. Babu Gopinath found out about her through his secret network and made off with her one night. A lot of legal wrangling ensued. For two whole months the police had a good time. At Babu Sahib's expense, of course, but in the end, he won the court case and brought her here . . . *dharan takhta!*'

The other woman, who sat quietly smoking a cigarette, was dark-complexioned and her red-streaked eyes oozed considerable brashness. Babu Gopinath pointed to her and said to Sando, 'Say something about her too.'

Slapping her on the thigh, Sando proclaimed, 'And this, gentlemen, is *teen patoti fulful boti*, Mrs Abdur Rahim "Sando", otherwise known as Sardar Begum. She too is a product of Lahore. Fell in love with me in 1936 and made a *dharan takhta* of me in two years flat. I fled Lahore. What do you know? Babu Gopinath sent for her to keep me amused. She too gets a daily ration of a tin of Craven A. She takes a morphine shot every evening, which costs two and a half rupees. Don't let her dark complexion deceive you; she's a real *tit for tat* woman.'

'Don't talk gibberish!' Sardar only said this much, though not without a certain air—the feigned air of a seasoned professional.

After introducing everyone, Sando began another round of my praises.

'Enough, yaar,' I said, 'let's talk about something else.'

'Boy!' he shouted with gusto. 'Some whisky and soda,' and then looking at the host, said, 'Babu Gopinath, out with the green.'

Babu Gopinath stuck his hand into his pocket, yanked out a wad of hundred-rupee bills and gave one to Sando. Sando stared at it with reverence, brandished it and said, 'Oh God! My Rabbul Alameen,[*] would that a day might come when I too can lick my thumb and peel off note after note! On your feet, Ghulam Ali! Bring two bottles of Johnnie Walker Still-Going-Strong.'

The bottles arrived in no time and we all began to drink. The evening lasted a good three hours, during which Abdur Rahim, as usual, talked the most. He downed the first glass in a single gulp and shouted, '*Dharan takhta*, Manto Sahib, now this is what I call perfect whisky. The second it goes blazing down my throat it inscribes "Long Live the Revolution!" inside my guts. Long Live Babu Gopinath!'

[*] Lord of the Universe.

Poor Babu Gopinath, he remained perfectly silent, though now and then he did chime in with Sando. I couldn't help thinking that the man had no opinion of his own and went along with whatever anyone else said. Ghaffar Sain—whom Sando had anointed as Babu Gopinath's 'legal adviser', which only meant Babu had faith in him—was the greatest proof of Babu's gullibility. Then too, I gathered from the conversation that Babu had spent a good part of his time in Lahore in the company of fakirs and dervishes. There was an air of absent-mindedness in him, as if he was perpetually lost in distant thoughts, so I asked him at one point, 'Babu Gopinath, what are you thinking about?'

Startled, he said with a smile, 'Me . . . nothing . . . nothing at all.' Then glancing at Zeenat with a look full of tender love he exclaimed, 'Just about these beauties. What else is there?'

'He is a formidable home-wrecker, Manto Sahib, really formidable. You won't find a single prostitute in all of Lahore who hasn't had *kuntinutely* with him.'

At this Babu Gopinath exclaimed with awkward modesty, 'I don't have it in me any more, Manto Sahib!'

Soon the conversation veered towards smutty talk: a discussion of all the popular families of Lahore prostitutes, who among them was well to do, who a nautch-girl, who an employee of a bawd, how much did Babu Gopinath pay for the ritual deflowering of a girl. Only Sardar, Sando, Ghaffar Sain and Ghulam Ali participated in the conversation, using the typical jargon of Lahore's bordellos. I understood most of it, though certain terms eluded me completely.

All the while Zeenat remained absolutely silent. She only smiled occasionally when some remark or other caught her fancy. It seemed she had no interest in this sort of gossip. She didn't drink any whisky either, not even watered down. And when she smoked, she didn't evince any liking for either tobacco or smoke, though, strangely, she went through more cigarettes than anyone else. Nothing she did gave any clue as to whether she had any feelings for Babu Gopinath, though the latter's considerable concern for her was quite evident. He had provided her with every item necessary for her comfort. Yet I sensed a certain tension between the two; instead of being close, they seemed somewhat distant.

At about eight in the evening Sardar left to get her morphine shot at Dr Majeed's. After three glasses of whisky, Ghaffar Sain picked up his rosary and dozed off on the carpet. Ghulam Ali was charged with bringing food from the restaurant. After Sando put the brakes on his interesting chatter, Babu Gopinath, fairly drunk by this time, shot the same loving glance at Zeenat and asked me, 'Manto Sahib, what do you think about *my* Zeenat?'

I wondered what to say and looked at her. She lowered her face with an endearing blush. Without thinking I blurted out, 'I think very highly of her.'

Babu Gopinath was pleased. 'Manto Sahib,' he began, 'she is a very nice girl. She isn't fond of jewellery or any of the other things women usually hanker after. I've asked her many times, "My dear, shall I buy you a house?" And do you know how she replied? "A house of my own, what for? I have nobody"... Tell me, Manto Sahib, how much would a car cost?'

'I don't have the foggiest idea.'

'What do you mean?' he said incredulously. 'Impossible, Manto Sahib, impossible that you wouldn't know the price of a car. Please come with me tomorrow. We'll buy a car for Zeeno. She can't do without a car in Bombay.'

Zeenat's face remained impassive.

Babu Gopinath was quite drunk now and growing increasingly more sentimental. 'You're a very erudite man, Manto Sahib. By comparison, I'm just an ignoramus. But tell me, please, how might I serve you! Yesterday Sando mentioned you in passing. I immediately sent for a taxi and told him, "Take me to Manto Sahib." Please forgive me if I've offended you in any way. I've done many wrongs . . . Shall I send for some more whisky?'

'Oh no. I've had enough.'

He grew even more sentimental. 'Have some more, Manto Sahib, please.' He again took out the wad of notes and began peeling off a hundred-rupee note. I snatched the whole wad and pushed it back into his pocket. 'What about the hundred-rupee note you gave to Ghulam Ali earlier?'

For some reason that wasn't clear to me, I was concerned about Babu Gopinath. How a bunch of suckers had stuck to this poor soul like leeches! I had taken him for a gullible fool, but he caught my meaning all right, looked at me and smiled. 'Manto Sahib, whatever was left of that note will either fall out of Ghulam Ali's pocket or . . .'

Just then Ghulam Ali entered and announced, painfully, that some bastard pickpocket had cleaned him out at the restaurant. Babu

Gopinath smiled at me. He quickly peeled off another hundred-rupee note and gave it to Ghulam Ali. 'Go, get some food. Come on, quick.'

It took me half a dozen meetings to discover Babu Gopinath's true personality. While it's not possible to know another person completely, I did discover quite a few interesting things about him. First, I must admit that my initial impression of him as an absolute moron turned out to be wrong. He knew well enough that Sando, Ghulam Ali, and Sardar who pretended to be his bosom buddies were, in fact, nothing more than a bunch of self-serving opportunists. He let them ride roughshod over him, accepted their curses and scorn, but never got angry. 'Manto Sahib, to this day I've never turned down anyone's counsel,' he told me. 'Whenever anyone offers his opinion, I say *Subhanallah*! They take me for a dullard, but I consider them wise. At least they had the wisdom to recognize in me the kind of ignorance that allows them to take advantage of me. You see, from early on, I've hung out with mendicants and *kunjars*.* I've developed a fellow feeling, a kind of affection for them. To tell you the truth, I can't imagine myself living apart from them. I've already decided that when my fortune runs out, I'll go and live in a shrine. A prostitute's kotha and a pir's *mazaar*—these are the two places that give me comfort and a sense of peace and serenity. Soon I shan't be welcome at any more kothas for I'll have exhausted all my money. But there's no lack of pirs in Hindustan. I'll retire to some mazaar or other.'

'Why are you so attracted to kothas and mazaars?' I asked.

After some thought he answered, 'Do you really want to know why? Because deceit, nothing but deceit resides there from floor to ceiling. Can you think of a better place for someone who wants to indulge in self-deception?'

I asked him another question, 'You're fond of listening to singing girls; are you a music buff?'

'No, not at all,' he answered. 'And it's just as well. That way I can listen to the most disagreeable voice and still sway my head in appreciation . . . Manto Sahib, I'm not interested in listening to music, but I do immensely enjoy pulling a ten- or hundred-rupee note out of my pocket and flashing it in front of the singer. I pull out a note and show it to her, she gets up to retrieve it with a delightful air, she draws near, I stick it into my socks, she bends over to pull it out—oh, you

---

* The offspring of a prostitute.

can't imagine the kick I get out of the whole routine! People like me love these triflings, otherwise who doesn't know that parents send their daughters to whorehouses to prostitute and people send their God to tombs and shrines to do the same.'

I don't know much about Babu Gopinath's folks except that his father was a penny-pinching moneylender who left him an estate worth ten lakh rupees. The minute he came into this fortune, he started squandering it however he pleased. He arrived in Bombay with fifty thousand rupees on him. Even though things were quite inexpensive, he still spent a hundred to a hundred and twenty-five rupees every day.

He bought Zeeno a Fiat car for, perhaps, three thousand, and hired a chauffeur for her, a goonish character. For some reason Babu Gopinath felt drawn to such people.

Over time our meetings became more frequent. While I merely found him interesting, he treated me with utmost deference, displaying greater courtesy and respect than anyone else.

One evening when I arrived at his place I was totally bowled over to find Shafiq hanging out there. Perhaps you will understand better if I spell out his full name: Muhammad Shafiq Tusi. Widely known as something of an avant-garde singer and an exceptional wit, there was an aspect of his life most knew nothing about: Before having relations with three sisters, one after the other for three or four years each, he had had their mother as a mistress as well. Still lesser known was the fact that he didn't like his first wife, who had died shortly after they were married, because she wasn't coy and flirtatious like professional prostitutes.

However, anyone even slightly acquainted with him knew that in his forty years (the normal lifespan for this period) literally hundreds of prostitutes had kept him as their lover. He dressed extremely well, ate the finest foods and drove the best cars, without spending a penny of his own money on any *fille de joie*.

His wit, which betrayed a trace of the ribald humour of the *miraasi*s, never failed to fascinate women, especially women of pleasure; they were instinctively drawn to him without his making any effort.

I wasn't surprised at all when I saw him talking pleasantly with Zeenat; what did surprise me though was how he had managed to drop in here so out of the blue. Only Sando knew him, but the two hadn't been on speaking terms for some time. (I later found out that it was Sando, in fact, who had hauled him along. Apparently, they had patched things up.)

Babu Gopinath sat in a corner puffing away at his hookah. I don't recall having mentioned this before: He never smoked cigarettes. Muhammad Shafiq Tusi was rolling out his smutty jokes about miraasis. Zeenat appeared to be listening to them with only slight, and Sardar with great, interest. Shafiq saw me and shouted with gusto, 'Welcome! Welcome! I didn't know you too have a fondness for this alley!'

Sando exclaimed, 'Come in, come in . . . Here comes Mr Angel of Death. *Dharan takhta!*'

I got his drift.

A short gossip session ensued. I noticed that the exchange of glances between Zeenat and Muhammad Shafiq Tusi was more than just that. It was telling another story. She was a mere novice at this art, but Shafiq's exceptional finesse more than made up for her lack of skill. Sardar was watching this exchange like a master trainer studying the manoeuvres of his pupils in the wrestling arena.

By now I had become rather informal with Zeenat. She called me 'brother', which was fine with me. She was affable, not at all chatty, artless, and very neat and clean.

I was dismayed to see her exchanging glances with Shafiq. For one thing, it was very awkward, for another . . . Let's just say that her calling me brother also had something to do with it. At one point, when Shafiq and Sando got up and went out, I asked her about leering at Shafiq, perhaps a trifle sternly because big fat tears immediately flooded her eyes and she withdrew to another room, crying. Babu Gopinath left his hookah and hastily followed her. Sardar communicated something to him with her eyes, which I couldn't fathom. He emerged after a short while and, saying, 'Come, Manto Sahib,' took me inside the other room.

Zeenat was sitting on the bed. When she saw me she covered her face with her hands and lay down. Babu Gopinath and I sank into chairs near the bed. 'Manto Sahib!' he began gravely, 'I love this woman dearly. She's been with me for two years. I swear by Hazrat Ghaus-e A'zam Jilani that she hasn't given me any cause for complaint, not even once. Her sisters, I mean the other women in the profession, have been relentlessly ripping me off, but she has never taken or asked for even one paisa more than her due. Once, when I stayed away for weeks at some other woman's, she pawned a piece of her own jewellery to meet her expenses. As I've told you before, it won't be long before I leave this world. My wealth isn't going to last much longer. I don't wish to see her ruined. In Lahore I begged her repeatedly to observe other prostitutes and learn from them. Today I have money; tomorrow I'll be a pauper. Women like her need many wealthy patrons. Unless she finds another lover like me after I'm gone, she'll be ruined. But, Manto Sahib, would she listen? She insisted on staying at home all day like high-born ladies. I consulted with Ghaffar Sain. He said that I should bring her to Bombay. I know why he said that. He's acquainted with two prostitutes who have made it into the movies here. I decided he was right. She's been here for two months. I sent for Sardar from Lahore to show her the ropes of her calling. She can also learn a great deal from Ghaffar Sain. Although nobody knows me in Bombay, she thinks this will disgrace me. I told her not to worry about me. "Bombay is a huge city," I said. "Many big cats live here. I've bought you a car. Go, find yourself someone good." Manto Sahib, how I wish for her to stand on her own feet, become more aware, more worldly-wise. I'm even prepared to open a bank account in her name and deposit ten thousand rupees in it right this minute. But I know that woman, Sardar, will bilk her of every paisa in ten days flat. Here, you try to make her understand that she needs to become smarter. Every evening since she's got the car, Sardar takes her out to Apollo Bunder. Alas! No luck so far. Sando had to practically drag Shafiq along this evening. What's your opinion of the guy?'

I was reluctant to give my opinion. Instead Babu Gopinath offered his. 'He looks quite well-off . . . and handsome. Well, Zeeno, my darling, do you like him?'

Zeeno remained silent.

My head whirled when I learned the real reason why Babu Gopinath had brought her to Bombay. I couldn't believe it. But my future observations removed all doubts. Babu Gopinath sincerely and ardently wished for Zeenat to become the mistress of some wealthy man here, or at least become artful enough to extract money from several such men.

If all he had wanted was to rid himself of Zeenat, well, that was easy enough. He could have accomplished it in a day. Since his intentions were pure, he tried every which way to secure her future. He went so far as to entertain several phony film directors in the hopes that they would find her a role in some movie. He even had a telephone installed at his place. But nothing worked.

Muhammad Shafiq Tusi kept coming for a month and a half, even spent a few nights with Zeenat, but he was not the kind of man to provide any woman with stability.

'Shafiq Sahib turned out to be such a hollow gentleman,' Babu Gopinath exclaimed one day with sorrow and regret. 'Just look at his nerve, he swindled poor Zeenat out of four bed sheets, six pillowcases and two hundred rupees in cash. I hear he's carrying on with some girl called Almas these days.'

It was true. Almas was the youngest daughter of Nazir Jan of Patiala. She was the last to be drafted into Shafiq's service. Her three older sisters had been his mistresses before. I know for a fact that the two hundred rupees he bamboozled out of Zeenat were spent on Almas, who subsequently had a terrible brawl with her sisters and took poison.

After Tusi stopped visiting, Zeenat rang me up several times asking me to find him and bring him to her. I tried to locate him but not a soul knew his whereabouts. Then one day, quite by chance, I ran into him at the radio station. He seemed quite agitated. When I told him that Zeenat wanted to see him, he said nonchalantly, 'I've already received this message from several others. I'm sorry, I don't have the time. She's a fine woman but, regrettably, far too prudish for my taste—I've no interest in women who act like wives.'

Disappointed, Zeenat resumed her outings to Apollo Bunder with Sardar. After fifteen days of sweating and umpteen gallons of petrol, Sardar managed to bag two men. Babu Gopinath interpreted this as a promising sign, for one of the men, the owner of a textile mill that manufactured silk fabrics, had promised Zeenat that he would marry her. An entire month passed and he never showed up again.

One day, I was at Hornby Road for some work when I saw Zeenat's car parked by the sidewalk. Muhammad Yasin, who owned the Nageena Hotel, was sitting in the rear. I asked him, 'Where did you get this car?'

He smiled. 'You know the owner?'

'Yes, I do.'

'Then you can figure out the rest. But, yaar, she's a hell of a piece!' He winked at me roguishly. I smiled.

Four days later, Babu Gopinath came to my office in a taxi. He told me how Zeenat had met Yasin. One day, Sardar and Zeenat had picked up some men from Apollo Bunder and gone to the Nageena Hotel.

There, they had a tiff about something and the men left in a huff, but somehow they struck up an acquaintance with Yasin.

Babu Gopinath was feeling quite optimistic. In a relationship only a fortnight old, Yasin had bought Zeenat six exquisite and very expensive saris. Babu Gopinath was now waiting for the affair to deepen so that he might eventually return to Lahore. Unfortunately, this didn't happen.

A Christian woman took a room in the Nageena Hotel and Yasin lost his head over her young daughter Muriel. While poor Zeenat languished alone at the hotel, Yasin took Muriel out for rides everywhere in Zeenat's car. Babu Gopinath was deeply hurt when he learned about it. 'Manto Sahib, what kind of people are they!' he said to me. 'If he's tired of her, why doesn't he tell her clearly? And this Zeenat, she's really very strange. She knows what's going on, but will she ever open her mouth to say, "Well, sir, if you want to carry on with this Kristan girlie, get your own car, why use mine?" What shall I do, Manto Sahib? She happens to be an exceedingly fine, noble-hearted woman. I'm totally lost. I wish she would at least try to be a tad bit smarter.'

Zeenat didn't take the end of her affair with Yasin badly.

Nothing of significance transpired for quite a while. When I rang up one day, I was informed that Babu Gopinath had gone to Lahore with Ghulam Ali and Ghaffar Sain to arrange for money because the fifty thousand he had brought with him had run out. He had told Zeenat that he might have to stay there longer because he would have to sell some of his property.

Sardar needed her morphine shots, Sando his Polson's butter. So they joined forces and managed to find two or three customers for Zeenat every day. They told her plainly that Babu Gopinath wasn't coming back and that she should fend for herself. They bagged a hundred to a hundred and twenty-five rupees a day, half of which went to Zeenat and the remainder they appropriated for themselves.

'What are you doing?' I asked Zeenat one day.

'Bhaijan, I have no idea what they do,' she replied naively. 'I just do whatever they say.'

I was assailed by the powerful urge to reason with her. Tell her that what she was doing was a mistake, that Sando and Sardar were looking out for only their own interests and wouldn't think twice about selling her off. But I didn't say anything. Zeenat, let's face it, was a tiringly dull-witted, listless and unambitious person. The unfortunate woman didn't

even know the value of her own life. She sold her body, but without the
style and panache so needed for her profession. Honestly, she was very
annoying. She showed no interest in anything, whether it was smoking
cigarettes, eating, drinking, telephoning or even the couch on which she
often reclined.

Babu Gopinath returned after a month—he had left Ghulam Ali
and Ghaffar Sain behind in Lahore—and found someone else living
in Zeenat's old place. At Sando and Sardar's behest, Zeenat had
moved into the upper storey of a bungalow in Bandra. He came to
me and I gave him the new address. When he asked about Zeenat, I
told him what I knew, though not that Sando and Sardar had pushed
her into prostitution. The taxi was waiting downstairs. He insisted
that I come along.

We reached Bandra after an hour's drive. As the taxi was climbing
Pali Hill, we spotted Sando up ahead on the narrow road. Babu Gopinath
yelled, 'Sando!'

The instant Sando saw Babu Gopinath all he could say was, '*Dharan
takhta*.'

Babu Gopinath invited him to ride with us, but he said, 'Ask the
driver to pull over to the side; I want to talk to you in private.'

The taxi parked along the edge of the road. Babu Gopinath got
out and the two of them walked together for some distance, talking all
the while. A little later Babu Gopinath returned to the taxi alone and
instructed the driver, 'Turn around, we're going back.'

He suddenly seemed happy. When we reached Dadar, he said,
'Manto Sahib, Zeenat is going to be married soon.'

Astonished, I asked, 'To whom?'

'To a big landowner from Haidarabad Sind. May they have a happy
life together. It's good that I've arrived in time. With the money I have
brought back I can give her a decent dowry. What do you think?'

What could I think? My mind was totally blank. I was only
wondering who that wealthy landowner from Hyderabad Sind could
be. Or was this some scheme that Sando and Sardar had hatched
together? Eventually, though, it was confirmed that the man was in fact
who he was claimed to be. He had met Zeenat through a music teacher
from Hyderabad who was trying in vain to teach her to sing. One day
the teacher brought along his patron Ghulam Husain (the wealthy
landowner from Hyderabad). Zeenat showed him great hospitality. At

Ghulam Husain's earnest request she sang Ghalib's ghazal which begins with the line *'Nukta-cheen hai gham-e dil usko suna'e na bane'*. He was smitten with her. The music teacher confided in her about Ghulam Husain's admiration and feelings. Sardar and Sando sprang into action and settled the marriage immediately.

Babu Gopinath was happy. He went to see Zeenat once, as a friend of Sando. He also met Ghulam Husain, which doubled his happiness. He said to me, 'Manto Sahib, he's a very handsome and able young man. Before leaving Lahore I had visited the shrine of Data Gang Bakhsh and prayed for her. Looks as though my prayer has been answered. May Bhagwan keep them both happy!'

Babu Gopinath made the arrangements for Zeenat's wedding with great sincerity and dedication. He gave her jewellery worth two thousand rupees, a trousseau worth an equivalent amount and five thousand rupees in cash. Muhammad Shafiq Tusi, Muhammad Yasin, the proprietor of the Nageena Hotel, Sando, the music teacher, Babu Gopinath and I were present at the wedding. Sando represented the bride.

When the ceremony of acceptance took place, Sando exclaimed in a hushed voice, *'Dharan takhta!'*

Ghulam Husain was looking very smart in his suit of blue serge, gracefully receiving congratulations from the attendees. He was tall and well built. Next to him, Babu Gopinath looked like a small partridge.

He had provided the customary food and drinks for the wedding banquet. After the meal, he himself was pouring the water to help the guests wash their hands. When I came to wash mine, he said to me with the exhilaration of a child, 'Manto Sahib, just go inside and see how breathtakingly beautiful Zeeno looks in her bridal dress.'

I lifted the curtain and stepped inside. She was clad in a shalwar-kameez of red brocade woven with gold thread and a matching dupatta with a gold-thread border. Her make-up was very light, and although I detest lipstick, it looked quite becoming on her lips. She looked very lovely when she blushed and greeted me with aadaab. My eyes caught sight of the flower-bedecked, canopied bed in one corner, and I couldn't resist laughing. 'What is this joke?'

Zeenat looked at me with the utter innocence of a little kabutri and said, 'Bhaijan, you make fun of me.' Her eyes welled up.

I hadn't yet realized my clumsy slip-up when Babu Gopinath entered. He lovingly wiped the tears off her cheeks with his kerchief and said to me in a voice saturated with grief, 'Manto Sahib, I have always considered you a wise and intelligent man . . . You should have at least thought a little before you said such words.'

I could clearly sense in his tone the crushed remnants of the deep reverence he had nurtured for me all along.

Before I could apologize to him, he lovingly patted Zeenat's head and exclaimed with heartfelt sincerity, 'May God bless you and keep you happy!'

He looked at me with bedewed eyes filled with reproach, a painful, anguished reproach, and walked out of the room.

Yazeed

The tumultuous events of 1947 came and flitted away like a few bad days appearing unexpectedly in an otherwise pleasant season.

Karim Dad hadn't simply attributed the upheavals to Providence, sat back complacently and done nothing; rather, he had faced the storm valiantly, like a man. He sparred with the enemy forces quite a few times, not so much to bring them to their knees, but only to offer vigorous resistance. He knew the enemy was far too powerful, but he also knew that to lay down his arms would be an insult not just to himself but to every man. This, at any rate, was how others thought of him, those who had seen him fighting with those brutes and willingly putting his life in harm's way. But if you asked Karim Dad whether he considered putting down his weapons before the enemy an insult, he would think long and hard, as though pondering a difficult mathematical question.

He didn't know how to add or subtract, any more than how to multiply or divide. After the riots of '47 were over, people sat down to take stock of the losses, both human and material. Karim Dad didn't involve himself in this computation. All he knew was that the war had claimed the life of his father Rahim Dad, whose corpse he had carried on his shoulders and laid to rest in the grave he had dug by a well with his own hands.

There had been more incidents like this in the village. Hundreds of young and old men had been butchered; several girls abducted, some brutally raped. Those who had suffered these wounds were crying as much over their own ill fate as over the exceptional ruthlessness of the enemy. But not a single tear was ever spotted in Karim Dad's eyes. He was proud of his father's gallantry. Exhausted from fighting against a pack of rioters armed with dozens of lances and hatchets, the old man's strength had given out and he had fallen. When the news of his death was brought to Karim Dad, he merely addressed his father's spirit thus: 'Look, yaar, this isn't a nice thing to do. Didn't I tell you to carry some weapon on you at all times!'

He then dug a pit by the well and interred his father's dead body. Standing by the grave, he uttered a few words by way of the Fatiha: 'Only God knows best about sins and recompense. But let me just wish you Paradise!'

The rioters had dispatched Rahim Dad—who had been not just a father but also a great friend to Karim Dad—with such fiendish cruelty, that any time people recalled his savage murder, they never failed to hurl obscenities at the murderers. At such times Karim Dad never spoke a word. Several of his flourishing grain fields had been completely laid to waste and two houses reduced to ashes, yet Karim Dad didn't spare his losses a second thought. Now and then, though, one did hear him utter this much: 'Whatever happened was due to our own failings.' When asked what those failings were, he chose to remain silent.

While the village folks were still lamenting over their dead, Karim Dad got himself married to the same blossoming Jaina he'd had his eyes on for some time. Jaina was grieving. Her brother, a strapping youth, had been killed in the riots. He had been the only person left whom she could count on for support since the death of their parents. That she also loved Karim Dad dearly was beyond doubt, but the pain of losing her brother had cast a pall over that love somewhat. Her eyes, lively and smiling before, now never seemed free of tears.

Karim Dad couldn't stand wailing and crying at all. The sight of a doleful Jaina annoyed him, but he chose not to mention it to her, thinking that, tender-hearted woman that she was, his words might hurt her feelings even more. However, one day he couldn't hold back any more. He caught up with her in the field and gave her a piece of his mind. 'Look, it's been a whole year since the dead were shrouded and buried. Even they are probably tired of all this keening and wailing over them. Let go of it, my dear. Who knows how many more deaths we're fated to see in this life. Save some tears for the future.'

Jaina took umbrage at his words, but what could she do? She was deeply in love with the man. During long bouts of solitude, she tried her best to conjure up some meaning in his words and, eventually, convinced herself that what he had said wasn't all that unreasonable after all.

The elders opposed their marriage when the proposal was run past them; however, their opposition turned out to be quite weak. Excessive mourning had sapped their energies so completely that they couldn't even hold on to oppositions that had every chance of success. And so Karim Dad got married. With the customary wedding fanfare and music, and after every ceremony was duly performed, Karim Dad brought his beloved Jaina home as his bride.

Since the rioting a year ago, the whole village had assumed something of the depressing air of a cemetery. Thus, when Karim Dad's marriage arrangements got under way with a lot of hullabaloo and excitement, a vague feeling of trepidation swept over some people. They cringed and felt as though it wasn't Karim Dad's but some *bhoot–pret*'s* wedding procession that was unfolding before them. Some friends informed Karim Dad about this reaction and he laughed his head off. One day, jokingly, he mentioned it to his new bride, who instantly began quaking with alarm.

'Well,' he said to Jaina, taking hold of her wrist with its beautiful, bright bracelet, 'you can't escape. You're stuck with this bhoot for the rest of your life. Even Rahman Sain's hocus-pocus can't rid you of him.'

Jaina stuck her hennaed finger between her teeth, blushed a little, and got out only this much, 'Kaimay, nothing seems to frighten you!'

Karim Dad ran the tip of his tongue over his reddish-brown moustache and smiled broadly. 'What is there to frighten anyone? Fear doesn't exist.'

By now, Jaina's grief had subsided quite a bit. She was soon to be a mother. To see her in the fullness of her blossoming youth made Karim Dad enormously happy. He would say to her, 'You were never so stunningly beautiful before, Jaina, I swear. If all this beauty is only for the sake of the baby who's coming, I'll have to fight with that little rascal, I'm telling you.'

Jaina would blush and quickly cover her big, bulging belly with her chador, which made him laugh and tease her even more. 'Why are you

* Malicious spirit.

hiding that thief? Don't I know that all this dolling up is just for that little swine?'

At that Jaina would become serious. 'Why are you swearing at the baby? After all it's your own.'

'And Karim Dad is the biggest swine of them all,' he would say, his reddish-brown moustache quivering from the rumble of his laughter.

The 'Little' Eid came along, followed a couple of months later by the 'Big' Eid. Karim Dad celebrated both with equal fanfare and great fuss. The rioters had attacked his village twelve days before the Big Eid and his father Rahim Dad and Jaina's brother Fazl Ilahi had both been murdered in that attack. Jaina cried a lot as she remembered their killings but, realizing how Karim Dad was predisposed to put any tragedy behind him, she couldn't grieve as much as her own temperament called for.

Sometimes when she thought about it, she wondered how she could have begun to forget the most tragic incident of her life so imperceptibly. She had absolutely no memory of how her parents had died. Fazl Ilahi was six years older than her. He wasn't just a brother; he had been both father and mother to her. She was absolutely sure that it was for her sake alone that he hadn't married. And it was to save her honour that he had lost his life fighting the enemy—a fact known to the whole village. His death was truly the greatest catastrophe of her life, a veritable hell suddenly let loose upon her just twelve days before the Big Eid. Whenever she thought about that calamity now, the realization that she was drifting further away from its effects never failed to surprise her.

As the month of Muharram approached, for the first time Jaina expressed her desire to Karim Dad. She was very interested in seeing the decorated horse and the *taziya*s of Muharram. She had heard a lot about them from her girlfriends. She asked Karim Dad, 'If I'm feeling up to it, will you take me to see the Muharram horse?'

'I will, even if you aren't feeling well, and the swine too,' he replied with a smile.

She hated the word 'swine', took immediate offence to it and often lost her cool. But it was uttered with such endearing honesty that her bitterness was instantly transformed into an indescribable sweetness and she would begin to see how the word 'swine' could be filled with genuine affection and love.

The rumour of an imminent war between India and Pakistan had been circulating for quite some time. Actually, almost as soon as Pakistan was established it had been taken for granted that there would definitely be a war, but *when* was something the inhabitants of the village couldn't say with any certainty. If anyone asked Karim Dad about it, his short answer invariably was, 'It will be when it will be. What's the point of losing sleep over it?'

But whenever Jaina heard about that dreaded event, it knocked the living daylights out of her. She was a peace-loving woman by nature. Even ordinary squabbles made her terribly nervous. Besides, during the previous mayhem she'd been witness to a great deal of carnage and bloodshed. Her own brother, Fazl Ilahi, had been mowed down in one such riot. She would cringe with an unknown fear and ask, 'Kaimay, what will it be?'

Karim Dad would smile. 'How would I know? Maybe a boy, maybe a girl.'

Such a cheerful reply made her feel even more helpless. Soon she would forget all about the dreaded war, focusing all her attention on whatever else Karim Dad was saying. He was a strong, fearless man who loved Jaina very much. After buying himself a rifle, he had quickly become an expert marksman. These things kept her spirits up. But now and then, when she was by the waterfront and heard from a terrified girlfriend of the rumours about war being spread by the village folk, she would instantly go into a daze.

One day, Bakhtu the midwife came for Jaina's daily check-up and brought along the news that the Indians were about to stop the river. Jaina couldn't understand. She asked, 'About to stop the river . . . which river?'

'The one that waters our fields.'

Jaina thought for a while and then said with a smile, 'Mausi, have you gone mad? Who can stop rivers? They aren't just any old street drain.'

Rubbing Jaina's belly gently, Bakhtu replied, 'Bibi, I don't know. I'm just telling you what I heard. This information has even appeared in newspapers.'

'What information?' Jaina was still finding it hard to believe.

Feeling Jaina's stomach with her wrinkled hand, the old woman said, 'The same . . . about stopping the river.' Then she pulled Jaina's shirt down over her stomach and said with the confidence of a seasoned obstetrician, 'God willing, you'll have your baby in exactly ten days.'

When Karim Dad came home, the first thing Jaina asked him about was this rumour about the river. At first he tried to evade the question, but when she persisted, he said casually, 'Yes, I've heard something like that.'

'Like what?'

'Just that the Hindustan-wallahs will divert the waters of our rivers.'

'Why?'

'To ruin our crops,' Karim Dad replied.

The answer convinced Jaina that rivers could be stopped from flowing. With a feeling of utter despondency she merely said, 'How cruel they are.'

This time around, Karim Dad took some time to smile. 'But tell me, did Mausi Bakhtu visit you today?'

'She did,' Jaina replied half-heartedly.

'What did she say?'

'That the baby will be born exactly ten days from today.'

'Zindabad!' Karim Dad cried out boisterously.

Jaina was furious. She muttered, 'You're making merry, while only God knows what calamity awaits us.'

Karim Dad got up and left for the *chaupal.** Here, practically all the men of the village were crowding around Chaudhry Natthu asking him about this news of cutting off the water to their river. One man was roundly swearing at Pandit Nehru, another was cursing Indians without letting up, a third was persistently denying that the waters of a river could be diverted. There were also some in whose opinion what lay ahead was punishment for their own sins, best averted by collective prayer in the mosque.

Karim Dad sat quietly in a corner listening to their exchange. Chaudhry Natthu was the most effusive among those swearing at the Indians. Karim Dad was shifting so often in his seat that it gave the impression this sort of conversation was making him very nervous. The men were all saying with one voice that cutting off the water was a very nasty act indeed, the height of meanness, downright vile, a most horrid oppression, a sin, the very same conduct as Yazeed's.

Karim Dad cleared his throat a few times as if preparing to say something. When another volley of the coarsest obscenities rose to

* Village community centre for consultation, discussion and for other social activities.

the Chaudhry's mouth, he yelled, 'Chaudhry, don't call anyone bad names!'

The swear word for doing something to the lower anatomy of the Indians' mother caught in the Chaudhry's throat. He turned around and directed a mighty strange look towards Karim Dad, who, meanwhile, had busied himself arranging his turban on his head. 'Huh . . . what did you say?'

In a soft but firm voice Karim Dad responded, 'Just that you shouldn't swear at anyone.'

The word that was caught in the Chaudhry's throat now shot out of his mouth with incredible force. He asked sharply, '*Anyone?* Who the hell are they to you?'

Now the Chaudhry addressed the folks gathered in the chaupal. 'You heard him, didn't you? He says don't rebuke anyone. Ask him: Who are they to him?'

With tremendous poise and self-control Karim Dad replied, 'Who are they to me? Well, they are my enemies.'

Something resembling raucous laughter rose from the Chaudhry's throat so loudly that the bristles of his moustache flew to either side of his lips from the force. 'You heard him. They're his enemies. So we should love them. Right, boy?'

And Karim Dad, in the manner of a deferential boy, answered, 'No, Chaudhry, I'm not asking you to love them. I only ask that they shouldn't be called bad names.'

Karim Dad's bosom buddy Miran Bakhsh, who was sitting right next to him, asked, 'Why?'

'What's the point of it, yaar? They want to make your fields barren and you think that all you need in order to get even with them is a few insults. That isn't smart, is it? Insults are the recourse of people who have run out of answers.'

'And you, do you have an answer?' asked Miran Bakhsh.

'Whether I have one or not is not the issue,' Karim Dad said after a pause. 'This matter concerns tens of thousands, indeed hundreds of thousands. A single person's answer can't stand as the answer for everyone. Such matters require a lot of deep thought and deliberation . . . to devise a solid plan of action. They cannot divert the course of the water in one day. It'll take them years. And, pray tell, is your strategy simply to hurl obscenities at them for a few minutes and let out all your rage?'

He put his hand on Miran Bakhsh's shoulder and added with genuine affection, 'All I know, yaar, is that, somehow, even calling Hindustan mean, despicable, vile and tyrannical is wrong.'

'Listen to this!' Chaudhry Natthu blurted out instead of Miran Bakhsh.

However, Karim Dad continued his conversation with Miran Bakhsh. 'It's foolishness to expect mercy from the enemy. Once the battle has begun, lamenting that the enemy is using large-bore rifles while we have small-bore, that our bombs are fairly small and theirs are much larger . . . Tell me, honestly, is that any kind of complaint? Whether it's a small knife or a large knife, both can be used to kill. Am I wrong?'

It was the Chaudhry, again, who started thinking, but got discombobulated in a second. 'But the issue . . .' he said with irritation, 'the issue is that they're stopping the water. They want to starve us to death.'

Karim Dad removed his hand from Miran Bakhsh's shoulder and spoke directly to the Chaudhry. 'Chaudhry, when you've designated someone as your enemy, why complain that he wants to kill you by means of hunger and thirst? Did you think he would send you great big pots of sumptuous pilafs and pitchers of ice-cooled fruit juice from across the border, rather than laying waste to your lush fields and crops? Did you think he would plant gardens for your enjoyment?'

The Chaudhry lost his cool. 'Damn you, what nonsense is this?'

Miran Bakhsh, too, asked Karim Dad softly, 'Yes, yaar, what nonsense is this?'

'It isn't nonsense, Miran Bakhsha,' Karim Dad attempted to reason with his friend. 'Just think a little: In a battle what wouldn't one opponent do to defeat the other. When a wrestler, all set for the bout, descends into the arena, he has every right to use whatever manoeuvres he sees fit . . .'

'Makes sense,' Miran Bakhsh agreed, shaking his shaven head.

Karim Dad smiled. 'Well then, stopping the river also makes sense. For us it's an atrocity, but for them it's entirely admissible.'

'You call it admissible?' the Chaudhry butted in. 'When your tongue is hanging out from thirst, we'll see whether such an atrocity is still admissible. When your kids are begging for a single morsel of food, will you still call it admissible?'

Karim Dad ran his tongue over his parched lips and replied, 'Yes, Chaudhry, even then. Why do you only remember that he's our enemy and conveniently forget that we're just as much his enemy? If we had it in our power, we would cut his food and water supply too. Now that the enemy is able and about to do that, we'll certainly have to think of a way to counter his move. And futile name-calling won't do that. The enemy won't send rivers of milk flowing your way, Chaudhry Natthu! If he could, he would poison every drop of your water. You call it plain inequity, plain bestiality because you don't like this way of killing. Isn't it a bit odd that even before the war has begun you're setting up conditions, as if it is a marriage contract and you have the freedom to set down your conditions? To tell the enemy, "Don't kill me by starvation and thirst, but, by all means, kill me with a gun that is of such and such bore." This, in fact, is the real *nonsense*. Think about it with a cool head.'

This was all that was needed to send the Chaudhry to the height of his irritation. 'So bring some ice and cool my head!'

'This too is my responsibility now.' Karim Dad laughed tapping Miran Bakhsh on the shoulder, and then got up and walked out of the chaupal.

Just as he was stepping inside the *deorhi* of his house, he saw Bakhtu coming out. A toothless smile appeared on her lips when she saw Karim Dad.

'Congratulations, Kaimay. You've got a boy, the very image of the moon. Now think about a nice name for him.'

'Name?' Karim Dad thought for a moment. 'Yazeed . . . that'll do, yes, Yazeed.'

Bakhtu the midwife was stunned, her face dropped, while an overjoyed Karim Dad barged into the house shouting jubilantly. Jaina was lying on the charpoy, looking paler than before, with a cotton-ball of a little baby boy beside her, sucking away at his thumb. Karim Dad looked at the baby with a mix of affection and pride. He tweaked the baby's cheek playfully with his finger and muttered, 'Oh my Yazeed!'

A shocked scream escaped from Jaina's lips, 'Yazeed?'

Looking closely at his son's face and its features, Karim Dad affirmed, 'Yes, Yazeed. That's his name.'

Jaina's voice suddenly dropped to a whisper, 'What are you saying, Kaimay—Yazeed?'

He smiled. 'So what's wrong with it? It's just a name.'

'But whose name . . . Think!' was all she could say.

Karim Dad replied in a grave tone of voice, 'It isn't necessary that he should turn out to be the same Yazeed, the one who cut off the water; this one will make it flow again.'

Ram Khilawan

After executing a slew of bedbugs, I was looking through some old papers when, suddenly, Saeed Bhaijan's photo popped out. An empty frame was lying on the table so I inserted the photo in it and then sat down in a chair and began waiting for the dhobi—my Sunday ritual.

I usually ran out of my stock of clean laundry by Saturday evening. I shouldn't say 'stock' because in those destitute days I barely had enough clothes to maintain the pretence of respectability for six or seven days.

Negotiations for my marriage were under way and this had necessitated that I make many trips to Mahim over the past several Sundays. My dhobi was a decent fellow; whether he got paid or not, he regularly delivered my freshly washed clothes on Sunday at exactly ten o'clock. Still, I was afraid that one day he might get tired of not being paid and sell my clothes in the bazaar where stolen merchandise is traded. I might then be forced to participate in my marriage negotiations without anything on my body, which, obviously, would be highly unseemly.

My kholi was reeking of the stench of dead bedbugs, but just as I was looking for a way to ventilate the room, the dhobi showed up.

He greeted me with 'Sab, salaam', opened the bundle of fresh laundry, took out my few items of clothing and deposited them on the table. As he was doing so his eyes fell on Saeed Bhaijan's photo. He seemed surprised and, upon taking a closer look, let out a startled 'Huh?'

'What's the matter, dhobi?' I asked.

'This is Saaeed Shaleem Balishtar,' he replied, his eyes still riveted on the photo.

'Why—you know him?'

'Yes.' He nodded vigorously. 'Two brothers. Their bungalow there
. . . in Colaba. Saaeed Shaleem Balishtar. Washed their clothes.'

This must have been two years ago, I concluded. Before they left for
the Fiji islands, my elder brothers Saeed Hasan and Muhammad Hasan
had practised law for about a year in Bombay. I said to him, 'You mean
two years ago?'

He again nodded vigorously. 'When Saaeed Shaleem Balishtar
leaving, he gave me pagri, dhoti, kurta, all new. Both very good. One
had beard . . . very big.' He indicated the length of the beard with his
hand and, pointing at Saeed Bhaijan's photo, continued, 'This one
younger. Had three *bawa log*, boy and girl . . . played with me lot. He
had big bungalow . . . very big . . . in Colaba.'

'Dhobi, they're my brothers,' I told him.

He made a strange sound, as if he was perplexed, 'Huh? Saaeed
Shaleem Balishtar?'

Attempting to allay his confusion I explained, 'This is Saeed Hasan
Bhaijan's photo. The one with the beard is Muhammad Hasan—our
eldest brother.'

The dhobi gawked at me and then looked around my kholi, taking
notice of the filth in the dingy little room that had only a table, a chair
and a cot made of gunnysack meshing that was full of bedbugs, and
no electric light. He was having difficulty believing that I was Saaeed
Shaleem Balishtar's youngest brother. But when I related certain things
about Saeed Bhaijan he shook his head and said, 'Saaeed Shaleem
Balishtar lived in bungalow; you live in kholi.'

'This is how the world is,' I said philosophically. 'Not all fingers of
the hand are alike.'

'Yes, Sab, you speak truth.' With that he picked up his bundle
and made to leave. I remembered about paying my account. I had
only eight annas in my pocket, hardly enough even for the fare
to and from Mahim for my marriage negotiations. I asked him to
hold on, just so he would know my intentions were good, and said,
'Dhobi, you're keeping the account? God knows how many washes
I owe you for.'

He adjusted the fold of his dhoti around his crotch area and said,
'Sab, don't keep account. Washed Saaeed Shaleem Balishtar clothes for
whole year. Took whatever he gave. Don't know what account is.'

He left and I started to get ready for Mahim.

The negotiations were successful. I got married. My situation also improved so I moved from my nine-rupees-a-month kholi on Sekend Pir Khan Street to a flat on Clare Road at thirty-five rupees per month and started paying the dhobi regularly.

He was happy that my situation was now relatively better so he said to my wife, 'Begum Sab, Sab's brother Saaeed Shaleem Balishtar big man. Lived there, in Colaba. When left, gave me pagri, dhoti, kurta. Your sab become big man one day.'

I had already told my wife about the photo incident and the magnanimity with which the dhobi had treated me in my impoverished days. He took whatever I gave him whenever I gave it and never complained or made a fuss. But the dhobi's indifference to keeping an account of the wash soon began to get on my wife's nerves. 'Look,' I said to her, 'he's been washing my clothes for four years now; he's never kept an account.'

'Why would he, indeed, when this way he can charge double, even quadruple.'

'How?'

'You don't know,' she said, 'they take advantage of the ones who don't have wives to watch over them.'

Almost every month she squabbled with the dhobi about not keeping an account, and each time he answered with his characteristic simplicity, 'Begum Sab, don't know how keep account. Don't lie to you. Saaeed Shaleem Balishtar, your sab's brother, worked for him whole year. His Begum Sab say, "Dhobi, you get this much," I say, "Fine."'

One month a total of two hundred and fifty items of clothing were given to him to wash. Just to test his honesty my wife said to him, 'Dhobi, you washed sixty pieces this month.'

'Fine. Begum Sab, know you won't lie to me.'

My wife paid him for sixty pieces. He thanked her with a salaam, touching the money to his forehead. As he was leaving, she stopped him, 'Wait, dhobi, it was not sixty, but two hundred and fifty items. Here, take the rest of your money. I was just joking.'

His only answer was 'Begum Sab, you won't lie to me.' He touched the additional money to his forehead, said salaam, and went on his way.

I moved to Delhi two years after my marriage, lived there for a year and a half and then decided to return to Bombay where I found accommodation in Mahim. We went through four dhobis in three

months. They were dishonest and cantankerous. A veritable argument
broke out after each load of washing. Either it fell short of the number
of items or the quality of the washing was atrocious. We started to miss
our old dhobi. We had nearly given up hope of finding a good dhobi
when one day our old dhobi showed up out of the blue. 'I saw Sab in
bus one day and said myself, "How can that be? Sab moved Delhi." I
inquired in Byekhalla.* Press-wallah told look for you here in Mahim.
Sab's friend live nearby. I asked him and here I am.'

We felt relieved, as did our laundry.

When the Congress party assumed power, alcohol was banned.
Imported liquor and wines were still available, but home brews could
neither be made nor sold. Now, about ninety-nine per cent of dhobis
were habitual drinkers. They spent the whole day standing knee-deep
in water and their evenings drinking anywhere from a quarter to half
a bottle. Liquor had, in a way, become part of their lives. Our dhobi
fell ill. He treated the illness with the home-brewed poison that was
made illegally and sold surreptitiously, with the result that it ruined his
stomach and brought him near death.

I was unusually busy with work in those days. I left early in the
morning, at about six, and returned around ten or ten-thirty in the
evening. When my wife learned about our dhobi's life-threatening
illness, she took a taxi and went to see him. She had the servant and the
taxi driver carry him to the taxi and brought him to a doctor. The doctor
was impressed by her concern for the dhobi and refused to accept his
fee, but my wife insisted. 'No, Doctor Sahib, you can't claim the whole
reward by yourself.'

The doctor smiled and said, 'Well then, let's split it fifty-fifty.'

He accepted half the fee.

The dhobi received proper medical treatment. A few injections
took care of his stomach ailment. Nutritional supplements gradually
restored his strength. Within a few months he had completely
recovered. He was grateful and invoked God's blessings on us all
the time. 'Bhagwan make Sab like Saaeed Shaleem Balishtar. Live in
Colaba. Have children, lots money. Begum Sab came visit dhobi in
car, took him to *kila* to see big doctor, who has *mem*. Bhagwan keep
Begum Sab happy . . .'

* Byculla.

Many years, full of political upheavals, went by, yet the dhobi came every Sunday without fail. He was in robust health now. A long time had passed since his illness but he still remembered the care we had given him and never failed to invoke God's blessings on us. He had given up drinking completely. Initially he did reminisce about his drinking days, but not at all now. He no longer felt the need for liquor after standing all day in water.

The situation in the country was deteriorating rapidly. Hindu–Muslim rioting followed Partition. Muslims were being slaughtered in Hindu areas and Hindus in Muslim neighbourhoods—not just in the darkness of the night but also in broad daylight. My wife left for Lahore.

When the situation grew even worse I told the dhobi, 'Look, dhobi, you'd better stop work now. This is a Muslim neighbourhood. God forbid that someone should kill you.'

He smiled. 'Sab, nobody kill me.'

Our neighbourhood witnessed several killings but the dhobi came regularly.

One Sunday, I was at home reading the newspaper. The sports page carried the cricket scores and the front page the tally of Hindus and Muslims murdered during the rioting. I was still wondering about the frightening similarity between the two counts when the dhobi showed up. I started checking the washed items against the notebook entry. Meanwhile, the dhobi kept chattering away light-heartedly: 'Saaeed Shaleem Balishtar good man. When he go he give pagri, dhoti, kurta. Your Begum Sab also good person. Gone away, right? Her country, right? When you write her, give my salaam. She come my kholi . . . in car. I had bad diarrhoea. Doctor put needle. Right away I good. When you write her, give my salaam. Say Ram Khilawan want you write him letter—'

I cut him off, rather sharply. 'Dhobi, have you started drinking again?'

He laughed. 'Drinking? Sab, find no drink now.'

I didn't think it was right to say anything more. He gathered the dirty laundry in a bundle, said salaam, and left.

Conditions grew really critical over the next few days. A barrage of wires descended from Lahore making urgent pleas that I drop everything and head straight there. On Saturday I made up my mind to leave the next day. I wanted to leave early in the morning but my clothes were with the dhobi. I decided to go to his place and collect them myself before the onset of curfew. In the evening I set out for Mahalakshmi in a victoria carriage.

The curfew was an hour away. Traffic was still flowing in the streets and trams were rumbling on. When my carriage approached the bridge a commotion erupted and a stampede broke out. It looked as though bulls had come to blows. When the crowd thinned, I saw a whole bunch of club-wielding dhobis in the distance, dancing and making loud noises near the buffaloes. I was headed in that direction but the coachman refused to go. I paid him and started walking. When I came close to the dhobis they abruptly stopped their hullabaloo.

I stepped forward and asked one of them, 'Where does Ram Khilawan live?'

Another dhobi, brandishing a club, came swaying his head and asked the one I had talked to, 'What does he want?'

'Wants to know where Ram Khilawan lives.'

This other fellow, completely inebriated, staggered forward and literally bumped into me in his drunken gait. 'Who are you?' he asked brusquely.

'I? . . . Ram Khilawan is my dhobi.'

'Ram Khilawan's your dhobi. And you're the offspring of which dhobi?'

Some of the others in the group yelled, 'A Hindu dhobi or a Muslimeen dhobi?'

All the dhobis, drunk to their teeth, gathered around me, ominously pumping their fists and swinging their clubs. I had to answer only one question—was I Muslim or Hindu?

I was frightened to death. It was impossible to get away as they had me completely surrounded. There wasn't even a policeman anywhere in sight whom I might have called for help. I was at a complete loss, so I started babbling in disjointed sentences: 'Ram Khilawan is Hindu . . . I'm asking where he lives . . . show me his kholi . . . he is my dhobi for ten years . . . he was very ill . . . we treated him . . . my wife . . . my memsahib came here . . . in a car . . .'

My babble had gone only this far when I felt an immense wave of self-pity wash over me. Embarrassment gripped my heart; how low a man could sink to save his skin. The thought gave me the courage to say, 'I'm Muslimeen.'

'Kill him! Kill him!'

The dhobi who was dead drunk threw his glance to one side and shouted, 'Wait! Let Ram Khilawan kill him!'

I turned around only to find Ram Khilawan standing behind me holding a stubby club in his hand. He looked at me and let loose with a tirade against Muslims, hurling the coarsest obscenities at them in his peculiar dhobi dialect. Raising the club above his head and mouthing abuses, he advanced towards me.

'Ram Khilawan!' I called out to him in a commanding voice.

'Shut up!—you Ram Khilawan's . . .' he thundered.

My last hope quickly ebbed away. When he was literally upon me, my throat went dry and I said in a hushed voice, 'Ram Khilawan, don't you recognize me?'

He raised his club higher to hit me. All of a sudden his eyes narrowed, dilated and narrowed again in quick succession. He let the club fall from his hand, came nearer, gaped at me and then shouted, 'Sab!' He turned to his people and accosted them, 'No Muslimeen. He my Sab . . . Begum Sab's Sab. Come to me . . . in car . . . took to doctor . . . he made my diarrhoea good.'

He reasoned with his fellows at length. But would they listen to him? Drunkards all. Soon they were arguing heatedly. A few sided with Ram Khilawan and the brawl escalated into fisticuffs. I quietly slipped away from the scene.

By nine o'clock the next morning my bags were packed and ready, only my boat ticket, which a friend had gone to buy on the black market, needed to arrive.

I was feeling anxious. Strange thoughts were colliding inside my mind. I wanted the ticket to fly over to me so I could set out for the pier at once. Even the slightest delay and I was convinced my flat would take me prisoner for life.

There was a knock at the door. My ticket has arrived, I thought. I quickly opened the door and who do I see—the dhobi.

'Sab salaam!'

'Salaam!'

'May I come in?'

'Sure.'

He walked in very quietly, took out my clothes from the bundle and laid them on the bed. Then he wiped his moist eyes and said in a voice hoarse with emotion. 'You leaving, Sab?'

'Yes.'

He started to cry. 'Sab, forgive. It's liquor doing. Liquor . . . these days . . . free. Seth log give . . . free . . . say drink and kill Muslimeen. Nobody not take free liquor, Sab. Forgive. I drunk. Saaeed Shaleem Balishtar kind man . . . gave pagri, dhoti, kurta . . . Begum Sab save my life. Dying from diarrhoea. Come to me . . . in car . . . took to doctor . . . spent money . . . big money. You go your country, Sab . . . don't tell Begum Sab . . . Ram Khilawan . . .'

His voice choked. He slung the bundle over his shoulder and made to leave. I stopped him, 'Wait, Ram Khilawan.'

But he walked out quickly, arranging the front fold of his dhoti.

Sahae

'Don't say that one lakh Hindus and one lakh Muslims died; say that two lakh human beings died. That two lakh human beings died is not such a great tragedy after all; the tragedy, in truth, is that those who killed and those who were killed, both have nothing to show for it. After killing one lakh Hindus, the Muslims may have thought that they had finished off Hinduism. But it lives, and will live on. Likewise, after killing one lakh Muslims the Hindus may have exulted over the death of Islam. But the truth is before you: This hasn't managed to put even a scratch on Islam. Those who think that religions can be killed by guns are foolish. *Mazhab, deen, iman, dharm,* faith, belief—these are found in our souls, not in our bodies. How can butchers' cleavers, rioters' knives and bullets annihilate them?'

Mumtaz was unusually excited that day. Just the three of us had come to see him off at the ship. He was leaving us for an undetermined period of time and was headed for Pakistan—a Pakistan we hadn't imagined even in our dreams would come into being.

We were Hindus, all three of us. Our relatives in West Punjab had incurred heavy losses in both property and lives—presumably, this was why Mumtaz had decided to leave. Juggal had received a letter from Lahore telling him that his uncle had died in communal riots; the news affected him in a bad way. Still reeling from its impact, he casually said to Mumtaz one day, 'I'm wondering what I would do if riots broke out in my neighbourhood.'

'Yes, what would you do?' Mumtaz asked.

'I might kill you,' Juggal said in all seriousness.

Mumtaz fell silent, dead silent. His silence continued for nearly eight days, breaking only when he suddenly announced that he was leaving for Karachi by ship at 3.45 p.m. that very afternoon.

None of us talked to him about his decision. Juggal was feeling contrite that the reason behind Mumtaz's departure was his comment: 'I might kill you.' Perhaps he was still wondering whether in the heat of passion he could really kill Mumtaz or not—Mumtaz who was one of his best friends. That's why he was now the silent one among the three.

Strangely enough, though, Mumtaz had become unusually talkative, especially in the few hours before his departure. He had begun drinking the moment he got up in the morning. His bags were packed as though he were going on a vacation. He would talk to himself and laugh for no apparent reason. If a stranger had seen him he would have thought that Mumtaz was feeling overwhelming joy at the prospect of leaving Bombay. But the three of us knew well that he was trying hard to deceive both us and himself in order to hide his true feelings.

I very much wanted to ask him about his sudden decision to leave. I even gestured to Juggal to bring up the subject, but Mumtaz never gave us a chance.

After downing three or four drinks Juggal became even quieter and went to lie down in the other room. Braj Mohan and I stayed with Mumtaz. He had quite a few bills to settle, give the doctors their fees, fetch his clothes from the cleaners—all these chores he did light-heartedly and easily enough. But as he was taking a paan from the stall next to the restaurant at the end of the street, his eyes began to well up with tears. When we moved away from the stall he put his hand on Braj Mohan's shoulder and said softly, 'You remember, don't you, how Gobind lent us a rupee ten years ago, when we were down on our luck?'

After this Mumtaz remained silent, but once we returned home he launched another endless stream of small talk—all totally unconnected, but nonetheless so full of feeling that Braj Mohan and I found ourselves fully participating in it. When the time for Mumtaz's departure drew near, Juggal joined us too. But the moment the taxi started for the docks, a hush fell over everyone.

Mumtaz's eyes continued to say goodbye to the wide, sprawling bazaars of Bombay, until the taxi pulled into the harbour. The place was terribly crowded. Thousands of refugees, a few of them affluent, most others poor, were leaving—it was a veritable crush of people. And yet Mumtaz alone seemed to me to be leaving, leaving us behind for a place he had never even seen before, a place which, no matter how hard he tried to get used to it, would still remain unfamiliar. That's what I thought at any rate. I couldn't tell what was going through Mumtaz's mind.

After his bags had all been taken to the cabin, Mumtaz took us out on to the deck. For a long time he gazed at the place where sky and sea came together. Then he took Juggal's hand in his and said, 'How perfectly deceptive . . . this meeting of the sky and the sea, and yet so incredibly delightful too!'

Juggal remained silent. Perhaps his earlier remark—'I might kill you'—was still tormenting him.

Mumtaz ordered a brandy from the ship's bar; that was what he had been drinking since morning. Drinks in hand, we stood against the guardrail. Refugees were piling on to the ship with a lot of noise and commotion, and seagulls were hovering over the water, which looked almost still.

Abruptly Juggal downed his glass in one huge gulp and said rather crudely, 'Do forgive me, Mumtaz—I think I hurt you the other day.'

Mumtaz paused briefly and asked him, 'When you uttered those words—"I might kill you"—was that exactly what you were thinking? You arrived at this decision with a cool head?'

Juggal nodded his head, and then said, 'But I feel sorry.'

'You'd have felt sorrier had you actually killed me,' Mumtaz said pensively. 'But only if you had paused to reflect that you hadn't killed Mumtaz, a Muslim, a friend, you had killed a human being. If he was a bad man, what you would have killed was not his badness, but the man himself. If he was a Muslim, you wouldn't have killed his Muslim-ness, but his being. If Muslims had got hold of his dead body, it would have added a grave to the cemetery, but the world would have come up one human being short.'

Stopping to think a bit, he resumed, 'Perhaps my co-religionists would have anointed me as a martyr, but I swear I would've torn through my grave and cried that I didn't accept the title, that I didn't want this diploma for which I had taken no exam. Some Muslim murdered your uncle in Lahore, you heard the news in Bombay and murdered me— just tell me: What medals do we deserve for this? What robes of honour do your uncle and his killer back in Lahore deserve?'

'If you ask me, the victims died the miserable death of a pie-dog, and their killers killed in vain, utterly in vain.'

Mumtaz became agitated as he spoke, but the emotional excess was matched by an equal measure of sincerity. His observation that mazhab, deen, iman, dharm, faith, belief—these were found in our souls, not in our bodies, and that they couldn't be annihilated by cleavers, knives and bullets had made an especially deep impression on me.

So I told him, 'You're absolutely right.'

This made Mumtaz think again. He said with some unease, 'No, I wouldn't say "absolutely right". I mean, yes, sure, this is all okay. But perhaps I haven't been able to say it all clearly, the way I want to. By "religion" I don't mean *this* religion, nor this dharm, which afflicts ninety-nine per cent of us. I rather mean that very special thing which sets one individual apart from all others, the special thing which shows that someone is truly a human being. But what is it? Unfortunately I can't put it on my palm and show it to you.' A sudden gleam appeared in his eyes and he said, as if to himself, 'But what exactly was special in him? A staunch Hindu, who worked the most abominable profession, and yet his soul—it couldn't have been more radiant.'

'Whose soul?' I asked.

'A certain pimp's.'

The three of us started. Mumtaz's tone was natural enough, so I asked him in perfect seriousness, 'A pimp's?'

Mumtaz nodded in affirmation. 'What a man! Amazing. And even more amazing that he was, as it is commonly called, a pimp—a procurer of women—and yet had an absolutely clear conscience.'

Mumtaz paused for a few moments, as if refreshing his memory of past events, and then added, 'I don't remember his full name. Something Sahae. He came from Benares. And he was extremely particular about cleanliness. It was a smallish place where he lived, but he had elegantly divided it into neat little sections. The customers' privacy was scrupulously maintained. There were no beds or cots, but instead mattresses and bolsters. The sheets and pillowcases were always clean and spotless. And even though he had a servant, he did all the cleaning and dusting himself. Not just cleaning; he did everything himself, and he always put his heart into it. He was not given to cheating or deception. If it was late at night and only watered-down liquor could be had in the neighbourhood, he would say outright, "Sahib, don't waste your money." If he had a suspicion about one of the girls, he'd let you know upfront. He even told me that he had earned twenty thousand rupees in three years, taking a two-and-a-half-rupee commission from every ten. He only wanted to make another ten thousand rupees. Why only that much? Why not more? He told me that after he had made his thirty thousand he would return to Benares and open a fabric shop. I don't know why he was so keen on opening a fabric shop, of all things.'

At this point in the narration I couldn't hold back my surprise, 'What a strange man!'

Mumtaz continued: 'I used to think he was a fake right down to his littlest toe. A huge fraud. Who could believe that he called all the girls who worked for him his "daughters". He had opened savings accounts at the post office for all the girls and every month he deposited all their income for them. It was just unbelievable that he actually paid out of his own pocket for the expenses of some ten to twelve girls. Everything he did seemed a bit too contrived to me.

'One day when I went to his place he told me that it was both Amina's and Sakina's day off. "I let them go out one day every week so they can go to some restaurant and satisfy their craving for meat. Here, as you know, everyone else is a Vaishnava." I smiled to myself thinking he was lying. Another day he told me that the Hindu girl from Ahmedabad whom he had married off to a Muslim customer had written him a letter from Lahore saying that she had made a request at the tomb of Data Sahib which had been granted. So now she had made another such petition on behalf of Sahae: that he might earn his thirty thousand rupees soon and return to Benares to open his fabric shop. I broke out laughing. I thought he was trying to win me over since I'm a Muslim.'

'Were you wrong about him?' I asked Mumtaz.

'Absolutely! There was no difference in his word and his deed. It's possible that he had some weakness and he may have erred before in his life, but on the whole, he was a very fine person.'

'And just how did you conclude this?' Juggal asked.

'At his death.' Mumtaz fell silent for a while. After some time he peered into the space where sky and sun had been gathered into a foggy embrace. 'The rioting had begun. Early in the morning one day I was passing through Bhindi Bazaar. There were few people around due to the curfew. Even the trams weren't running. I walked along looking for a taxi. Near J.J. Hospital, I saw a man rolled into a bundle by the large bin on the sidewalk. I thought it must be some labourer sleeping, but when I saw the blood and gore splattered on the cobblestones, I stopped. It was clearly murder. I thought it best to get out of there, but then I perceived a slight movement in the body. I stopped again. Not a soul was around. I peered down at the body. It was the familiar face of Sahae, but with blood all over it. I sat down beside him on the sidewalk and looked closely. His twill shirt, which was always spotless, was soaked in blood. The wound was perhaps in the area of the ribs. He started to moan faintly. I carefully shook his shoulder, as one does to wake someone from sleep. I even called him a few times by the only name I knew. I was about to get up and leave when his eyes opened. For a long time he stared at me with those half-opened eyes. Then his entire body started twitching and, recognizing me, he said, 'You? You?'

'One after another I asked him all kinds of questions: Why had he come to that area? Who had wounded him? How long had he been lying on the sidewalk? The hospital was right across from us—did he want me to let them know?

'He was too weak to talk. Once I'd exhausted all my questions, he groaned out these words with the greatest difficulty: "It was my time. This is how Bhagwan willed it!"

'Who knows what Bhagwan wanted, but being a Muslim, I didn't want to see a man I knew to be a Hindu die in a Muslim neighbourhood, thinking that his murderer might be a Muslim, as was the man who now stood watching his life ebb away. I'm not a coward, but at the time I felt worse than a coward. On the one hand, I was afraid of being arrested for the murder, and on the other I was scared that even if I wasn't arrested, I could still be detained for interrogation. It also occurred to me that if I took him to the hospital he might implicate me to avenge himself. After all, he was dying, why not take me along too? Assailed by such thoughts, I was about to flee when Sahae called my name. I stopped. I didn't want to, but my feet simply froze. I looked at him as though saying, "Get on with it, mister, I have got to go." Doubling over with pain, he unbuttoned his shirt with great difficulty and put his hand inside, but then his strength gave way. At that point he said to me, "In the waistcoat under the shirt . . . in the side pocket . . . there is some jewellery and twelve hundred rupees. It . . . is Sultana's property . . . I'd left it with a friend for safekeeping . . . Today . . . I was going to send it to her . . . you know it's getting ever more dangerous these days. Please give it to her and . . . please tell her to leave right away . . . but . . . be careful about yourself!'"

Mumtaz fell silent, but I felt as though somewhere far away, where the sky and the sea were curled up in a foggy embrace, his voice was slowly dissolving into the voice of Sahae as it rose on the sidewalk pavement near J.J. Hospital.

The ship's horn sounded. Mumtaz said, 'I did go and see Sultana. When I gave her the jewellery and money, she broke into tears.'

We said goodbye to Mumtaz and walked off the ship. He was standing on the deck by the guardrail, waving his right hand. I said to Juggal, 'Don't you feel as though Mumtaz is calling after Sahae's spirit—to make it his mate during his trip?'

Juggal only said, 'How I wish I were Sahae's spirit!'

Khushia

Khushia was thinking.

After buying a paan with a pinch of heady black tobacco in it, he was sitting on the stoop of the shop adjacent to the paan-wallah's stall. During the daytime the stoop was piled high with tyres and a myriad of auto parts, but at about eight-thirty in the evening the auto supply shop closed for the day leaving the stone platform for Khushia's exclusive use.

He was chewing on his paan, slowly, deliberately, and thinking. Thick jets of sticky, tobacco-mixed glob was swishing everywhere in his mouth. He felt as though his teeth were grinding his thoughts and blending them with his saliva. Maybe that was why he didn't wish to spit out the glob of chewed-up paan.

Khushia kept rolling the spittle around in his mouth as he pondered what had happened to him half an hour ago.

Just before coming over to sit on the stoop, as was his wont, he had gone to Fifth Lane in Khetwadi. Kanta, a new girl from Mangalore, lived at the corner of this lane. Someone had informed him that she was planning to change her accommodation; he had gone to find out about it first-hand.

He knocked at the door of her kholi. A voice responded, 'Who is it?'

'Khushia,' he replied.

Since the voice had come from somewhere deep inside the house, it was a while before the door opened. Khushia entered. After Kanta closed the door, Khushia turned around. What he saw shocked him.

Kanta was standing before him in the nude. Yes, in the nude, for the small towel she had thrown around her body could hardly be called a covering. Whatever needed to be covered was in plain view before his astonished eyes.

'Well, Khushia, what brings you here? I was about to bathe. Anyway, do sit down. You should have asked the *bahar*-wallah to send over some tea. I believe you know that accursed Rama has run away.'

Khushia had never seen a woman naked so unexpectedly, and lost his bearings; he didn't quite know what to say. His eyes, confronted with such nakedness so abruptly, wanted to hide themselves somewhere.

'Go,' he said nervously, 'go take your bath.' Then, finding that he was no longer so tongue-tied, he continued, 'Why did you have to answer the door if you were naked? You could have let me know you were bathing. I would have come back another time. Anyway, go, take your bath.'

Kanta smiled. 'When you said it was Khushia, I thought, "What's the harm. It's just our Khushia. Let him come in."'

Now, hours later, her smile was still embedded in his mind, creating havoc, and her naked body, standing right in front of his eyes, seemed to be melting into his own as if moulded from wax. It was stunningly beautiful. For the first time ever, it had dawned on him that women who sold their bodies could have such shapely figures. The realization surprised him, and even more surprising was the fact that she had stood before him stark naked without feeling a shred of shame or modesty. Why?

Kanta had already provided the answer when she said, 'When you said it was Khushia, I thought, "What's the harm. It's just our Khushia. Let him come in."'

Kanta and Khushia were part of the same profession. He was her pimp, so, in a manner of speaking, he was like one of her own. But this was no reason for her to have appeared in front of him naked. There had to be another reason behind it. Khushia tried to dig up some other meaning in her words.

The meaning was so obvious and yet so obscure that he failed to conclude anything definite.

Even now the vision of her completely naked body was etched on his mind—a body as firm and taut as the skin on a drum. And she entirely indifferent to his faltering gaze. Even in that confused state, his probing eyes had gone over her rich brown figure several times, but not a single atom of that body had displayed the slightest tremor. She had stood as immobile and unfeeling as a bronze figurine.

'Damn it, a man was standing in front of her—a man whose eyes could see a woman's body even through clothes, whose thoughts might take him God knows where. But she didn't bat an eyelid! Instead her eyes seemed as fresh as newly washed fabric. She should have blushed— just a little. Her eyes should have wavered—at least a bit. Granted, she was a prostitute, but prostitutes don't just drop their clothes like that!'

Khushia had been soliciting clients for girls for ten years, long enough to know all their quirks, hidden and otherwise. He knew, for instance, that the girl who lived at the end of Pydhonie with a man she called brother and who was fond of playing the song 'Kahe karta moorakh pyar, pyar, pyar' from the film *Achhut Kanya* on her malfunctioning gramophone was, in fact, madly in love with the movie star Ashok Kumar. Some clever boys had wheedled what they wanted out of her by promising to introduce her to the superstar. He also knew why the Punjabi woman who lived in Dadar wore pants and a coat. One of her lovers had once told her, 'Your legs are just like the legs of the English actress who was in the movie *Morocco*, also known as *Khun-e Tamanna*.' She watched the film many times. When her lover told her that Marlene Dietrich wore slacks because she had beautiful legs which she had insured for two lakh rupees, this Punjabi woman immediately started wearing hip-hugging slacks. And that girl from the south who lived in Mazgaon—the only reason she seduced handsome college boys was that she wanted to have a pretty baby, even though she knew full well she'd never be able to because she was barren. Or that swarthy Madrasi woman who always wore diamond earrings—Khushia knew she was just wasting her money on bleaching agents, her skin would never become white.

He knew the ins and outs of all the girls on his circuit, but he didn't know that one day Kanta Kumari, whose real name was impossible to remember, would stand in front of him completely naked and throw him into the greatest turmoil of his life.

So much spittle had now collected in his mouth that he was finding it increasingly difficult to chew on the tiny pieces of betel nut which kept escaping through the crevices of his teeth.

Tiny beads of perspiration had sprouted up on his narrow forehead, like fresh curds that had been gently squeezed through a piece of cheesecloth. His manly pride had been hurt. Every time he recalled the image of Kanta's naked body in his mind, he felt he'd been disgraced.

'If this isn't disgrace, what is it?' he asked himself. 'A girl standing in front of you naked tells you to your face: "Well, what's the harm. It's just our Khushia." As if I'm not Khushia, but that idiotic tomcat who sits around on her bed dozing all the time. Yes, what else?'

By now he was pretty convinced that he'd been insulted. He was a man and unconsciously expected that every woman, whether respectable or not, would consider him just that—a man—and, therefore, guard her modesty around him. He had only come to her place to find out when she was going to change her lodgings and where her new place would be. It was strictly a business call. The most he might have imagined was that when he knocked at her door she would be lying on her bed with her hair in curlers, or removing lice from her tomcat, or depilating unwanted hair from her underarms with the powder that gave off such a horrible odour that it stung his nostrils, or playing patience with the cards spread out on her bed. That's about it. She didn't keep anyone with her in the house, so anything along that line was out of the question.

But Khushia hadn't thought about any of these things; he had merely visited her to get some information when Kanta, whom he had always seen clothed, suddenly came and stood in front of him completely naked. Yes, it should be called completely naked. That itty-bitty towel couldn't possibly have covered everything. He had the strange feeling that the inside of a banana had suddenly dropped down in front of him leaving the peel in his hands. No, he'd actually felt something else; it was as if he himself had been stripped naked. Well, if the matter hadn't gone beyond this point, it would have ended right there. He could have found some way to allay his perplexity. But what was eating away at him was that she had smiled and said, 'When you said it was Khushia, I thought "What's the harm. It's just our Khushia. Let him come in."'

He kept mumbling over and over, 'She was smiling, the saali!' To him her smile seemed as naked as her body. In fact, both looked contrived.

Khushia's thoughts repeatedly went back to his childhood when a neighbour often asked him, 'Khushia, my son, run along and fetch me a bucket of water.' After he filled the bucket and brought it back, she would tell him from behind the threadbare screen of her dhoti, 'Bring it here and put it next to me. I have soap on my face; I can't see.' When he lifted the dhoti to place the bucket near her, he would see a naked woman covered in soapsuds, but that sight had never stirred up such excitement.

'Well, I was just a little boy then. There's got to be a big difference between a simple, innocent little boy and a grown man! Who hides their body from a mere boy? Now I'm almost twenty-eight years old; not even an old hag would stand naked in front of a twenty-eight-year-old man.'

What the hell had Kanta taken him for? Did he lack any of the things a strapping youth could lay claim to? It's true that the unexpected sight of Kanta's naked body had thrown him off balance. But had he not surreptitiously scanned the assets of that body, which in spite of being subjected to repeated harsh treatment had retained their shapeliness and firmness? Had the thought not crossed his mind, because he was a man, that she was a steal at ten rupees? And hadn't he labelled that bank clerk who visited her on Dussehra an unlucky fool because he left without touching her when he couldn't get her to lower her rate by two rupees? On top of all that, hadn't all his muscles felt a strange sensation of tautness, so much so that he thought his bones would crack under the pressure? Then why hadn't this dusky girl from Mangalore considered him a *man*, not 'just our Khushia', and had let him see all of her?

In a fit of anger, he spat out a stream of paan juice, which splashed on to the sidewalk painting flowery patterns. Then he got up, hopped on the tram and went home.

He took a bath and donned a brand new dhoti. One of the shops in his building was a barbershop. Khushia went in and began combing his hair in the mirror. Then, giving in to a sudden impulse, he plunked himself down in one of the chairs and asked the barber earnestly for a proper shave. Since this was Khushia's second request for a shave that day, the barber reminded him, 'Khushia, did you forget, I just shaved you this morning?' Khushia quickly ran the back of his hand along his cheeks and said in all seriousness, 'Yes, but it isn't close enough.'

After he got a close shave and a little bit of powder dusted on his face, he left the shop. There was a taxi stand directly across from it. He hailed a taxi in the peculiar manner of Bombay-wallahs, calling out 'Chhi-chhi!' After he sat down, the driver turned around and asked, 'Where to, Sahib?'

These three words, but especially 'Sahib', sent a wave of exhilaration through Khushia. He smiled and said in an exceedingly friendly tone,

'I'll tell you in a second, but first go towards Opera House . . . by way of Lamington Road. Got it?'

The taxi driver pushed the red flag on his meter down and headed for Lamington Road with a honk. After they had come to the tail end of the road, Khushia instructed him, 'Turn left.'

The taxi turned left. Before the driver could switch gears, Khushia abruptly ordered, 'Stop for a minute, there, near the lamp post.' The taxi pulled up right in front of the lamp post. Khushia got out of the vehicle and walked over to a paan-wallah's stall. He bought a paan, exchanged a few words with a guy who was standing by the stall, guided him into the taxi and told the driver, 'Now go straight.'

They drove for quite a while, the driver turning whichever way Khushia ordered, through several bustling bazaars full of glittering lights, finally entering a dimly lit lane with very little traffic. Some people had rolled their beds out on to the sidewalk and were stretched out on them. Others were getting a leisurely massage. The taxi motored past these people and came to stop outside a wooden house fashioned somewhat like a bungalow. 'Okay, go. I'll wait here in the taxi,' Khushia told his companion in a hushed voice. Gaping at Khushia like a fool, the man got out, walked over to the bungalow and went inside. Khushia sank down into his seat, putting one leg on top of the other. Then he took out a biri, lit it, took a few drags and tossed it out of the window. He was feeling very restless. His heart was beating so wildly that he was certain the driver had left the engine running to boost the fare. 'How much more do you expect to make by letting the engine run?' he asked.

The driver turned and said, 'But, Seth, the engine isn't running.'

The realization that the engine wasn't running only heightened Khushia's agitation and he started chewing on his lip. Then, setting the boat-shaped cap tucked under his arm on his head, he tapped gently on the driver's shoulder and said, 'Look, a girl will come out soon. You take off as soon as she steps inside the cab. Understand? Don't be afraid. There won't be any trouble.'

Just then two figures came out of the wooden house. Khushia's companion was in front and Kanta was right behind him, dressed in a screaming-red sari.

Khushia quickly moved to the part of the seat that was dark. His companion opened the door, helped Kanta climb in, and then shut it.

Suddenly a perplexed voice, somewhat resembling a shout, shot from Kanta's throat. 'You—Khushia?'

'Yes, it's me, Khushia, so what? You got your money, didn't you?' His thick voice rose. 'Driver, take us to Juhu.'

The driver turned the key in the ignition. The engine sputtered, drowning out whatever it was that Kanta said. The taxi lurched forward, leaving Khushia's befuddled companion behind, and disappeared in the shadows of the dimly lit lane.

From that day forward no one ever saw Khushia on the stoop of the auto supply shop again.

Toba Tek Singh

A few years after Partition, the thought occurred to the governments of Pakistan and Hindustan that, as with ordinary prisoners, an exchange of lunatics was in order. Muslim madmen in Indian asylums should be sent over to Pakistan and the Hindu and Sikh lunatics languishing in Pakistani madhouses should be handed over to Hindustan.

Whether the proposition was smart or dumb only God knows. Anyway, following the decision of some wise men, a bunch of high-level conferences were convened on either side and concluded with the fixing of a date for the transfer. A thorough scrutiny was mounted. Muslim lunatics with relatives still living in Hindustan were allowed to stay there; others were shepherded to the border. In Pakistan, the question of keeping anyone didn't even arise since nearly all Hindus and Sikhs had already migrated to Hindustan. The remaining Hindu and Sikh lunatics were rounded up and brought over to the border under police escort.

Regardless of what did or didn't happen across the border, in the Lahore asylum the news of the coming exchange stirred up rather interesting speculation among the inmates. There was one Muslim lunatic who had never missed reading the newspaper *Zamindaar* during the last twelve years. When a friend asked him, 'Molbi Sab, what is this thing called Pakistan?' he gave the matter prolonged, deep thought and said, 'It's a place in India where they make straight razors.'

The explanation satisfied his friend.

Likewise, one Sikh inmate asked another Sikh, 'Sardarji, why are we being sent to Hindustan? We don't know their language.'

The latter smiled. 'But I know the Hindustoras' language. They are absolute rascals—these Hindustanis. They strut around.'

One day, as he was bathing, a Muslim lunatic shouted 'Pakistan Zindabad!' so loudly that he slipped, fell to the floor and was knocked out.

There were some inmates who weren't really mad. Most of them were murderers. Their relatives had had them committed after bribing the officers so that they would be spared the hangman's noose. They did seem to have some inkling of why Hindustan was partitioned and what this Pakistan was, but even they didn't understand the matter clearly enough. Newspapers weren't much help and the watchmen were idiots and completely illiterate; nothing definite could be gleaned from conversations with them. All they knew was that there was this man Muhammad Ali Jinnah whom everyone called Quaid-e Azam. He had made a separate country for Muslims called Pakistan. But they knew nothing about where it was located. So these inmates, whose minds hadn't fused entirely, were continually in a fix about whether they were in Pakistan or Hindustan. If they were in Hindustan, then where was Pakistan?

One inmate got so mixed up about this business of Pakistan–Hindustan, Hindustan–Pakistan that he became even crazier. One day, while sweeping the floor, he suddenly climbed a tree, perched on a limb, and for the next two hours held forth non-stop on the delicate matter of Pakistan and Hindustan. When the guards tried to coax him down, he climbed even higher. When he was threatened, he told them in no uncertain terms, 'I don't want to live in Hindustan and I don't want to live in Pakistan; I'll live here in this tree.'

Finally, when the bout of madness subsided, he decided to come down, whereupon he started hugging his Hindu and Sikh friends deliriously, crying all the while because he was overcome by the thought that they would leave him here and go to Hindustan.

A Muslim radio engineer with a Master of Science degree always kept himself aloof from other inmates and walked quietly on a particular path of the asylum's garden all day long. Suddenly, one day, he took off all his clothes, gave them to an officer and started frolicking in the garden stark naked.

A plump Muslim lunatic from Chiniot, once a very active worker for the Muslim League, used to bathe fifteen or sixteen times a day. He abruptly gave up bathing altogether. His name was Muhammad Ali, and one day he announced from his cubicle that he was Muhammad Ali Jinnah. A Sikh followed suit and declared himself Master Tara Singh. This nearly led to a bloodbath, but designating both men as highly dangerous and confining them to separate quarters averted the crisis.

A young Lahori Hindu lawyer who had lost his mind after failing in love was terribly hurt upon hearing that Amritsar had now been moved to Hindustan. His beloved was a native of that city. Although she had snubbed him, even in his madness her memory was fresh in his mind. He constantly hurled obscenities at the Hindu and Muslim leaders who had conspired to eviscerate Hindustan, making him a Pakistani and his beloved a Hindustani. When talk of the exchange began, many of the other lunatics tried to bolster his sagging spirits. They told him not to lose heart; he would be packed off to the Hindustan where his love lived. But he didn't want to abandon Lahore. He was afraid he wouldn't be able to set up a successful law practice in Amritsar.

There were two Anglo-Indian inmates in the European ward. They literally went into shock hearing that the English had freed India and gone back home. For hours they secretly discussed the grave matter of their status in the asylum now that the English had left. Would the European ward be kept or liquidated? Would they get a 'real breakfast'? Or would they be obliged to force the bloody Indian chapatti down their gullets in place of the double-roti?

A Sikh inmate had arrived in the asylum fifteen years ago. He could be heard uttering strange gibberish all the time: '*Upar de gurgur de aiynks de be-dhyaana de mung de daal aaf de laaltain.*' Day or night, he never slept. The watchmen could vouch for the fact that he hadn't slept even a wink in fifteen years. Whenever he heard talk in the asylum of the coming exchange, he always listened to it intently. If someone asked him his opinion, he would answer with complete seriousness: '*Upar de gurgur de aiynks de be-dhyaana de mung de daal aaf de Pakistan government.*'

Later, though, he changed *aaf de Pakistan government* to *aaf de Toba Tek Singh government*, and started asking the other loonies where Toba Tek Singh, the place he came from, was. But no one knew whether Toba Tek Singh was in Pakistan or Hindustan. And if someone tried to explain, he inevitably got confused, thinking that Sialkot, which used to be in Hindustan, was now said to be in Pakistan. Who knew, perhaps

Lahore, currently in Pakistan, would shift to Hindustan tomorrow, or maybe all of Hindustan would become Pakistan. And who could say with any surety that both Hindustan and Pakistan would not disappear altogether.

Over time this lunatic's kes had become so scraggly that it almost seemed to have disappeared. He hardly ever bathed, so the hair of his beard and head had become matted and stuck together, giving his features a frighteningly grotesque look. However, he was a harmless man. During his fifteen years in the asylum he had never had a brawl with anyone. The old staff knew that he had owned quite a bit of land in Toba Tek Singh. He had been a prosperous landowner until one day, suddenly, he went berserk. His relatives brought him to the asylum in heavy chains and had him admitted. They came to visit him once a month, inquired after him and then went back. Their visits continued for a long time, but stopped when the Pakistan–Hindustan *garbar* started.

His name was Bishan Singh, but everyone called him Toba Tek Singh. Although he had no awareness of the day or month or how many years had passed, somehow he always knew the day his relatives were expected. He would tell the officer that his 'visit' was coming that day. He would take a long bath, scrub his body vigorously with soap, oil and comb his hair, have his clothes, which he hardly ever wore, brought out and slip into them, and meet his visitors thus, looking all prim and proper. If they asked him something, he remained quiet or mumbled his incomprehensible '*Upar de gurgur de aiynks de be-dhyaana de mung de daal aaf de laaltain*' now and then.

He had a daughter who, growing a little at a time, had become a young woman in fifteen years. Bishan Singh never recognized her. As a little girl, she would cry when she saw her father, and now, as a young woman, tears still welled up in her eyes at the sight of him.

When this confusing business of Pakistan and Hindustan began, he started asking his fellow lunatics where Toba Tek Singh was located. His curiosity grew by the day when he didn't get a satisfactory answer. Now the 'visits' had also stopped. Where before he would instinctively know when his relatives were coming to see him, now that inner voice no longer intimated such a visit to him.

He fervently wished those people who talked with him with such kindness and warmth and who brought him gifts of fruits, sweets and clothes would visit him. If he were to ask them, they would surely have told him whether Toba Tek Singh was located in Pakistan or Hindustan because he thought they themselves came from Toba Tek Singh.

One lunatic called himself 'God'. One day Bishan Singh asked him about Toba Tek Singh: Was it in Pakistan or Hindustan? As usual, 'God' burst out laughing and said, 'Neither in Pakistan nor Hindustan because we haven't yet given the orders.'

Bishan Singh begged 'God' many times to give the order so the dilemma could be laid to rest, but he said he was too damn busy because he had many other orders to give first. So one day, fed up with 'God's' dilly-dallying, Bishan Singh let him have a piece of his mind: *'Upar de gurgur de aiynks de be-dhyaana de mung de daal aaf Wahe Guruji da Khalsah and Wahe Guruji ki fateh—jo bole so nihal, sat siri akaal!'* Perhaps he meant to say: You're the Muslims' God, had you been the God of the Sikhs you would surely have heard my plea.

Some days before the scheduled exchange of lunatics, a Muslim friend of Bishan Singh came to see him. He had never visited him before in all these years. Bishan Singh saw him but shrugged and started to turn back. The guards stopped him and said, 'He's come to visit you. He's your old friend Fazl Din.'

Bishan Singh hardly glanced at the man and started to mumble something. Fazl Din drew closer and put his hand on Bishan Singh's shoulder. 'I've been thinking of visiting you for quite a while now but was pressed for time. All your relatives have safely left for Hindustan. I helped them as much as I could. Your daughter Roop Kaur . . .' He suddenly held back.

Bishan Singh looked as though he was trying to remember something and then mumbled, 'Daughter Roop Kaur.'

Fazl Din said falteringly, 'Yes . . . She . . . she's all right . . . she went with them.'

Bishan Singh remained quiet. Fazl Din continued, 'Your family asked me to keep inquiring after your well-being. Now I hear that you're also leaving for Hindustan. Give my salaams to brother Balbeer Singh and brother Vadhwa Singh . . . and, yes, to sister Amrit Kaur as well. Tell brother Balbeer Singh that Fazl Din is doing well. The two brown buffaloes they had left behind—one of them gave birth to a male calf. The other also had a calf, a female, but it died after six days . . . And if there's anything more he'd like me to do, tell him I'm always ready. And this, here, a little *morandas* for you.'

Bishan Singh took the small sack of sweets and handed it to the guard standing nearby. He then asked Fazl Din, 'Where is Toba Tek Singh?'

Fazl Din was a bit bewildered. 'Where . . . where it's always been.'

Bishan Singh asked him again, 'In Pakistan or in Hindustan?'

'In Hindustan . . . No, no, it's in Pakistan.' Fazl Din was flummoxed.

Bishan Singh left, mumbling, '*Upar de gurgur de aiynks de be-dhyaana de mung de daal aaf de Pakistan and Hindustan aaf de durfatte munh.*'

Preparations for the exchange had been completed. The list of lunatics who would be swapped had been sent over to the country receiving them and the day when the exchange would take place had been fixed.

On a blistering cold morning, lorries packed with Hindu and Sikh lunatics started out from the Lahore asylum under police escort along with the officials overseeing the exchange. At the Wagah border, the superintendents of both sides met, concluded the preliminary formalities, and the exchange began, continuing well into the night.

Getting the lunatics out of the lorries and handing them over to the officials on the other side turned out to be a gruelling job indeed. Some resisted getting out, others who were willing to come out became impossible to control because they took off in different directions. As fast as the stark naked ones were clothed, they tore the clothes right off again. One rolled out a torrent of obscenities, another broke into song. Some got into fisticuffs, while others cried their hearts out, sobbing inconsolably. The hullabaloo was deafening. The female lunatics were raising their own separate hell. And all this in a cold so punishing that it made one's teeth chatter non-stop.

The majority of lunatics were against the exchange. They couldn't understand why they were being uprooted. Those who still had some sanity left were shouting *Pakistan Zindabad!* or *Pakistan Murdabad!*— which so enraged some Muslim and Sikh lunatics that they nearly came to blows.

When Bishan Singh's turn came and the official across the Wagah border began to enter his name in the register, he asked, 'Where is Toba Tek Singh—in Pakistan or in Hindustan?'

The official laughed. 'In Pakistan.'

Bishan Singh jumped, withdrew to one side and ran to his fellow inmates. Pakistani guards grabbed him and started pushing him towards the other side of the border. He dug his heels in, refusing to budge. 'Toba Tek Singh is here!' and then he started to spew out loudly: *'Upar de gurgur de aiynks de be-dhyaana de mung de daal aaf Toba Tek Singh and Pakistan.'*

They did their best to coax him into believing by saying 'Look, Toba Tek Singh has now moved to Hindustan, and if it hasn't yet, it will be sent there right away,' but he stubbornly refused to accept that. When they attempted to drag him forcibly across the border, he dug in with his swollen legs with such determination on the patch of earth that lay in the middle that no force in the world could move him from it.

Since he was entirely harmless, the guards didn't force him and let him stand where he was while the rest of the exchange continued.

Just before sunrise an ear-splitting cry shot out of Bishan Singh's throat. Officials from both sides of the border rushed over to him, only to find that the man who had stood on his feet day and night for the past fifteen years was lying face down. There, behind the barbed wires, was Hindustan, and here, behind the same barbed wires was Pakistan. In between, on the thin strip of no-man's land, lay Toba Tek Singh.

The Testament of Gurmukh Singh

From isolated incidents of stabbing, news began to trickle down of full-blown skirmishes between parties in which kirpans, swords and guns were being used, not to mention knives and cleavers. Now and then one also heard of homemade bombs going off.

Everyone in Amritsar was of the opinion that these communal riots would not last long. Once passions had cooled down the situation would return to normal. Riots had erupted in Amritsar before, but they had had a short life. Deathly commotion, in which murder and carnage took place, raged for a few days and then subsided on its own. If past experience was any indication, people believed that the fire, after it had spent its fury, would die down. This, however, didn't happen. The rioting grew worse by the day.

Muslim residents of largely Hindu neighbourhoods began to flee. Likewise, Hindus in predominantly Muslim areas abandoned their homes for more secure locations, convinced that such moves were temporary, only until the atmosphere had been cleansed of its rioting furore.

Retired sub-judge Mian Abdul Hayy was not overly worried. He was absolutely sure that the situation would normalize before long. He lived with his eleven-year-old son, a daughter who was seventeen, and a servant of about seventy who had been with him for a long time. It was a small family. Notwithstanding his confidence, at the first signs of rioting the prudent Mian Sahib had stockpiled food. He didn't have to worry about food supplies in case the situation—God forbid—took a turn for the worse and shops closed down for an indefinite period.

His daughter Sughra, on the other hand, wasn't quite as relaxed about the matter. Their three-storey house was quite a bit taller than the surrounding buildings. You could easily see almost three-quarters of the city from its upper floor. Sughra had noticed that not a day passed without some conflagration or other starting somewhere in the distance or close by. Earlier, the blare of fire engines could be heard as they sped by, but no longer. There were just too many fires.

The view at night was something else again. In the pitch dark, tall flames shot up like so many devas spewing fire, followed by strange noises that sounded dreadful with their mixture of ear-splitting cries of *Har Har Mahadev!* and *Allahu Akbar!*

Sughra did not mention her premonitions and fears to her father. He had already advised them not to be afraid; everything would be all right. And since Mian Sahib had been right most of the time before, she felt somewhat reassured. However, when the power and water supply was cut off, she couldn't hold back and mentioned her anxiety to him, diffidently suggesting that they move temporarily to Sharifpur where other neighbouring Muslims were headed. But Mian Sahib stood firm by his opinion. 'No need to panic,' he said calmly. 'The situation will get better very soon.'

The situation didn't get better very soon. In fact, it rapidly worsened. The entire neighbourhood became empty of Muslims. On top of that, suddenly one day, Mian Sahib suffered a stroke that confined him to his bed. Basharat, his son, who had earlier spent most of his time playing alone inside the house, now scarcely left his father's side and began to understand the precariousness of the situation.

The bazaar next to their house lay deserted. Dr Ghulam Mustafa's dispensary had been shut some time ago, and from the balcony Sughra had seen padlocks hanging from Dr Gorand's farther down. Mian Sahib's condition was critical. Sughra was feeling terribly anxious, unable to think straight. She took Basharat aside and begged him, 'For God's sake, do something. I know it isn't safe to step outside, but please go and fetch someone. Abbaji is very ill.'

Basharat did go, but returned immediately with a terribly pale face. He had seen a blood-drenched corpse in the chowk and a bunch of masked men busy pillaging a nearby shop. She hugged her terrified brother and tried to be patient, but she couldn't bear the sight of her father. Mian Sahib's right side had become totally paralysed, as if it had no life left in it. His speech had also become slurred. He talked mostly through gestures and seemed to be telling her not to worry, everything would be all right by the grace of God.

Nothing became all right. Ramzan Eid was two days away. Mian Sahib was sure that the current crisis would end before Eid, but now the atmosphere was thick with the premonition that the day of Eid might prove to be doomsday. From the top of the house only clouds of smoke could be seen rising from practically every part of the city. The horrifying sound of exploding bombs kept Sughra and Basharat on edge all night. Sughra had to stay awake to look after her father; the bombs seemed to be exploding inside her head. Panic-stricken, she looked now at her paralysed father, now at her terrified brother. The male servant Akbar, being an old man of seventy, wasn't really much help. He just lay in his dingy little room coughing and spitting big globs of phlegm day and night. Finally, one day, Sughra had had enough with him and gave him a piece of her mind. 'What are you good for, anyway? Don't you see Mian Sahib's condition? You are, to say the least, a thankless lout. Now, when you're most needed to serve him, you laze about, faking asthma. Oh, those servants who eagerly laid down their lives to serve their masters are long gone!'

After she had vented her anger, Sughra left the old servant, only to begin to regret letting herself go when the poor man had done nothing wrong. She laid out his food on a tray and carried it to his room but found it empty. Basharat went through the entire house looking for him but the servant was nowhere to be found. The latch on his door was unfastened on the outside, which gave the impression that he had perhaps gone out to do something for Mian Sahib. Sughra prayed ardently for his success. Two days passed but Akbar didn't return.

It was evening. The siblings had seen many such evenings in the past, enlivened by the boisterous commotion of the coming Eid, when their eyes stayed glued to the sky expecting to sight the new moon.

Eid was to be the following day, only the new moon needed to announce its arrival. How impatient they used to be for the announcement. And how annoyed when a stubborn piece of cloud wandered across the night sky and refused to budge from where the sighting of the moon was likely. Now it was clouds of smoke everywhere. Both climbed to the upper floor. Here and there on faraway roofs they saw human figures, but only as shadowy blotches. They couldn't tell whether these figures were looking for the moon or watching the leaping flames.

The moon turned out to be one brazen body. It managed to peek through the cloud cover. Sughra quickly raised her hands and offered a prayer to God to restore her father's health, while Basharat twisted inside with displeasure over the riots that had ruined the delights of Eid.

The sun hadn't yet gone down fully, in other words, the evening darkness hadn't quite set in. Mian Sahib's cot, on which he lay immobile, was set out on the floor sprinkled with water. His eyes were fixed on the distant sky, thinking something difficult to guess. After sighting the moon Sughra came and said salaam to him. He acknowledged it with a movement of his hand. As she bowed her head, he patted it with his good hand with tender affection. Tears dripped from her eyes, and Mian Sahib was so overcome with emotion that his own eyes also became moist. He laboured with his paralysed tongue to console her. 'The blessed and gracious God will put everything right.'

Just then they were surprised by a sudden knock at the door. Sughra was struck with terror. She glanced at Basharat. His face blanched.

The knock came again. 'Go and see who it is,' Mian Sahib told Sughra.

Sughra thought that the old man Akbar had returned. A flicker ran through her eyes. She grabbed Basharat's arm and said, 'Go and see. Perhaps it's Akbar.'

Mian Sahib shook his head, as if he meant to say, 'No, it's not Akbar.'

'Who else could it be, Abbaji?'

As Mian Abdul Hayy was struggling to say something, Basharat returned, looking terribly frightened and breathless. He moved Sughra away from Mian Sahib's cot and said in undertones, 'It's some Sikh.'

'A Sikh!' Sughra screamed. 'What does he want?'

'He's asking me to open the door.'

Trembling, Sughra pulled Basharat to her bosom and plunked down on Mian Sahib's cot, looking at her father with listless eyes.

A strange smile swept over Mian Abdul Hayy's thin, lifeless lips. 'Go open the door. It's Gurmukh Singh.'

Basharat shook his head. 'No, it's someone else.'

'It's him,' Mian Sahib slurred decisively. 'Sughra, go and open the door.'

Sughra stood up. She knew Gurmukh Singh. Before retiring, her father had done something for him, but her memory about the favour was hazy. Perhaps he had saved Gurmukh Singh from some fraudulent case that was brought against him. Since then he had always brought them a gift bag of *rumaali sevaiyan* on Chhoti Eid. Her father told the man several times, 'Sardarji, there really is no need to inconvenience yourself.' But the latter would respectfully join his hands and say, 'Mian Sahib, by the grace of Wahe Guruji you have everything. It's just a small gift that I bring on the occasion of Eid to express my gratitude. Even a hundred generations of mine could never pay you back for the immense favour you did for me. May God keep you happy!'

Sardar Gurmukh Singh had been bringing this gift on the eve of Eid from as far back as Sughra could remember. She wondered why she hadn't thought of him when the knock sounded. And why did Basharat say, 'No, it's someone else,' when he, too, had seen Gurmukh Singh many times? Who else could it be? Thinking along these lines, she approached the deorhi. Should she open the door or just ask from inside. She hadn't made up her mind quite yet when there was a louder, more insistent knock. Her heart began to pound loudly. With great difficulty she asked, 'Who is it?'

Basharat was standing close by. He pointed at a chink in the door and asked her to peek through it.

She peeked. It was not Gurmukh Singh; he was quite old. The man who stood outside on the stoop looked young. Her eyes were still glued to the chink when the man knocked again. She saw he had a paper bag in his hands, just like the one Gurmukh Singh used to bring.

She took her eyes off the chink and asked in a loud voice, 'Who are you?'

'I . . . I'm Gurmukh Singh's son Santokh.'

Much of her fear had subsided by then. 'What brings you here today?' she asked politely.

'Where is Judge Sahib?' he asked.

'He is ill.'

'Oh,' Sardar Santokh said regretfully. 'These,' he shook the paper bag, 'these are sevaiyan. Sardarji is no longer with us. He passed away.'

'Passed away?' Sughra quickly asked.

'Yes, about a month ago. As he was dying, he told me, "Son, I've been bringing sevaiyan to Judge Sahib every Chhoti Eid for the past ten years. You should do the same when I'm gone." I promised him. I'm making good on my promise. Here, please accept this.'

Sughra was so touched her eyes welled up with tears. She opened the door a crack and took the proffered bag. 'May God give Sardarji a place in Heaven,' she said.

After a pause Gurmukh Singh's son asked, 'Judge Sahib is ill?'

'Yes.'

'What is wrong?'

'He had a stroke.'

'Oh! Had Sardarji been alive, he'd have felt very sad. He remembered Judge Sahib's kindness to his dying day. He used to say, "He is not a human but a god." May God give him long life. Please give him my salaams.'

Before Sughra could decide whether to ask him to arrange for a doctor to visit Judge Sahib, Santokh Singh had gone. He had walked a few steps when four masked men approached him. Two of them held burning torches and the other two a can of kerosene and other flammable materials. One of them asked, 'So, Sardarji, you're done with your job?'

'Yes.'

'Well then, shall we take care of the Judge Sahib now?' the man asked, laughing behind his mask.

'Yes . . . as you like,' Sardar Gurmukh Singh's son said and walked away.

For Freedom's Sake

I don't remember the year but it must have been when Amritsar was reverberating everywhere with the cries of 'Inqilab Zindabad!' These cries, I recall, were filled with a strange excitement, a gushing energy one saw only among the blossoming milkmaids of the city as they tore through its bazaars with baskets of *uplas* carefully balanced on their heads. It was a wild and woolly time. The dread, tinged with sadness, which had hung in the atmosphere since the bloody incident at Jallianwala Bagh, had completely disappeared and a dauntless fervour had taken its place: the desire to fling oneself headlong, regardless of where one might land.

People chanted slogans, staged demonstrations and were sent to prison by the hundreds. Courting arrest had become a favourite pastime: You were apprehended in the morning and released by the evening. You were tried in court and thrown in jail for a few months. You came out, shouted another slogan, and got arrested all over again.

Those days were so full of life! The tiniest bubble when it burst became a formidable vortex. Somebody would stand in the square, make a speech calling for a strike, and a strike would follow. A tidal wave would sweep through requiring everybody to wear only homespun khadi to put the textile factories of Lancashire out of business, and all imported cloth would be boycotted. Bonfires would go up in every chowk, and in the heat of the moment people would peel off their clothes then and there and throw them into the flames. Now and then, when a woman tossed one of her ill-chosen saris down from her balcony, people would go wild with applause.

I remember one conflagration across from the main police station by the Town Hall. My classmate Shaikhu became so excited that he took off his silk jacket and tossed it on to the pyre of imported clothing, setting off a round of thunderous applause because he was the son of a noted toady. The applause excited him even more. He peeled off his silk shirt and offered it to the flames too, realizing only later that the shirt had gold buttons and links.

Far be it from me to make fun of Shaikhu. The fact is that I felt just as passionate in those days. I'd dream of getting hold of handguns and forming a terrorist group of my own. That my father was receiving his pension from the government never crossed my mind. Something inside me was boiling to spill out, akin to the heady feeling of a game of flush.

I had never cared much for school anyway, but in those days I came to positively detest it. I'd leave the house with my books and make straight for Jallianwala Bagh. Here I'd watch whatever was happening until school ended. Or I would sit under a tree and stare at the women in the windows of houses some distance away, hoping that one of them would fall in love with me. Why such a thought entered my head I have no idea.

Jallianwala Bagh was the scene of much activity at the time. Canvas tents and enclosures were set up everywhere. People would choose somebody as 'dictator' every few days and install him with due ceremony in the biggest tent. He would receive a military salute from his ragtag army of volunteers. In mock seriousness, he would receive the greetings of khadi-clad men and women for three or four days, at most a fortnight. He would collect donations of flour and rice for the soup kitchen from the banias, and one day while drinking his lassi (God only knows why it was so readily available in the Jallianwala Bagh area) he would be grabbed by the police, arrested, and whisked away to prison.

I had an old classmate, Shahzada Ghulam Ali. You can get some idea of how close our friendship was from the fact that we flunked our high school exams together twice. We had even run away to Bombay once. Our plan was to reach the Soviet Union eventually, but when our money ran out and we were forced to sleep on the streets, we had to write home, asking to be forgiven, and returned.

Shahzada Ghulam Ali was a handsome young man: tall and fair as Kashmiris generally are, with a sharp nose and playful eyes. There was something particularly regal in the way he walked, as well as a trace of the swagger of professional goondas.

He had not been a 'Shahzada' during our schooldays. But as revolutionary fervour picked up and he participated in a dozen or so rallies, the slogans, garlands of marigold, songs of patriotic zeal and the opportunity to talk freely with female volunteers turned him into a sort of half-baked revolutionary. One day he delivered his first speech. The next day I found out from the newspaper that Ghulam Ali had become a 'Shahzada'.

Soon he became known all over Amritsar, which is a fairly small city where it doesn't take long to become famous or infamous. Its residents—quite critical of ordinary people, and determined to find fault with them—couldn't be more forgiving to a religious or political leader. They always seem to be in need of a sermon or speech. One can survive here as a leader for a long time. Just show up in different clothes each time: now black, now blue.

But that was a different time. All the major leaders were already in prison and their place was free for the taking. The people of course had no need for leaders, at least not much, but the revolutionary movement certainly did. It urgently needed people who would wear khadi, sit inside the biggest tent in Jallianwala Bagh, make a speech, and get arrested.

In those days Europe was going through its first 'dictatorships'. Hitler and Mussolini had gained quite a bit of notoriety. Perhaps that's what led the Congress party to create its own 'dictators'. When Shahzada Ghulam Ali's turn came, forty 'dictators' had already been arrested.

I headed off to Jallianwala the minute I heard that the strange mix of circumstances had made our Ghulam Ali a 'dictator'. Volunteers stood guard outside the large tent. Ghulam Ali saw me and called me in. A mattress was laid out on the ground with a khadi bedcover on it, and there, leaning against cushions and bolsters, sat Ghulam Ali talking to a group of khadi-clad banias about, I believe, vegetables. He finished the session quickly, gave instructions to his volunteers and turned towards me. He looked far too serious, which prompted me to tease him. As soon as the volunteers had cleared away, I laughed and said, 'Hey, Prince, what's up?'

I made fun of him for quite a while. Yet, there was no denying the change in him; it was palpable, and what's more, he was aware of it.

He kept telling me, 'Saadat, please don't make light of me. I know I'm a small man and don't deserve this honour. But from now on I want to keep it this way.'

I returned to Jallianwala Bagh in the evening. It was packed with people. As I had come early I found a place close to the platform. Ghulam Ali appeared amidst tremendous applause. He looked dashing in his immaculate white khadi outfit, the slight swagger mentioned earlier adding to his attraction. He spoke for nearly an hour. Goose pimples broke out on my body several times during his speech. I even felt the overwhelming need to explode like a bomb then and there a few times. Perhaps I was thinking that such an explosion might free India.

God knows how many years have passed since then. Our emotions and events were in a state of flux. It is difficult to describe their precise modulations now. But as I write this story and recall him making that speech, all I see is youth itself talking, youth that was innocent of politics and filled with the sincere boldness of a young man who suddenly stops a woman on the street and tells her outright, 'Look, I love you,' then surrenders himself to the law.

I've heard many more speeches since. But in none of them have I heard even a faint echo of the bubbling madness, reckless youth, raw emotion and naked challenge that filled Shahzada Ghulam Ali's voice that day. Speeches today are laced with laboured seriousness, stale politics and prudence dressed in lyricism.

At the time neither side, the government or the people, was experienced. They were at each other's throats, unaware of the consequences. The government sent people to prison without understanding the implications of such a step, and those who submitted to voluntary arrest showed equal ignorance of the true significance of their act.

It was wrong-headedness, and potentially explosive. It ignited people, subsided, and ignited them all over again, creating a surge of fiery exuberance in the otherwise dull and gloomy atmosphere of servitude.

All of Jallianwala Bagh exploded with loud applause and inflammatory slogans when Shahzada Ghulam Ali ended his speech. His face was gleaming. When I met him alone and shook his hand to congratulate him, I could feel that it was trembling. A similar warm throbbing was evident on his bright face. He was gasping a bit. His eyes were aglow with the heat of passion, but they also hid traces of a search that had nearly exhausted itself. They were desperately looking for somebody. Suddenly he snatched away his hand and darted towards the jasmine bushes.

A young woman stood there, wearing a spotless khadi sari. The next day I came to know that Shahzada Ghulam Ali was in love with her. It was not a one-sided love because she, Nigar, loved him madly in return. Nigar, as is obvious from her name, was a Muslim girl; an orphan. She worked as a nurse in a women's hospital. She was perhaps the first Muslim girl in Amritsar to come out of purdah and join the Congress movement.

Partly her khadi outfit, partly her participation in the activities of the Congress, and partly also the atmosphere of the hospital—had all slightly mellowed her Islamic demeanour, the harshness which is part of a Muslim woman's nature, and softened her.

She wasn't beautiful, but she was a model of femininity in her own way. Humility, the desire to respect and worship, and *adarsh*, so characteristic of a Hindu woman's nature, had come together in Nigar in a most pleasing combination. Back then the image would never even have occurred to me, but now whenever I think of her, she appears to me as a beautiful confluence of the Muslim namaz and the Hindu *aarti*.

She practically worshipped Shahzada Ghulam Ali. He too adored her. When I asked him about her, he told me they had met during the Congress rallies and after a brief time together had decided to tie the knot.

Ghulam Ali wanted to marry her before his imminent arrest. I had no idea why. He could just as easily have married her after his release. Prison sentences used to be quite short in those days. Three months, at most a year. Some were let go after only a fortnight to make room for others. Anyway, he'd told Nigar of his plan and she was willing. All that was needed was Babaji's blessing.

Babaji, as you must know, was a major figure. In those days he was staying outside the city in the palatial lodgings of the city's richest jeweller, Lala Hari Ram. Ordinarily he lived in his ashram in a neighbouring village. But whenever he came to Amritsar, he encamped at Hari Ram's. For the duration of his stay this house became a shrine for his devotees, who would stand in long lines, patiently waiting for his darshan. In the evening, seated on a wooden platform laid out under a cluster of mango trees some distance from the house, Babaji gave a general audience and accepted donations for his ashram. This was followed by the chanting of bhajans, and the session would end at his bidding.

Babaji was an abstemious and God-fearing man. He was also very learned and intelligent. These qualities had endeared him to everyone— Hindu, Muslim, Sikh and Untouchable alike. Everybody considered him their leader.

On the face of it, Babaji was indifferent to politics, but it was an open secret that every political movement in Punjab began and ended at his behest. The government found him intractable, a political riddle that even the brainiest government functionaries could never hope to solve. His barest smile stirred up widespread speculation, but when he proceeded to interpret it himself in an entirely novel way, the populace, already in thrall, felt truly overwhelmed.

The civil disobedience movement in Amritsar, with its frequent arrests, quite clearly owed a lot to Babaji's influence. Every evening at darshan, he'd drop an innocuous word from his toothless mouth about the freedom movement in the whole of Punjab and about the fresh and increasingly harsh measures being taken by the government, and the mighty leaders of the time would scramble to pick it up and hang it around their necks like a priceless amulet.

People said that Babaji's eyes had a magnetic quality, his voice was magical, and he had a cool head—so cool indeed that the worst obscenities, the sharpest sarcasm, could not provoke him, not even for the hundredth of a second—which made his opponents writhe in frustration.

He must have taken part in hundreds of demonstrations in Amritsar, but, strangely, I hadn't caught a glimpse of him, from near or far, although I'd seen every other leader. Thus when Ghulam Ali mentioned that he was planning to seek Babaji's permission to marry, I asked him to take me along.

The very next day Ghulam Ali arranged for a tonga, and we arrived at Lala Hari Ram's magnificent mansion.

Babaji was done with his morning *ashnan** and worship, and was listening to a beautiful *panditani*† sing patriotic songs. He was seated on

* Bath.
† Pandit woman.

a palm mat spread out on the immaculate white tile floor. A bolster lay near him but he wasn't leaning against it.

The room had no other furnishings besides the mat. The panditani's light brown complexion looked stunningly beautiful in the light reflecting off the tiles.

In spite of being an old man of seventy or seventy-two, Babaji's entire body—clad only in a tiny red ochre loincloth—was free of wrinkles. His skin had a rich dark colour. I learned later that he had olive oil rubbed into it before taking a bath.

He greeted Shahzada Ghulam Ali with a smile, and glanced at me. He acknowledged our greetings by a slight widening of his smile and then made a sign for us to sit down.

Today when I recall that scene and examine it closely, I find it quite intriguing. A half-naked old man sitting on a palm mat in the style of a yogi; his posture, his bald head, his half-open eyes, his soft tawny body, indeed every line in his face radiated a tranquil contentment, an unassailable conviction that he could not be dislodged, not even by the worst earthquake, from the summit on which the world had placed him. And beside him sits a just-opened bud from the vale of Kashmir, her head bowed partly out of respect for the elderly man, the effect of the patriotic song, and her own boundless youth yearning to spill out of the confining folds of her coarse white sari and sing not just a song for the country, but to her youth as well; she wanted to honour not just the nearness of this elderly man, but also that of some healthy young man who would have the courage to grab her hand and jump head first into life's raging fire. Opposite the elderly man's granite confidence and serenity, her light brown complexion, her dark lively eyes, her bosom heaving inside her coarse khadi blouse—all seemed to throw a silent challenge: Come, pull me down from where I stand, or lift me up to sublimity.

Nigar, Shahzada Ghulam Ali and I sat somewhat off to one side; I was frozen like an idiot, equally flustered by Babaji's imposing personality and the unblemished beauty of the young Kashmiri woman. The glossy tiles also had an effect on me, indeed quite an effect. Would the pandit girl let me kiss her eyes, just once? The thought pulsated through my body, and my mind immediately darted off to my maidservant, for whom I'd begun to feel something lately. I felt like leaving the assembly and heading directly home—perhaps I would succeed in stealthily luring her upstairs to the bathroom. I just might. But the second my glance fell on Babaji and the passionate strains of the nationalistic song filled my ears, a different thought began to course through my body: If I could just get hold of a handgun, I'd rush to the Civil Lines area and make short work of the English.

And next to this idiot sat Nigar and Ghulam Ali, a pair of hearts in love, somewhat tired of their long and uneventful throbbing, ready to melt into each other's embrace and find those other shades of love. In other words, they'd come to ask Babaji, their uncontested political leader, for permission to marry. Obviously it was not the song of the nation that resonated in their ears at that moment. It was their own song, beautiful, but as yet unsung.

The song ended. With a hand gesture Babaji gave his blessing to the panditani and then turned, smiling, to Nigar and Ghulam Ali, again managing a small glance at me as well.

Ghulam Ali was perhaps about to introduce himself and Nigar but Babaji—goodness, his memory!—quickly said to him in his sweet voice, 'Prince, you haven't been arrested yet?'

'No, not yet,' Ghulam Ali replied, his hands folded in respect.

Babaji picked out a pencil from a box and toyed with it as he said, 'But you *are*—I think.'

The remark went over Ghulam Ali's head. So Babaji looked at the panditani and said, pointing at Nigar, 'Nigar has captured our Prince.'

Nigar blushed. Ghulam Ali's mouth fell open. And the panditani's light brown complexion flushed with good wishes. She gave the pair a look that seemed to say, 'How wonderful!'

Babaji looked at the panditani once again. 'These children,' he said to her, 'have come to ask for my permission. How about you, Kamal, when are you going to get married?'

So she was called Kamal! The abrupt question caught her off guard, and she turned red in the face. 'Me?' she said in a trembling voice. 'I've decided to join your ashram.'

She said this with a trace of regret, which Babaji's perceptive mind registered instantly. He gave her a smile, the soft smile of a yogi, and then turned to Ghulam Ali and Nigar and asked, 'So have the two of you made up your minds?'

'Yes,' they answered softly in unison.

Babaji scanned them with his politician's eyes. 'Sometimes,' he said, 'one is obliged to change the decisions one has made.'

For the first time in Babaji's lofty presence, Ghulam Ali unleashed the boldness of his coltish youth, saying, 'Even if our decision is put off for some reason, it will never change!'

Babaji closed his eyes and proceeded to question him in the manner of a lawyer. 'Why?'

Surprisingly, Ghulam Ali didn't lose his nerve at all. His ardent love for Nigar made him say, 'Circumstances may force us to put it off, but our decision to free India is irrevocable. Absolutely!'

Looking back, I now feel that Babaji hadn't thought it worthwhile to query him further on the subject and just smiled—a smile which everyone present must have interpreted in his or her own way. And if asked, Babaji would have given it a radically different meaning. Of that I'm sure.

Anyway, stretching the smile which evoked a thousand different meanings, he said, 'Nigar, come join our ashram! It is only a matter of days before Prince is sent to jail.'

'All right, I will,' she answered softly.

Babaji changed the subject and asked about the revolutionary activities in the Jallianwala Bagh camp. Ghulam Ali, Nigar and Kamal filled him in for what seemed like a long time about various arrests, releases, and even about milk, lassi and vegetables. During this time I sat there like a bumpkin, wondering why Babaji was dilly-dallying so much in giving his blessing to Ghulam Ali and Nigar. Did he have doubts about their love for each other? About Ghulam Ali's sincerity? Had he invited Nigar to the ashram just to help her get over the pain she'd feel upon her husband's incarceration? But then, why had Kamal responded to Babaji's question, 'Kamal, when are you going to get married?' with 'I've decided to join your ashram'? Didn't men and women marry at the ashram? These kinds of questions kept raging inside my head as the four of them speculated on whether the number of lady volunteers was enough to deliver chapattis for five hundred militants on time. How many stoves were there? How large were the griddles? Couldn't one get a griddle big enough for six women to bake chapattis on all at once?

This pandit girl, Kamal, would she just chant national songs and religious bhajans for Babaji's edification once she was admitted to the ashram, I wondered. I had seen the male volunteers of the ashram. True enough, they all took their ritual bath and brushed their teeth every morning, spent most of their time out in the open air and chanted bhajans in accordance with the rules of the ashram, but their clothing still reeked of perspiration, didn't it? Quite a few had bad breath to boot. And I never saw on anyone even a trace of the good nature and freshness one associates with outdoor living. Instead, they looked stooped and repressed, their faces pallid, eyes sunken and bodies ravaged—as blanched and lifeless as the udders of a cow from which even the last drop of milk has been squeezed out.

I'd seen these ashram-wallahs on numerous occasions in Jallianwala Bagh. I couldn't imagine Kamal, who was moulded in her entirety out of milk, honey and saffron, being subjected to the gaze of these men with nothing but filth in their eyes. Would she—a being swathed all over in the scent of *lobaan*—have to listen to these men with their mouths smelling worse than the stench of rotting mulch? Perhaps, I thought, the independence of India was above all this.

But this 'perhaps' was not something I could understand, what with my patriotism and passion for the country's freedom. I thought of Nigar, who was sitting very close to me and telling Babaji that turnips usually took quite a long time to cook. For heaven's sake, what had turnips got to do with marriage? She and Ghulam Ali had come for Babaji's blessing to get married, hadn't they?

My thoughts wandered off to Nigar and the ashram, which I had never visited. Ashrams, *vidyalayas*, *jamat-khanas*, *takiyas* and *darsgahs*, all such places inspire only the deepest revulsion in me. I don't know why. I've often seen boys and the caretakers of orphanages and schools for the blind walking in a row along streets asking for handouts. I have also seen jamat-khanas and darsgahs: Boys in *shar'i* pyjamas worn well above their ankles, their foreheads marked with calluses despite their tender age, the slightly older boys sporting thick bushy beards, the younger ones with a revolting growth of sparse bristles on their cheeks and chins—all absorbed in prayer, but their faces reflecting pure beastliness.

Nigar was a woman, not a Muslim, Hindu, Sikh or Christian, just a woman. No, she was more than that, a woman's prayer intended for her lover, or for one whom she herself loved with all her heart. I couldn't imagine her—she who was herself a prayer—raising her hands in supplication every morning as required by the rules of Babaji's ashram.

Today as I recall Babaji, Nigar, Ghulam Ali, the ravishingly beautiful pandit girl, indeed the entire atmosphere of Amritsar, engulfed as it was in those days in the fine romantic haze created by the movement for independence—all appear like a dream, the sort one longs to have over and over again.

I still haven't seen Babaji's ashram, but I hate it as passionately today as I did then. I don't care at all for a place where people are subjected to an unnatural way of life. To strive for freedom is fine. I can even understand dying for it. But to turn living people into mere vegetables, without passion or drive, is beyond me. To live in poor housing, shun amenities, sing the Lord's praises, shout out patriotic slogans—fine! But to stifle in humans the very desire for beauty! What kind of humans have no feeling for beauty, no zest for life? Show me the difference between the ashrams, madrasas and vidyalayas that accomplish this and a field of horseradishes!

Babaji sat talking about the other activities in Jallianwala Bagh with Ghulam Ali and Nigar for a long time. Finally he told the couple, who, apparently, had not forgotten the purpose of their visit, to return there, and promised to wed them himself in the evening on the following day.

The two were elated. What greater fortune could there be than to have Babaji himself perform their marriage! Ghulam Ali later told me that he had become so overjoyed he thought it couldn't be true. Babaji's slightest gesture turned into a historic event. He couldn't believe that such a great man would personally come to Jallianwala Bagh for the sake of an ordinary man, a man who had become the Congress's 'dictator' merely by accident. Precisely the headline which splashed across the front pages of newspapers throughout India.

All day long Ghulam Ali wondered whether Babaji would really show up. Wasn't he a terribly busy man after all? But the doubt, which he had raised as a psychological precaution, proved wrong. Promptly at 6 p.m., just as the bushes of *raat ki rani* were beginning to pour forth their fragrance, and a band of volunteers who had set up a small tent for the bride and groom was decorating it with jasmines, marigolds and roses, Babaji walked in, supporting himself on his lathi, with the patriotic song-spouting pandit girl, his secretary and Lala Hari Ram in tow. The news of his arrival came moments before when Lala Hari Ram's green car pulled up at Jallianwala Bagh's main entrance.

I too was there. In another small tent, lady volunteers were helping Nigar into her bridal attire. Ghulam Ali had made no special arrangements. He'd spent the whole day negotiating with the city's banias for provisions to feed the volunteers, after which he'd stolen a few moments to talk briefly with Nigar in private, and then, as I recall, told the officers under his charge only that at the end of the wedding ceremony he and Nigar would raise the flag together.

Ghulam Ali was standing by the well when he heard that Babaji had arrived, and, if I remember correctly, I was asking him, 'You know, Ghulam Ali, don't you, how this well was once filled to its mouth with the bodies of people slain in the firing? Today everybody drinks from it. It has watered every flower in this park. People come and pluck those flowers. But strangely, not even a drop carries the salty taste of blood. Not a single petal of a single flower has the redness of blood in it. Why is that?'

I vividly remember that as I spoke I had looked at the window of a neighbouring house where, it is said, a young girl had been shot dead by General Dyer as she stood watching the massacre. The streak of blood had begun to fade on the old lime wall behind the window.

Blood had become so cheap that spilling it no longer affected people as it once had. I remember I was in the third or fourth standard at school, and six or seven months after the bloody massacre our teacher had taken us to see Jallianwala Bagh. It hardly looked like a park then, just a dreary and desolate stretch of uneven earth, strewn all over with clods of dried dirt. I remember how the teacher had picked up a small clod, reddened I believe from paan spittle, and showed it to us, saying, 'Look, it's still red from the blood of our martyrs!'

As I write this story myriad things keep coming to mind. But it is the story of Ghulam Ali and Nigar's marriage that I want to write, isn't it?

Anyway, upon hearing that Babaji had arrived, Ghulam Ali rushed to gather the volunteers in one place. Together they gave Babaji a military salute. The two inspected different camps for quite some time. All the while Babaji, who had a keen sense of humour, fired off numerous witty remarks during conversation with female volunteers and other workers.

In the meantime, the evening haze began to settle over Jallianwala Bagh and lights came on here and there in nearby houses. A group of volunteer women started to chant bhajans. They sang in unison, some sweetly, but most harshly and out of tune. Together, though, they sounded pleasant enough. Babaji was listening with his eyes closed. Roughly a thousand people must have gathered. They sat on the ground around the platform. Except for the bhajan-singing girls, everyone else was quiet.

The chanting tapered off into a silence which seemed anxious to be broken. So when Babaji opened his eyes and trilled sweetly, 'Children, as you already know, I'm here to unite these two freedom lovers in marriage,' the entire Bagh resonated with loud cries of jubilation.

Nigar, in her bridal attire, sat in a corner of the platform, her head bowed low. She looked very lovely in her tricoloured khadi sari. Babaji motioned for her to come closer and sat her next to Ghulam Ali, which caused more cries of delight.

Ghulam Ali's face was unusually flushed. When he took the wedding contract from his friend and handed it over to Babaji, I noticed his hand was shaking.

A maulvi sahib was also present on the platform. He recited the Qur'anic verse customary at weddings; Babaji listened to it with closed eyes. The custom of 'proposal and acceptance' over, Babaji gave his blessing to the bride and groom. Meanwhile, the congratulatory showering of the couple with *chhuwaras*—dried dates—traditional at such events, had begun. Babaji snatched a dozen or so for himself and tucked them away.

Smiling shyly, a Hindu girlfriend of Nigar's gave Ghulam Ali a tiny box as a present and whispered something in his ear. He opened the box and covered the parting in Nigar's hair with powdered sindoor. The drabness of Jallianwala Bagh was enlivened again with a round of loud applause.

Babaji got up amidst all the noise. A hush instantly fell over the crowd.

The mixed fragrance of raat ki rani and jasmine wafted by on the light evening breeze. The scene was absolutely breathtaking. Babaji's voice had acquired an extra measure of sweetness today. After congratulating the couple on their wedding, he said, 'These two will work for their country and nation with even greater dedication now, because the true meaning of marriage is nothing but true friendship between a man and a woman. Ghulam Ali and Nigar will work together as friends for swaraj. Such marriages are commonplace in Europe—I mean marriages based on friendship and friendship alone. People who are able to exorcize carnal passion from their lives are worthy of our respect.'

Babaji explicated his concept of marriage at length. He firmly believed that the true joy of marriage was something above and beyond the bodily union of husband and wife. He didn't consider sexual union as important as people generally made it out to be. Thousands of people ate just to satisfy their craving for flavour. But did this mean that to do so was incumbent on humans? Although few people ate solely out of the need to stay alive, they alone knew the true meaning of eating. Likewise, only those people who married out of the desire to experience the purity of this emotion and the sanctity of this sacred relationship truly enjoyed connubial bliss.

Babaji expounded on his belief with such clarity and profound sincerity that an entirely new world opened up before his listeners. I too was deeply touched. Ghulam Ali, who sat opposite me, was so engrossed in Babaji's speech that he seemed to be drinking in every word. When Babaji stopped, Ghulam Ali briefly consulted with Nigar, got up, and declared in a trembling voice:

'Ours will be just such a marriage. Until India wins her freedom, our relationship will be entirely like that of friends.'

More shouts of applause followed, brightening the dreary atmosphere in Jallianwala Bagh with cheery tumult for quite a while. Shahzada Ghulam Ali grew emotional, and streaks of red blotched his Kashmiri face. 'Nigar!' he addressed his bride in a loud voice. 'Could you bear to bring a slave child into this world?'

Dazed in equal parts by the wedding and by Babaji's lecture, Nigar lost what little presence of mind she had when she heard this question. 'No! Of course not!' was all she could get out.

The crowd clapped again, transporting Ghulam Ali to an even higher pitch of emotion. The joy at saving Nigar from the ignominy of birthing a slave baby went to his head, and he wandered off the main subject into the tortuous byways of how to free the country. For the next hour he spoke non-stop in a voice weighed down by emotion. Then, suddenly, his glance fell on Nigar, and he was struck dumb. He couldn't get a word out. He was like a drunkard who keeps pulling out note after note without any idea of how much he is spending and then suddenly finds his wallet empty. The abrupt paralysis of speech irritated him greatly, but he immediately looked towards Babaji, bowed and again found his voice: 'Babaji, bless us to remain steadfast in our vow.'

Next morning at six Shahzada Ghulam Ali was arrested. In the same speech in which he had vowed not to father a child until the country gained her freedom, he had also threatened to overthrow the English.

A few days after his arrest Ghulam Ali was sentenced to eight months' imprisonment and sent to the Multan jail. He was the forty-first 'dictator' of Amritsar and, if I remember correctly the figures quoted in the newspapers, the forty-thousandth political activist apprehended and imprisoned for taking part in the movement for independence.

Everybody thought that freedom was just around the corner. The astute British politicians, however, let the movement run its course. The failure of the major national leaders of India to reach an agreement pretty much took the teeth out of it.

Following their release, the freedom lovers tried to put the memory of their recent hardships behind them and get their interrupted business back on track. Shahzada Ghulam Ali was let go after only seven months. Even though the revolutionary fervour had subsided considerably by then, people did show up at the Amritsar railway station to greet him, and a few parties and rallies were held in his honour. I attended all of them. But they were largely lacklustre affairs. A strange fatigue seemed to have come over people, like runners returning listlessly to the starting line after being suddenly told, 'Stop! We'll have to do it over,' in the middle of a dash.

Several years passed. The listlessness, the exhaustion still hung over India. My own life went through a series of upheavals, some major, some minor. A beard and moustache sprouted on my face. I entered college and twice failed in my FA. My father died. I knocked about looking for a job and found work as a translator for a third-rate newspaper. Fed up, I decided to go back to school and enrolled in Aligarh University, but I contracted tuberculosis and found myself wandering around rural Kashmir three months later, recuperating. Then I headed for Bombay. Witnessing three Hindu–Muslim riots in two years was enough to send me packing to Delhi. But that city, by comparison, turned out to be terribly drab, with everything moving at a snail's pace. Even where there was some sign of activity, it had a distinctly feminine feel to it. Maybe Bombay isn't so bad after all, I thought, even if your next-door neighbour has no time to ask your name. What of it? Where there is time, you see a lot of hypocrisy, a lot of disease. So after spending two uneventful years in Delhi I returned to fast-paced Bombay.

It had been eight years since I left home. I had no idea what my friends were doing; I barely remembered the streets and by-lanes of Amritsar. How could I? I hadn't kept in touch with anybody from home. As a matter of fact, I'd become somewhat indifferent to my past in the intervening eight years. Why think about the past? What good would it do now to total up what was spent eight years ago? In life's cash, the penny you want to spend today, or the one another may set his eyes on tomorrow is the one that counts.

Some six years ago, when I wasn't quite as hard up, I'd gone to the Fort area to shop for a pair of expensive dress shoes. The display cases in a shop beyond the Army & Navy Store on Hornby Road had been tempting me for some time. But since I have a particularly weak memory, I wasn't able to locate the shop in question. Out of habit I started to browse in other stores, even though I'd come specifically to buy shoes. I looked at a cigarette case in one store, pipes in another, and then I strolled on until I came to a small shop that sold footwear. I stopped and decided to look for a pair there. The attendant greeted me and asked, 'Well, Sahib, what may we show you?'

For a moment or two I tried to remember what I had come to buy. 'Oh, yes. Show me a pair of dress shoes with rubber soles.'

'We don't stock them.'

The monsoons will start any day now, I thought. Why not buy a pair of gumboots? 'Well then, how about gumboots?'

'We don't sell those either,' the man said. 'Try the shop next door. We don't stock any rubber footwear at all.'

'Why?' I asked out of curiosity.

'Orders from the boss.'

There was nothing I could do but leave after that brusque but definitive reply. As I turned to go, my eyes fell on a well-dressed man with a child in his arms standing outside on the footpath buying a tangelo from a street vendor. I stepped out just as he turned towards the store. 'You! Ghulam Ali!'

'Saadat!' he shouted and hugged me, the child in his arm sandwiched between us. Unhappy with the situation, the infant started to cry. Ghulam Ali called the man who had attended me, handed the child over to him and said, 'Go! Take him home!' Then he said to me, 'It's been ages, hasn't it?'

I probed his face. The swagger, the ever-so-slight trace of rakishness that had been such a prominent feature of his appearance had entirely disappeared. It was a common family man who stood before me, not the fiery young khadi-clad speech-maker. I remembered his last speech, when he had energized the otherwise bleak atmosphere of Jallianwala Bagh with his sizzling hot words, 'Nigar! Could you bear to bring a slave child into this world?' Instantly I thought of the child Ghulam Ali was holding in his arms until a few moments ago.

I asked him, 'Whose child is that?'

'Mine, of course,' he answered, without the least hesitation. 'I have an older one too. And you, how many do you have?'

For a second I felt it was somebody else talking. Hundreds of questions rattled in my mind: Had Ghulam Ali completely forgotten his vow? Had he dissociated himself entirely from political life? The ardour, the passion to win freedom for India—where had they gone? Whatever happened to that naked challenge? Where was Nigar? Had she been able to bear giving birth to two slave children after all? Maybe she'd died and Ghulam Ali had remarried.

'What are you thinking?' Ghulam Ali smacked me on the shoulder and said. 'Come on, let's talk. We've met after such a long time.'

I started, let out an elongated 'Yes-s-s', and fumbled for words. But Ghulam Ali didn't give me a chance and began speaking himself instead: 'This is my shop. I've been living in Bombay for two years. Business is good. I can easily save three, even four hundred rupees a month. What are *you* doing? I hear you've become a famous short story writer. Remember the time we ran off to Bombay together? But, yaar, that was a different Bombay. It was small. This one is huge. Or it seems so to me, anyway.'

Meanwhile, a customer walked in, looking for tennis shoes. Ghulam Ali told him, 'No rubber stuff here. Please go to the shop next door.'

'Why not?' I asked Ghulam Ali as soon as the customer left. 'I was looking for a pair of shoes with rubber soles myself.'

I'd asked the question only casually, but his face fell. 'I just don't like them,' he said, softly.

'What do you mean, "them"?'

'Rubber—I mean things made of rubber.' He tried to smile, but couldn't. He let out a laugh instead, loud and dry. 'Okay, I'll tell you. It's a silly thing, but somehow it's had a significant impact on my life.'

Traces of deep reflection appeared on his face; his eyes, playful as ever, dimmed for a second and then lit up again. 'That life—it was absolutely phoney! To tell you the truth, Saadat, I've completely forgotten the days when this thing about being a leader had gotten into my head. The past four, five years have been pure bliss. I can never thank God enough for all He's given me. I have a wife, children . . .'

'Thanking God enough' got him started about his business venture: the initial investment, the profit he'd made in a year's time, the money he had in the bank now.

I interrupted him. 'But what's this "silly thing" that had a profound impact on your life?'

The glow once again disappeared from his face. 'Ye-e-e-s,' he said. 'It *had* a profound impact. Thank God it no longer does. I guess I'll have to tell you the whole thing.'

Meanwhile, the attendant returned. Ghulam Ali left him in charge of the store and ushered me into his room in the rear. Here, leisurely, he told me why he had developed such a dislike for rubber goods.

'You know how I got started on my political career. And you also know what kind of character I had. We were pretty much alike. I mean, let's be honest, our parents couldn't brag about us being without blemish. I don't know why I'm telling you this. Maybe you get my drift. I wasn't endowed with a strong character. But I had this desire to do something. That's what drove me to politics. I swear to God that I was not a fake. I could have laid down my life for the country. I still can. All the same, I feel—in fact, it's a conclusion I've come to after much serious thought—that India's politics and her leaders are all pretty green, as green as I used to be. A tidal wave rises, but I think it doesn't rise on its own, it's deliberately created . . . Perhaps I haven't been able to lay it all out for you clearly.'

His thoughts were terribly muddled. I gave him a cigarette. He lit it, took a few long drags and continued, 'What do you think? Doesn't every effort India has made to free herself look unnatural? Perhaps not the effort, maybe I should say the outcome of the effort. Why have we failed to achieve freedom? Are we a bunch of sissies? Of course we aren't. We're men. But the environment is such that our energies fall short of what's needed to reach our goal.'

'As if there is a barrier between us and freedom?' I asked.

His eyes gleamed. 'Absolutely. But not like a solid wall or an impenetrable rock. It's like a membrane at the most, a cobweb, created by the way we conduct our politics and live our sham lives. Lives in which we deceive others, and ourselves even more.'

His thoughts were still in a jumble. He seemed to be trying to make an accounting of all his past experiences on the spot. He stubbed out the cigarette, looked at me and said, 'A person should stay the way God made him. He does not need to shave his head, wear red ochre clothes, or cover his body with ash to perform good deeds, does he? You might say a person does all those things out of his own free will. That's just it. This novelty, "out of his own free will", is precisely what leads people astray, at least that's what I think. Their lofty position makes them indifferent to natural human weaknesses. But they completely forget that it is not their character, thinking or beliefs that will endure in the minds of simple people—as a matter of fact, these disappear into thin air in no time at all. What does endure, rather, is the image of their shaven heads, red ochre garb and ash-smeared bodies.' Ghulam Ali grew terribly excited. 'The world has seen a whole host of reformers. Nobody remembers their teachings. But crosses, sacred threads, beards, bracelets and underarm hair survive. We're more experienced than our ancestors a thousand years ago. I can't understand why none of these contemporary reformers can see that he's disfiguring humans beyond all hope of recognition. There are times when I feel like screaming: "For God's sake, haven't you deformed him enough already? At least take pity on him now and let him be! You want to make him a God, while the poor thing, he's having a hard time just holding on to his humanity."

'Saadat, I swear to God this is how I feel. If it's wrong and false, then I don't know what is right and true. For two full years I've wrestled with my mind. I've argued with my heart, with my conscience, in fact with every pore of my body. In the end, I feel humans must remain humans. If a couple wants to curb their carnal passion, let them. But the entire human race? For God's sake! What good will all that "curbing" accomplish?'

He stopped briefly to light another cigarette, letting the entire matchstick burn itself out, shook his head ever so slightly, and continued: 'No, Saadat, you cannot know the incredible misery I've been through, in my body and in my soul. But it couldn't be otherwise. Whoever attempts to go against nature is bound to come to grief. The day I made that vow in Jallianwala Bagh—you remember, don't you, that Nigar and I would not bring any slave children into this world—I felt an electrifying surge of happiness. I felt that with that declaration my head had started to soar upward until it touched the sky. However, when I got out of jail the painful realization slowly took hold of me that I had curbed a vital part of my body and soul, that I had crushed the prettiest flower in my garden between my palms. At first the thought brought an exhilarating sense of pride: I had done what others could not. Slowly, when my reasoning became clear, the bitter truth began to sink in. I went to see Nigar. She had given up her job at the hospital and joined Babaji's ashram. Her faded colour, her altered mental and physical condition—I thought I was mistaken, that my eyes were being deceived. Spending a year with her convinced me that her torment was the same as mine, although neither of us wanted to mention it to the other, feeling the noose of our vow tighten around us.

'All that political excitement simmered down within a year. Khadi clothes and the tricolour flag no longer seemed so attractive. And even if the cry of "Inqilab Zindabad" did go up now and then, it had lost its previous resonance. Not a single tent could be seen anywhere in all of Jallianwala Bagh, except for a few pegs left in the ground here and there as reminders of a time gone by. The political fervour had pretty much run out of steam.

'I spent most of my time at home, near my wife . . .' He stopped, the same wounded smile playing on his lips once again. I kept quiet so as not to interrupt his train of thought.

After a while he wiped the perspiration off his forehead, put out his cigarette and said, 'We were both struck by a strange curse. You know how much I love Nigar. I'd think: "What kind of love is this? When I touch her, why don't I allow the sensation to peak? Why do I feel so guilty? As if I'm committing a sin?" I love Nigar's eyes so much. One day when I was feeling normal . . . I mean just how one should feel, I kissed them. She was in my arms—or rather I should say, I had the sensation of holding a tremor in my arms. I was about to let myself go, but managed to regain control in time. For a long while afterwards, several days in fact, I tried to convince myself that my restraint had given my soul a pleasure few had experienced. The truth was that I'd failed. And that failure, which I wanted to believe was a great success, made me the most miserable man on earth. But as you know, people eventually find ways to get around things. Let's just say I found a way around it. We were both drying up. Somewhere deep inside a crust had started to form on our pleasures. "We are fast turning into strangers," I thought. After much thinking we felt that we could . . . without compromising our vow . . . I mean that Nigar wouldn't give birth to a slave child . . .' The wounded smile appeared a third time, dissolved immediately into a loud laugh, with a distinct trace of pain in it; then he continued in an extremely serious tone of voice: 'Thus started this strange phase of our married life. It was like a blind man suddenly had sight restored in one eye. I was seeing again. But soon the vision blurred. At first we thought . . .' He seemed to be fishing for the right word. 'At first we felt satisfied. I mean we hadn't the foggiest idea that we'd start feeling terribly dissatisfied before long. As though having one eye wasn't enough. Early on we felt we were recovering, our health was improving. A glow appeared on Nigar's face, and her eyes shone. For my part, my nerves no longer felt so hellishly strung out all the time. Slowly, however, we turned into rubber dummies. I experienced this more than she did. You wouldn't believe it, but, by God, every time I pinched the flesh of my arms, it felt like rubber. Absolutely. As though I didn't have any blood vessels. Nigar's condition, I believe, was different. Her perspective was different too. She wanted to become a mother. Every time a woman in our lane had a baby, Nigar would sigh quietly. I didn't much care about having children. So what if we didn't have any? Countless people in the world don't either. At least I had remained steadfast in my vow. And that was no mean achievement. Well, this line of thinking did comfort me quite a bit, but as the thin rubbery web began to close around my mind, I became more and more anxious. I grew overly pensive, the feel of rubber clung to my mind. At meals the food felt chewy and spongy under my teeth.' A shudder went through his body as he said this. 'It was disgusting! All the time it felt as though soap lather had stuck to my fingers and wouldn't wash off. I started to hate myself. I felt all the sap had drained out of me and something like the thinnest of skins was left behind—a used sheath.'

He started to laugh. 'Thank God I'm rid of that abomination now, but at what cost, Saadat! My life had turned into a dried-up, shrivelled-up piece of sinew, all my desires smothered. But, oddly, my sense of touch had become unusually keen, almost unnaturally keen. Maybe not keen, but focused, in one direction only. No matter what I touched, wood, glass, metal, paper or stone—they all had the same clammy tenderness of rubber that made me sick! My torment would grow even worse when I thought about the object itself. All I needed to do was grab my affliction in my two fingers and toss it away, but I lacked the courage. I longed for something to latch on to for support, for the merest straw in this ocean of torment, so that I might reach the shore. I kept looking for it desperately. One day as I sat on the rooftop in the sun reading, rather browsing, through a religious book, my eyes caught a Hadith,[*] and I jumped for joy. The "support" was staring at me. I read the lines over and over again. I felt as if water had gushed through the desiccated arid landscape of my life. It was written: "It is incumbent on man and wife to procreate after they are married. Contraception is permissible only in the event of danger to the lives of parents." Then and there I peeled off my affliction and threw it aside.'

He chuckled like a child. I did too, because he had picked up the cigarette with his two fingers and tossed it aside like some infinitely revolting object.

All of a sudden he became serious. 'I know what you'll do, Saadat,' he said. 'You'll turn all I've told you into a story. But, please, don't make fun of me in it. I swear to God, I've told you only what I've felt. I won't get into a debate over this with you. But the substance of what I've learned is this: It's no bravery to fight nature, no achievement to die or live starving, or to dig a pit and bury oneself in it for days on end, or sleep for months on a bed of sharp nails, or hold one arm up for years until it atrophies and turns into a piece of wood. This is show business. You can't find God or win freedom with show business. I even think the reason India hasn't gained freedom is precisely because she has more showmen than true leaders. And the few leaders she does have are going against the laws of nature. They have invented a politics that stops faith and candidness from being born. It is this politics which has blocked the womb of freedom.'

[*] A saying of the Prophet Muhammad.

Ghulam Ali wanted to say more when the attendant walked in. He had a child, perhaps Ghulam Ali's second boy, in his arms. The boy was holding a colourful balloon. Ghulam Ali pounced on it like a madman and it burst with a loud boom. A piece of rubber dangling from a little bit of string remained in the boy's hand. Ghulam Ali snatched it with two fingers and threw it away like some infinitely revolting object.

The Last Salute

This battle for Kashmir was nothing like any other battle. It had confused Subedar Rub Nawaz so much that he couldn't think clearly. He felt as though he had turned into a rifle, but one whose trigger was jammed.

He had fought on many fronts in the last Great War and knew how to kill and be killed. All the high- and low-ranking officers regarded him with admiration and respected his wits, daring and pluck. The platoon commanders always assigned him the most hazardous duty and he never failed to live up to their expectations. But this battle . . . it was so strange. He had joined it with great fervour and passion, obsessed with the single thought—annihilate the enemy at any cost. But when he confronted the enemy, he saw familiar faces. Some had once been his friends, his bosom buddies in fact. They had fought alongside him against the enemies of the Allied forces, but now they seemed to have become sworn enemies hell-bent on killing him.

Sometimes it all seemed like images in a dream: the declaration of the last Great War, enlistment, the usual physical tests, target practice, being packed off to the front and moved from one theatre of war to another, and, finally, the war's end. And close upon its heels the creation of Pakistan, followed immediately by the Kashmir war—so many events occurring in dizzying succession. Could it be that all this was done to confound people, to prevent them from taking the time to grasp it all? Why else would all these momentous events occur so rapidly that it made your head spin?

Subedar Rub Nawaz understood one thing: They were fighting to win Kashmir. Why did they need to win Kashmir? Its annexation was

vital for the survival of Pakistan. But as he took aim to shoot and a
familiar face appeared on the opposite side, he forgot for a moment why
they were fighting, why he had lifted his gun and aimed. At such times
he had to remind himself repeatedly that he was no longer fighting for
the wages, a parcel of land or medals, but for his country. But this was
his country before too, wasn't it? He belonged to this same region that
had now been included in Pakistan. Now he had to fight the very person
who, not long ago, had been his countryman—why even his next-door
neighbour, and their two families had bonded for generations. All of a
sudden that man's country had become an alien piece of land where he
had never set foot before, whose water he had never tasted. He had been
given a gun and ordered, 'Go fight for this land where you still haven't set
up your home, acquired a taste for its water or gotten used to the feel of
its air. Go fight Pakistan—where you've lived so many years of your life.'

Rub Nawaz's thoughts drifted off to the Muslim soldiers who
had been forced to abandon their homes and property to come here.
Whatever they owned had been taken away. And what had they found
here? Nothing, except guns, of the same weight and calibre, even the
same make.

Whereas before they had fought together against a common enemy,
whom they had merely imagined to be their enemy for the sake of their
stomachs and rewards and recognition, now they had themselves split
into two groups. They were no longer Indian soldiers, but Indian and
Pakistani soldiers. The thought that there were still Muslim soldiers back
in India flummoxed his mind, and when he thought about Kashmir his
mind became even more muddled. It just refused to think further. Were
Pakistanis fighting for Kashmir or for Kashmiri Muslims? If the latter,
why not also fight for the Muslims of Hyderabad and Junagarh? And
if this was purely a war for Islam, why weren't other Muslim countries
fighting alongside of them?

After thinking long and hard, Rub Nawaz concluded that these
matters were far too subtle for the intelligence of an ordinary soldier,
who needed to be a little thick in the head if he wanted to be a good
soldier. It was best not to think about them. There were times, though,
when his disposition got the better of him and he did pursue these
thoughts furtively only to have a hearty laugh about his lapse.

The battle for control of the road that led from Muzaffarabad to
Kiran had been raging along the banks of the Kishan Ganga for some

time. It was a strange battle. At night, rather than the sound of bullets, a crescendo of abuses, each one smuttier than the last, rose from the neighbouring hills.

One evening, as Subedar Rub Nawaz was getting his platoon ready for a surprise assault, a barrage of obscenities shot up from a trench below their position. Initially he freaked out. It seemed as if a gang of afreets were jitterbugging and laughing raucously. 'Pig's ass,' he muttered. 'What the hell's going on?'

One member of his platoon responded with a filthy abuse and said to Rub Nawaz, 'Subedar Sahib, the motherfuckers are swearing at us.'

At first, when he heard the provocative insults, Rub Nawaz thought of throwing himself headlong into the fray, but decided to hold back. His men couldn't stay quiet for very long. Soon they had had enough and began returning the enemy's noxious abuse with their own, equally hideous, invectives at the top of their lungs. It was a peculiar battle for Subedar Rub Nawaz. He tried a few times to restrain his men, but the profanities got so vicious it wasn't possible to hold back.

Naturally the enemy couldn't be seen at night, but it also couldn't be spotted in daylight because of the cover of thick vegetation. Only their foul abuse rose from the foothills, crashed against the rocks and melted into thin air. Rub Nawaz felt that his men's counter-abuses probably weren't making it all the way down the valley but were simply evaporating overhead. This rattled his nerves and in a huff he ordered them to attack.

He noticed something rather peculiar about the hills. Some were densely covered with trees and vegetation on the upward slope and entirely barren on the downward, while others were the reverse, with tall, sturdy pines on the downward side. The needles on these pines were so damp that the boots of the soldiers lost all traction so his men kept slipping again and again.

On the hill occupied by the Subedar's contingent, the slope provided no cover as it was completely without trees or brush. It was obvious the attack would be quite hazardous, but his men, chomping at the bit to get even for the blistering obscenities hurled at them, were more than willing to go for it anyway. As it turned out, they were successful. Their losses included two men dead and four wounded. The enemy lost three men and the rest took to their heels, leaving their provisions behind.

The Subedar and his men were terribly disappointed that they were unable to capture even a single enemy soldier alive whom they would have treated to their choicest profanities for as long as they liked. However, they did succeed in capturing a major enemy fortification. Rub Nawaz immediately relayed the outcome of the attack to his platoon commander, Major Aslam, over the wireless and received his commendation.

Almost every hill had a pond at the top, including the one they had captured. This one was quite a bit larger than the others and had crystal clear water. Everyone took a dip despite the frigid weather. Their teeth chattered, but they didn't care. They were still splashing when the sound of a gunshot rang through the valley. They all immediately dropped flat on the ground, completely naked. A little while later Subedar Rub Nawaz scanned the downward slope with his binoculars, but failed to spot the enemy hideout. As he was looking, another gunshot rang out. He saw smoke rising from a relatively low hill just beyond the bottom of the slope. Without delay he ordered his troops to open fire.

A volley of bullets rained down and was returned from the other side. Subedar Rub Nawaz tried to study the enemy position through his binoculars. Most likely they were huddled behind a pile of large stones but this provided scanty cover. He was sure they couldn't remain there much longer. The second any of them decided to make a move, they would come within range of his men's guns.

Firing continued for a while. Eventually he ordered his men to save their ammunition and shoot only when the enemy made a move and was exposed. Just then he noticed his naked body and muttered under his breath, 'Goddamn it . . . Without clothes a man looks like an animal!'

Now and then the enemy fired a random bullet that was returned just as sporadically from this side. This silly game continued for two whole days. The weather had suddenly turned brutally cold, so cold that it froze your blood even in the daytime. Subedar Rub Nawaz got round after round of tea going to stay warm. The kettle was kept at a boil all the time, but they never took their eyes off the enemy. When one soldier had to move, another took the binoculars and kept watch.

A bone-piercing wind was gusting. When the soldier on lookout said there was some surreptitious movement behind the stone fortification, Subedar Rub Nawaz took the binoculars himself and peered through them. He didn't detect any movement. Suddenly a call tore through the air, its echo ricocheting for a long time against the rocks in the clump of neighbouring hills. He couldn't make out what it was saying. He fired a shot in exchange. Once the echo of his fire had died out, the same voice rose again. Clearly, it was calling him. 'You pig's ass!' he shouted back. 'What do you want?'

'Don't call me bad names, brother,' the enemy shouted. Apparently he wasn't too far away.

Rub Nawaz looked at his men and repeated 'brother . . .' just as surprised as he was pissed off. Then he cupped his hands around his mouth and yelled, 'No brothers here, only your mottha's, fuckers.'

'Rub Nawaz,' a wounded voice rose quickly from the other side.

Rub Nawaz trembled.

The pained voice kept crashing against the hills, repeating 'Rub Nawaz . . . Rub Nawaz' like a refrain, each with a different cadence, before it evaporated into the freezing air.

Rub Nawaz came around after a long time. 'Who might that be?' he said to himself, and then muttered, 'Pig's ass!'

He knew that the bulk of the Tetwal front was made up of troops from the old 6/9 Regiment; he had been one of them too. But the voice—whom did it belong to? Many people had been his close friends, and there were others he bore enmity towards on account of some personal matters, but who was this person who had taken his abuse to heart and was calling out loudly to him? He brought the binoculars to his eyes and peered through them again. He couldn't see anyone in the sparse, swaying vegetation on the hill. He cupped his hands around his mouth again and blared, 'Who is it? This is Rub Nawaz . . . Rub Nawaz.'

And this 'Rub Nawaz' also kept bouncing off the rocks. 'Pig's ass!' he muttered again.

Instantly a voice boomed, 'It's me . . . it's Ram Singh.'

Rub Nawaz jumped, as if he wanted to leap over to the other side right away. 'Ram Singh,' he first said to himself, and then he screamed at the top of his voice, 'Ram Singh! Hey you, Ram Singha . . . Pig's ass!'

Before 'pig's ass' had time to crash against the hills and disappear altogether, Ram Singh's cracking voice shot up, 'You, potter's ass!'

Rub Nawaz fumed. With commanding presence he looked at his troops and muttered, 'He's talking shit, pig's ass.' And then he retorted to Ram Singh, *'Oaye, Baba Tal ke karah parshad—Oaye, khinzeer ke jhatke!'*

---

* The term used in the story refers to the halva offering made at Baba Tal and to the meat of an animal slaughtered by one blow of the sword. Muslims consider this method of slaughter religiously unlawful.

Ram Singh started to laugh uncontrollably, so did Rub Nawaz.
The hills tossed their exchange playfully back and forth. Subedar Rub
Nawaz's men were dead silent.

When the hysterical bout of laughter subsided, Ram Singh's voice
rose. 'Look, yaar, we'd like to drink some tea.'

'So drink. Have fun.'

'How can we have fun?' Ram Singh shouted. 'All our stuff is over
there.'

'Over where?' Rub Nawaz asked.

'Over there, where your bullets can make us into mincemeat.'

Rub Nawaz laughed. 'So what do you want, pig's ass?'

'Just let us retrieve it.'

'All right, go get it.' Rub Nawaz looked at his men.

Ram Singh's anxious voice came back, 'You'll fire on us, potter's
ass.'

An irritated Rub Nawaz shot back, 'Damn you, you lousy turtle,
stop raving!'*

Ram Singh let out a big laugh. 'Swear that you won't fire.'

'Swear by what?'

'By anyone, doesn't matter.'

'Okay, send someone out to grab your stuff,' Rub Nawaz said
grinning.

Silence pervaded the atmosphere for a few moments. Rub Nawaz's
man, who had the binoculars trained on the enemy, gave him a look
and was about to fire when Rub Nawaz stopped him emphatically, 'No!
Don't!'

He snatched the binoculars from the man's hand and squinted
into it. He saw a man slithering out from behind the pile of stones and
advancing gingerly on tiptoe. He walked like this for some distance and
then suddenly took off at a gallop, disappearing quickly into the bushes. A
couple of minutes later he emerged carrying some stuff in his hands. He
stopped for a moment before bolting towards the makeshift fortification
and slipping into the precarious safety of that buffer. The second he
disappeared from sight Rub Nawaz pulled the trigger of his gun. His loud
laughter and the bullet's ping rose almost simultaneously, reverberating
in the valley for a while, followed by Ram Singh's 'Thank you!'

---

* Originally, 'Stop babbling, you Santokh Pond turtle!'

'Don't mention it,' Rub Nawaz acknowledged. Then, looking at his men, he said, 'What do you say, shall we have a round?'

A few rounds of gunfire were exchanged playfully and then a hush fell over the landscape for some time. Rub Nawaz looked through the binoculars again and spotted a cloud of smoke curling up from the hill. 'So have you fixed your tea, Ram Singha?' he shouted.

'Not yet, potter's ass,' came the answer.

Rub Nawaz was a potter by caste. His blood boiled whenever anyone even vaguely hinted at his origins. Only with Ram Singh it was different. Rub Nawaz didn't let it get on his nerves with him because Ram Singh was a special chum of his. They had grown up in the same village and were born only a few days apart. Not just their fathers, even their grandfathers had enjoyed close, friendly ties. Rub Nawaz and Ram Singh had gone to the same primary school and enlisted in the army on the same day. In the last Great War they had fought side by side on several fronts.

Feeling embarrassed before his men Rub Nawaz mumbled, 'Pig's ass, he never gives it up.' And then he hollered at Ram Singh, 'Don't go shooting off your mouth, you lice-infested donkey.'

Ram Singh's loud laugh shot through the air. Rub Nawaz had his gun aimed in the direction of the enemy and let it go off playfully. A scream tore through the air. He quickly peered into the binoculars and saw a man rise and hobble out from behind the stone bulwark, doubled over. Holding his stomach, the man crumbled to the ground after going a short distance. It was Ram Singh.

'Ram Singh!' Rub Nawaz screamed and jumped to his feet. Immediately, three or four shots were fired from the other side. One bullet brushed past his right arm. He quickly threw himself on the ground face down. His men started firing back but failed to hit the enemy, so he ordered them to attack. Three lost their lives within seconds but the rest kept advancing and, with great difficulty, finally managed to capture the other hill.

Ram Singh was lying on the rocky ground in a pool of blood, groaning. He had been hit in the stomach. A gleam appeared in his eyes when he saw Rub Nawaz. Smiling he said, 'You potter's ass, you did this . . . Whatever for?'

Rub Nawaz felt as if he was the one who had been shot in the stomach and was now writhing in agony. He smiled, bent over Ram

Singh and started to unfasten his belt. 'Pig's ass, who asked you to
stand up?'

As his belt was loosened, Ram Singh cried out from the intensity
of the pain. Rub Nawaz examined the wound. It was very nasty. Ram
Singh pressed Rub Nawaz's hand and mumbled in a feeble voice, 'I only
got up to show myself to you and you fired, you son of a gun.'

'I fired just for the heck of it. I swear to God, the One and Only
One,' Rub Nawaz said in a choking voice. 'I knew you, always an ass,
were getting up . . . I'm so sorry.'

Ram Singh had lost a lot of blood. It had taken a few hours for Rub
Nawaz and his men to get over here, long enough for Ram Singh to
lose a whole bucket's worth of blood. Rub Nawaz was amazed that Ram
Singh was still alive. He didn't expect him to last long. Moving him was
out of the question. He got on the wireless and requested his platoon
commander to dispatch a medic immediately; his friend Ram Singh had
been wounded badly.

Rub Nawaz knew it would be impossible for the medic to arrive in
time and that it was a matter of minutes before Ram Singh's life ebbed
away. After sending the message he smiled and said to Ram Singh, 'The
medic is on his way. Don't worry.'

In a sinking voice, Ram Singh said pensively, 'Why would I
worry . . . But tell me, how many of my men have you killed.'

'Only one.'

'And yours?' Ram Singh inquired still more feebly.

'Six,' Rub Nawaz lied, giving his men a meaningful look.

'Six . . . six,' Ram Singh counted in his heart. 'My men lost their
spirit when I was wounded. But I told them to fight on, risking their
lives . . . Six, yes.' Then his mind drifted off into a hazy past. 'Rub Nawaz
. . . you remember those days, don't you?'

And he went down memory lane, talking about their childhood,
their village, the stories of their schooldays and of their time in the
6/9 Jat Regiment, the jokes about their commanding officers and their
affairs with strange women in foreign lands. Somewhere along the way
he remembered something interesting and let out a big laugh, which
sent a wave of excruciating pain through his body, but he paid no
attention to it and said, still laughing, 'You, pig's balls, you remember
that madam?'

'Which one?'

'The one in Italy. We used to call her . . . What was it now? Some woman she was, a real man-eater . . .'

Rub Nawaz remembered her right away. 'Yes, yes, that . . . Madame Moneyto Finito, "no money, no action". But now and then she let you have a ride for less, that daughter of Mussolini.'

Ram Singh laughed loudly, some clotted blood gushing from his wound as a result. Rub Nawaz's makeshift bandage had slipped off. He secured it in place and admonished Ram Singh, 'Don't talk.'

Ram Singh was running a high fever and this made his brain work faster. Although he had no strength left, he was babbling on and on, stopping briefly now and then as if to check how much petrol was still left in his tank. Soon afterward he lapsed into a delirium punctuated by moments of perfect lucidity. During one lucid moment, he asked Rub Nawaz, 'Yaar, tell me honestly, do you people really want Kashmir?'

Rub Nawaz replied in all earnestness, 'Yes, Ram Singha, we do.'

'No, no, I can't believe it. You've been taken for a ride.'

'No, it's you who's been taken for a ride,' Rub Nawaz said emphatically to convince him. 'I swear by Panchtan Pak.'

'No, yaar, don't swear.' Ram Singh grabbed his hand as he said, 'Maybe you're right.' But it was evident from his tone that he didn't believe Rub Nawaz.

Major Aslam, the platoon commander, arrived with some of his soldiers a little before sundown, but there was no medic. Floating between semi-consciousness and the throes of death, Ram Singh was babbling about something, but his voice was so weak and broken that it was difficult to make out his words. Major Aslam had also been part of the 6/9 Jat Regiment and knew Ram Singh quite well. He had Rub Nawaz tell him the details about what had transpired and then he called out, 'Ram Singh! Ram Singh!'

Ram Singh opened his eyes and came to attention still lying on the ground. He raised his arm with great difficulty and saluted. For a moment he looked at the major closely and then his rigid arm fell limply to his side. He started to murmur in visible irritation, 'O Ram Singha, you pig's balls, you forgot this is a war . . . a war . . .'

He couldn't finish. His slowly closing eyes looked at Rub Nawaz with bewilderment and then he turned cold.

A Tale of the Year 1919

'This, brother, is about an event that occurred in 1919. All of Punjab—Amritsar, to be more exact—was in the throes of awful turmoil due to the Rowlatt Act. Under the Defence of India Rules, Sir Michael O'Dwyer had banned Gandhiji's entry into the Punjab. Gandhiji was on his way there when he was stopped at Palwal, arrested, and sent back to Bombay. In my opinion, had the British not acted so rashly, the Jallianwala Bagh incident wouldn't have added such a gory chapter to the dark history of their rule.

'Whether Muslim, Hindu or Sikh, everyone held Gandhiji in the highest esteem and considered him a Mahatma. The minute the news of his arrest reached Lahore, all business came to a dead stop. And in Amritsar the news led to an almost immediate general strike.

'It is said that the Deputy Commissioner had already received orders for the expulsion of Dr Satyapal and Dr Kitchlew on the evening of 9 April but he was unwilling to enforce them. He didn't think anything untoward was likely to happen in Amritsar. Protest demonstrations had been generally peaceful so far; the question of violence didn't arise. I'm telling you what I witnessed myself. It was the day of the Ram Navami festival. A procession was taken out, but no one dared take a single step against the wishes of the rulers. However, brother, this Sir Michael—he had lost his mind. Obsessed as he was with the fear that these leaders were simply waiting for a sign from Mahatma Gandhi to overthrow British rule, and that a conspiracy was lurking behind all these demonstrations and strikes, he ignored the wishes of the Deputy Commissioner.

'The news of Dr Satyapal's and Dr Kitchlew's expulsion had spread through the city like wildfire. Every heart was tense with apprehension, fearing that something dreadful was about to happen. Yes, brother, there was a palpable feeling of heightened emotion everywhere. All businesses had come to a standstill and a deathly silence had enveloped the city, the kind that pervades cemeteries. However, the surface calm was not without the resonance of the passion raging beneath it. Following the news of the expulsion orders, people began to assemble in thousands, intending to march to the Deputy Commissioner Bahadur and petition him to rescind the orders seeking the banishment of their beloved leaders. But, my brother, those were not the times when petitions were heard; a tyrant in the guise of Sir Michael was the chief administrator. Would he hear the petition? Not a chance. He declared the gathering itself in violation of the law.

'Amritsar, once the biggest centre of the freedom struggle, wearing the wounds of Jallianwala Bagh like a proud emblem—ah, what straits it is in today! But let's not linger over that painful story. It weighs heavily on the heart. People blame the British for the ghastly events that were visited upon this great city five years ago. Maybe they were. But, brother, if the truth be told, our own hands were equally stained with the blood that was shed there. But that's another matter . . .

'Like every other big officer and all the toadies of the British, the Deputy Sahib's bungalow was located in the exclusive area of the Civil Lines. Now, if you are familiar with Amritsar, you would know that a bridge connects the city with this quarter. Once you cross this bridge, you come on to the Mall where the British rulers had built themselves this earthly paradise.

'Anyway, when the procession was nearing the Hall Gate it came to be known that mounted British troops were posted on the bridge. However, the crowd marched on undaunted. I can't even begin to describe how excited they were. But every last one of them was unarmed; no one had even a measly stick on him to speak of. They only wanted to lodge a collective protest against the arrest of Dr Satyapal and Dr Kitchlew and press for their unconditional release. The procession kept advancing on the bridge. The goras opened fire when the protesters got close. Suddenly a stampede broke out. There were only a few dozen troops and the crowd numbered in the hundreds, but, brother, bullets can knock the daylights out of anyone. An unimaginable confusion erupted. Some were wounded by gunshots, others trampled underfoot.

'I was standing near the edge of a filthy ditch on the right. A violent push threw me into it. After the firing stopped I pulled myself out. The people had scattered. The wounded were lying on the road and the gora soldiers were on the bridge, laughing. What my mental state was at the time I have no idea, but I couldn't have been in full possession of my senses. The fall into the ditch had completely disoriented me. It was only after I had pulled myself out that the whole event began to slowly reconstruct itself in my mind.

'I could hear a terrible noise rising far in the distance, as if some people were screaming and yelling angrily. I crossed the length of the ditch and, going through the tomb-sanctuary of Zahira Pir, arrived at Hall Gate. There I saw a group of thirty or forty extremely agitated young men throwing rocks at the big clock above the Gate. When the glass on the clock shattered and fell to the ground, one of the young men shouted to the rest of his mates, "Let's go and smash the Queen's statue!"

'Another one suggested, "No, yaar, let's set the police headquarters on fire instead."

'"And all the banks," added a third.

'A fourth young man stopped them. "Wait! What's the point of that? Let's go to the bridge and make short work of the goras."

'I recognized this fellow; he was Thaila Kunjar, tall, athletic and quite handsome. His real name was Muhammad Tufail, but he was better known as kunjar because he was the offspring of a prostitute. He was quite the tramp and had become addicted to gambling and drinking at a young age. His sisters Shamshad and Almas were the most beautiful prostitutes of their time. Shamshad had an exquisite voice and the filthy rich travelled great distances just to attend her *mujras*. The sisters had had enough of their brother's unseemly conduct. It was known throughout the city that they had more or less disowned him. Even so, one way or other, he always managed to trick them into giving him whatever he needed. He always looked dapper, ate and drank well, had refined tastes, and was full of wit and humour, with none of the ribald vulgarity associated with *bhand*s and miraasis.

'The agitated young men paid no heed to his words and started advancing towards the Queen's statue. "I said don't waste your energy,"

Thaila admonished them again. "Come with me. Let's beat the hell out
of the goras who murdered our innocent people. Together we can easily
wring their necks. Come on!"

'By then some boys had already left for the statue, the rest halted
and followed Thaila as he started for the bridge. I thought to myself,
these boys, their mothers' darlings, are walking towards certain death.
From my hiding place near the fountain, I called out to Thaila, "Don't
go, yaar, why do you want to risk your life and theirs?"

'He let out a strange, raucous laugh and said, "Thaila wants the
goras to know that their bullets won't scare him away." He then turned
to his companions and added, "If you're afraid, you're free to leave."

'In a situation such as this it's hard to go back once you've started,
especially when your leader is going forward fearlessly, showing little
regard for his life.

'The bridge isn't all that far from the Hall Gate, some sixty or seventy
yards at most. Thaila was ahead of everyone. Twenty steps away, where
the railings of the bridge began, two mounted goras stood on guard.
When Thaila approached the railings, shouting slogans, a shot was fired.
I thought he had fallen, but he continued to advance undaunted. His
pals panicked and took to their heels. He turned around and shouted,
"Don't run away. Come on!"

'He was facing me as he said that, but then he turned to look at
the goras while reaching with his hand to feel his back. In spite of the
distance, I saw that red spots had appeared on his white bosky shirt.
He darted forward like a wounded tiger. Another gunshot rang out.
He wobbled a little and then pounced on one of the mounted goras.
Within a second, the saddle was empty and the gora was flat on the
ground with Thaila on top of him. The other soldier, a bit confused at
first, tried to rein in his horse, which was bolting from fright, and then
started shooting wildly. I haven't the foggiest idea what happened next
for I blacked out and fell to the ground by the fountain.

'When I came to, brother, I found myself in my own house.
Apparently some people who knew me had carried me there. I
learned from them that the crowd, after being fired upon at the
bridge, had become so enraged that it had attempted to knock down
the Queen's statue. The Town Hall and three banks were torched.
About half a dozen Europeans were butchered and widespread
looting had ensued.

'The Brits didn't care much about the looting; it was the murder of half a dozen Europeans that raised their hackles. The result was the bloody massacre at Jallianwala Bagh. Deputy Commissioner Bahadur had handed over the city to General Dyer and, on 12 April, General Sahib marched with his troops through numerous bazaars in the city, arresting many dozens of innocent citizens.

'The following day some twenty-five thousand people gathered at Jallianwala Bagh in a peaceful meeting. General Dyer arrived at the scene towards evening with a contingent of armed Gorkha and Sikh soldiers who opened fire on the unarmed civilians.

'No one had a clear idea of the number of casualties. Later, when the matter was investigated, it was revealed that about a thousand people had been mowed down and three to four thousand were wounded. . . . But I was talking about Thaila. I'm telling you about what I saw myself . . . God alone is perfect. Thaila, of course, couldn't be. On the contrary, he had all four major shar'i faults. Though a prostitute's womb had nurtured him, he was exceptionally brave. I can now say without a doubt that when he turned around, looked at his companions and urged them to keep their spirits up, he had already taken the first bullet fired by that accursed gora. In the heat of the moment, he likely hadn't realized that red-hot lead had penetrated his chest. The second bullet hit him in the back, the third again pierced his chest. I didn't see it myself but I've heard that when Thaila's corpse was disengaged from the gora, his fingers were still dug so deeply into the throat of the gora who'd already gone to hell that only with tremendous effort could the two be pulled apart.

'The next day his body, riddled with bullet holes, was delivered to his family for burial. Apparently the other gora had emptied his revolver into a dead Thaila merely for target practice.

'People say that when his corpse arrived it stirred up quite a commotion among the residents of his neighbourhood. True, he was not well liked by his folks, but the sight of his mangled body made everyone burst into loud crying. His sisters Shamshad and Almas fainted on the spot. As the bier was carried out for burial, their agonized wailing touched everyone so deeply that they couldn't stop their tears— tears of blood.

'Brother, I've read somewhere that it was a prostitute who was struck down by the first shot fired during the French Revolution.

Muhammad Tufail was the son of a prostitute. No one has bothered to find out whether it was the first bullet, the fifth or the fiftieth that felled him in this struggle for freedom, likely because the poor man didn't pull much weight in society and amounted to nothing. I doubt Thaila Kunjar's name appears in the record of those who were drenched in this bloodbath of Punjab, or even that such a record was ever compiled.

'Those were stormy days. A military government was in power. The monster called martial law was bellowing in every street and alley of the city. The poor man was interred in great confusion and a big hurry, as if his doleful relatives were guilty of this grievous crime and wanted to erase every last trace of it.

'Brother, that's how Thaila died . . . and was buried . . . and . . .'

My fellow traveller hesitated and paused for the first time. The train was thundering along, the rattling wheels repeating the same refrain, 'Thaila died, Thaila buried . . . Thaila died, Thaila buried.' It was as if there was no space between dying and being buried, as if here he died, here he was buried. The two words blended with the rattle with such a lack of feeling that I had to expel them from my mind. I asked my chance companion, 'You were about to say something more.'

He looked at me with a start. 'Yes, the most painful part of the story remains to be told.'

'What's that?' I asked.

'As I already mentioned, Thaila had two sisters, Shamshad and Almas, both stunningly beautiful. Tall, with very delicate features and big beautiful eyes, Shamshad was a superb singer of thumris. People say that she had taken lessons from Khan Sahib Fateh Ali Khan. Musically not much to speak of, Almas was an exquisite dancer, entirely peerless in her ability to express different emotional states through her movements. In mujra performances it seemed that every atom of her body participated in the dance and every gesture carried a meaning. The beauty of her eyes never failed to captivate her audience.'

My companion was taking more time than I thought was necessary in praising the accomplishments of the two sisters, but I didn't interrupt him as it didn't seem proper. After a while he broke out of this lengthy adulation and came to the most tragic part of the story.

'Well, brother, it's like this: Some bootlicker out to ingratiate himself with the British told the army officers about the ravishing beauty of the sisters. A memsahib—what was the witch's name? Yes,

Miss Sherwood—had been killed in the riots. It was decided to send
for the sisters and . . . and . . . take it out on them for the death of the
Englishwoman . . . You know what I mean, brother?'

'Yes, I do,' I said.

'In times such as this,' he said, heaving a deep sigh, 'even dancing
girls and prostitutes are like our mothers and sisters. Their honour must
be protected. But, brother, would this country ever give a damn about
respect and honour? The minute the police chief received the orders
from his superiors, he immediately went into action. He went to the
sisters himself and told them that the sahib-logs had summoned them
. . . to perform. Just think about it, brother. Thaila hadn't been dead
two days, the earth on his grave was still moist, and they were ordering:
Come and dance in our imperial presence, for our entertainment.
Could there be a more cruel method of exacting revenge? You won't
find any example of a more atrocious way of belittling someone! The
people who issued these orders, didn't they think that even a prostitute
has, could have, her honour, her dignity? Of course she could—why
not?' He asked himself, though, clearly, I was his audience.

'Yes, surely, she could have her honour.'

'Quite right. After all, Thaila was their brother. And he hadn't
lost his life in a gambling-den brawl or in a bout of drunkenness
at some sleazy tavern. He had courageously quaffed the wine of
martyrdom for the sake of his country. He was a prostitute's son
but that prostitute was also a mother; Shamshad and Almas were
her daughters, Thaila's sisters first, prostitutes later. And they had
fainted at the sight of his corpse, they had poured their hearts out
at his funeral to such an extent that whoever heard their wails had
broken into tears—tears of blood.'

'So did they go?' I asked.

He didn't answer for some time and then said in a voice laden with
sadness, 'Yes . . . yes they did . . . Fully decked out.' Sadness suddenly
gave way to a sharp tone of bitterness. 'They went to their callers all
dolled up and prettied. It was a lively soiree full of fun and . . . So I've
heard. Both sisters put on a stunning performance. In their glittering
peshwaz dresses they looked like the proverbial fairies of Mt Caucasus.
Wine flowed freely and they sang and danced with abandon. The
merrymaking continued well into the night until the party ended at a
sign from a senior officer.'

My fellow traveller abruptly stood up and began staring at the trees as they flitted by outside the window frame.

The train chugged on. The metallic clatter of the wheels on the tracks seemed to be repeating his words, 'Party ended . . . party ended.'

Tearing those words from my mind I asked him, 'What happened then?'

Taking his eyes off the trees and electric poles as they flew by, he replied in a firm voice. 'What happened? They tore off their glittering dresses and, standing there stark naked, said, "Here, take a good look at us . . . we are Thaila's sisters . . . you riddled his body with your bullets only because it harboured a patriotic spirit. We're his beautiful sisters. Come, defile our perfumed bodies with your vile passion . . . But before you do . . . allow us to spit in your faces!"'

He fell silent, as if he had nothing more to say.

'What happened after that?' I asked quickly.

His eyes welled up with tears. 'They were shot . . . shot dead on the spot.'

I didn't say anything. The train slowed and pulled into the station. He hailed a coolie to carry his bags. As he was leaving, I asked, 'The ending of the story you just told . . . it seems as if you made it up yourself?'

He started and looked at me. 'How did you know?' he asked, surprised.

'How? Your tone was filled with incredible agony.'

Swallowing his bitterness with a glob of saliva, he replied, 'Yes, those bitches . . .' He held himself back from cursing and added after a pause, 'They disgraced their brother's selfless martyrdom.'

With that he got off the train and walked away.

Frozen

The instant Eshar Singh stepped into the room Kalwant Kaur sprang up from the bed, walked over to the door and bolted it, glaring at him. It was midnight. The suburbs were sunk in an eerie quiet.

Kalwant Kaur sat down on the bed and crossed her legs. Eshar Singh stood quietly in a corner holding his kirpan, perhaps trying to straighten out his muddled thoughts. A tense silence prevailed for some moments. Kalwant Kaur didn't like the way she was sitting, so she lowered her legs and started swinging them. Still Eshar Singh didn't say a word.

Kalwant Kaur was a plump woman with a heavy, broad rear end and oversized, fleshy breasts projecting upward a bit too much. A bluish shadow covered her upper lip and the shape of her chin betrayed that she was no less than an Amazon.

Eshar Singh still stood in the corner with his head drooping downward. His tightly wrapped turban was beginning to come loose and the hand holding his kirpan was trembling a bit. Despite that, his tall frame and his appearance left no doubt that he was every bit the man for a formidable woman like Kalwant Kaur.

The relentless silence raised her hackles and her patience soon ran out. She glowered at Eshar Singh but could only exclaim, 'Eshar *saiyaan*!'

He raised his head and looked at her, only to quickly turn his face away from the penetrating intensity of her sharp gaze.

'Eshar saiyaan,' she started to scream, but quickly stifled it. Hopping off the bed, she walked over to him and asked, 'Where have you been hanging out all these days?'

'I have no idea,' he replied, running his tongue over his parched lips.

'What kind of fucking answer is that?' she asked in a rage.

He tossed the kirpan aside and slumped down on the bed, looking as though he'd been feeling ill for some time.

She glanced at the bed, now dwarfed by his big, burly body. A surge of compassion for the man swelled in her heart. She touched his forehead and lovingly asked, '*Jaani*, what's wrong?'

Eshar Singh was staring up at the ceiling but turned his gaze and probed the face he knew so well. 'Kalwant.'

She could sense a distinct pain in his voice. The whole of her seemed to have gathered in her upper lip. 'Yes, jaani?' she said tenderly, biting her lip.

Eshar Singh took off his turban and looked at her, his eyes begging for understanding and comfort. He slapped her big, fleshy bottom, jerked his head and said to himself, 'I'm going nuts.'

His kes came undone with the jerk. Kalwant Kaur started combing her fingers through it and asked lovingly, 'Eshar saiyaan, where have you been all this time?'

'At my enemy's mother's!' he said, looking at her intently. All of a sudden he started kneading her fleshy buttocks vigorously. 'I swear by Wahe Guru, you're one awesome woman!'

She pushed his hands away indifferently and asked, 'Tell me, on my life, where have you been? In the city?'

With a single movement Eshar Singh wound his hair into a bun and answered, 'No.'

She was ticked off. 'Damn it, you did go there. And you stole a lot of money that you don't want to tell me anything about.'

'May I not be my father's son if I'm lying to you!'

That seemed to quiet her down, but only for a while. Within seconds she flared up again. 'But I can't understand what got into you that night. You lay beside me after you gave me all that jewellery you looted in the city . . . you were madly kissing me all over . . . And then, abruptly, you just got out of bed, put on your clothes and dashed out.'

Eshar Singh blanched. She was quick to notice how his colour had paled and immediately said, 'Look how your face has changed. Eshar saiyaan, by Wahe Guru, something is fishy here.'

'Nothing is fishy, I swear by your life.'

But his voice lacked conviction, which reinforced her suspicions. Pursing her lips and enunciating every word emphatically, she asked, 'Eshar saiyaan, come clean. You're not the man you were eight days ago.'

He sat up with a start, as if he'd been attacked. Gathering her in his robust arms, he started gnawing at her vigorously. 'Jaani, I'm the same Eshar. Squeeze me harder, so it cools off the heat in your bones.'

She didn't resist him, but kept up her earlier litany. 'What happened to you that night?'

'The enemy's mother got fucked, that's all.'

'Come on, won't you tell me?'

'There's nothing to tell.'

'May you cremate my body with your own hands if you don't tell me the truth!'

He flung his arms around her neck and pressed his lips to hers. A few bristles of his bushy moustache tickled her nose and she sneezed. They both laughed.

He took off his quilted vest and ogled her lustily. 'Come on, let's play a round of cards,' he said.

Tiny beads of perspiration sprouted on Kalwant Kaur's upper lip. She rolled her eyes coquettishly and blurted out, 'Get lost!'

He pinched her ample bottom hard, making her flinch. She withdrew to one side. 'Don't do that, Eshar saiyaan, it hurts.'

He went over to her and pulled her upper lip between his and started to nibble at it. She melted away. He took off his shirt and tossed it away, saying, 'Well then, let's get on with a round of trumps.'

Her upper lip began to quiver with anticipation. With one quick movement Eshar Singh peeled off her shirt like an experienced butcher pulling the hide right off the body of a slaughtered animal in a single perfect motion. Staring lasciviously at her naked form, Eshar pinched her arm and said, 'Kalwant, I swear by Wahe Guru, you're one hell of a delicious woman!'

Kalwant looked at the red welt slowly appearing on her arm. 'You're really a brute, Eshar saiyaan.'

He laughed through his bushy moustache. 'So let brutality reign tonight,' and with that he launched into more of the same. He scraped his teeth against her upper lip, nibbled at her earlobes, ravaged her voluptuous breasts, whacked her bottom resoundingly, kissed her cheeks raw, sucked her nipples so much that the drool was smeared over her entire chest, until she began to boil. But none of this foreplay helped rouse him, to create even the slightest tremor of passion. Like a beaten wrestler flat on his back, he tried all the holds and manoeuvres he knew. None worked. Taut as a string ready to be strummed, and frustrated with all these unnecessary preliminaries, Kalwant Kaur said, 'That's enough shuffling, Eshar saiyaan, throw the card now!'

Eshar Singh felt as though the entire deck had slipped from his hands, and plopped down on to the floor. He gasped and threw himself down beside Kalwant Kaur, his forehead drenched in a cold sweat. Kalwant Kaur made frantic efforts to instil some passion into him but failed. So far everything had proceeded without a word, but when her overheated female parts didn't receive the expected gratification, she got out of bed in a huff. Pulling the sheet hanging from the peg, she quickly threw it around herself. Her nostrils flared and she fumed. 'Eshar saiyaan, who's the bitch you've been with who's squeezed you dry?'

Eshar Singh remained in bed, panting, and didn't answer.

She exploded angrily, 'I'm asking you—who's the whore? Your lover, your trump card?'

'No one, Kalwant,' Eshar Singh mumbled, his voice sounding drained, 'no one.'

With her arms akimbo Kalwant Kaur thundered resolutely, 'Eshar saiyaan, I'll get the truth out of you today, I swear by Wahe Guru. Isn't there a woman lurking behind all this?'

Eshar Singh wanted to say something but Kalwant Kaur didn't let him. 'Before you swear, don't forget, I'm Sardar Nihal Singh's daughter. If you lie to me, I'll make mincemeat out of you. Now, swear by Wahe Guru. Isn't there a woman behind all this?'

In great agony Eshar Singh nodded in affirmation. Kalwant Kaur went completely wild. She leapt towards the corner and grabbed his kirpan. Ripping away the sheath like a banana peel and tossing it away, she struck Eshar Singh.

Jets of fresh, warm blood flowed down his body. Still not satisfied, Kalwant Kaur started pulling his kes like a wild cat, all the while hurling obscenities at her anonymous rival.

After some time, Eshar Singh said in a tired, meek voice, 'Let it go, Kalwant, let it go.'

The pain in his voice was heart-rending. Kalwant Kaur took a step back.

The blood spurting from his neck was staining his moustache. He opened his trembling lips, and looking at her with both protest and gratitude he said, 'My darling, you acted hastily, but I guess I deserved it.'

Kalwant Kaur's jealousy flared up again. 'Who is she—that . . .' she screamed.

The blood had now reached his mouth. As he tasted it a shiver ran through his body. 'I've killed six men with this very same kirpan . . .' he said.

Kalwant Kaur's mind was completely occupied with the other woman. 'Who is she—the bitch? I'm asking you.'

A glint appeared in Eshar Singh's eyes, which had begun to glaze over. 'Don't call her bad names.'

'I'm asking you to tell me who she is!' Kalwant Kaur screamed again.

'I'll tell you,' he began but his voice choked. He ran his hand over his neck and smiled as he looked at his fresh, warm blood. 'What a motherfucking creature man is!'

Kalwant Kaur, waiting for his answer, yelled with impatience, 'Eshar saiyaan, get to the point.'

His smile widened behind his blood-soaked moustache. 'I am coming to the point . . . My fucking throat is slit . . . I can only talk slowly.'

A cold sweat broke out on his brow as he spoke. 'Kalwant, my darling, I can't tell you what happened with me. Man is one weird creature. When looting broke out in the city, I joined in. Whatever jewellery and money I was able to lay my hands on, I gave to you, but I didn't tell you one thing.'

A jab of sharp pain in his wound made him groan in agony. Kalwant Kaur paid no attention to him and asked ruthlessly, 'What one thing?'

He blew away the specs of clotted blood from his moustache and continued, 'The house we broke into had seven people inside. I killed six of them . . . with this very same kirpan you've . . . But never mind. Listen . . . There was a girl . . . ravishingly beautiful . . . I threw her over my shoulder and . . . walked away with her. . .'

Kalwant Kaur listened attentively. Once again Eshar Singh blew the blood off his moustache. 'Kalwant jaani, I can't begin to tell you how staggeringly beautiful she was. I would have killed her too, but I thought, "No Eshar saiyaan, you enjoy Kalwant Kaur every day, have a taste of this fruit too."'

Kalwant Kaur only muttered, 'Huh!'

'I slung her across my shoulder and kept walking. On the way . . . What was I saying . . . yes, on the way, near the riverbank, I put her down under some cactus bushes. I first thought to shuffle her some, but then I changed my mind . . .' His throat went completely dry.

Kalwant Kaur swallowed nervously and asked, 'What happened then?'

He could hardly get the words out in his faltering voice, 'I threw the trump . . . but . . . but . . .'

His voice sank.

Kalwant Kaur shook him violently. 'What happened?'

Eshar Singh laboured to open his eyes and stared at Kalwant Kaur, her whole body quaking with rage. 'She was dead . . . a corpse . . . a hunk of cold flesh . . . Give me your hand, jaani . . .'

Kalwant Kaur put her hand on his, which was colder than ice.

Open It!

The special train left Amritsar at two in the afternoon, taking eight hours to reach Mughalpura. Quite a few passengers were killed along the way, several received injuries, and some just wandered off to God knows where.

At ten in the morning, when Sirajuddin opened his eyes on the bare, ice-cold ground of the refugee camp, he saw a surging sea of men, women and children swirling around him, and whatever little remaining ability he had to think and comprehend deserted him. He stared at the murky sky for the longest time. Despite the incredible din, his ears seemed to be deaf to any sound. Seeing him in this state anyone would have concluded that he was deeply engrossed in thought. That, of course, was not the case. He was totally numb. His entire being seemed to be suspended in space.

Gazing blankly at the dull sky his eyes collided with the sun and a shaft of intense light penetrated every fibre of his being. Suddenly he snapped back into consciousness. A series of images flitted across his mind—images of plunder, fire, stampede, a train station, gunshots, night, Sakina . . .

Sirajuddin jumped up with a start and made his way through the seemingly endless sea of humanity around him like a man possessed.

For three full hours he scoured the camp calling out 'Sakina! Sakina!' but found no trace of his teenage daughter. The whole area was rife with ear-splitting noises. Someone was looking for his child, another for his mother, still another for his wife or daughter. Finally Sirajuddin gave up and sank to the ground off to one side from sheer exhaustion, straining his memory to retrieve the precise moment when Sakina had separated from him. However, each effort to recall ended with his mind closing up at the sight of his wife's mangled body, her guts spilling out, and he couldn't go any further.

Sakina's mother was dead. She had died right in front of Sirajuddin's eyes. But where was Sakina? As she lay dying, Sakina's mother had urged him, 'Don't worry about me. Just grab Sakina and run!'

Sakina had been with him. Both of them were running barefoot. Her dupatta slipped off and when he stopped to pick it up, Sakina shouted, 'Abbaji, leave it!' He retrieved it anyway. Thinking about it now, his eyes spontaneously drifted to the bulge in the pocket of his coat. He plunged his hand in and brought out a piece of cloth. It was the same dupatta. There could be no doubt about it. But where was Sakina herself?

Sirajuddin strained his memory but his tired mind was muddled. Had he been able to bring her to the station? Was she with him aboard the train? Did he pass out when the rioters forced the train to stop and stormed in? Was it then that they carried her off?

His mind was bursting with questions, but there were no answers. He needed sympathy, but everyone around him needed it too. He wanted to cry, but couldn't; his tears had dried up.

Six days later, when Sirajuddin had recovered somewhat, he met a few people who were willing to help him. Eight young men equipped with a lorry and rifles. He blessed them and described Sakina to them. 'She is fair and exceedingly pretty. She takes after her mother, not me. She is about seventeen, with big eyes and dark hair. She has a beautiful big mole on her right cheek. She's my only daughter. Please find her. May God bless you!'

The young volunteers assured old Sirajuddin fervently that if his daughter was alive he would be reunited with her in a few days.

The volunteers didn't spare any effort. Putting their lives in harm's way, they went to Amritsar. They rescued several women, men and children and brought them to safety. Ten days passed but they found no trace of Sakina.

One day they were heading off to Amritsar on their rescue mission aboard the same lorry when they spotted a girl trudging along the road near Chuhrat. The sound of the lorry startled the girl and she took off in a panic. The boys stopped the lorry and ran after her. Eventually they caught up with her in a field. She was stunningly beautiful and had a big black mole on her right cheek.

'Don't be afraid,' one of the boys tried to reassure her. 'Are you Sakina?'

The girl turned deathly pale. She didn't reply. When the boys, all of them, reassured her gently, her fear subsided and she admitted that she was indeed Sakina, Sirajuddin's daughter.

The young men tried everything to lift her spirits. They fed her, gave her milk to drink, and then helped her into the lorry. One of them even took off his jacket and gave it to her because she was feeling quite awkward without her dupatta, and was making repeated but futile attempts to cover her chest with her arms.

Several days went by, but Sirajuddin received no news of Sakina. He spent his days making the rounds of different camps and offices but had no success in tracing his missing daughter. At night he prayed for the success of the volunteers who had assured him that if she was alive they would find her in a matter of days.

One day he saw those volunteers at the camp. They were sitting inside the lorry. Sirajuddin rushed over to them just as the lorry was about to take off, and asked, 'Son, did you find my Sakina?'

'Oh, we will, we will,' they said in unison and the lorry took off.

Once again Sirajuddin prayed for the success of these young men, which took some of the weight off his heart.

That evening he noticed a hullabaloo close to where he was sitting. Four men were carrying a stretcher. Upon inquiring he was told that a girl was found lying unconscious by the train tracks. He followed them. The men handed the girl over to the hospital staff and left.

For a while he stood leaning against the wooden post outside the facility and then he slowly walked inside. There was no one in the room. All he could see was the stretcher with a corpse lying on it. Sirajuddin advanced towards it, taking small, hesitant steps. All of a sudden the room lit up. 'Sakina!' he screamed, spotting the big black mole gleaming on the blanched face of the dead girl.

'What is it?' the doctor who had turned on the light asked him.

'I . . . sir, I . . . I'm her father!' the words came out with a rasp.

The doctor glanced at the body lying on the stretcher. He felt the pulse and, pointing at the window, told Sirajuddin, 'Open it!'

Sakina's body stirred ever so faintly on the stretcher. With lifeless hands she slowly undid the knot of her waistband and lowered her shalwar.

'She's alive! My daughter is alive!' Old Sirajuddin screamed with unbounded joy.

The doctor broke into a cold sweat.

Empty Bottles, Empty Cans

Why singles are so taken with empty bottles and cans continues to amaze me even now. By singles I mean men generally not interested in getting married—ever.

Granted, this breed tends to be eccentric and fosters idiosyncrasies; however, what throws me off is their exaggerated fondness for empty bottles and cans. Often they also keep birds and animals. I can understand their need for companionship, but empty bottles and cans? In heaven's name, what possible companionship can these inanimate objects offer?

Call it the result of transgressing nature if you wish to find a reason for such strange habits and eccentricities, but you can't explain it as easily in psychological terms. Indeed it's hugely difficult.

I have a relative, about fifty now, who is fond of keeping pigeons and dogs as pets. There's nothing odd about that. His affliction is this: Every day he goes to the bazaar to buy cream which he boils down to clarified butter. *This* is what he uses to cook his food. He believes this is how pure ghee is distilled.

He also keeps a reserve pot of water especially for his personal use. It's always covered with a piece of a thin, gauzy fabric to prevent insects from getting in while still allowing the continuous passage of fresh air. Before going to the toilet, he takes off all of his clothes, wraps a small towel around himself and slips on his wooden clogs. Now, if you want to understand the psychology behind the clarified butter, the thin, gauzy fabric over the mouth of the water pot, the towel and the wooden clogs—be my guest.

I have a friend—a single. He appears to be quite normal. He works as a reader at the high court. His affliction: He smells foul odours everywhere all the time. So, as a consequence, his kerchief is never far from his nose. He's fond of keeping rabbits.

There's another single. He drops down to offer namaz whenever and wherever the opportunity presents itself. But he's perfectly sane. He has a profound understanding of world politics. He's an expert in training parrots to speak.

And this wealthy old major in the military—he's fond of collecting hookahs. *Gurguri*s, *pechwan*s, you name it; he's got quite a collection. Although he owns several houses, a rented room in a hotel is where he lives. Pheasants are his passion.

And this retired Colonel Sahib, he lives in a spacious bungalow with his dozen or so dogs, big and small. He keeps a collection of whiskies, of all types and brands. He drinks four glasses every evening with one or another of his favourite canines and treats the dog to some as well.

All the singles I've mentioned so far are, without exception, fond of empty bottles and cans to one degree or another. Whenever my kinsman, the one who distils pure ghee from cream, spots an empty bottle anywhere in the house, he washes it thoroughly and puts it in his cupboard, thinking that it might come in handy some day. The high court reader, who only smells foul odours everywhere, all the time, collects only bottles and cans that he has made absolutely sure will never smell bad. The fellow who is ready to pray anywhere and any time keeps dozens of bottles to wash himself after going to the toilet and tin cans to use for ablutions. He thinks that these items are both inexpensive and clean. The major, who is given to stockpiling hookahs, collects empty bottles and cans for the sole purpose of selling them to scrap merchants. The retired colonel is only fond of collecting empty bottles of whisky. If you happen to visit him, you will see these whisky bottles neatly arranged inside several glass cabinets in a small, tidy room. No matter how antiquated the brand, you can be sure to find it in his rare collection. Just as some people are fond of collecting stamps and coins, he has a passion—or rather obsession—for collecting empty whisky bottles and displaying them.

The Colonel Sahib has no relatives. If he does have anyone, I'm certainly not aware of it. Even though he's all alone in the world, he doesn't suffer from loneliness at all. He's happy with his dozen or so dogs and he cares as much for them as an affectionate father for his children. He spends his entire day with his pets, and whatever free time he has is spent rearranging his darling bottles in their cabinets.

Now, you might say, well, all right, empty bottles make sense, but why have you tacked on empty cans along with them? Why in the world should it be necessary for a bachelor to be interested not just in empty bottles but also in empty cans? And whether bottles or cans—why should they be empty? Why not full?

Haven't I already told you that I wonder about that too? This and similar questions often assail my mind. Yet I'm unable to come up with an answer, no matter how hard I try.

Empty bottles and cans represent a void. The only logical connection between them and celibate men is perhaps that the latter's life is characterized by a gaping emptiness. This doesn't help, for it begs the question: Do such men try to fill one void with another? A person can at least say that dogs, cats, rabbits and monkeys fill the emptiness of a man's life to some degree. They can amuse with their funny antics and airs, and even respond to love. But what possible enjoyment can empty bottles and cans afford?

It's possible that the following might offer you an answer to these questions.

Ten years ago, when I went to Bombay, a film produced by a famous studio had been running for twenty weeks. The heroine was an experienced actress, but the hero was a complete novice and looked very young in the advertisements. After reading great things about his acting skills in the newspapers, I decided to go see the film. It was quite all right. The story was interesting enough and, considering that the hero was appearing before the camera for the first time in his life, his acting was okay.

It is generally difficult to guess the true age of an actor or actress on the screen. Thanks to the wonders of make-up, a young man can look years older, an old man like a strapping youth. But this newcomer was in fact quite young, vibrant and very agile, like a college student. Although not exactly handsome, every limb on his firm body was well proportioned and finely shaped.

In the years that followed I saw many more films with the same actor. He had become more mature in his work. The raw, boyish softness of his features had gelled into the firmness that comes with age and experience. He was now among the finest film stars in Bombay.

Scandals are nothing new in the film world. Every day brings the news that some actor has become amorously involved with some actress or other, or that actress X has ditched her lover for director Y. No actor or actress is immune from a romantic affair at some time or other. However, the life of this new actor was entirely free of any such entanglements. This fact, though, was not talked about much in the newspapers. No one ever mentioned, even in passing, that Ram Saroop's life was absolutely free of any kind of gossip in spite of his close involvement with the film world.

To tell you the truth, I'd never given much thought to these matters because I had absolutely no interest in the personal lives of film people. Watch a film, form a good or bad opinion of it, that was the extent of my involvement. However, when I met Ram Saroop, I learned many interesting things about him. This meeting took place nearly eight years after I saw his first film.

During his early days in the film industry he lived in a village quite far from Bombay. With his increasing involvement in motion pictures, he was obliged to move into a modest flat in the Shivaji Park neighbourhood near the sea. This flat was where I met him. It had four rooms, including the kitchen.

The family that lived here comprised eight members: Ram Saroop himself, his servant who doubled as the cook, three dogs, two monkeys and one cat. Ram Saroop and the servant were both bachelors; the dogs and the cat were also without mates of the opposite sex; the monkeys were the exception, but they stayed in their separate wire mesh cages most of the time.

Ram Saroop loved his six animals dearly. He also treated his servant kindly, which had little, if anything, to do with emotion. He had a set routine, and performed tasks at fixed times with the cold regularity of a machine, as if automatically. It almost seemed as though Ram Saroop had jotted down the set of rules and regulations governing his life and handed them over to his servant, who had then memorized them.

If Ram Saroop took off his clothes and slipped into a pair of shorts, the servant immediately placed a few bottles of soda and some flasks of ice on the glass-topped teapoy. This meant that the sahib would now drink rum and play with his dogs. If the phone rang in the meantime, he was supposed to say that the sahib was not home.

An empty bottle of rum or can of cigarettes was never to be trashed or sold. It was put away carefully in the sahib's room, which was already crowded with piles of empty bottles and cans.

If a woman came to the door, she would be turned away with the excuse that the sahib had spent the night shooting for a film and was asleep. If she showed up in the evening she was told that the sahib was out on a shoot.

The ambience of Ram Saroop's place wasn't very different from that of any bachelor who lives alone. It lacked the decor and tidiness beholden to a woman's delicate touch. Yes, it was neat and clean, but in a coarse sort of way. The first time I entered, the feeling that I'd stepped into the part of a zoo where tigers and cheetahs and such are kept overwhelmed me; it exuded the same animal odour.

One of the rooms was a bedroom, another a sitting room, and the third was where the empty bottles and cans were kept—all the rum bottles and cigarette cans that Ram Saroop had emptied himself. They were just sitting around haphazardly without any particular order, bottles and cans, one on top of the other, face up or face down. Some stood in a line in one corner, while others were just heaped up in another, coated with dust, giving off the pungent odours of stale tobacco and equally stale rum blended together.

I must say I was bowled over when I first saw this room, crowded as it was with numberless bottles and cans—all empty.

'What's going on?' I asked Ram Saroop.

'Whatever do you mean?'

'I mean this junk?'

'It just kind of piled up,' was all he could say.

'It would take seven or eight years to collect so much junk'—I thought out loud.

I was mistaken. As I later found out, it had taken ten. When he moved over to Shivaji Park he had hauled along all the bottles and cans that had accumulated in his old house. Once, I asked him, 'Saroop, why don't you sell these. In the first place, they shouldn't have been allowed to get out of hand, but now that they have, and you can get a good price on account of the war, you'd better get rid of this junk.'

His only answer: 'Drop it, yaar! It's just too much bother.'

This sort of gave the impression that he really had no interest in empty bottles and cans, but his servant let me in on the fact that Ram

Saroop raised hell if even a single bottle or can was moved from its place.

Ram Saroop had no interest in women. We had become close friends. Several times I asked him casually, 'So my friend, when are you getting married?' and each time I was given the same type of answer: 'Whatever for?'

'Yes, indeed, whatever for—really?' I thought. 'Will he shut her up in his junk room? Or play with her in his shorts as he sipped his rum?' While I did bring up the subject of marriage with him now and then, try as hard as I could, in my imagination I couldn't picture him with a woman.

Our association was now several years old. During this time the rumour went round several times that he had fallen in love with some actress named Sheela. I absolutely didn't believe in the veracity of the story. For one thing, it wasn't something one could expect from Ram Saroop; for another, Sheela wasn't quite the woman any sane young man would lose his heart to. She always looked lifeless, as though she was suffering from tuberculosis. She did look tolerable in her first few movies, but eventually lost whatever panache she might have had, morphing into a totally insipid, bland character, now consigned to appear only in third-class movies.

I asked him just once about this Sheela woman. He replied with a smile, 'Do you think she's the only woman left for me?' About this time his dearest dog Stalin caught pneumonia. Ram Saroop had it treated in the best way he knew, but the poor animal's days were numbered. Its death pained him deeply. His eyes remained teary for quite some time. Then one day he gave away his other dogs to a friend. I thought it was due to the terrible shock of Stalin's death, otherwise he would never have parted with them. However, it surprised me a bit when, not long afterwards, he also got rid of the monkeys. Must be because he didn't want to go through another harrowing experience in the future, I concluded. Now he only played with his cat Nargis, as usual, in his shorts while sipping rum. The cat loved him equally in return because she had no competition; she alone was the recipient of his affections.

Soon, his living quarters no longer smelled of tigers and cheetahs and reflected a noticeable order and taste in their decor. His face, too, now assumed a slightly fresher look. However, all this happened so slowly that it was difficult to determine the exact time of the onset of the change.

Time rolled on. His new film was released. I observed a marked freshness in his acting. When I congratulated him, he smiled and said, 'Come, have some whisky?'

'Whisky?' I asked, surprised. Didn't he always drink rum . . . only rum?

His earlier smile shrank somewhat on his lips as he answered, 'I'm tired of drinking rum.'

No further questioning was necessary.

A week later when I went to see him, he was drinking as usual, not rum but whisky, not in his shorts but in a kurta–pyjama. We played cards and drank for a long time. After a while I noticed his tongue and palate were having difficulty accepting the taste of the new drink, for with every sip he made a face as if he was drinking something foreign. I said to him, 'Looks as if you haven't got used to whisky yet, have you?'

'Oh, I will. Give it some time,' he said smiling.

Ram Saroop's flat was on the second floor. As I was passing by one day I saw great big piles of empty bottles and cans near the garage being loaded on to a couple of rickety carts by a few junk dealers. I was aghast; this treasure could only have belonged to Ram Saroop. I felt a tinge of indescribable pain to see it being hauled away. I ran up to his flat and rang the bell. The door opened, but when I tried to step inside his servant uncharacteristically stopped me, saying, 'Sahib was out on a shoot last night; he's sleeping now.'

I left in surprise and anger, muttering something under my breath.

That very evening Ram Saroop came to my house with Sheela in tow, draped in a new crisp Banarasi sari. 'Meet my wife,' Ram Saroop said, pointing at Sheela.

Had I not already downed four pegs of whisky I would certainly have been knocked out.

Both of them sat for a short while and then left. For a long time afterwards I kept ruminating: What did Sheela remind me of? A papery, beige sari over a sparse, thin body, puffed out here, shrunk there? Suddenly the image of an empty bottle floated before my eyes, an empty bottle wrapped in paper.

Sheela was a woman—totally empty, but it was possible that one void had filled another.

A Progressive

When Joginder Singh's short stories became popular it occurred to him that he could throw a party for famous prose writers and poets. He thought this would probably widen the scope of his popularity and acceptance.

Joginder Singh was nothing if not astute. After inviting the renowned litterateurs to his home and offering them great hospitality, he finally sat down with his wife Amrit Kaur and allowed himself to forget, at least for a moment, that he was just a clerk at the local post office where his real job was sorting mail. After he had relieved his head of the burden of carrying a three-metre-long, Patiala-style, coloured turban and put it aside, he invariably felt that the smallish head hiding under his long, jet-black hair was utterly filled with progressive literature. This feeling filled both his heart and mind with a strange elan. He believed the entire tribe of the world's short story writers and novelists was connected to him in a subtle relationship.

What Amrit Kaur had a hard time understanding, though, was why, every time her husband invited these people, he never failed to say to her, 'Amrit, these people who are coming for tea today, well, they're India's top-notch poets. Do you understand? Now don't you go cutting corners in showing them proper hospitality, okay?'

Sometimes it was India's top-notch poet, sometimes its greatest short story writer. Anyone less than that just didn't cut it. Then there was all that raucous conversation that went on at the party, every word of it went over her head. Progressivism was talked about with great gusto and Amrit Kaur was unable to understand any of it.

One time, after Joginder Singh finished entertaining a very great short story writer and came to sit in the kitchen area, Amrit Kaur asked, 'This blasted progressivism—what is it?'

With his turban still mounted, Joginder Singh shook his head slightly and said, 'You can't understand what it means just like that. A "Progressive" is someone who promotes "progress". It's a Persian word. In English such a person is called a "radical". *Afsana-nigars*— meaning short story writers—who seek "progress" in story writing are called *taraqqi-pasand*.* In all of India today there are only three or four progressive short story writers and I'm counted among them.'

Joginder Singh liked to express himself using English words and phrases and it had become second nature over time. So now, without the least bit of hesitation he thought in an English that was made up of the choicest and most pithy phrases taken from the writings of some famous English novelists. In about fifty per cent of ordinary conversation he used words and phrases culled from English books. He always called Aflatun, Plato and Arastu, Aristotle. He threw Freud, Schopenhauer and Nietzsche into every one of his important conversations for good measure, though in ordinary speech he never mentioned these philosophers, and when talking to his wife he took special care not to allow English words or these philosophers to come anywhere near.

Amrit Kaur was terribly disappointed when Joginder Singh finally explained the meaning of progressivism to her. She was under the impression that this subject so hotly debated by her husband with distinguished poets and fiction writers would be something truly great. But after she realized that all of India boasted only a smattering of progressive short story writers, a soft glint appeared in her eyes. When Joginder Singh saw it, his bushy-moustached lips quivered a bit in a faint smile. 'Amrit,' he said, 'you'll be pleased to know that a great man of India wants to see me. He's read my stories and likes them very much.'

'Is this great man a poet or a story writer like you?' Amrit Kaur asked.

Joginder Singh promptly took out an envelope from his pocket. Patting the back of his hand with it he said, 'He's both. But he's most famous for something entirely different.'

'And what might that be?'

* Progressive.

'Well, he's a wanderer.'

'A wanderer?'

'Yes, a wanderer . . . he's made drifting the sole aim of his life. He's always on the go. Now in the chilly valleys of Kashmir, now on the sun-swept plains of Multan. Sometimes in Sri Lanka, other times Tibet.'

Amrit Kaur's curiosity shot up. 'But what does he do?'

'He collects folk songs, from all over India. Punjabi, Gujarati, Marathi, Peshawari, Frontier, Kashmiri, Marwari . . . However many languages are spoken throughout India, and whatever folk songs he can find in those languages, he collects them.'

'So many songs! What will he do with them?'

'He writes books, articles . . . so others can also hear about those songs. Many English-language magazines have published his articles. To collect folk songs and then present them skilfully is no ordinary task. Amrit, he's a very great man, a truly great man. And look how cordially he's written to me.'

Joginder Singh read out the letter to his wife, the letter that Harendarnath Tirpathi had written to him at his post office address. Harendarnath Tirpathi had praised Joginder Singh's short stories in a delightfully sweet manner and written, 'You're a progressive writer of India.' When Joginder Singh read this phrase he couldn't resist commenting, 'Now see, Tirpathi Sahib also says that I'm a progressive.'

After reading the entire letter aloud Joginder Singh looked at his wife for a few seconds and then asked what she thought of it. 'So?'

Her husband's sharp, piercing gaze made Amrit Kaur blush a bit and then she smiled and said, 'What do I know? This is big man's talk, only a big man can understand it.'

Joginder Singh didn't catch the subtlety of her comment; he was somewhat preoccupied with the thought of inviting Harendarnath Tirpathi to stay with him for a while. 'Amrit,' he said, 'shouldn't we perhaps invite Tirpathi Sahib? What do you think? I wonder whether he might turn down our invitation. After all, he's a great man. He may think we're just trying to flatter him.'

On such occasions he always included his wife in the project so the work involved in inviting someone might be shared by both. As soon as he used the word 'our' Amrit Kaur, no less naive than her husband, started taking an interest in this Tirpathi fellow, although not only was the man's name something of a riddle for her, she also failed to comprehend how wandering around collecting folk songs could make someone great. When she was first told that Harendarnath Tirpathi collected folk songs, she was reminded of something her husband had once told her, namely, there were quite a few people in Vilayat* who earned a lot of money catching butterflies. The thought crossed her mind that maybe Tirpathi Sahib had learned collecting folk songs from some fellow from Vilayat.

Joginder Singh expressed his anxiety: 'Who knows, he might think our invitation is just some kind of flattery.'

'How could it be just flattery? Other great men come to visit you, don't they? Write him a letter. Something tells me that he *will* accept your invitation. Why, he's also eager to meet you, isn't he? But tell me: does he have a family? I mean a wife and children.'

'Family?' Joginder Singh mumbled, his mind busy composing the contents of the invitation in English. 'Perhaps. No, I'm sure he does. Come to think of it, I once read in an article that he has a wife and a little girl.'

Now that what he wanted to write in the letter had jelled in his mind, he got up, walked to the other room, took out a small letter pad—the one he used to correspond with only very special people—and started writing to Harendarnath Tirpathi in Urdu, or rather an Urdu translation of what he had thought up in English during the conversation with his wife.

In just three days he received Harendarnath Tirpathi's response. Joginder Singh opened the envelope with a throbbing heart. Upon reading that his invitation had been accepted, his heart throbbed even faster. His wife was outside in the sunlight rubbing yogurt into their young boy's hair when Joginder walked over to her with the envelope in hand. 'He's accepted my invitation. Says he was coming to Lahore anyway. He's got some important work to do here . . . Wants to arrange for the publication of his new book. He sends his greetings to you.'

A feeling of immense happiness washed over Amrit thinking that such a great man, who collected folk songs, had sent her his greetings. She thanked God from the depths of her heart for having been married to a man known to every great man in India.

It was the early days of a wintry November. Joginder Singh woke up around seven in the morning but lingered in bed with his eyes wide open. His wife and son lay on a cot nearby under a warm quilt. Joginder

* England.

started thinking about how immensely happy he would feel meeting
Tirpathi Sahib, and the latter no less happy meeting Joginder Singh,
India's youthful, up-and-coming short story writer and progressive
man of letters. He would engage Tirpathi Sahib on every subject under
the sun: folk songs, village dialects, short stories, recent events of the
war, etc., etc. He would tell him how, despite being just a hard-working
office clerk, he became a good writer. Amazing, wasn't it, that someone
who sorted mail was by disposition an artist?

Joginder Singh was mighty proud that even after toiling half the day
like a common labourer at the post office he could still find the time to edit
a monthly magazine, and contribute stories to two, even three publications,
to say nothing of those long letters he sent off to friends weekly.

He lay in bed for quite a while, preparing himself mentally for
his approaching meeting with Harendarnath Tirpathi. He had read
his stories and essays and had also seen his photograph. Usually, just
reading someone's stories and seeing his photo made Joginder Singh feel
that he had come to know the person quite well. But in Harendarnath
Tirpathi's case, he couldn't trust himself. Sometimes he felt that
Tirpathi was a complete stranger. In his fiction writer's mind, the man
appeared wrapped in reams of paper rather than clothes. And the paper
reminded him of the wall in Anarkali bazaar. It was plastered from one
end to the other with so many layers of cinema ads that it seemed as if a
second wall had sprung up in front of the original.

What if Tirpathi Sahib turned out to be such a man—Joginder
Singh wondered still lying in bed. In that case it would be very difficult
to understand him. Later, when he remembered his own penetrating
intelligence, all his uncertainties evaporated in an instant. He got up
and began preparing for Tirpathi's reception.

It had been settled in their correspondence that Harendarnath
Tirpathi would make his way to Joginder Singh's house himself; this
because he hadn't yet decided whether to travel by lorry or train. And
that Joginder Singh would take Monday off and wait for his guest at
home the whole day.

After bathing and changing, Joginder Singh walked into the kitchen
and sat with his wife for a long time. They took their tea quite late,
thinking that Tirpathi might arrive soon. But when he didn't, they put
the cake and other food back into the cupboard and just drank tea while
they waited for the guest.

Eventually, Joginder Singh got up and went into the other room. He was standing in front of the mirror sticking hairpins into his beard to keep it neatly pressed down when there was a knock at the door. He left his beard half-finished and dashed to the deorhi to open the door. As expected, it was Harendarnath Tirpathi's lush, black jungle of a beard, at least twenty times bigger than his own, that first came into view.

A smile fluttered across Harendarnath Tirpathi's lips, buried as they were under the thick mop of his moustache. One of his eyes, which was slightly crooked, became even more crooked. He jerked his unbelievably long hair and stuck out his hand—as calloused as a peasant's—towards Joginder Singh, who was greatly impressed by the steely grip and equally so by his leather bag that was as distended as a pregnant woman. 'Tirpathi Sahib, I'm very pleased to meet you' was all he could get out of his mouth.

It has been fifteen days since Harendarnath Tirpathi's arrival. His wife and daughter had been with him on the journey but they decided to stay at the home of a distant relative who lived in the Mozang area of Lahore. Tirpathi didn't think it proper for them to stay there long; two days later he had them move into Joginder Singh's house.

They spent the first four days talking many quite interesting things. Joginder Singh was very pleased to hear Harendarnath Tirpathi applaud his short stories. He read him an unpublished piece and received great praise. He even read him two stories he hadn't quite finished and Tirpathi expressed a good opinion about these as well. They also discussed progressive literature, noted technical flaws in a number of writers, and made a comparison of old and new poetry. In short, those four days brought them a surfeit of enjoyment. Tirpathi's personality left a deep impression on Joginder Singh. What he particularly liked about the man was his way of talking, at once childish and wise. The man's beard, twenty times bigger than his own, totally overwhelmed his thoughts, and the image of his long, jet-black hair, that had something of the flow of folk songs, never left Joginder Singh's eyes, not even when he took care of the mail at the post office.

Tirpathi completely claimed Joginder Singh's heart during these four days. He was so enamoured of the man that even his crooked eye now seemed infinitely beautiful to him, so beautiful in fact that he concluded that had the eye not been crooked, Tirpathi's face could never have looked so graceful.

Every time Tirpathi's thick lips moved under his bushy moustache, Joginder Singh imagined a bevy of birds warbling sweetly in the bushes. Tirpathi spoke slowly and gently, and now and then when he caressed his beard, Joginder Singh felt a sense of immense comfort, as though his own heart was being caressed with tender love.

The atmosphere during those four days was such that, had he even tried, Joginder Singh couldn't have succeeded in describing it in any of his stories. But—voila!—on the fifth day Tirpathi suddenly opened his leather bag and started reading his own short stories aloud and kept it up relentlessly for the next ten days. He must have read out the equivalent of several books.

Joginder Singh was mightily fed up. He developed an absolute aversion to short stories. Tirpathi's leather bag, puffed up like some moneylender's protruding belly, became a source of unending torment. Every evening, as he was returning from work, the fear that he might run into Tirpathi the moment he stepped through the doorway gripped his heart. When he reached home, they would exchange a few words and Tirpathi would open his bag and subject Joginder Singh to a couple of his short stories.

Had Joginder Singh not been a progressive, he would have told his guest flatly, 'Enough, enough, Tirpathi Sahib, that's quite enough. I have no more strength left to listen to your stories. Please . . .' But he thought, 'No, no, I'm a progressive. I shouldn't say this. It's my own fault that I no longer like his stories. They must have something good in them. After all, I did like his stories before. In fact, I thought they were excellent. I . . . I've become biased.'

For one whole week this conflict continued to ravage Joginder Singh's progressive mind. He thought so hard and so much that he reached a point where he couldn't think any more. All kinds of thoughts assailed his mind, but he'd lost the ability to sort them out properly. Slowly his confusion grew so intense and unforgiving that he began to hallucinate: he imagined he was stranded in a gigantic house during a hurricane, the numerous windows being blown open by gusts of merciless wind and he didn't know how to close them all at once.

A full twenty days passed but Tirpathi showed no sign of leaving. Joginder Singh began to feel edgy. Every evening when Tirpathi treated him to a fresh story he'd written during the day, Joginder only heard flies buzzing in his ears and his mind began to wander.

One evening Tirpathi read out a brand new story that focused on the sexual relations of a man and a woman. Joginder Singh was shocked to realize that for exactly three weeks he had spent every night sleeping under the same covers with a long-bearded man rather than with his own wife. The thought stirred up a veritable riot inside of him, at least for a moment. 'Heavens, what a guest I'm stuck with!' he said to himself. 'Is he a leech or something? Why doesn't he leave? And why am I forgetting his Begum Sahiba and daughter. The whole family has moved in. He hasn't even considered that it will crush us poor people. I'm an ordinary employee of the post office. All I make is fifty rupees a month. How long will I have to play host to him? And listen to his short stories that just keep coming one after the other? I'm a human being after all, not some metal footlocker. And worst of all, I can't even sleep with my wife. These long winter nights, my God, how they've been wasted!'

After twenty-one days Tirpathi began appearing to him in a completely new light. Now everything about the man repulsed him. His crooked eye was now just a crooked eye. His long, lush, raven-black hair no longer seemed quite as soft and silky; his inordinately long beard an unforgivable stupidity.

After twenty-five days a strange condition swept over Joginder Singh: he began to think he himself was a stranger. Surely he had known a Joginder Singh once, but not any more. And his wife—after Tirpathi left and everything finally returned to normal, he would marry her all over again. His old life, which these people had been using like a tatty old rag, would be restored to him and he would be able to sleep with his wife, and . . . and . . .

Thinking beyond this point brought tears to the man's eyes and something bitter caught in his throat. The desire to rush to Amrit Kaur, who used to be his wife in the good old days, to take her into his arms and start crying would overwhelm him, but he lacked the courage to do it because he was a progressive writer.

Now and then a crazy thought bubbled up inside of him like milk come to a boil: why not tear off this mantle of progressivism he'd wrapped around himself and start screaming, 'To hell with Tirpathi! Damn progressivism! You and your folk songs are all phoney! I want my wife back! All your desires have shrivelled up in your folk songs, but I'm still young. Have pity on me. Just think about it: I, who couldn't stay away from his wife for even a minute before, have had to sleep with you under a common quilt for the last twenty-five days! If this isn't tyranny, what is?'

But no matter how much he raged inside, he never could utter those words. Come evening, impervious to his miserable condition, Tirpathi would unload a fresh story without fail and then slip under the same quilt with him. After a whole month had passed, Joginder Singh had about had it. Finding an opportunity, he met his wife in the bathroom. His heart throbbing violently, afraid Tirpathi's wife might interrupt, he planted a hasty kiss on her lips like he was franking an envelope at the post office and said, 'Stay awake tonight. I'll tell Tirpathi that I have to go out and won't be back before two-thirty, but I'll come back early, say, around midnight. Open the door when you hear a soft rap. And then . . . The deorhi is somewhat secluded, but do lock the door that opens towards the bathroom.'

After firmly instructing his wife he went to Tirpathi and took his leave.

Twelve o'clock was four dark, chilly hours away. He spent two of them pedalling around aimlessly on his bike and didn't feel cold at all. The thought of the coming intimacy kept him warm. Then he decided to spend the rest of the time sitting in the open area across from his house. There, he felt himself becoming romantic. The hushed silence of the cold evening seemed familiar. Stars shone overhead in the frosty sky, like heavy droplets of water congealed into pearls. The occasional scream of a locomotive tore through the quiet, prompting his writer's mind to think of the silence as a massive chunk of ice and the sound of the whistle as a nail being driven through its heart.

For quite a while he let this unprecedented feeling of romance spread through his mind and heart and meditated on the darkened beauties of the night. Suddenly he was jolted out of his reverie. He quickly looked at his watch; only two minutes before midnight. He promptly got up, went to the door and knocked softly. Five seconds went by. The door didn't open. He knocked a second time.

The door opened and he whispered, 'Amrit . . .' But when he raised his eyes, whom did he see but Tirpathi. Joginder Singh was overwhelmed by the feeling that the man's beard had grown so long it seemed to touch the ground. Then he heard Tirpathi say, 'Wonderful! Couldn't have asked for more. I've just finished writing a new story. Come, let me read it to you.'

Pleasure of Losing

People take pleasure in winning. But he, well, it was losing that gave him the greater thrill, especially when it came in the wake of winning. Winning was easy enough; it was losing that made him sweat. Earlier, when he used to work in a bank, he too had thought about making piles of money. His relatives and friends had pooh-poohed the idea though. Soon afterwards he left for Bombay and, before long, he was sending wads of money to relatives and friends to help them financially.

Bombay was teeming with possibilities. He chose to go into films as they promised both money and fame. He could make a bundle in this world, and lose it just as easily. He's still marching on in that world. He made thousands, crores even, and squandered all of it. Making it took no time at all, losing it did. He wrote the lyrics for a film and earned one lakh rupees, but it took a long time to lose this stupendous sum—in prostitutes' balconies, their pimps' assemblies, in races and gambling dens.

One of his films yielded a tidy profit of ten lakh. The big question then was how to squander this windfall. So he wittingly bumbled every step along the way. He bought not one but three cars, one brand new and two shabby old ones that he was absolutely sure were worthless. He left them outside the house to rot away, locking the new one in his garage on the pretext that petrol was hard to come by. So a taxi was the answer. You hailed one in the morning and had the driver stop a mile or so down the way near one gambling place or another, emerging the next day after burning two or two-and-a-half thousand rupees. You took another taxi and went home, purposely

236 Saadat Hasan Manto

forgetting to pay the fare so that when you stepped out in the evening the taxi would still be standing at the door. You yelled at the driver, 'Wretched man, you're still here. All right, let's go to my office . . . I'll have them pay the fare.' But arriving at the office, you once again forget to pay, and . . .

Two or three of his films back to back turned out to be terrific hits and broke all records. He was swimming in money and his popularity soared sky-high, which greatly annoyed him. So he deliberately made a couple of films that failed miserably, indeed, so miserably that the failures became proverbial. In ruining himself, he had taken a few others along. But he wasn't one to give up. He put some zing into the sagging spirits of those he'd wrecked and made another film that proved to be a gold mine.

His relations with women followed the same pattern of loss and gain. He would pick up a prostitute from some song-and-dance soiree or some kotha, spend lavishly on doing her up, and catapult her to the height of fame. Then, after he'd sucked every ounce of womanhood out of her, he would deftly set up opportunities for her to leave him for the embrace of some other man.

He would take on the awfully rich and many handsome, amorous young men in a deathly struggle to win some beauty's favour, and always come out ahead. He would plunge his hand into the thorniest bramble and pluck the blossom of his choice. He would stick that blossom on his lapel, only to gladly let his rival snatch it away.

Back when he was visiting a Faras Road gambling den every day for ten days in a row, he was obsessed with losing, despite the fact that he had just recently lost a very beautiful actress and kissed goodbye to a sum of ten lakh on a film. But his thirst for losing still wasn't quenched as both losses had come much too suddenly. This time around his calculations had obviously misfired. Perhaps this was the reason he was now cautiously losing a fixed amount every day in the Faras Road gambling establishment.

He would set out for Pawan Pul in the evening with two hundred rupees in his pocket. The taxi would course past the line of prostitutes' display windows, which had iron bars running horizontally across them, and halt some distance away by a utility pole. He would get out of the taxi, adjust his heavy eyeglasses and arrange the front fold of his dhoti, and then, glancing to his right at the terribly ugly woman behind the iron bars busily applying her make-up in front of a broken mirror, he would climb up to the *baithak*.

He had been visiting this gambling den at Faras Road regularly for the last ten days, determined to lose two hundred rupees on every visit. Sometimes it took only a few hands, sometimes it took until the wee hours of the morning.

After the taxi pulled up beside the utility pole on the eleventh day, he got out, fixed the heavy glasses on his nose and the front fold of his dhoti, and looked to his right. Suddenly he had this strange feeling about the fact that he had been looking at this ugly woman for the past ten days. As usual, she was seated on a wooden takht, busily applying her make-up in front of the broken mirror.

Coming abreast of the iron bars, he peered at the middle-aged woman: swarthy complexion, oily skin, cheeks and chin tattooed with blue circles more or less blending in with her terribly dark skin. Her teeth were awful and her gums were practically melting away from chewing paan and tobacco regularly. What kind of man would go to her, he wondered.

When he took another step towards the bars, the ugly woman smiled at him, put her mirror off to one side and said to him awkwardly, 'Well, Seth, want to come in?'

He inspected the woman, who regardless of her attributes and age still hoped for customers, even more closely. Greatly surprised, he asked her, 'Bai, how old might you be?'

This hurt her feelings. She made a face and perhaps swore at him in Marathi. He quickly realized his mistake and apologized sincerely. 'Bai, please forgive me. I just asked. That's all. But I do find it quite surprising that you sit here day after day all decked out. Do people visit you?'

The woman didn't answer. He again realized his mistake and asked her in a matter-of-fact voice free of curiosity, 'What's your name?'

The woman was about to lift the curtain to go inside but stopped short and said, 'Gangu Bai,'

'Tell me, Gangu Bai, how much do you make in a day?'

The woman felt a note of compassion in his voice and came over to the window bars. 'Six, sometimes seven rupees . . . sometimes nothing.'

As he repeated Gangu Bai's words—'Six, sometimes seven rupees . . . sometimes nothing'—he thought of the two hundred rupees in his pocket that he'd brought along to burn. An idea suddenly flashed across his mind.

'Look, Gangu Bai, you make six or seven rupees a day. What if I gave you ten?'

'For the work?'

'No, not for the work. But you could think of it as for the work.' He quickly pulled out a ten-rupee note from his pocket and pushed it across the bars. 'Here, take it.'

Gangu Bai took the banknote, but she was gawking at him wonderingly.

'Look, Gangu Bai, I'll give you ten rupees every evening at about this time, but on one condition.'

'Condition? What condition?'

'That after you get your ten rupees, you'll have your meal and go inside to sleep. I don't want to see your lights on.'

A strange smile splashed across Gangu Bai's lips.

'Don't laugh. I mean it. I never go back on my word.'

Then he headed for the gambling den. As he was climbing the stairs he thought, 'I came here to blow two hundred anyway, so what if it's one ninety now.'

Several days passed. The taxi stopped by the electric pole each evening. He got out, fixed the glasses on his nose, looked to his right at Gangu Bai ensconced on the takht behind the grillwork, arranged the front fold of his dhoti, pulled out a ten-rupee note and handed it to her. She touched it to her forehead, thanked him with a salaam, and he went upstairs to drop hundred and ninety rupees in card games. A couple of times on his way out, about eleven in the evening or two or three in the morning, he found Gangu Bai's shop closed.

One evening after giving her ten rupees he went up to the den and finished early, by ten o'clock. He'd ended up with such unlucky cards on every hand that he'd lost that day's quota within a few hours. He came down from the kotha and was getting into the taxi when his eyes fell on Gangu Bai's shop. He was astonished to see that it was open and she was sitting on the takht behind the grillwork. It looked as if she was waiting for customers. He got out of the taxi and approached her. She panicked when she saw him, but by then he was already in front of her.

'What's this, Gangu Bai?'

She didn't answer.

'What a pity that you didn't live up to your promise. Didn't I say I wanted your lights off in the evening? And here you sit like . . .'

His voice was filled with disappointment and sadness. Gangu Bai became thoughtful.

'You're bad,' he said and started walking away.

'Don't go, Seth, stop,' she called after him.

He stopped. Gangu Bai started with slow deliberation, measuring every word carefully. 'Yes, I'm bad, very bad. But who is good here? Seth, you pay ten rupees to keep one light off, but look around you, how many more lights are still on.'

He looked through his thick lenses, first at the light bulb glaring right above Gangu Bai's head and then at her tawny face. He bent his head and said, 'No, Gangu Bai, no.' He got into the taxi with a heart with no pleasure in it.

God–Man

Chaudhry Maujo was sitting on a cot of coarse string-matting under the shady banyan and leisurely puffing away at his hookah. Wispy balls of smoke rose from his mouth and dissipated slowly in the stagnant air of the scorching afternoon.

Ploughing his little patch of land all morning had left him totally exhausted. The sun was unbearably hot, but there was nothing like the cool smoke of the hookah to suck away all the fatigue within seconds.

The sweat on his body had dried, and although the stagnant air was hardly any comfort for his overheated body, the cool and delicious smoke of the hookah was spiralling up to his head in indescribable waves of exhilaration.

It was nearing the time when Jaina, his daughter, would bring his repast of bread and lassi from home. She was very punctual about it, even though she didn't have a soul to help her in her work. She'd had her mother, but Maujo had divorced her two years ago following a lengthy and particularly nasty argument.

Young Jaina was a very dutiful girl. She took good care of her father. She was diligent in finishing her work so there would be time to card cotton and prepare it for spinning, or to chat with the few girlfriends she had.

Maujo didn't own much land, but it was enough to provide for his needs. His was a very small village, tucked away in a far-flung spot with no access to the railway. There was just a dirt road that connected it to a large village quite some distance away. Twice a month Chaudhry Maujo mounted his mare and rode there to buy necessities at a couple of shops.

He used to be a happy man, blissfully free of worries, except for the thought that sometimes assailed him: He had no male offspring. At such times he contented himself by thinking that he should be happy with whatever God had willed for him. But, after his wife had gone back to her parents, his life was no longer the same. It had become unspeakably cheerless and drab. It was as if she had carried all its delicious coolness and exuberance away with her.

Maujo was a religious man, but he knew only a few fundamentals of his faith: God is One and must be worshipped; Muhammad is His Prophet and it is incumbent to follow his teaching; and the Qur'an is the word of God which was revealed to Muhammad. That's about it.

Ritual daily prayers and the Ramzan fast—well, these he had dispensed with. The village was far too small to afford a mosque; there were only a dozen or so houses, situated far apart. People did repeat 'Allah! Allah!' often enough in their speech and carried His fear in their hearts, but that was the extent of their devotion. Nearly every household had a copy of the Qur'an, but no one knew how to recite it. Everyone had placed it high up on a shelf, reverentially wrapped in its velvet sheath. It was only brought down from its sanctum when it was needed for someone to swear by it or take an oath to do something.

The maulvi was called in only when a boy or girl needed to be married. The village folk took care of the funeral prayer themselves, that too in their own tongue, not Arabic.

Chaudhry Maujo came in especially handy on such occasions. He had a way with words. They never failed to affect the listener deeply. No one could equal his manner of eulogizing the deceased and praying for his deliverance. Just last year when the strapping son of his friend Deeno died and was laid to rest in his grave, Maujo eulogized him thus:

'Oh, what a handsome young man he was! When he spat, the spittle landed twenty yards away. No one, and I mean no one, in any villages far or near could match the sturdy projectile of his piss. And what an accomplished wrestler he was! He could wriggle out of an opponent's hold as easily as unbuttoning a shirt.

'Deeno, yaar, this is the worst day of your life! This terrible blow will affect you for the rest of your life. Was this the time for such a robust young man to die . . . such a handsome young man? How the goldsmith's lovely and headstrong daughter Neti had cast magic spells on him to win his love, but, bravo, your boy, Deeno, remained steadfast.

He never gave in to her wiles. May God present him with the loveliest houri in Heaven, and may your boy never be tempted by her. And may God shower him with his mercy and blessings! Amen!'

Several people, Deeno included, were so affected by this oratory that they started crying inconsolably, and even Maujo couldn't stop his tears from bubbling out.

Maujo didn't feel the need to send for the maulvi when the idea of divorcing his wife got hold of his mind. He'd heard from elders that repeating the word 'talaq' three times over ended the matter then and there. So he ended the matter accordingly. Next day, though, he felt very sorry and ashamed that he had committed such a heinous blunder. Such squabbles were, after all, common among husbands and wives. They didn't always end in divorce. He should have been more forgiving.

He liked his Phataan. She was no longer young, but Maujo was in love with her body. He also liked the things she talked about. Above all else, she was his Jaina's mother. But it was too late now; the arrow had already left the bow. There was no way for it to fly back. Whenever he thought about the episode, the otherwise refreshing smoke of his beloved hookah caught in his throat like something bitter.

Jaina was a beautiful girl, the very image of her mother. In the space of just two years, she had suddenly blossomed from a little girl into a stunningly beautiful young woman. Her effervescent youth was spilling out from every pore of her body. Her marriage was among Maujo's constant worries, which made him miss Phataan even more. How easily she could have taken care of everything!

Rearranging his *tehmad* and himself on the cot, Maujo took a rather long drag on his hookah and started to cough. Just then he heard a voice, '*As-salamu alaikum*, and may God's mercy and blessings be upon you!'

Maujo started and turned around to look. He saw a long-bearded elderly man in flowing lily-white clothes. He returned the greeting and wondered where the man had materialized from.

The stranger had big, commanding eyes smeared with kohl and long, flowing locks of hair. His hair and beard were a blend of grey and black, with the grey predominating, and he wore a snow-white turban. An embroidered, saffron-coloured silk sash was thrown over his shoulder and he held a thick staff with a, silver ball at the top. He had a pair of delicate shoes of soft red leather on his feet.

The man's appearance inspired immediate respect in Maujo. He quickly got up and asked courteously, 'Where are you from and when did you arrive?'

The man's lips, shadowed by a moustache trimmed in the fashion recommended by Islamic custom, curved into a smile. 'Where do fakirs come from? They have no place to call home, and there is no fixed time for their arrival, or for when they leave. They go wherever God wills them to, and stop where He orders them to halt.'

The words affected Maujo deeply. He took the elder's hand in his with great reverence, kissed it, and then touched it to his eyes, saying, 'Consider Chaudhry Maujo's house your own.'

The elderly man smiled and sat down on the cot, lowering his head over his staff and wrapping his hands around the ball. 'Perhaps some good deed you did has so pleased God, eminent is His majesty, that He has sent this sinner your way.'

An overjoyed Maujo asked, 'So you have come here at His behest?'

The maulvi raised his head and said in a huff, 'Who else's? You think I came here at your command? Am I your servitor or His whom I have worshipped for a good forty years to reach my insignificant station?'

Maujo shivered. He asked in his coarse but entirely sincere way to be forgiven for his unintended lapse. 'Maulvi Sahib, we uncouth village folk, who don't even know how to offer our prayer properly, often end up making such mistakes. We are sinners. But to forgive, and have God also forgive us, behooves you.'

'Precisely. That's why I'm here,' said the maulvi, closing his big, kohl-lined eyes.

Chaudhry Maujo sat on the bare ground and started massaging the maulvi's legs. Meanwhile Jaina appeared. The minute she saw the other man, she quickly pulled her veil over her head and face. His eyes still closed, the maulvi asked, 'Who is it, Chaudhry Maujo?'

'Jaina, my daughter, Maulvi Sahib.'

The maulvi looked at Jaina through his half-closed eyes and said to Maujo, 'Tell her that we are fakirs, there is no need to observe purdah before us.'

'Of course not. No purdah at all, Maulvi Sahib.' Then, looking at Jaina he said, 'He is Maulvi Sahib, among God's most favoured devotees. Remove your veil.'

Jaina lifted her veil. The maulvi looked at the girl for as long as his heart desired and told Maujo, 'Chaudhry Maujo, you've got a beautiful daughter.'

Jaina blushed.

'She takes after her mother,' Maujo said.

'Where is her mother?' The maulvi looked again at the girl's blossoming youth.

Maujo felt out of his wits. He didn't know what to say.

The maulvi asked again, 'Where is her mother?'

Flabbergasted, Maujo blurted out, 'She died.'

The maulvi, his eyes riveted on the girl, noticed her reaction and said in a thundering voice, 'You're lying!'

Maujo timidly grabbed the maulvi's feet out of contrition. 'Yes, I lied,' he said, feeling remorseful. 'Please forgive me. I'm a big liar. I divorced her, Maulvi Sahib.'

With a long 'hu-u-u-u-h' the maulvi turned his eyes away from Jaina's veil and trained them on Maujo. 'You're a big sinner! What was the poor woman's fault?'

Drowned in utter shame, Maujo said meekly, 'I'm really confused. It was just a trifling, nothing serious, but it got out of hand and ended up in divorce. I'm truly a sinner. I was regretting my action the very next day. I told myself it was a fool thing to do, but it was already too late. It was pointless to dwell on regret.'

The maulvi put his staff on Maujo's shoulder. 'The sublime and lofty God is full of mercy and grace. If He wills, he can fix what is spoiled. If He wills, He will order this lowly fakir to find a way out of this difficulty for you.'

A grateful Maujo fell on the maulvi's feet and began to cry. The maulvi again glanced at Jaina, who was also in tears. 'Come here, girl!'

His voice was so commanding that Jaina simply couldn't ignore it. She put the food and lassi aside and approached the cot. The maulvi grabbed her arm and ordered her to sit down.

When she lowered herself to the ground, he pulled her up by her arm. 'Come, sit by my side.'

Jaina drew her body together as she sat next to him. The maulvi threw his arm around her waist and pulled her closer, pressing her to his side. 'What have you brought for us to eat?' he asked.

Jaina tried to pull away a little but she found the hand on her waist quite unyielding. 'Roti, saag, and lassi,' she replied.

The maulvi squeezed her firm, slender waist. 'Okay, lay it out for us.'

Jaina got up to lay out the food. Meanwhile, the maulvi tapped the silver hilt of his staff on Maujo's shoulder a couple of times. 'Get up, Maujo, and wash our hands.'

Maujo sprang to his feet, drew water from the nearby well and, like the devoted acolyte of a holy man, washed the maulvi's hands. The girl laid out the meal on the cot.

After the maulvi had devoured all the food himself, he ordered Jaina to wash his hands. She couldn't very well refuse. After all, the maulvi's bearing and appearance and his manner of talking were so commanding.

The maulvi belched noisily and pronounced loudly, '*Al-hamdu lillah!*' He then ran his wet hands over his beard, belched a second time, and stretched out on the cot, all the while gazing at Jaina's chador that had slid down from her face. Jaina quickly gathered the pots and left. The maulvi closed his eyes and announced, 'Maujo, we're going to take a nap now.'

Maujo massaged the maulvi's legs until he dozed off and then withdrew. Going off to one side, Maujo lit a couple of cow dung cakes, gave his chillum a fresh piece of tobacco, and started smoking the hookah on an empty stomach. But he was happy. He felt that a heavy burden had been lifted off his chest somehow. In his characteristic rustic but sincere manner he thanked God, the Most High, Who had sent along His angel of mercy in the guise of Maulvi Sahib.

Initially he was of a mind to stay by the maulvi, in case he needed some service, but when the man didn't wake up for quite some time, Maujo went to his field and resumed his work. He didn't care at all that he was hungry; rather, he was beside himself with happiness because the maulvi had eaten his share of the food, which he considered a great blessing for himself.

When Maujo returned from the field before sundown it pained him to see that Maulvi Sahib was nowhere in sight. He cursed himself roundly for his negligence. Why had he left the maulvi? Why hadn't he stayed near him? Perhaps the maulvi was displeased and decided to go away. He might even have called down God's curse upon Maujo. With that thought his simple peasant's soul began to tremble with fear and tears appeared in his eyes.

Maujo looked for Maulvi Sahib everywhere but couldn't find him. No trace of him either even after it got quite dark. Maujo gave up exhausted, lamenting and cursing himself. Homeward bound, his head hung low, he saw two harried young men coming along the road. He asked what the matter was. After some hemming and hawing they blurted out the truth: They had dug up a pot of wine stashed in a dirt heap and were about to drink from it when, all of a sudden, an elderly man with the luminous face of a divine being confronted them with wrathful eyes. This was a downright unlawful act. God had forbidden the consumption of intoxicants. They were committing a sin for which there was absolutely no forgiveness. The young men were so intimidated that they couldn't utter a word and just took to their heels.

Maujo told them that that heavenly figure was in fact a man of God. Then he gave voice to his fear: all this didn't bode well for the village. No telling what calamity might descend on it now. First he'd acted discourteously by leaving the maulvi alone; now these boys had attempted to imbibe the forbidden drink.

The Chaudhry mumbled, 'Only God can save us now, my boys, only God,' and headed home.

He didn't exchange any words with Jaina, just sat down quietly on the cot and began smoking his hookah. Tumultuous thoughts were swirling around in his head. He was sure that both he and the village were in for some unspeakable calamity.

The evening meal was ready. Jaina had cooked extra for Maulvi Sahib. When he didn't come, she asked about him. Maujo replied with sorrow, 'He's gone. Why would he want to stay among us sinners!'

Jaina felt very sorry because Maulvi Sahib had promised to find a way to bring her mother home. He was gone. Who would find a way to do that now? She sat down quietly on the low wooden stool. The meal started to get cold.

A while later the deorhi came alive with the sound of movement and the two started. Maujo got up and went to the deorhi, returning moments later with Maulvi Sahib. In the dim light of the oil lamp Jaina noticed the maulvi's unsteady gait and the small earthen pot he held in his hands.

Maujo helped him to the cot. Maulvi Sahib handed the pot over to Maujo and stammered, 'God put us through the worst ordeal today. We stumbled upon two young men from your village. They had dug up a pot of wine from the earth and were about to drink. The minute they saw us they ran. Their conduct shocked us. So young and on the verge of committing such a grave sin! But then we thought: At their age one does sometimes stray from the straight path. So we entreated God, the Most High, to forgive the boys their sin. And lo, He replied . . . Do you know what he said?'

'No,' said Maujo, trembling all over.

'He said, "Do you agree to take their sin upon yourself?" I said, "I do, Sublime Lord." His voice came, "Well then, drink the whole pot yourself and We will pardon the boys."'

Maujo drifted off into the world his imagination had conjured up. His hair stood on end. 'So you drank?' he asked timidly.

The maulvi's voice trembled, 'Yes, I did. I d-d-d-rank . . . to assume their sin . . . to save them . . . to please God Almighty. There is still some left in the pot. I have to drink that too. Put it away carefully. Make sure not a drop disappears.'

Maujo put the pot in a small room, tying a piece of cloth tightly over its mouth. When he returned to the courtyard he saw Maulvi Sahib making Jaina massage his head while he told her, 'If a man does something good for the sake of others, God, eminent is His glory, is very pleased with such a man. Right now, He is also very pleased with you. So am I.'

As an expression of his pleasure, he made Jaina sit next to him and kissed her forehead. She cringed and hurried to get up, but the maulvi's grip was firm. He clasped her to his chest and said to Maujo, 'Chaudhry, fate is smiling on your daughter.'

The Chaudhry was overwhelmed with gratitude. 'It is all due to your prayer . . . your kindness.'

Once again the maulvi pressed the girl to his chest. 'When God is kind, everyone else is kind too. Jaina, I'll teach you a prayer. Keep saying it and God will be kind to you.'

The maulvi got up quite late the next morning. Out of deference tinged with a feeling of awe, Maujo hadn't dared to go to work in his field and had remained beside the maulvi's cot in the courtyard. When, finally, the man's sleep broke, Maujo helped him brush his

teeth with a twig and wash his hands and face. Then he brought the
pot of wine over to him as ordered. The maulvi mumbled some pious
words, removed the cloth from the pot, blew into it a few times, and
emptied a few bowls. Now he looked at the sky, again mumbled some
words, and said in a loud voice, 'Oh Lord, we will prevail in whatever
test you put us to.' Addressing the Chaudhry, he said, 'Maujo, we've
just been ordered to tell you, go right now and bring your wife back!
We've found a way.'

Maujo was overjoyed. He hurriedly saddled his mare. Promising to
return early the next day and advising Jaina to look to the maulvi's every
comfort and not shrink from serving him as best as she could, he left.

Jaina got busy scrubbing the dirty dishes. The maulvi, comfortably
settled on the cot, kept staring at her and drinking wine by the bowlful.
Eventually he pulled out a string of large beads and started to roll them
through his fingers. When Jaina was finished, he said to her, 'Look here,
Jaina, do your *wuzu*.'*

'I don't know how to, Maulvi Sahib,' she replied innocently.

He chided her softly, 'You don't know how to make wuzu? Tut-tut-
tut. How will you face God then?' He stood up from the cot and taught
her to perform wuzu, scouring every last nook and corner of the girl's
body with his eyes as he went over the different acts of ritual washings
with her.

This done he asked for the prayer rug. There was none. He chided
her again with the same tenderness. He asked her to get a sheet instead,
spread it out in an inner room of the house and then latch the main
door. When she had done so, he asked her to bring the wine pot and
the bowl over. She did that. He drank half a bowlful of wine, set the still
half-full bowl down in front of him, closed his eyes and resumed telling
his beads. Meanwhile Jaina sat quietly near him.

His remained busy with his beads for a long while. Then he opened
his eyes, blew into the half-full bowl three times over and offered it to
Jaina. 'Drink!'

Shaking, Jaina took the bowl with hesitant hands.

'Didn't we say drink?' the maulvi commanded in his awe-inspiring
voice. 'It will rid you of all your miseries.'

---

* The ritualistic washing in a prescribed manner before performing namaz and other
  religious acts.

Jaina quickly downed the liquid. A smile spread across the maulvi's thin lips. 'Look, we're about to start our *wazifa** again. When you see our index finger rise it is a sign for you to fill the bowl about halfway and drink from it immediately. Understand?'

The maulvi didn't wait for her to answer; he closed his eyes and sank back into his meditation.

A terribly bitter taste exploded in Jaina's mouth; she felt as if the inside of her chest was on fire. She desperately wanted to get up and drink some cold water. But how could she? So she just sat there, enduring the stinging sensation in her throat and chest. Suddenly the maulvi's index finger rose with a snap. As if hypnotized, the obedient girl quickly filled half the bowl and drank the wine. She wanted to spit it out but she just couldn't get up.

Meanwhile, the maulvi continued rolling his beads, deep in meditation, his eyes closed in rapture. Jaina felt as if her head was spinning and she was succumbing to the relentless onslaught of drowsiness. In her semi-conscious state she saw herself in the arms of a youth with neither beard nor moustache who was taking her along to enjoy the pleasures of paradise.

When she opened her eyes, she saw herself stretched out on the coarse sheet. With her half-open, inebriated eyes she looked around herself and wondered: When did I lie down here, and why? Everything seemed shrouded in fog. She fought back another wave of sleep and abruptly got up. Maulvi Sahib—where was he? . . . And that paradise?

It was an empty space that confronted her. She stepped into the courtyard and found the maulvi making his wuzu. He turned around at the sound of her footsteps and smiled. Jaina withdrew to the room. She sat down on the sheet and began thinking about her mother, whom her father had gone to bring back home. There was still a whole night before they returned.

And to top it all, she was feeling quite hungry. She hadn't cooked a meal. Many thoughts were crowding into her agitated mind. After a while the maulvi appeared and said, 'I have to do a wazifa for your father. It will require an all-night vigil by some grave. I'll also pray for you.' Then he left.

---

* A prescribed prayer formula performed daily by Muslims, not to be confused with the five mandatory daily prayers (the namaz).

He returned at the crack of dawn. His great big eyes, now bereft of their line of kohl, were bloodshot. His voice was faltering, his tread wobbly. As he entered the courtyard, he looked at Jaina with a smile, approached her and pressed her against his chest. He kissed her and plopped down on the cot. Jaina sat on a stool in a far corner and began mulling over the events of the previous evening, her recollection of which was quite hazy. She was also waiting for her father who should have been back by now. A full two years had passed since she had been separated from her mother . . . And, yes, the paradise . . . that paradise . . . How was it? Was her companion Maulvi Sahib? She could vaguely remember that whoever it was didn't sport a beard; he was someone young.

'Jaina,' the maulvi said to her after some time, 'Maujo hasn't returned yet.'

She remained quiet.

'And there I was, performing the wazifa especially for his sake throughout the desolate night, sitting with bowed head by a dilapidated grave!' he told the girl. 'When will he return? Do you think he'll be able to bring your mother back?'

Her only answer: 'Perhaps he'll be here soon. He will come home. So will Mother. But I can't say anything for sure.'

Suddenly the sound of footsteps was heard. Jaina got up quickly. The moment she saw her mother she immediately wrapped her arms around her and broke into tears. When Maujo came in, he greeted the maulvi with the greatest courtesy and reverence and commanded his wife, 'Phataan, say salaam to Maulvi Sahib!'

Phataan disengaged herself from her daughter and, wiping her tears, offered salaams to the maulvi. The latter gaped at her with his red fiery eyes and said to Maujo, 'I've just returned after performing a night-long wazifa for you by a grave. God has heard me. Everything will be all right.'

Chaudhry Maujo dropped down to the floor and quickly started pressing the maulvi's calves. So overwhelmed was he by feelings of deep gratitude and reverence that he couldn't say anything to the maulvi; instead, he said to his wife tearfully, 'Come here, Phataan, you thank Maulvi Sahib for I don't know how to.'

She came and sat next to her husband. All she could say was, 'We poor folk, how can we ever thank you enough.'

The maulvi looked closely at Phataan. 'Maujo Chaudhry,' he said, 'you were absolutely right. Your wife is truly beautiful. In spite of her age, she looks young. Exactly like Jaina . . . even more beautiful. We will put everything right, Phataan, for God is inclined to be merciful and giving.'

Both husband and wife sank into silence. Maujo continued pressing the maulvi's calves, while Jaina busied herself with getting the fire going in the hearth.

After a while the maulvi rose from the cot, patted Phataan's head gently and said to Maujo, 'God commands that if a man wants to remarry the wife he has divorced, he must, in punishment, have her first marry another man and seek divorce from him. Only then is it lawful for her first husband to remarry her.'

'I've heard this before, Maulvi Sahib,' Maujo said softly.

The maulvi made Maujo get up and placed his hand on his shoulder. 'I entreated God tearfully not to put your poor soul through such harsh punishment; I said that you erred without meaning to. But God answered, "How long do you expect Us to go on listening to your intercessions? If there is anything you want for yourself, well, We'll give it to you." I submitted, "My Lord, Lord of the Sea and the Earth, I don't ask anything for myself. You've already given me everything. But Maujo Chaudhry—he loves his wife dearly . . ." He proclaimed, "Well then, We want to test his love and your faith. You marry her for a day and hand her over to Maujo the next day after divorcing her. This is the best We can do for you, and that too because for the past forty years you have been unfailing in your devotion to Us."'

An overjoyed Maujo cried out, 'I accept, Maulvi Sahib, I accept.' He looked at his wife with a twinkle in his eyes and asked, 'So Phataan, what do you say?'

But without waiting for her answer, he blurted out again, 'We both accept.'

The maulvi closed his eyes, mumbled something, breathed over the two, and raised his eyes to the sky. 'God, the Blessed, the Most High, may we triumph over this ordeal with Your help!' Then he said to the Chaudhry, 'Well, Maujo, I'm going out now. When I return, I'd like you and Jaina to leave here and spend the night somewhere else. Come back in the morning.' And he went out.

When he returned in the evening, Jaina and Maujo were ready. He exchanged a few short words with them and started mumbling something. A little later, after a sign from him, father and daughter promptly exited the house.

The maulvi fastened the door latch and said to Phataan, 'For this one night you're my wife. Go bring the bedding and spread it out on the cot. We will sleep.'

Phataan did as commanded. The maulvi said, 'Bibi, you sit here, I'll be along shortly.'

He then went into the other room. In the light of the earthen oil lamp he spotted his wine pitcher in a corner near the stack of pots and pans. He shook the pitcher. There was some wine left. Still standing, he impatiently gulped a few mouthfuls of the intoxicant directly from the pitcher and used the embroidered saffron-coloured silk sash that was slung across his shoulder to wipe his lips and moustache. Then he closed the door.

He re-emerged after quite some time with the bowl in hand. Phataan was sitting on the cot. He blew into the bowl three times and offered it to her. 'Come on, drink it up!'

Phataan gulped down the liquid and instantly felt queasy. The maulvi tapped on her back a few times and said, 'There, okay!'

Phataan tried to feel better, and to a degree she did. The maulvi stretched out on the bed.

In the morning, when Maujo and Jaina returned, they found Phataan sleeping alone in the courtyard with no sign of the maulvi anywhere. Maybe he's gone out for a bit . . . to the fields, Maujo thought. He tried to wake Phataan. Mumbling some inarticulate sounds, she slowly opened her eyes. Then, in a clear distinct voice, she mumbled, 'Paradise! Oh, sheer paradise!' But as soon as she saw Maujo, she sat up in the bed, eyes wide open.

'Where is Maulvi Sahib?' Maujo asked.

Phataan, who still hadn't fully recovered her senses, replied, 'Maulvi Sahib? What Maulvi Sahib? Oh he, God knows where he's gone . . . Isn't he here?'

'No,' Maujo said. 'Okay, I'll go out and look for him.'

Just as he was leaving he heard Phataan's muffled scream. He turned around to look at her. She was pulling out something black from under the pillow. 'What the hell is this?' she asked, looking at the object in her hand.

'Hair,' Maujo replied.

Phataan quickly threw that tangled clump of hair down on the floor. Maujo picked it up and gave it a close look. 'It's a beard and sideburns.'

Jaina, who was standing near them, said, 'Maulvi Sahib's beard and sideburns.'

'Yes, his beard and sideburns,' affirmed her mother from the bed.

Maujo was nonplussed. 'But where is the Maulvi Sahib himself?' Suddenly a thought came into his simple, trusting peasant mind, 'Jaina, Phataan, you don't understand. He was a godly person, full of saintly graces. He fulfilled what we most yearned for and left us this memento to remember him by.'

He reverently kissed that clump of hair, touched it to his eyes, and, handing it to Jaina, told her, 'Go, wrap it in a clean piece of cloth and put it in the big chest. God willing, it will bring blessings to our household forever.'

Once Jaina left, he sat down next to his Phataan and told her lovingly, 'I will learn to say my namaz and always pray for the saintly elder who again brought us together.'

Phataan just sat there in hushed silence.

I'm No Good for You!

A heated discussion about Chaudhry Ghulam Abbas's latest speech was in full swing in the Tea House. The atmosphere inside was cosy and as warm as the tea. We were in agreement about one thing: We should grab Kashmir no matter what and Dogra rule must end immediately.

They were all *mujahids*, God's valiant soldiers, who didn't know the first thing about fighting but were ready to jump into the battlefield at any moment. The consensus was that if we launched a surprise attack, Kashmir would be in our hands in a blink.

Well, I was among those mujahids. My problem, though, is that I'm a Kashmiri right down to the hilt, and no less a Kashmiri than Pandit Jawaharlal Nehru, which makes it my greatest weakness. I just chimed along with the other mujahids. It was decided that the minute war broke out we would join and fight at the very front.

Although Haneef showed great enthusiasm, I sensed that he was feeling rather melancholy, but I couldn't figure out the reason for his downcast mood.

Everyone left after the tea, only Haneef and I stayed on. By now the Tea House had become nearly empty with only two boys chatting over their breakfast in a far corner.

I had met Haneef a while back. He was about ten years younger than me. He had finished his BA and was undecided whether to opt for an MA in English or in Urdu. Sometimes he got it into his head to stop his studies altogether and set out to travel.

I looked at him closely. He was picking up the used matchsticks from the ashtray and nervously breaking them into small bits. As I've already mentioned, he was feeling rather blue. It appeared to be a good opportunity to ask him about it. 'Why are you feeling so glum?'

He lifted his head, tossed the broken pieces to one side, and replied, 'Oh, no particular reason.'

I lit up. 'What do you mean "no particular reason"? That's no answer. There's always a reason for everything. Perhaps you're reminiscing about some old event.'

He nodded. 'Yes.'

'And that event has something to do with Kashmir?'

He started. 'How did you know that?'

I smiled. 'I'm a Sherlock Holmes too. My good man, weren't we just now talking about Kashmir? When you agreed that you were thinking, and thinking about some past event, I immediately guessed that this event must have to do with Kashmir. It's got to be. So, did you fall in love there?'

'Love . . . I don't know . . . God knows what it was. Anyway, something did happen and the memory of it still haunts me.'

I was eager to hear his story. 'If you don't mind, tell me about that "something".'

He asked me for a cigarette and lit it. 'Manto Sahib,' he said, 'it isn't an especially interesting incident. But if you promise to listen quietly without interrupting, I'll tell you everything, down to the last detail, about what transpired three years ago. I'm not a storyteller, all the same I'll try.'

I promised not to interrupt. Actually he wanted to narrate his story by going into the depths of his heart and mind.

After a pause he began, 'Manto Sahib, it happened two years ago, when Partition wasn't even in our imagination. It was summer time. I was feeling down, God knows why. I guess all unattached, single men feel gloomy in the summer. Anyway, one day I decided to go to Kashmir. I packed a few essentials and went to the lorry stand. I bought a ticket and boarded. When the lorry arrived at Kad, I changed my mind. What is there in Srinagar, I thought. I've already seen it many times; I'll get out at the next stop, Batut. It's a salubrious place. Tuberculosis patients especially go there and leave cured. So I got off at Batut and stayed in a hotel, a rather bare-bones one, but all right. I was quite taken with Batut. I went climbing on the slopes every morning, ate a breakfast of toast and pure butter on my return from the hike, and then read some book or other lying down.

'I was spending my days pleasurably in the salubrious environment of the place. I'd become friends with all the shopkeepers in the area around the hotel, especially Sardar Lahna Singh who was a tailor. I would spend hours at his shop. He was a fanatic about listening to and telling love stories. His sewing machine would keep whirring and he'd be absorbed in those stories.

'He knew every last thing about Batut. Who was having an affair with whom, who'd had a tiff, which girls had just started to put on airs—you name it. His pocket was always full of such gossip.

'In the evenings, the two of us went for a stroll on the downward slopes, all the way to the Banihal Pass, and then walked back up slowly. There was a cluster of mud dwellings to the right of the first bend in the road if you were coming from the hotel and headed towards the slopes. One day I asked Sardarji whether those quarters were meant to be lived in. I asked because they had caught my fancy. Yes, they were for living in, he told me. "A railway babu from Sargodha is staying there these days. His wife is ill."

'She must have tuberculosis, I concluded at once. God knows why I'm so scared of this disease. From that day on I never passed by those quarters without covering my nose and mouth with a kerchief. I don't want to prolong the story. In short, eventually, I became friends with Kundan Lal, the railway babu. I soon realized that he wasn't at all concerned about his wife's condition. He was simply going through the motions of being a caring husband. He visited her occasionally and lived in a separate dwelling, which he disinfected with phenyl three times a day. It was his wife's younger sister Sumitri, hardly fourteen years old, who took care of her with unflinching devotion.

'I first saw Sumitri by the Maggu stream. A big pile of dirty laundry lay by her side and she was perhaps washing a shalwar when I passed by. The sound of my footsteps startled her. She quickly joined her hands and said namaste to me. I returned her greeting and asked, "You know me?" "Yes," she said in her shrill voice, "you're Babuji's friend." What stood before me, I felt, was not Sumitri, but suffering itself, moulded into her form. I felt like talking to her, to help her with her washing, to lessen her burdens just a little, but such informality seemed out of place at our very first meeting.

'The second time I met her, again by the very same stream, she was rubbing soap into some clothes when I said namaste and sat down on top of a bed of fallen apples. She felt somewhat nervous, but her trepidation disappeared once we started talking. She became so friendly that she started telling me all about the affairs of her household:

'It'd been five years since her elder sister got married to Babuji, she told me. During the first year of their marriage, Babuji treated her sister well, but when he was suspended from his job for allegedly taking bribes, he wanted to sell her jewellery and gamble with it, hoping it would double the amount. Her sister wouldn't agree, so he started beating and abusing her. He would shut her up in a small dark room all day long without food for months. Finally, when she couldn't take it any more, she handed him the jewellery. He disappeared with it and didn't show his face for six months, during which time she was reduced to starvation. Had she wanted to, she could have gone back to her parents. Her father was quite wealthy; he even loved her a lot. But she didn't think it was proper to go back. She ended up contracting tuberculosis. When Kundan Lal finally reappeared six months later, he found his wife bedridden. He had been reinstated. When asked where he'd been all this time, he hedged and fudged.

'Sumitri's sister didn't ask him about her jewellery. She was happy that God had heard her entreaties and sent her husband back to her. Her health improved a little, but a month later her condition deteriorated sharply. It was only then that her parents somehow learned about her illness. They immediately came over and forced Kundan Lal to bring her to the mountain right away and said they would bear the expenses. Kundan Lal thought, why not, let's have some recreation. He brought Sumitri along for his amusement and landed in Batut.

'Once here, he took absolutely no notice of his wife. He stayed out the whole day playing cards. Sumitri prepared the special diet for her sister. Every month Kundan Lal wrote to his in-laws that the expenses were mounting, and every month they added extra to the amount they sent.

'I don't wish to let this story drag on. I was now seeing Sumitri practically every day. The area by the stream where she washed clothes was pleasantly cool, just like the water of the stream. The shade under the apple trees was heavenly, and I wished I could sit there all day long, picking up the lovely round apples and tossing them into the clear water of the stream. The reason for this rather crude lyricism that has crept into my account is that I'd fallen in love with Sumitri and somehow sensed that she had accepted it. So one day, overwhelmed by a sudden surge of emotion, I clasped her to my bosom and kissed her on the lips with my eyes closed. Birds were twittering on the branches of the apple trees and the stream was humming gently.

'She was pretty, though a bit skinny. But if you thought deeply, you'd have felt that this is how she had to be. If she had been a bit fleshy, she wouldn't have looked so delicate. She had the eyes of a gazelle, which nature had lined with a dark eye shadow. She was short but infinitely pleasing, and her long, thick, dark hair reached down to her waist. A virgin, blossoming youth. Manto Sahib, I was lost in her love.

'As she was expressing her love for me, I told her what had been sticking like a thorn in my heart for some time. "Look, Sumitri," I said, "I'm Muslim and you're Hindu. What would be the end of this love? I'm not a libertine or rake that I could take advantage of you and be on my way. I want to make you my mate for life." She threw her arms around my neck and told me firmly, "Haneef, I'll convert."

'The weight on my heart lifted and I felt light. We decided that as soon as her sister got well she would leave with me. But it was not in her sister's fate to get well. Kundan Lal had told me plainly that he was waiting for his wife to die. In a manner of speaking, what he said had a ring of truth to it, though thinking such a thought and then blaming yourself for thinking it didn't seem right. Reality was staring us in the face. The disease being what it is, there was no way to escape from it.

'Sumitri's sister's condition worsened by the day. However, Kundan Lal couldn't care less. With more money coming from his in-laws and expenses reduced, or being purposely reduced, he had started going to the Dak Bangla to booze it up, and had even started coming on to Sumitri.

'My blood boiled, Manto Sahib, when I heard about that. Had I not lacked the courage, I'd have thrashed him black and blue with my shoes right there in the middle of the street. I hugged Sumitri to my chest, wiped away her tears and started to talk of love.

'As I passed by their quarters one morning on my walk, I had the uncanny feeling that Sumitri's sister was no longer in this world. I halted and called out to Kundan Lal. I was right. The poor woman had passed away at eleven o'clock the night before.

'He asked me to stay there a while so he could go and make arrangements for her last rites. He went out. As I stood there I was reminded of Sumitri. Where was she? The room with her sister's corpse was deathly quiet. I walked over to the adjoining quarters and peeked in. Sumitri was curled up on the bed like a bundle. I went in and shook her shoulder. "Sumitri! Sumitri!" I called her name. She didn't respond. Just then I spotted her shalwar stained with big splotches of blood. I shook her again. Again she didn't answer. I asked her tenderly, lovingly, "What's the matter, Sumitri?" She burst into tears. I sat down beside her. "What's the matter, Sumitri?" She said through her sobs, "Go, Haneef, go!" "But why?" I asked. "I know your sister has died. But please don't kill yourself crying." She choked on her words as she said, "She's dead, but I can't grieve over her. I've died myself." I didn't understand. "Why must you die? You have yet to become my lifemate, remember?" At this she started to cry bitterly. "Go, Haneef, go! I'm no good for you any more. Last night . . . last night Babuji finished me off. I screamed. Jiji screamed from her quarters. She had guessed everything. The shock killed her. Oh, how I wish I hadn't screamed. She couldn't have saved me. Go, Haneef, go!" She got up from the bed, grabbed my hand like someone possessed and dragged me out of the room. She quickly went back in and bolted the door. That son-of-a-bitch Kundan Lal returned after some time with four or five men in tow. I would have stoned him to death then and there had he been alone, I swear.

'This, then, is my story . . . Sumitri's story. Those three words of hers, "Go, Haneef, go!" never leave my ears. They're filled with such pain, such anguish.'

Tears had appeared in Haneef's eyes.

'Well, what happened, happened,' I said. 'You could still have married her . . .'

He lowered his eyes, uttered a coarse invective directed at himself, and said, 'Call it my weakness. Man turns out to be such a coward when it comes to that. God's curse upon him.'

The Revolt of Monkeys

The alarming news that 'monkey-ism' was on the rise was trickling in from all parts of the country. The government turned a blind eye to it at first but when it noticed that the matter was threatening to become serious it immediately sprang into action.

It is appropriate that the reader should be told right in the beginning what 'monkey-ism' or 'apishness' stands for. Of course we can't go into much detail here because it's a fairly long story, but briefly, the apish movement was set in motion by none other than the monkeys themselves and was directed squarely against humans.

Their gripe was: 'Now, when it's an incontrovertible fact that humans are our descendants, why do they treat us so coldly, and not just coldly but entirely contrary to the manner of apes? They tie ropes around our necks and make us dance to the tune of their *dugdugies*[*] in every lane and by-lane while they stick their hands out to beg for money . . . as though we're humans . . . Furthermore, while it is indisputable that we're their ancestors and that our blood flows in their veins, it is pretty dubious to say that *they* have climbed the evolutionary ladder to become humans. If there is such a thing as evolutionary stages, then why didn't we, billions of monkeys (you may call us a minority if you like, but if a census were ever taken, we would outnumber humans by far), go through them?'

The monkeys maintained: 'Why should these evolutionary stages remain the exclusive prerogative of only certain monkeys? Evolution!

[*] Kettledrums.

Hah, it's pure hogwash. Hell, they haven't evolved at all; if anything, they've regressed. They failed to hold on to the status that was bestowed on them; they tumbled so far down from apishness that they became humans.

'Their evolution is a sign of their downfall. We want these fallen monkeys to revert to their original apishness all over again. And we have started this movement to do just that: bring them back to the fold. We bear them no ill will or enmity; in fact, we consider them our siblings. The purpose of our movement is to compel these monkeys who strut around as humans nowadays, and who've grabbed power and influence because of our laxity, to recognize their true primary nature and return to our social habitat.'

Speeches were given publicly, out in the open, and in the privacy of homes, and sometimes even in clandestine meetings. In essence, they underscored the point that vigorous protests should be made against the tyranny and violence the monkeys had unleashed in the guise of man and that demonstrations should be staged in every part of the city, raising cries of *Down with humanity! Long live apishness!*

At first humans thought this was some kind of comedy show and had a hilarious time of it. Gradually, though, the monkeys' speeches, their irrefutable arguments and their point of view began to find a place in the hearts of some humans. As a result, those in power discovered from the reports of the secret police that several humans had become the monkeys' disciples, and, as trustworthy sources verified, thousands had renounced their humanity and returned to being apes; they had sprouted long tails and started walking on all fours.

High officials in the government dismissed this as pure nonsense. That a monkey can become human is an established fact, but how can a human become a monkey? Such reverse progression had never been seen or heard. So, after consulting their superiors, they countered the monkeys' claims by unleashing an equally relentless propaganda campaign of their own: A human can never morph into a monkey.

There was no dearth of able and resourceful personalities among the monkeys. To squash the government propaganda their savants came up with the ingenious argument that if in this time man can be transformed into woman and woman into man, why not man into monkey, which is his true form.

Still man's arguments didn't entirely fail to have an effect on the monkeys. Those humans who hadn't yet completely transformed found themselves hesitating about whether to complete the process of transformation or revert to being humans. But the monkeys' powerful rejoinder sustained them in their wavering mental and physical state.

The monkeys' propaganda secretary promptly mounted an especially vehement campaign. The one incontrovertible truth was: 'Humans have come forth from us, and only because of some regrettable deviationist streak. Can they deny that they are a distorted form of us?'

In truth, humans had no answer to this crushing argument. But they kept babbling: 'Well, no, we don't deny that we were once monkeys. But we had to toil hard and go through difficult stages to achieve our status as humans. It was our granite willpower, our protracted effort, our spiritual awakening, our thought and action, our evolutionary struggle that has brought us to this sublime and lofty state . . . a race that we won and others lost. The losers are still wallowing in their simian state. When these lower primates see us in our lofty state, they burn with jealousy. So let them stew. We'll march ahead on our evolutionary path until one day, who knows, we might even become gods.'

Quick came the answer from the apes' camp: 'Brethren, what lofty state have you reached? As we see it, you're plunging ever deeper into the depths of degradation. Evolution is something we don't deny, but just tell us, where do you stand today after climbing so many steps of the evolutionary ladder and after centuries of setting up one society after another? Your entire history is filled with warfare and carnage, murder and bloodshed, with rape and the defilement of women's honour, with ruling others and being subjugated by them.

'On the other hand, look at our—your ancestors'—history. Can you cite one such dark episode in our history? Yes, we frisk about from one branch to another, but have we ever fought over them as our property? You, you humans, have been writing story after story about us in your books—including the well-known story of how we grabbed on to one another's tails to build a bridge over the river. You too build bridges, so massive that your human brains are knocked out in astonishment. But then you blow them up. Whereas who can blow up the bridge we devised? Not a single monkey's tail has behaved treacherously to this day, nor has a single monkey's wife gotten into bed with another monkey. Our wives pick lice from our bodies and comb our hair daily, but they don't forfeit their rights doing so; they continue to be the same as ours. You're not unaware of the way your wives idle away their time, nor are your wives unaware of how you mess around. What you imply by calling us monkeys applies more appropriately to your own selves. Conversely, 'human' is an apt term for us considering the meaning you give it in describing yourselves. The plain fact is that you belong to our race. The same blood runs in our veins. No wonder if at times some resemblance should crop up and, equally, no wonder that it should result in the kind of row that has erupted between us now. We invite you to return to our fold. Come back to us, and raise the cry "*Down with humanity! Long live apishness!*" You'll be the better for it.'

The retort from the human side came loud and clear: 'These monkeys are shouting nonsense. They're green with envy that we've reached such glorious heights. A single story written about them under God knows what perverse influence, and that too for our children, cannot be taken as the definitive word about them. Otherwise who isn't aware of the kind of justice this monkey doled out to two cats regarding their quarrel over a piece of cheese? He weighed the piece on his scale and, little by little, gobbled it up himself.'

The monkeys rejoined: 'Scales and weights are human inventions; we don't use them at all, we don't even know how to use them. Now, if you want the truth, it was no monkey who swindled the cats out of their cheese, it was a human. There's no wonder that he would dupe the poor cats. We can show thousands of such cats whom these humans, once our brothers, are feeding lentils and cauliflower instead of their natural diet of sinews and membranes and thus, having already screwed up their own nature, are hell-bent on destroying that of others. Instead of ridiculing our sense of fairness, have a look at the institutions of justice you've created. Don't your courts ride roughshod over any notion of justice every day by sending hundreds, indeed, thousands of people who have committed no crime to the gallows? We say again, they are our brothers who have somehow gone astray. Our arms are forever open to take them back, our prayers forever for them. We wish to take no revenge.'

Gradually this amicable statement changed and, instead, this cry rose from the monkeys' camp: 'We want to take revenge . . . for this evolution . . . for this so-called progress these monkeys have foisted on themselves and turned into humans.'

The humans took severe measures of their own. Thousands of apes were taken into custody; hundreds dragged to the courts and subsequently hanged. But the movement in support of apishness continued unabated, until, finally, the human government declared it illegal. As a result, while some apes were arrested, the rest just melted away into the trees, frustrating every attempt to apprehend them. Who had the mind or the foolhardiness to chase after them in their jungle hideouts? Some monkeys, rumour had it, settled in the trees around the bungalows of some high officials, where they were well looked after and provided every comfort. This because those officials were themselves secret partisans of apishness, but loathed embracing it openly for fear of losing their high positions.

This went on for quite some time. Arrests continued, gallows were erected in the middle of chowks, the culprits were whipped, skinned and forced to crawl on their stomachs. Numerous acts and ordinances were put into effect. Nothing worked. But the monkeys were not about to call it quits. They stubbornly stuck to their position. Now and then they organized agitations, got together and stormed humans, chewed through electric cables, snatched bread from people's hands, smashed the little dugdugies to whose beat their monkey-masters made them dance, chewed through their ropes and fled.

They secretly converted several humans over to apishness, detonated home-made bombs, spread terror and, as often, risked their lives. Though the powers had broken up their organization, still they were as relentlessly united and well organized in their dispersal as ever. When man is faced with this sort of situation, he nearly goes mad. I say this because I too am one of the humans. But the strange truth is that the monkeys appeared smugly impervious to any change. They remained what they had been all along—monkeys. Their antics lost none of the playfulness. They would swoop down and snatch from the hands of humans whatever caught their fancy. Grab a gun from someone and march on like an army cadet. Batons, tear-gas grenades, nothing stopped them. They were, one might say, as restless as mercury. If you drew a gun on them, took aim and fired, they would take a leap and, before you knew it, would be sitting comfortably on your shoulder laughing their monkey heads off. If you threw a tear-gas shell at them, they'd jump and quickly turn it towards you.

The government was thoroughly fed up with their antics. A secret intelligence service report claimed that this monkey movement, or conspiracy, or whatever, could never have been launched by the monkeys themselves. A group of influential humans, supporting apishness just for kicks, must be working behind the scenes and, on further investigation, this fact was established beyond the shadow of a doubt. This disclosure was even more upsetting for the government; some officials panicked lest they should fall into the trap of apishness and, after reaching the top of the evolutionary ladder, lapse into being apes, a state their forefathers had fought long and hard to escape.

In spite of the government's countless strategies, the rising tide of the monkey movement couldn't be stemmed. Some monkey or other would appear on a rooftop or a steeple somewhere in the city several times during the day or night and shout through his megaphone: *Down with humanity! Down with dugdugies! Long live apism!*

One day the matter got out of hand. An audacious monkey stole into the living room of none other than the country's highest authority, opened the cigar box, picked one up, lit it and started puffing away leisurely. His Honour was furious. The monkey screeched at him. His Honour scolded and threatened. The monkey couldn't care less and leaped, landing on the sofa. The next moment he took another leap and alighted on one of the chairs, leaving His Honour with the distinct feeling that the monkey's movements were mimicking his own image in the mirror. He felt so riled up and incensed, writhing inside with anger and utter helplessness, that he finally broke down in tears.

We heard about this episode from our special sources, otherwise the next day's papers had a different story to tell: *An audacious monkey made an attempt to break into the government palace but the sentries gunned him down on the spot. After the incident, all pertinent government departments have been issued strict orders to take whatever steps necessary to quell the uprising of the monkeys.*

The chief of the secret police wasn't worried so much about the monkeys. He called together his subordinates and told them, 'These antics of the monkeys don't scare me. What I'm afraid of are the humans who have already reverted to being monkeys. I'm a man of keen intelligence. I think that if we can, as the descendants of monkeys, kick up so much trouble in the world and wreak such utter chaos, what might we do if we ever went back to being monkeys? Evolution, even when reversed, cannot but spell danger, no matter how one looks at it. So my instruction to you is this: Go and ferret out the humans who have embraced apism. If you can round them up, that will kill apism.'

Now the secret, as well as the ordinary, police intensified their efforts to apprehend the neo-monkeys who were wreaking havoc every night with one mischief after another. Several monkeys were caught and were given the 'third degree' inside the fort to make them squeal the whereabouts of the neo-monkeys. But they didn't let a word slip out of their mouths and bore the harshest torture with fortitude. They didn't relent even when their females were raped before their eyes. Exasperated, the police mowed them down and their corpses were doused with kerosene and set afire.

The next morning cyclostyled copies of a poster appeared everywhere in the city. In moving language it revealed the atrocities humans had committed and appealed to those who felt compassion to abandon their humanity and return to the fold of the monkeys, which was their original place.

Within minutes the posters were pulled down, but by then thousands of humans had already seen them, and hundreds chose to join apism. None of the countermeasures of the government worked. All the zoos, now converted into prisons, were filled with monkeys. One count put the figure of thirty thousand behind bars, but the incarcerated monkeys couldn't be happier.

The authorities were caught in a strange predicament: If they turned a blind eye to the monkeys, it was feared they would unleash a veritable revolution; if the authorities tightened their control and resorted to torture and atrocities, more and more humans would feel disgusted and turn against the government—after all, the same blood flowed in their and their ancestors' veins.

At long last, the authorities felt pressed to collectively think the matter over and devise some way that the ban on the monkey organization could be lifted; and further, the monkey leaders were to be invited to a conference and asked to explain their point of view so that some step towards reconciliation might be taken.

Gilgit Khan

Shahbaz Khan had had it with Jahangir, who worked in his restaurant and also ran errands. He couldn't stand the man's indolence any more, so one day he gave him his marching orders. Actually, Jahangir wasn't lazy or slow at all; he was so agile and fast that his movements seemed stationary to Shahbaz Khan.

Shahbaz Khan paid him the salary he was due. Jahangir said goodbye to him, bought a train ticket and went straight away to Baluchistan where coal had been discovered. Some of his friends had already made it there. He wrote to his brother Hamzah Khan in Gilgit and suggested he seek employment with Shahbaz Khan because he liked the man quite a bit.

Hamzah Khan went to Shahbaz Khan's restaurant one day, showed him the postcard he had received and said, 'I want to work for you. My brother says that you're a good and pious man. I'm also a good and pious man. How much will you pay?'

Shahbaz Khan looked at the man. He didn't look like Jahangir's brother at all—dwarfish, snub-nosed, and terribly ugly to boot. After reading Jahangir's letter and taking a look at him, Shahbaz Khan's immediate thought was to send him packing. But being a good-hearted man who had never turned away anyone in need, he took Hamzah Khan on for a salary of fifteen rupees a month. 'Look,' he told him, 'whatever work is given to you, do it honestly.'

With a smile on his ugly lips, Hamzah Khan assured his employer, 'Khan Badshah, I'll never give you any trouble. I'll do whatever you ask me to do.'

The assurance pleased Shahbaz Khan.

At first Hamzah Khan's work left a lot to be desired, but soon he learned all the ropes: how to brew tea, how much gur to throw in with refined sugar, how to bargain for coals with the itinerant coal-peddling women, how to treat each customer in an appropriate manner—everything.

He only had one shortcoming: his unbearably bad looks. He was also a little ill-mannered, which put the customers slightly ill at ease. But when they got used to his bad looks, it stopped bothering them. In fact, some even started taking an interest in him because he was, after all, an amusing fellow. However, their interest didn't please Hamzah Khan, who thought it was a sham. It was just for their own fun and amusement, to have a good time at his expense.

The customers had christened him Gilgit Khan, not only because he was from Gilgit but also because he referred to his native place far too often in his speech. He didn't mind his new name at all. While he had no inkling what 'Hamzah' meant, he knew quite well what Gilgit was.

It had been a year now since he started working for Shahbaz Khan. During this time it didn't escape his notice that his employer hated his looks, and the thought gnawed at him constantly.

One day he saw a puppy outside the restaurant—a creature even more unsightly than he was. He picked it up and brought it to his dingy little room above the restaurant, which the owner had allowed him to live in. The room was so small that one more puppy and Gilgit Khan would not have been able to fit inside.

The puppy's legs were terribly misshapen, its snout awful to look at. Strangely, Gilgit Khan's own legs, or rather, his lower half, were disproportionately smaller than his upper half. He and the puppy were both bent out of shape.

Gilgit loved his pup a lot. And though Shahbaz Khan hated the sight of the animal and threatened many times to put a bullet through him, Gilgit was not about to part with it, come hell or high water. Initially he kept quiet and listened patiently to Shahbaz Khan. But one day he told his employer flat out, 'Khu, you're the owner of the restaurant, you don't own my friend Tan-Tan.'

Shahbaz Khan eased up. After all, Gilgit was a workhorse. He got up at five in the morning, got the two braziers going, hauled water from the handpump across from the restaurant, and then got busy taking care of the customers.

In three months Gilgit Khan's Tan-Tan grew into a sizeable dog. He slept with his master in the same room, in his bed in fact, which Gilgit didn't mind given the punishingly cold nights of winter. Indeed, he felt immensely happy that the dog loved him so much that he didn't want to part with him even at night.

It was a special customer of Gilgit who had given the pup his name Tan-Tan. Never mind the pup's terrible looks, the man took an interest in him. Gilgit had saved some pennies from his meagre wages and bought a collar studded with tiny bells for the little pup. This special customer, who was probably a columnist for some daily paper, heard the tinkling bells and started calling the puppy Tan-Tan.

As Tan-Tan grew, his legs began to look even shorter, not unlike his owner's appearance. Gilgit's legs also seemed to shrink with amazing rapidity, while his torso grew normally. Shahbaz Khan did not like his appearance, but what could he do. Gilgit was an exceedingly hard-working man who toiled like a donkey from five in the morning till eleven or even twelve at night without a minute's rest—although during this time he did go up to his dingy quarters three or four times to look in on his darling puppy, now grown quite a bit bigger. He would feed him leftovers from the restaurant kitchen, give him water to drink, cuddle him, and then promptly return to work.

One day Tan-Tan fell ill. The majority of the restaurant's patrons were students from the neighbouring medical college. Gilgit overheard one of them saying that quail or chicken meat was especially good for someone suffering from a stomach ailment, and that starving the patient was pure foolishness.

Since the dog had diarrhoea, Gilgit hadn't given him anything to eat since the morning. He started looking everywhere for a chicken but couldn't find any. No one in the entire neighbourhood raised chickens.

Now, Shahbaz Khan was very fond of quail fights and owned a quail that he cared for more than his own life. Gilgit Khan stealthily opened the cage and grabbed the bird, and slaughtered it while reciting the *kalima* over it. He then fed it to his dear Tan-Tan.

The sight of the empty cage made Shahbaz Khan very anxious. How could the bird have flown away from its cage, he wondered nervously. The quail was so used to acting on his cues. How wondrously it had won many fights. He asked Gilgit Khan, who promptly replied, 'Khu, how would I know where your quail went. It must have run away somewhere.'

On pursuing the matter further, Shahbaz Khan found patches of blood and some feathers by the open drain in front of the restaurant. No doubt was left in his mind that they were the remains of his beloved quail. Anguish swept over him at the thought that some monster had roasted his quail and gobbled it up.

He gathered the bird's remains lovingly, dug a small pit in the open field behind the restaurant and laid them to rest. Then he recited the Fatiha over the grave. At the restaurant he offered food to the poor, hoping the reward for the good deed would go to his quail.

If anyone inquired about the quail, Shahbaz would tell them, 'It has attained martyrdom.'

Gilgit pretended not to have heard these words and continued with his work. He was overjoyed to see that his Tan-Tan had recovered fully and no longer suffered from his ailment. As a gesture of thanksgiving, Gilgit fed two beggars at his own expense. When Shahbaz asked him why he didn't charge them for the food, he said, 'Khan, a little charity now and then is a good thing.' Shahbaz kept quiet.

One day a fledgling mynah came flying from somewhere and fell right in front of Gilgit Khan as he was taking the breakfast tray to some college student. He put the tray to one side, picked up the frightened chick and put it in the cage that was formerly the home of his employer's quail. He began nurturing the chick, and in little over a month it grew quite plump and chirruped a lot. One day Tan-Tan wandered in, saw the chick and became restless: How could he reach it and chew it up?

Gilgit saw his Tan-Tan staring at the chick with such longing, but with no possibility of reaching it. He looked at the cage hanging from a hook on the wall, and without another thought, he took the chick out, wrung its neck, plucked its feathers and offered it to his darling dog.

Tan-Tan sniffed at the corpse of the plucked bird a couple of times, emitted a powerful sneeze, and took off.

Gilgit felt terribly sad. The same day, two college girls who came to the restaurant for tea regularly, and whom Gilgit cared about immensely, arrived. They always talked to him with light-hearted smiles; today, though, they seemed somewhat annoyed. One of them, Gilgit Khan's favourite, asked him, 'Why did you kill the mynah?'

Gilgit was confused for a moment but pulled himself together and replied, 'Khu, I wanted to feed my dog.'

'So did he eat it?'

'That swine . . . he just sniffed it and let it be.'

'So what did you gain by killing it? Before, you killed Khan's quail and fed it to him. Did he eat it?'

'Yes, he did,' Gilgit replied proudly. 'He even chewed up the bones.'

Shahbaz Khan was standing nearby. The minute he heard this he slapped Gilgit on his neck with all his might. 'You bastard . . . now you're admitting it. Why did you keep denying it before?'

Gilgit kept quiet.

Both girls burst out laughing. Gilgit didn't much care about the slap, but their laughter wounded him deeply.

Shahbaz Khan was beside himself with anger. The blow alone wasn't enough. He now assailed him verbally, unloading all the obscenities he knew on his employee. And finally, 'Why do you love that Tan-Tan or Chan-Chan so much, bastard? You call that thing a dog, huh! He's uglier than you, so ugly it turns my stomach!'

When Gilgit Khan went up to his hovel some time later, his ears were still buzzing with the girls' laughter. Tan-Tan was lying in a corner with his legs, which couldn't be more crooked, resting against the wall.

He thought for some time and then pulled out his jackknife and took a step towards the dog. A sudden thought made him snap the knife shut and put it back in his pocket. He called the dog to him lovingly and took him out for a walk.

The train was fast approaching when the two reached the tracks. Gilgit ordered his loving dog to go stand right in the middle of the tracks. The animal obeyed his master.

The train was considerably closer. Tan-Tan, planted in the middle of the tracks, was looking at Gilgit, his eyes brimming with loyalty. Gilgit glanced at himself. He felt his dog was infinitely better looking than he was.

When the train was almost upon them, Gilgit Khan quickly pushed Tan-Tan off the tracks, but got caught himself in the process. He was turned into minced meat. The dog sniffed at that pile of raw meat and started crying loudly in a heart-wrenching howl.

Martyr-Maker

I am a native of Gujarat, Kathiawar, and belong to the bania caste. Recently, when *tanta* broke out over the partition of India, I happened to be unemployed. Forgive me for using the word tanta. But does it matter? I should think not. After all, Urdu should accept non-Urdu words, even if they are borrowed from Gujarati.

So yes, I was unemployed, except for my small cocaine business, which still yielded a dribble of an income. When the country split and people from both sides started moving across the border in thousands, I thought, why not go to Pakistan. Even if I couldn't deal in cocaine there, I would at least be able to set up some other business. So I set out for Pakistan, doing all kinds of small deals along the way.

I arrived in Pakistan with the intention of starting a big business. After studying the situation closely I decided to get into allotments.* I was already adept at easing my way using flattery and bootlicking. I licked butt and sweet-talked, struck up a friendship with some fellows, and managed to get a small house allotted to me. I made a great deal of money by selling this property, and my success gave me the courage to visit different cities and acquire more allotments of residential houses and shops.

Every kind of job requires hard work. I had to run around quite a bit for allotments: sucking up to one person, greasing the palm of another, taking a third to dinner, and yet another to music and dance

---

* Allotment of evacuee Hindu and Sikh properties to Muslims to replace the properties they had left behind in India.

shows. In short, I had to go through a hell of a lot of trouble. I would
wander around sizing up spacious bungalows all day long, scouring the
entire city to decide on a big beautiful house whose allotment would
bring in a sizeable profit.

Hard work never goes unrewarded. Within a year I'd made piles of
money. By God's grace I had everything now: One of the finest bungalows
in the city, hoards of *maal-pani* in the bank—forgive me for using the
peculiar Gujarati jargon, but what's the harm. Urdu must welcome non-
Urdu words. So yes, by God's grace I had everything that one could
hope for: the finest bungalow, servants, a Packard, two and a half lakh
rupees in the bank, not to mention several factories and shops. Yes, I
had everything, but for some reason my peace of mind had vanished.
Even during the days of my small cocaine business I had sometimes felt
a certain heaviness sweep over my heart; now, though, it seemed as if I
no longer had a heart, or that if there was one it had been pressed under
a heavy weight.

What was this weight?

I'm an intelligent man. If a question agitates my mind, I try to
look for an answer and always find one. I started thinking with a cool
head about what was causing this *garbar-ghotaala*,* but where was my
head?

A woman? Could be. But I had no woman of my own. The one I
used to have had met her lord already in Kathiawar Gujarat. However,
there were others, but they belonged to other men, for instance, the wife
of my gardener. Well, everyone has their own taste. If truth be told, all
I care about in a woman is that she must be young—her being educated
or a dancer isn't a must. As long as she's young, any woman will do
for me.†

I'm an intelligent man. Whenever I'm confronted by a thorny
problem, I try to get to its root. My factories were running smoothly,
my shops were doing extremely well; money was being generated as
if on its own. I put all these aside and thought objectively about the
matter. All this garbar, I concluded after much thought, springs from
my never having performed a good deed.

---

* Conundrum, confusion.

† Manto uses 'apan ko sari javan aurten chalti hain' and adds in parentheses '[it is a]
Kathiawar, Gujarat's expression which has no equivalent in Urdu'.

In Kathiawar Gujarat, I had done many good deeds: such as when my friend Pandorang died, I sheltered his widow in my own home, thus keeping her from selling herself for two full years; or when Vinaik's wooden leg broke and I bought him a brand-new prosthesis, for which I had to spend forty rupees; or when Jamna Bai came down with venereal disease—saali (forgive me for using it) had no idea what it was—and I took her to a doctor and paid for her treatment for six months. But I hadn't done anything good for humanity in Pakistan so this had to be what was causing all this garbar in my heart.

So what shall I do, I asked myself. I thought of giving alms. I wandered through the city one day and saw that just about everyone looked like a beggar. Some were starved, others were without a scrap to wear. Whom to feed? Whom to clothe? There were so many. I might just as well have opened an almshouse. But what would a single almshouse accomplish? And where would I get the grain to feed all these people? Should I buy it on the black market? Which begged the question: What's the point of sinning with one hand and doing a pious deed with the other?

For hours I listened to the woes of countless people about their hardship and suffering. In truth, everyone was suffering: those who slept on shop stoops at night as well as those who slept in their tall mansions. A barefoot fellow was unhappy because he didn't have a proper pair of shoes, while someone who had a car was losing sleep over not having the latest model. In his own way each person was right about what was eating away at him, and everyone's needs made perfect sense.

I had once heard Ameena Bai Chitlekar of Solapur—may God have mercy on her—recite one of Ghalib's ghazals, a line of which has stuck in my memory: *Kis ki haajat rava kare ko'i* (whose need should one fulfil). Forgive me, this is the second line of the she'r, or maybe the first.

So there I was, wondering whose need I could take care of when a hundred out of a hundred were in need. Then again, the thought occurred to me that almsgiving wasn't really a meritorious act. You may not agree with me, but honestly, my many trips to refugee camps and my close scrutiny of the conditions there convinced me that welfare aid had turned many refugees into perfect slobs who sat around doing nothing all day, or wasted their time playing card games or *jagaar* (forgive me, jagaar means gambling), shouting obscenities at one another, and freeloading—what role could these loafers possibly have played in giving strength to Pakistan. I concluded that almsgiving was

absolutely not the right thing to do. But then what could I do that would
be a virtuous deed?

People were dying from cholera and plague in great numbers in
these camps. The hospitals were bursting already. The dearth of medical
facilities tore at my heart. I thought I might establish a hospital, but on
second thoughts decided against it even though I'd already devised the
whole plan in my head: I would call for bids for the hospital building
and a lot of money would pour in from prospective shareholders. I'd set
up my own construction company and accept its bid. My idea was to
spend one lakh rupees on the building. Obviously, it would have been
built for only seventy thousand and leave me a neat thirty thousand.
But the whole scheme came crashing down as soon as it dawned on me
that my effort to save the dying would only lead to overpopulation in
the country.

If you thought about it deeply, you would know that all this *lafra*
was caused by overpopulation. Lafra means problem, dilemma, one
that leads to scandal. Still I haven't been able to capture the entire range
of its meanings.

So yes, if you thought about it deeply, it would turn out that all this
lafra was caused by overpopulation. It was not a given that an increase
in population would, by some magic, result in a corresponding increase
in the land area or in the expanse of the sky, or in a precipitous increase
in rainfall so fields would yield more foodgrain. Well, I decided that
building a hospital was definitely not the good deed to undertake.

Then the idea occurred to me that I might build a mosque. But
thank God I was saved from the foolishness by the sudden memory of a
she'r sung by Ameena Bai Chitlekar of Solapur—may God have mercy
on her—namely: *Naam manjur hai to faij ke asbaab bana*. She used to
pronounce *manzur* as *manjur* and *faiz* as *faij*. The whole *she'r* went like
this: *Naam manzur hai to faiz ke asbaab bana / pul bana chaah bana,
masjid-o-taalaab bana.*

What wretch was after celebrity or a good name? It wouldn't be a
virtuous act for someone to build a bridge if the underlying motive was
to earn a good name, would it? Not at all. I told myself that the idea
of building a mosque was entirely wrong. The presence of too many

---

* If you want to earn a good name, do charitable works/build a bridge, a mosque or
water tank, or sink a well.

mosques, far away from each other, could in no way be good for the country. It would split up the population into many factions.

In desperation, I decided to go for the hajj. Just as I was making preparations for the trip, God Almighty showed me a way. A rally took place in the city which ended in a terrible commotion and in the ensuing stampede thirty people were trampled to death. The next day's papers carried the news of the incident and mentioned that the victims hadn't died, they'd achieved martyrdom.

That got me thinking. But I didn't just think, I also consulted several maulvis. They enlightened me about the fact that victims of accidents received the status of martyrs—the loftiest status a mortal could ever achieve. Wouldn't it be wonderful, I thought, if people didn't die but, instead, achieved martyrdom? Dying an ordinary death was like dying in vain. If people died as martyrs, well, that would be something— wouldn't it?

I gave this delicate matter still deeper thought.

Wherever you looked, you only saw people in pitiable shape: pale faces, ground down by sorrow and worries over their livelihood, listless and with sunken eyes, tattered clothes, lying about in crumbling huts like *kandam maal** or wandering around bazaars aimlessly with their heads sticking out in front like stray cattle. They have no idea why they're alive and for what, or for whom or how. An epidemic breaks out, thousands die. If not that way, by starvation and thirst; freeze in winter, shrivel up in summer. Lucky the one whose death provoked a few tears, but the majority remained unmourned.

Okay, you didn't understand what life was all about. It's also okay if you didn't enjoy its pleasures, but—now whose line was it that Ameena Bai Chitlekar, may God pardon her, used to intone in such a heartbreaking voice, '*Mar ke bhi chain na paaya to kidhar ja'inge*'†—I mean to hell with life if it still didn't get better after dying.

So the thought came to me: why not let these poor, ill-fated members of humanity who were spurned at every door they knocked on, who so desperately longed for every good thing in this world, find in that other world a station that will be the envy of those who would not deign to give them even a sidelong glance in this world. There was only one way

---

* Junk.

† Where would we go if we found no peace even after dying.

to ensure that: They should be spared a common, ordinary death and be made into martyrs.

Now the question was: Would they consent to be martyred? Of course they would, I thought. What Muslim does not long for martyrdom? Even Hindus and Sikhs have caught up with Muslims in coveting this lofty status. But imagine my disappointment when I asked this emaciated half-dead old coot, 'Would you like to become a martyr?' and he flatly refused with a resounding 'NO.'

For the life of me I couldn't understand why he wanted to go on living. I tried to reason with him, 'Look, old man, you'll be dead anyway in a month or so at the most. You have no strength left to walk. When you lose consciousness in the throes of a hacking cough it looks as if you're dead. You don't have even a broken cowrie to your name. You haven't seen any comfort in life and probably won't see any in the future either, the question doesn't even arise. Why do you want to live longer? You can't enlist in the army in hopes of laying down your life for your country fighting at the front. Isn't it better that you arrange for your martyrdom right here in the bazaar, or in the dump where you flop down for the night?'

'And how might I do that?' he asked.

'You see that banana peel up ahead,' I said. 'Suppose you slipped on it . . . It's obvious that you would die. You'll attain martyrdom.'

He failed to grasp my meaning. 'And why would I want to do that? Why would I want to knowingly step on the peel when I see it clearly? Don't you think I love my life?'

My, my, what a life! A pack of bones! A meshwork of wrinkles!

I felt sorry for the man, and sorrier when I heard that he, who could so easily have attained the lofty status of martyr, died, coughing away in the steel-frame bed of a charity hospital a few days later.

Then there was this decrepit old hag, practically toothless and in her last moments. I felt compassion for her. She had spent most of her life in abject poverty and suffering. I picked her up and brought her over to the railway *paata* (forgive me, back where I come from paata stands for railway tracks). But sir, what do you know, the moment she heard the whistle of the approaching train, she bounded clear of the tracks like a wound-up doll and fled.

It broke my heart, but I didn't let go of my resolve. After all, the son of a bania doesn't quit so easily. I didn't let the clear Path of Virtue slip out of my sight.

A big compound dating from the times of the Mughals lay vacant. It had a hundred and fifty-one small chambers, now in an advanced state of decay. My experienced eyes immediately estimated that their roofs would cave in during the first blast of torrential rain. So I bought the enclosure for ten thousand rupees and settled one thousand indigent tenants there, charging them two months' rent upfront at the rate of one rupee a month. Come the third month, as per my calculation, the roofs caved in during the first onslaught of heavy rains. Seven hundred people were martyred at one fell swoop, including old men and children.

That strange heaviness I was carrying around in my heart eased somewhat. The population decreased by seven hundred and the victims became martyrs in the bargain. Not a bad deal, eh!

I've been running this business ever since. Every day, according to my God-given ability, I manage to have two, sometimes three people quaff the wine of martyrdom. As I said before, everything requires gruelling hard work. For instance, this fellow whose life was as useless and meaningless as the fifth wheel of a rickety pushcart, I had to drop banana peels everywhere for ten full days to send him skidding to his martyrdom. But, I've come to believe now that just like death, the day of martyrdom is also foreordained. It was on the tenth day when this fellow finally fell over the peel on the hard cobblestoned ground and received martyrdom.

These days I'm having a gigantic building erected. The contract for two lakh rupees has gone to my own company. I'm sure I'll be easily able to pocket a neat seventy-five thousand from that amount. I've also taken out an insurance policy on the building. By my calculations, the entire building will crumble when the work on the third floor gets going because of the poor quality mortar I've used. Three hundred men are working on it. By God's grace, I dearly hope they'll all perish as martyrs. If anyone walks out unscathed, I will think he must be the worst kind of sinner and his martyrdom is not acceptable to the Lord.

Recite the Kalima!

La ilaha il-lal-lah, muhammadur rasul ul-lah—
   You are a Muslim, believe me, I speak only the truth. Pakistan has nothing to do with it. Honest. I'm ready any time to lay down my life for Quaid-e-Azam Jinnah. Please, don't be so hasty. Yes, of course, I know you don't have time, especially during these turbulent days of rioting. But, for God's sake, at least hear me out. Yes, I killed Tikka Ram, slashed his stomach with a sharp kitchen knife as you say, but not because he was Hindu. Well then, if I didn't kill him, who did, you might ask. All right, let me relate the whole story.
   Recite the kalima: *La ilaha* . . . What wretch knew that he would be embroiled in this mess? I killed three Hindus during the last Hindu–Muslim riots. But that was different, believe me. I'll tell you what happened, why I killed this Tikka Ram.
   Well, sir, what's your opinion of this breed called woman? I think our elders have spoken the truth: Only God can save us from their wiles, their shenanigans. If I'm spared the hangman's noose, I swear I'll never come anywhere near a woman—ever. But, sir, a woman is not the only one to blame; men are no less guilty. The minute they see a woman, any woman, they start drooling all over the place. Inspector Sahib, I have to die one day and face my Lord. The moment my eyes fell on Rukma, I just crumbled.
   Now one should ask: Man, you're a petty employee who makes only

---

* There is no God but Allah; Muhammad is the messenger of Allah. The Muslim profession of faith.

thirty-five rupees, what have you got to do with love? Collect the rent and be on your way. Call it my misfortune, Sahib, that one day when I went to collect the rent for kholi no. 16 and knocked at the door, Rukma Bai came out. I had seen her several times before, but that day her body was glistening with rubbed oil under a loosely wrapped gauzy sari. God knows why, a sudden impulse gripped me to yank on her sari and start massaging her body with all my strength. Well, that was the day when this wretch surrendered his heart and mind to her.

My, my, what a woman she was! Her body—so firm I thought I was massaging a piece of granite. I was gasping from exertion within minutes, but she kept saying, 'A while longer.'

Married? Yes, she was married. And if Khan the watchman is to be believed, she was also carrying on with a lover. But listen to the whole story; the lover will figure in it and so will everything else.

So, I lost myself to her that day. And she seemed to have guessed as much. She would give me a sidelong glance and smile. But, as God is my witness, every time she smiled a tremor of fear ran through my whole body. At first I thought it was the result of seeing one's love so close, but it was only later that I realized . . . But you should listen from the very beginning.

As I mentioned, I had exchanged many amorous glances with Rukma Bai. Now my entire effort was focused on how to get further along with her. Her husband, the bastard, remained glued to the kholi all the time, carving his puny wooden toys, and never gave me a chance.

One day I saw—what was her husband's name . . . yes, Girdhari—I saw Girdhari headed for the bazaar carrying a bundle of toys wrapped in a chador. Here was my chance. I immediately ran to kholi no. 16 and knocked on the door. My heart was pounding so hard it seemed as though it would jump out of my chest. The door opened. Rukma Bai stared at me. I trembled right down to the roots of my hair, I swear. I would have fled then, but she smiled and signalled to me to step inside.

She closed the door behind me and said, 'Sit!' I sat down. She came near me. 'Look, I know what you're after. It's not likely that you'll get it, not while Girdhari is alive.'

I stood up at once. Her closeness was scorching me. Even my temples were buzzing. She had rubbed oil over her body again today and had thrown the same gauzy sari loosely around her. I grabbed her shoulders and squeezed them hard as I said, 'I don't know what you're talking about.' Oh, those biceps, by God, they felt as hard as steel! I can't even begin to tell you what kind of woman she was.

Anyway, please listen to what happened.

I was so worked up I was sizzling. I hugged her tightly and blurted out, 'Girdhari can go to hell . . . You've got to be mine.'

She pushed me away. 'Watch out, you'll get oil all over you.'

'Who cares,' I said and clasped her to my chest again. Even if somebody had flayed my back raw with a whip, I wouldn't have let go of her then. But boy, oh boy, did she have a way with words! I cooled off and quietly sat down where she told me to sit. I knew she was thinking. That saala, Girdhari, is away at the moment. What is she so afraid of? When my patience ran out, I said, 'Rukma, we won't get such a fine chance again.'

She ran her hand over my head lovingly and said with a smile, 'Oh we will, we will, an even finer chance, you'll see. But tell me this: Will you do as I say?'

Sahib, I was like someone possessed. I was burning with passion. 'Yes, yes. I can kill for you, not one but fifteen people . . . if I have to.'

She smiled. 'Of that I'm sure.'

I swear to God, once again I trembled all over. I thought it was because of my inflamed passions.

Well, I stayed with her a little while longer, engaged in some love-talk, ate her fried bhajia, and then quietly slipped out. That thing? Well, it didn't happen, but, Sahib, that sort of thing doesn't happen the very first time anyway. Some other time, I told myself.

Ten days went by. On the eleventh day at two—yes, it must have been two in the morning, someone woke me up gently. I sleep down by the staircase.

When I opened my eyes I was surprised to see Rukma Bai in front of me. My heart started to pound. 'What's going on?' I asked in a hushed voice. And she said very softly, 'Come with me.'

Barefoot, I followed her to her kholi. I flung every thought to the wind and then and there clasped her tightly to my chest. And she whispered, 'Wait a little.' She turned on the light, the sudden glare blinding my vision somewhat.

When I was able to see again, I noticed someone lying on the floor on a mat; the face was covered with a piece of cloth. I gestured with my hand asking Rukma who it was. She said, 'Sit down.' I obeyed like an uncomprehending fool. She came close to me and, caressing my head lovingly, said something that knocked the living daylights out of me. I was frozen stiff, as if all the blood had coagulated in my veins.

Recite the kalima: *La ilaha* . . . I've never seen a woman like her in my life. '*Kambakht*,' she said smiling, 'I've bumped off Girdhari.'

Believe me, she'd murdered the sturdy man with her own hands. What a woman, Sahib! Whenever I recall that night every hair on my body stands on end. The heartless woman showed me the braided electric cord she had used to strangle Girdhari. She had attached a piece of wood to the cord and twisted it over and over again with such force that the poor man's tongue and eyes had popped out. It only took minutes to finish him off, she told me.

She removed the piece of cloth and showed me Girdhari's face, and I froze down to the marrow of my bones. What a woman! There, in front of her dead husband, she hugged me. I swear by the Qur'an. I immediately felt as though I'd become a dud forever. But, Sahib, the minute her body rubbed against mine and she gave me a strange sort of kiss, I was revived like never before. I'll remember that night for the rest of my life. Oblivious of the corpse lying in front of us, Rukma and I were deeply absorbed in each other.

In the morning we hacked Girdhari's body into three pieces. That was no trouble; the poor man's tools came in handy. Yes, we made a lot of banging noise, but people must have thought that Girdhari was working. Well, now, you might ask: Why did you participate in such a gruesome deed? Sahib, if you want the truth, she'd made me her slave in just one night. Had she asked me, I would have had no trouble making short work of fifteen men. Remember, I'd told her as much.

The big problem now was how to dispose of the chopped-up body. Rukma, regardless of her pluck and nerve, was a woman after all. I told her, 'Darling, don't you worry. Let's just dump the pieces in the trunk for now. I'll carry it out at night and get rid of them.' As luck would have it, a riot broke out that day and a lot of fighting and killing took place in five or six areas of the city. A thirty-six-hour curfew was imposed. I told myself, 'Abdul Karim, you must dispose of the body today no matter what.' So I got up at two in the morning and hauled the trunk out of her kholi. God, it was heavy! I was afraid of running into a khaki turban any minute somewhere on my way and be arrested for breaking the curfew. But, Sahib, no one harms him whom God wishes to protect.

Every single bazaar I passed through was deathly still. I spotted a small mosque near one bazaar. I opened the trunk, threw the pieces inside the mosque's courtyard and went back.

Oh, wouldn't a man sacrifice his life to the Lord's absolute power! Come morning it was discovered that Hindus had set fire to that mosque. Girdhari must have been burned up with it, I imagined. Now, Sahib, there was no impediment. I advised Rukma to let it be known in the chawl that Girdhari had gone out with his toys. I would visit her about two-thirty in the morning and we'd have action. She said, 'Abdul, let's not be hasty. Let's not meet at all for a fortnight.' That made sense. I kept quiet.

Seventeen days passed. Girdhari stole into my dreams to frighten me, but I told him, 'Saala, you're finished, dead. You can't do a thing to me now.' On the night of the eighteenth day, as I was sleeping at the foot of the stairs as usual, Rukma came, woke me up and led me to her quarters. It must have been around twelve, or at most one.

She stretched out naked on the mat and said, 'Abdul, my body is aching. Come, give me a massage.'

I quickly took some oil and started rubbing it over her body. I was out of breath within half an hour and a few drops of my perspiration dripped on to her clammy body. But would she ever say, 'You can stop now, you must be tired'? Eventually, I had to say, 'Rukma, that should do it.' She smiled, and what a smile it was! After catching my breath I sat down on the mat. She got up, turned off the light, and snuggled up to me. I was so exhausted from the hard work of massaging her that I couldn't think straight. I just put my arm on her breast and dozed off.

At some point I woke up with a start, feeling confused. I felt something hard digging into my neck. The thought of that twisted electric cord ran through my mind. Before I could free myself from the tightening noose, she had already mounted my chest. She pulled the cord with such force that my throat began to make cackling sounds. I tried to scream, but my voice couldn't leave my throat. After that I passed out.

I believe it must have been around four when I slowly came to. My neck was hurting badly. I stayed put and started unravelling the cord around my neck slowly. Suddenly I heard noises. Holding my breath with my eyes wide open, I probed the pitch-dark room but saw nothing. The noises gave the impression that two men were wrestling.

Rukma was gasping. Breathless, she said, 'Tikka Ram, turn on the light!' A frightened Tikka Ram peeped feebly, 'No, no. Rukma, no.' She said in a mocking tone, 'So timid! How will you cut him up and carry the pieces out in the morning?' My body froze stiff. I have no idea what Tikka Ram's response was.

God knows at what point the light suddenly came on. I sat up, rubbing my eyes. Tikka Ram let out a scream, hurriedly opened the door and took off. Rukma quickly closed the door behind him and latched it securely. Sahib, how can I ever tell you about my state then. Although my eyes were wide open and I was seeing and hearing everything, I had absolutely no strength to move.

Tikka Ram was not somebody I didn't know. He often came to our chawl hawking mangoes. I have no idea how Rukma managed to hook up with him.

She was gaping at me as if she didn't believe her eyes. She thought she had killed me. But there I was, alive and breathing right in front of her. She was about to pounce on me when there was a knock at the door followed by a crescendo of voices. She quickly grabbed my hand and dragged me into the bathroom. Then she opened the front door. The people outside were all chawl-wallahs. They asked her, 'Is everything all right? We just heard a scream.' 'Everything is fine,' she replied. 'It's just that I have this habit of walking in my sleep. When I opened the door and came out, I dashed against the wall. I panicked and screamed. That's all.' The people felt satisfied with her explanation and left.

Rukma shut the door and latched it tightly. I was worried sick thinking of what lay in store for me. Believe me, sir, the thought that the wretch wouldn't spare me produced a burst of energy in me, spurring me to fight her with all my might. In fact, I decided to hack her to pieces. When I managed to get out of the bathroom and saw her peering out of the big window, I rushed over to her, lifted her rear end and pushed her out. All this happened in a blink. I heard a heavy thud, quickly opened the door and cleared out. Lying on my cot, for the rest of the night I kept rubbing oil on my badly frayed neck to sooth it—here, you can see the bruises. None of the neighbours would have a clue about what happened, I thought with satisfaction. Didn't she herself tell them that she walked in her sleep? Her corpse lying on the other side of the chawl would convince them that she must have been sleepwalking and had fallen out the window. Dawn broke, taking all the time in the world. I wrapped a kerchief around my neck to hide the bruises. Nine o'clock, and then twelve, but nobody was talking about her dead body. She had landed in a long, narrow space wedged between two tenements with a door at either end to stop people from using it as a toilet. Still quite a heap of trash tossed out of the windows of the two buildings collected here and the sweeper woman carried it away every morning and evening. Perhaps she hadn't come to collect garbage that day, I thought, for if she had, she would have noticed Rukma's dead body as soon as she entered and would have made quite a hullabaloo. What the hell was going on? I wanted people to know about it without delay. By two o'clock, I couldn't hold back any more. I opened the door and peeked. I was stunned. No dead body, no garbage either. Wonders! Where the hell had Rukma disappeared? I swear by the Qur'an, if I ever walk away from the hangman's noose a free man, it won't surprise me more than her inexplicable disappearance. I'd pushed her from the third floor on to the cobbled ground below. How could she have survived? But then who had carried her corpse away? Reason refuses to accept it, but who knows, Sahib, the kind of woman she was, she might have walked out alive. Chawl-wallahs think that some Muslim either made off with her or killed her. Good for him if he killed her, but if he's keeping her in his house, you can imagine what end he'll come to. God save him, Sahib.

Now let me tell you about Tikka Ram. He met me twenty days later and asked, 'Where's Rukma?' I told him I had no idea. 'No, you damn well know,' he insisted with a veiled threat in his voice. I said, 'Brother, I swear by the Qur'an, I know nothing about her.' 'No,' he said, 'you're lying. You've killed her. I'm going to file a report with the police. I'll tell them that first you dispatched Girdhari, then Rukma.' He left. I broke into a sweat from sheer terror. I thought long and hard about what to do, but couldn't think of anything except that I should get rid of him. You tell me, what else could I have done? So I took a kitchen knife and sharpened it in absolute secrecy. Then I went out looking for Tikka Ram. By chance I found him near the urinal at the corner of the street. He had just put his empty boxes of oranges down outside and gone in. I darted in after him. He was just untying his dhoti when I yelled, 'Tikka Ram!' The moment he turned around, I plunged the knife into his stomach. He tried with both hands to keep his guts from spilling out but doubled over and crumpled to the ground. I should have made my escape immediately, but look at the foolhardy thing I did. I started to check for his pulse to make sure he was dead. All I'd heard was that everyone has this vein, but whether it was on the left or right of the thumb I didn't know. I was taking a long time figuring it out and that was my undoing. A constable entered unbuttoning his trousers. He grabbed me. Well, Sahib, this is the whole story, pure and simple, without a grain of falsehood. Recite the kalima: *La ilaha . . .*!

Barren

Our first encounter took place exactly two years ago today at Apollo Bunder. It was evening. In the distance, the last remnants of the sun had disappeared behind the waves, which resembled the folds of a thick, coarse fabric when looked at from the benches on the beach. I was sitting on the other side of the Gate of India on a bench next to where a man was getting a head massage. I was looking at the ocean, stretched out as far as the eye could see. At the furthermost point, where the sky and the sea came together, huge waves rose gradually, as if the sides of a dark-coloured carpet were being folded up.

The beach lights were all on, their reflection over the water spreading thick, quivering lines on it. Below me, along the stone wall, masts and rolled-up sails swayed gently. The sound of the waves and the voices of the sightseers permeated the atmosphere like a hum. Now and then the horn of an approaching or receding car split the air like an intrusive 'hunh!' in the middle of the telling of an absorbing tale.

Such a pleasant atmosphere calls for a smoke. I pulled out a packet of cigarettes but couldn't find any matches. God knows where I had left them. I was about to put the packet back in my pocket when I heard someone nearby say, 'Here are some matches.'

I turned around and saw a young man standing behind the bench. Bombay residents are normally pale, but this man looked frighteningly so. I thanked him. 'That's very kind of you.'

He handed me the matches. I thanked him again and said, 'Please sit down.'

'Please light your cigarette,' he said, 'I have to go.'

He seemed to be lying; it was obvious from his tone that he was neither in a hurry nor was there any particular place where he needed to be. True, you might ask how one can tell such things from a tone. But the truth is that was precisely how I felt at the time. So I said once more, 'What's the hurry. Have a seat,' and offered him a cigarette. 'Have one.'

He looked at the packet and said, 'Thanks, but I only smoke my own brand.'

I could have sworn that he was lying again. And again it was his tone that betrayed him. This piqued my interest and I resolved firmly that I would make him sit down beside me and smoke one of my cigarettes. I believed this wouldn't be too difficult because in just two sentences he had made it plain to me that he was deluding himself. He, in fact, *wanted* to sit down and smoke but, at the same time, he felt he should do neither. This dichotomy between yes and no was clear to me in his tone. Believe me, his very existence seemed to be suspended between being and non-being.

His face, as I've already mentioned, looked incredibly pale. Apart from that, the outlines of his nose, eyes and mouth were so faint that it seemed as if someone had drawn a portrait and then given it a wash. As I looked at him, his lips would swell at times but then fade away like a spark buried under layers of ash. It was the same with his other features: eyes like two puddles of muddy water with sparse lashes drooping over them; black hair that had a hue resembling burnt paper and appeared dry and brittle like straw. You could make out the contours of his nose more easily, but from a distance it looked pretty flat, because, as I mentioned earlier, his features were not very distinct.

He was of average height, neither tall nor short. However, when he stood a certain way, relaxing his spine, there was a marked difference in his height. Likewise, when he would suddenly stand erect, he appeared to be much taller than his true size.

His clothes were shabby, though not grimy. His jacket sleeves were frayed at the cuffs from constant wear and tear; you could see the threads unravelling. His collar was unbuttoned and his shirt looked as though it would not survive even one more washing. Yet, despite such clothing, he was trying hard to present himself as a respectable man. I say 'trying' because when I had looked at him, a wave of anxiety seemed to wash over his entire being, leaving me to wonder if he wasn't really trying to keep himself hidden from my eyes.

I got up, lit a cigarette, and offered the packet to him. 'Help yourself!' The way I said it and the quickness with which I lit the match and held it out to him somehow made him forget everything. Taking a cigarette, he stuck it in his mouth and started to smoke. But then he immediately realized his mistake. He promptly removed the cigarette from his mouth, pretending to cough. 'Cavenders don't agree with me,' he said. 'They have such strong tobacco that it irritates my throat right away.'

I asked, 'So what brand do you smoke?'

He stammered, 'I . . . I actually smoke very little because Dr Arolkar has advised me not to. Otherwise I buy 555, which is pretty mild.'

The doctor he mentioned was famous throughout Bombay; he charged a fee of ten rupees per visit. The 555 brand he mentioned, as you may well know, is very expensive. He'd now lied twice in one breath, which I found difficult to digest. Still, I kept quiet, even though I would have liked nothing better than to pull off his mask, expose his lies, and shame him into apologizing to me. However, when I looked at him I realized that whatever he said became a part of him. I didn't see the kind of blush that usually sweeps across the face of a liar. Instead, I sensed that he truly believed whatever he said. His lies were spoken with complete sincerity. He lied with such conviction that he didn't experience the slightest bit of guilt. Anyway, let's drop this. Recounting all these details will require reams of paper and I would never get around to the story itself.

After a little polite conversation that seemed to put him at ease, I offered him another cigarette and mentioned how exquisite the ocean looked. Being a storywriter, I was able to talk to him about the ocean, about Apollo Bunder and all the visitors there in such an engaging way that even after six cigarettes his throat failed to become the least bit irritated. He asked me my name. When I replied he stood up and said, 'Oh you . . . you're . . . Mr . . . I've read many of your stories . . . I didn't know it was you. I'm very pleased to have met you. Really very pleased.'

I wanted to thank him but he continued, 'In fact, I remember reading one of your stories just recently. I can't recall the title though. It's the one about the girl who's in love with a man but the fellow deceives her. There's another man in the story, the narrator, who's in love with her. When he discovers the girl's misfortune he tells her, "You must go on living. Turn the memory of the moments you spent engrossed in his love, when you were happy, into a foundation you can build your life on." I don't remember it word for word, but do tell me one thing: Is it possible . . . forget possible, tell me straight up whether, by any chance, you are that man. Forgive me, I shouldn't be asking such a question. I really shouldn't . . . but were you the person who had a tryst with her on the rooftop and then went downstairs to sleep in your own room, leaving her alone in the slumbering moonlight with all the passions of her youth?' Here he suddenly halted and then added, 'I really shouldn't be asking this sort of thing. After all, who opens up his heart to strangers!'

'I will tell you,' I said. 'But somehow it does seem a bit odd to be asking and telling everything when one has just met someone for the first time.'

His earlier excitement cooled suddenly. He said softly, 'You're right, but who knows whether we'll ever meet again.'

I said, 'Bombay is, of course, a very large city but we can meet again, not just once but many times. I'm an idle person, I mean short story writer . . . you'll find me here every evening, provided I'm not sick. Many young women come here to stroll and I come here to find one of them to fall in love with. Love's not a bad thing!'

'Love . . . love! . . .' He wanted to say something more but couldn't, and like a rope on fire he fell tortuously silent.

I had brought up 'love' just to be funny. And given the absolutely delightful surroundings, I would have had no regrets about actually falling in love with someone. When the waning daylight and evening shadows meet, when the rows of street lights begin glimmering in the encroaching darkness, when the air becomes slightly chilled and the feeling of romance permeates the atmosphere—a man naturally longs to be close to a woman. It is that feeling, that need, which lies hidden in our unconscious.

God knows which story he was referring to. I don't remember all of my stories, especially the romantic ones. I've known very few women in my life. The stories I wrote about women were either because of a particular need or just to indulge in mental gratification of the senses. Since they lack sincerity, I don't think much of them. I have observed women of a certain class and written a few stories about them, but those aren't romances. In any case, the story he was alluding to must be one of those mediocre romances, the kind I might have written to calm my own ardour. But—what's this?—I've started telling my own story.

So when he fell silent after uttering 'love', I felt the urge to expand further on that subject. I began: 'Well, it just so happens that our forefathers have enumerated many kinds of love, but as far as I'm concerned, whether love is born in Multan or on the icy plains of Siberia, whether it's born in winter or summer, in the heart of a rich man or a poor man, whether it's beautiful or grotesque, or whether those who fall into it are degenerate or pious, love remains love. It doesn't change. Just as the manner of a child's birth remains basically the same, so does love's. Of course, it's an entirely different matter if Saeeda Begum gives birth in a hospital while Rajkumari gives birth in a jungle, or if a sweeper-woman stirs the feelings of love in a Ghulam Muhammad while a Natwar Lal is smitten by the love of a princess. Just as children who are born prematurely remain weak after birth, so too a love born before its time suffers from weakness. Some children are born after excruciating labour; well, so are some loves—they cause a lot of pain. Just as some women miscarry, so does love miscarry for some people. And just as sterility results in an inability to conceive a child, you will find people who turn out to be incapable of love. This doesn't necessarily mean that the desire to love has completely vanished from their hearts, or that the feeling of love has been completely smothered. No, the desire may still be there, but they lack the ability to translate that into love. Just as some women are unable to conceive because of some physical problem, so these people are unable to ignite the spark of love in the hearts of others because of some spiritual handicap.'

I was finding my own harangue rather interesting, so I kept lecturing away without even looking at him. When I finally looked at him, I found him gazing off into space across the ocean, entirely lost in his own thoughts. I fell silent.

The sound of a particularly loud horn suddenly jolted him out of his reverie and he blurted out absent-mindedly, 'Yes, you're absolutely right!'

I thought of asking him, 'Absolutely right? . . . Forget that. Just tell me what I've been saying.' But I kept quiet, allowing him a chance to shake off his weighty thoughts.

He went on thinking for a while and then said, 'What you said is absolutely correct, but . . . Let's drop this topic. It . . . well, never mind.'

I liked what I'd been talking about. I wanted nothing more than to have someone go on listening to me, so I repeated, 'Well, as I was saying, some men, too, turn out to be barren when it comes to love. I mean they do desire to love, but are never able to fulfil that desire. I tend to think this is due to some spiritual shortcoming. What do you think?'

He turned even paler, as though he'd seen a ghost. The change came over him so suddenly that I became worried and asked, 'Is everything all right? You aren't feeling ill, are you?'

'No . . . no . . .' He sounded even more worried. 'I'm not ill or anything like that. What makes you think I am?'

I replied, 'Anyone who saw you now would assume that you're ill, extremely ill. You look frightfully pale. I think you'd better go home. Come, I'll take you there.'

'No, I'll go myself. But I'm not ill . . . I do feel a slight pain in my chest now and then. Maybe it's just . . . I'll be okay. You can continue.'

It didn't look as though he would be able to concentrate on my words so I remained silent, but when he insisted, I resumed. 'I was asking what you thought about people who are unable to love. I have no idea what they feel, what their inner thoughts are. But when I think of those barren women who, in the hope of conceiving a child, make fervent entreaties to God and, disappointed by Him, resort to spells and charms—bringing ash from cremation grounds, reciting night-long incantations that were given to them by sadhus, and making votive offerings—to gain the pearl of their desire, it occurs to me that a person who's unable to love must experience a similar ordeal. Such people truly deserve compassion. I feel more for them than I do for the blind.'

His eyes brimmed with tears. He swallowed and quickly stood up. Turning his face away he said, 'Oh, it's late. I have an important errand to run and I seem to have lost quite a bit of time talking.'

I also got up. He turned towards me and pressed my hand but spoke without looking at me, 'I really must leave now,' and walked away.

The second time I met him was again at Apollo Bunder. Although I'm not one for taking walks, back in those days an evening stroll to Apollo Bunder had somehow become part of my daily routine. A month later, though, a longish letter from an Agra poet—which, among other things, made lewd comments about the beauties who crowded Apollo Bunder's beaches and how lucky I was to be living in Bombay—pretty much destroyed whatever interest I may have had in the place. Now, whenever someone asks me to go there, I'm reminded of that poet's letter and feel like throwing up. But I was talking about a time before that letter. Then, I used to go there every evening and sit on the bench next to the place where many people were in the habit of having masseurs give their skulls a good workout, rubbing and knocking.

Day had given way to evening, with no trace of light left anywhere. The October heat was still intense, but a breeze was now blowing. Strollers, like exhausted travellers, made up most of the crowd. Behind me cars and more cars had lined up. All the benches were taken. Two chattering men, one Gujarati, the other Parsi, had settled on the bench next to me and were blabbering away in Gujarati, each with a different accent. The Parsi's voice had only two notes, one shrill, one deep that he alternated. When they both talked rapidly at the same time, it sounded as if a parrot and a mynah were having a duel.

Getting tired of their endless chatter, I got up and was about to head towards the Taj Mahal Hotel when I saw him coming my way. I didn't know his name so I couldn't call him. But when he saw me his eyes locked on, as though he'd found what he was looking for.

There were no empty benches, so I proposed, 'It's been a long time since we last met. Let's go over to the restaurant. All the benches here are taken.'

He said a few things by way of formality and came along. We walked a bit and then sat down in the large cane chairs in the restaurant. After I had ordered tea, I offered him my tin of cigarettes. Coincidentally, I had been to see Dr Arolkar just that day and he had advised me to quit smoking altogether, or, failing that, to switch to smoking better quality cigarettes, like 555. So, following the doctor's advice I had bought this tin that very evening. He stared at the tin, then at me. He started to say something but then decided against it.

I broke into a laugh. 'Don't think that I've started smoking these on your advice. Actually you might call it coincidence. Today, I too ended up going to Dr Arolkar because lately I've been feeling this pain in my chest. Anyway, he advised me to smoke these, but far fewer.'

As I said this I stole a peek at him and realized that my words had upset him, so I took Dr Arolkar's prescription out of my pocket and put it on the table. 'I can't read his handwriting but he seems to have crammed every vitamin into this one prescription.'

He glanced at the prescription which showed Dr Arolkar's name and address embossed in black letters and also the date. His erstwhile look of agitation quickly faded. He smiled and said, 'Why do most writers

suffer from vitamin deficiencies?' I replied, 'Certainly not because they
don't get enough to eat. It's more likely because they work a lot and get
paid a pittance.'

Meanwhile the tea had arrived and we started talking about other
things.

An interval of a month, maybe a month and a half, had passed
between our first and second meetings. His face now looked even paler
than before and there were dark circles around his eyes. Apparently he
was suffering from some spiritual crisis which troubled him constantly.
Every now and then he would stop short in the middle of his sentence
and, quite unconsciously, let out a sigh. Even when he tried to laugh his
lips hardly seemed to move.

Seeing him in this condition, I asked abruptly, 'You look sad . . .
Why is that?'

'Sad . . .' A faint smile, like one you might see on the face of a person
who's dying but wants to show that he isn't afraid to die, appeared on
his face. 'No, I'm not sad. Could it be that you're in a sombre mood
yourself?'

He finished his tea in a single gulp and quickly got up. 'All right,' he
said, 'I've got to go. I have an important matter to take care of.'

I was certain that he didn't have 'an important matter to take
care of'. Yet, I let him leave without trying to stop him. Once again, I
had failed to find out his name, but I did find out that something was
bothering him—mentally and spiritually. He was sad, or rather sadness
had completely permeated his being. But he didn't want anyone to
know. He wanted to live two lives: one that was real and the other that
he was busy creating every minute, every second. Both of his lives were
a failure. Why? That I don't know.

It was again at Apollo Bunder that we ran into each other for a
third time. This time, however, I took him to my place. Although
we didn't say anything on the way, we did talk quite a bit once we
reached home. The moment he entered the room a look of despair
appeared on his face and lingered there for a few seconds. He quickly
steadied himself and, unlike in the past, tried to appear unusually
cheerful and chatty, which made me feel even sorrier for him. He
seemed to be denying the reality of something as certain as death.
What's even worse, he sometimes seemed to be quite satisfied with
his self-deception.

As we talked away, he noticed the framed photograph on my table. Getting up and moving closer to the photograph, he asked, 'May I take a look . . . with your permission, of course?'

'By all means!'

He gave the photograph a fleeting look and then sat down. 'Quite a good-looking woman. I guess she's your . . .'

'No, no. It was a long time ago. I was attracted to her; rather, I should say I almost fell in love with her. Unfortunately, she never knew about it, and I . . . No, she was married off to . . . Anyway, this is a memento of my first love, which died even before it had a chance to be born.'

'A memento of your first love! You must have had quite a few affairs since.' He ran his tongue over his dry lips. 'I mean you must have had many loves in your life—requited and unrequited.'

I was about to set him straight and tell him that this humble man was just as barren in the matter of love as he was. But, God knows why, I held back. Instead, I lied to him for no reason at all. 'Of course! Such affairs do come along, don't they? You must have had quite a few yourself.'

He didn't say anything and fell completely silent, as though he had plunged into deep waters. After he'd been submerged in his own thoughts for a long time and his silence began to weigh on me, I said, 'Well, sir, where have you gotten lost?'

He was startled. 'I . . . Nowhere. I was just thinking about something.'

'Were you reminded of something that happened to you in the past?' I asked. 'Stumbled on a lost dream? Some old wounds starting to hurt again?'

'Wounds? Old wounds? Well, not wounds. Just one—very deep and vicious. And I have no desire for more. One is enough.' Saying that, he got up and attempted to pace inside my room. 'Attempted' because my place was small and cluttered with chairs, a table, a cot and what all—there was really no room to pace. He could only go as far as the table and then he had to stop. This time, though, he looked at the photograph closely and said, 'How much she resembles her! Her face wasn't quite as playful though. She had big eyes, the kind which can see as well as understand.' He heaved a sigh and sat back down. 'Death is beyond comprehension, especially when it seizes someone in the prime of their youth. I believe there's another power besides God—extremely jealous and begrudging anyone's happiness. But never mind . . .'

'No, no, please go on,' I insisted, 'if you don't mind. To tell you the truth, I thought you had probably never fallen in love.'

'What made you think that? A few minutes ago you said I must have had quite a few affairs myself, didn't you?'

He looked at me with questioning eyes. 'If I haven't loved, then why this sorrow that keeps gnawing at my heart? Why this affliction? This sadness? This state of being oblivious to myself? Why am I melting away like wax day and night?'

Ostensibly he was asking me, but in fact he was asking himself.

I told him, 'I lied when I said that you must have had quite a few affairs. But you lied too, when you said you weren't sad and that nothing was bothering you. It's not easy to know what's inside another person's heart. There could be any number of reasons for your sadness and, unless you choose to tell me yourself, I can't very well come to any conclusion, can I? That you're becoming frailer and frailer by the day is obvious. Surely you've suffered a big shock, and I do sympathize with you.'

'Sympathize!' Tears rushed to his eyes. 'I don't need sympathy. Sympathy can't bring her back, can't pull the woman I loved out of the abyss of death and return her to me. You've never loved. No, you have not. Of that I'm certain. For you are unscathed by its failure. Look at me,' he demanded, and looked down at himself. 'Do you see any spot where love hasn't left its scars? My entire existence is nothing more than the rubble of love's crumbling abode. How can I relate this tale to you? And why should I? You wouldn't understand. The words, "My mother died," are not likely to affect a stranger as much as the deceased's son. To you, indeed to anybody, my tale of love would seem commonplace. But the way it has affected me, how can anyone understand it! Only I have experienced this love and only I have borne its brunt.'

He fell silent. His throat had become dry; this was obvious from his repeated attempts to swallow.

'Did she deceive you?' I asked him. 'Or was there something else?'

'Deceive? She could never deceive. For God's sake don't use that word. She wasn't a woman, she was an angel. But woe to Death that couldn't bear to see us happy and gathered her up in its wings and took her away forever . . . Ah! You've opened my wounds. So now listen. I'll tell you part of that distressing tale. She came from a distinguished, wealthy family. When we first met, I'd already squandered away the whole of my ancestral property on a life of debauchery. Nothing remained. I left my home and went to Lucknow. Since I used to own a car, driving was the one skill I had. So I decided to become a chauffeur. My first job was at the residence of the Dipty* Sahib and she was his only daughter.'

He drifted off into his own thoughts and stopped talking. I remained silent. After some time he snapped out of his reverie and said, 'What was I saying?'

'That you worked for a dipty sahib.'

'Yes. She was the Dipty Sahib's only daughter. Every morning at nine I'd drive her, Zohra, to school. She observed purdah, but how long can one remain hidden from one's chauffeur! I was able to see her face on the very second day. She wasn't just beautiful; she had something quite special about her. She was a serious, poised young woman. The straight parting in her hair gave her an unusual aura of dignity. She . . . she . . . How do I explain to you what she was really like. I don't have words to describe her inner and outer beauty.'

He kept reciting his Zohra's accomplishments for a long time, making several attempts along the way to describe her in words, but failing repeatedly. It seemed that too many thoughts had crowded into his head. Now and then his face would light up in the middle of a sentence, only to be quickly clouded over by a gloom that left him talking in sighs. He told his story extremely slowly, as if relishing it himself. His story, which he recounted one piece at a time, went something like this:

He fell madly in love with Zohra. He spent the first few days looking for opportunities to steal a glance at her and working out all kinds of plans. But when he thought about it seriously, he recognized that he and Zohra were just too far apart. How could a chauffeur even think of falling in love with the daughter of his employer? That bitter realization clouded his days with unrelenting sadness. One day, though, he dared to scribble a few lines to Zohra on a piece of paper.

> Zohra! I know I'm your servant. Your father pays me a salary of thirty rupees a month. But . . . I'm in love with you. What shall I do? I'm so confused.

---

* Urdu pronunciation of deputy.

He stuck the scrap of paper inside one of her books. The next morning when he drove her to school his hands shook, and many times he very nearly lost control of the steering. But, thank God, no accident occurred. He spent the whole day in a strange state of mind. In the evening, when he was driving her back from school, she asked him to pull over. When he did so, she spoke in an extremely serious tone. 'Look, Naim, don't repeat this ever again. I haven't told my father about the letter you slipped inside my book. But if you ever do this sort of thing again, I'll be forced to report the matter to him. Understand? Okay, now drive on.'

After that, he tried to quit working for the Dipty Sahib and to extinguish his love for Zohra, but he didn't succeed. This tug of war went on for a month. One day he gathered his courage and wrote her another letter. He slipped it into her book and waited for the decree of his fate. He was sure that he'd be dismissed from his job the very next morning, but that didn't happen. On their way back from school that evening, Zohra once again spoke to him and admonished him. 'If you don't care about your own honour, at least care about mine.' She said all this with such gravity and firmness that Naim's hopes were completely dashed. Immediately he resolved to quit his job and leave Lucknow for good. At the end of the month he wrote one final letter to Zohra by the dim light of his lantern. Filled with pain and anguish he told her,

> Zohra! I've tried my best to act on your advice. Believe me, I have. But I cannot control my heart. This is the last time I shall ever write to you. I'll leave Lucknow by tomorrow evening so you need not say anything to your father. Your silence will decide my fate. I'll live far away from you . . . but don't think that I'll ever stop loving you. My heart will always be at your feet no matter where I live. I will always remember the days when I drove the car carefully and slowly in order to spare you any jolts. What else could I have done for you anyway?

This letter, too, he slipped into her book as soon as an opportunity presented itself. As they drove to her school in the morning, Zohra didn't say a word to him. Nor did she speak to him on their way back in the evening. He went to his room utterly dejected, packed the few belongings he had and put the bundle away in a corner. Then he sat down on his cot and, in the pale light of the lantern, thought about the precipitous gulf that separated him from Zohra.

He was very despondent, well aware of his own insignificance. After all, he was just a lowly servant! What right did he have to fall in love with his employer's daughter? But the thought occurred to him from time to time that it wasn't his fault that he'd fallen in love with her. And besides, his love was not a deception. Around midnight, as he was mulling over these thoughts, he heard a knock on the door. His heart jumped to his throat, but then he thought it must be the gardener. It was possible someone had fallen sick at his home and he'd come for help. But when he opened the door, Zohra was standing across from him— yes, Zohra—in the December chill, without even her shawl.

He was tongue-tied. He didn't know what to say. There was a deathly silence for a few moments and then, finally, her lips moved and she said in a trembling voice, 'Well, Naim, I'm here. Tell me what you'd like me to do. But before you tell me, I have a few questions of my own.'

Naim was silent.

Zohra asked, 'Do you really love me?'

Naim was hurt. His face flushed. 'Zohra,' he said, 'you're asking a question which would debase my love if I attempted to answer it. Instead, let me ask you: Don't I?'

Zohra didn't respond. After a brief silence she said, 'My father has a lot of money, but I don't have a single paisa to my name. Whatever is said to be mine is, in reality, not mine but his. Without wealth would you still love me as dearly?'

Being an overly sensitive man, Naim felt as if the question was an affront to his dignity. In a voice weighed down by sorrow, he said, 'For God's sake, Zohra, please don't ask questions whose answers are so commonplace that you can even find them in third-rate romance novels.'

Zohra stepped into the room and sat down on the cot. 'I'm yours,' she said, 'and always will be.'

She kept her word. After she and Naim moved to Delhi, married and set themselves up in a small house, the Dipty Sahib came looking for them. As Naim had already found work, he wasn't home. The Dipty Sahib scolded Zohra, accusing her of sacrificing her honour. He wanted her to leave Naim and put all that had happened behind her. He was even willing to pay Naim as much as two or three thousand rupees. But Zohra wasn't ready to leave her husband, no matter what. She said to her father, 'Daddy! I'm truly happy with Naim. You could never have found a better husband for me. We don't ask you for anything. But if you can, give us your blessing; we'll be grateful for that.'

The Dipty Sahib became very angry when he heard these words. He threatened to have Naim arrested. Zohra, however, asked him matter-of-factly, 'But Daddy! What is Naim's crime? The truth is we're both innocent. We love each other and he's my husband. This isn't a crime. And I'm no longer a minor.'

The Dipty Sahib was a shrewd man. He quickly realized that he wouldn't be able to prove Naim guilty when his own daughter was a willing partner. He left Zohra forever. Later on he tried to put pressure on Naim indirectly through other people and even tried to buy him off, but failed in that as well.

Zohra and Naim were living happily, even though Naim's salary was dreadfully small and Zohra, who'd been brought up in great comfort and luxury, now had to be content with wearing homely clothes and doing all the household chores on her own. But she was happy and found herself in a new world where she continually discovered fresh dimensions of Naim's love. She was pleased, very pleased, and so was Naim. But one day, as God had willed it, Zohra felt a severe pain in her chest and before Naim could do anything about it, she passed away, leaving his world dark forever.

It took him four hours to recount this story. He had spoken haltingly, as if relishing every word he uttered. By the time he finished, his face no longer looked pale. It was flushed, as though blood had been injected into him slowly, but his eyes had tears in them and his throat was dry.

His tale told, he got up quickly, as if in a terrible hurry, and said, 'I made a big mistake. I shouldn't have told you the story of my love. I made a terrible mistake. All this about Zohra should have remained sealed inside my heart, but . . .' His voice became hoarse. 'I'm alive and she . . . she . . .' He couldn't say anything more. He shook my hand quickly and left the room.

I never saw him again. Many times I went to Apollo Bunder with the express purpose of looking for him, but I never found him there. I did receive a letter from him six or seven months later in which he wrote:

Sir!

You will recall that I told you the story of my love at your place. It was only a story, an untrue story, for there's no Zohra, nor is there a Naim. Although I do exist, I'm not the same Naim who was in love with Zohra. One day you said there were people who were truly barren of love. I am one of them, someone who has spent his entire life merely deluding his heart. Naim's love for Zohra was a distraction and Zohra's death—I still don't understand why I killed her—it's quite possible that that too had something to do with my inner darkness.

I don't know if you believed my story to be true, but let me tell you something very strange. I, the creator of that story, believed it to be true, to be based completely on reality. I believed that I had really loved Zohra and she had really died. It might surprise you even more to hear that the story became increasingly real to me as time passed. I could clearly hear Zohra's voice, even her laughter, ring in my ears, and I could feel her warm breath on my body. Every little detail of the story came to life and so, in a manner of speaking, I dug my grave with my own hands.

Even if Zohra isn't fiction, I am. She's dead, so I must die too. This letter will reach you after my death. Farewell. I will find Zohra, I'm sure. But where? Of that I'm not so sure.

The only reason I've scribbled these lines to you is that you're a writer. If you can turn all of this into a story you may be able to sell it for seven or eight rupees, since you once said you can make that much from a story. That will be my gift to you. Goodbye.

Your acquaintance,
Naim

Naim created Zohra for himself and died. I created a story for myself and lived. It's not fair.

Co-translated with Moazzam Sheikh

Behind the Reed Stalks

As far as I'm concerned, it isn't necessary for me to tell you or for you to ask what city it was. Let's just say that this story is set in the suburbs of Peshawar, close to the border, where she lived in something like a mud hut behind a dense thicket of reeds. The reeds, located some distance from the cottage, more or less hid the sparse dwelling and anyone passing by on the dirt road in front could hardly see it.

The reeds were dried up, but they had burrowed into the ground in such a way that they formed a thick screen. God knows whether the woman had stuck them there herself or whether they'd been there all along. Whatever, at least they worked like an iron curtain.

Call it what you will, a house or a hut—it was just a cluster of three small but very immaculate and tidy rooms, with few furnishings to speak of. The room at the back had a *niwari palang*.* In a tiny niche above it, a small earthen lamp, its cotton wick dipped in mustard oil, burned all night long. The niche, too, looked quite clean and tidy, as did the oil lamp. It was given a new wick and filled with fresh oil every day.

Shall I tell you her name now, the one who lived in this little place behind the reeds with her young daughter?

All manner of rumours circulated about the girl. According to some she wasn't the woman's own daughter but rather an orphan the woman had adopted and brought up as her own. Others thought the girl was a child born out of wedlock, and still others claimed that she was, in fact, the woman's own flesh and blood. Whatever the truth may be, one

* A bedframe with broad cotton-tape meshing.

cannot be certain about it. Anyway, you'll have formed some opinion yourself by the time you're done reading this story.

Ah, yes, I forgot to tell you the woman's name. Actually, the name isn't important. You may call her by any name, Sakina, Mahtab, Gulshan, or whatever. What's in a name? However, for your convenience, let me call her Sardar.

Sardar was middle-aged. She must have been quite beautiful in her youth. Although her healthy-looking, rosy cheeks had become a bit marred by wrinkles now, she still looked several years younger than her age. But we shouldn't be concerned with her cheeks, should we?

Her daughter—never mind whether she actually was or wasn't *her* daughter—was a breathtaking specimen of blossoming youth. There was absolutely nothing in her features that betrayed, even faintly, any suggestion that she was a trollop, but the fact is her mother had set her up as a prostitute and was making good money. And Navab—again for your ease, let me give her this name—wasn't averse to her profession.

Because of her upbringing in a fairly secluded area, tucked far away from the nearest habitation, the girl had no inkling of the true joys of conjugal life. When Sardar introduced Navab's first man to her—on that very palang, of all places—the girl perhaps thought this was how all young women were initiated into their youth, so she became accustomed to her prostitute's existence and believed that her life's ultimate purpose lay in sleeping with men who came to visit her from far away.

On the face of it, she was every bit an indecent young woman— which is how our noble and chaste ladies are wont to look upon her and her ilk—but truth be told, she didn't even realize for a moment that she was living a life of sin. Realize? She never even had the chance to think about it.

She was very giving, and she gave of herself with utmost sincerity to every man who came to her in a week or ten days from far distances. She thought this was precisely what every woman was supposed to do. And she saw to her visitor's every comfort with unflinching devotion. She couldn't bear his facing even the slightest discomfort.

She was unaware of the lavish lifestyle of the city folk. She had no idea that the men who came to her riding in cars were used to cleaning their teeth with a brush in the morning and, first thing upon waking up, taking a cup of tea before going to defecate. Gradually, though, in her own girlish ways, she acquired some familiarity with the habits of these men. But it confused her a lot that they weren't all alike. One would ask for a cigarette when he woke up, another for tea, and some didn't want to get up at all. Some stayed awake all night and took off in their cars at the crack of dawn.

Sardar was blissfully free of all cares. She had full confidence in her daughter, or whatever she was, and knew the girl was quite capable of handling her clients. So Sardar took an opium pill and lolled around on her cot all evening. Now and then when she was needed, like when a client suddenly felt out of sorts because he'd had too much to drink, she would drowsily get out of bed and advise Navab to have the fellow taste some especially tart pickle, or to give him lukewarm salty water to induce vomiting and then put him to sleep with gentle strokes on his body.

Sardar was quite careful about one thing. She would have the client pay upfront, and tuck the money into her waistband. She would bless the fellow and pray for his well-being with her characteristic 'May you rock comfortably in your swing!' and then take an opium pill and collapse on the bed.

All the proceeds belonged to Sardar; however, all gifts remained with Navab. Because her clients were filthy rich, she dressed well and ate all kinds of fruits and sweetmeats.

She was happy. As she saw it, she was living an interesting and pleasant life in that mud-plastered dwelling of three small rooms. One of her clients, an army officer, had given her a gramophone and a bunch of records. She played film songs in her free time and tried to mimic the lyrics. She didn't have a good voice, but perhaps she was unaware of it. As it was, she was unaware of just about everything, and had no desire to learn about anything. She had accepted, totally unawares, the path she had been flung down.

The world on the other side of the reeds—she knew nothing about it except that in the space beyond the reeds was a dirt road that came to life every second or third day when a car came along amidst swirling clouds of dust, stopped, honked. Her mother, or whatever she was to Navab, would rise from her cot, go out and tell the man to park the car some distance away and then come in. The man would enter, sit by Navab's side on the niwari palang and begin to talk sweetly.

She didn't have many customers, maybe half a dozen or so, but they were her regulars. And Sardar, with her superior skills, had arranged matters so that they never ran into each other. She was one cunning woman! She'd fixed a day for each of them with such finesse that they found no reason to complain.

She also made sure, on occasions when it seemed imminent, that Navab didn't get pregnant. The circumstances of Navab's life were calling for it and it would happen sooner or later, but for some two and a half years now, Sardar had been dealing successfully with this eventuality.

The business was running quite smoothly behind the reeds for this period of time. The police hadn't caught even a whiff of it. The only ones who knew about it were the clients and Sardar and her daughter, Navab, or whatever she was.

One day all hell broke loose in this mud house behind the reeds. A big car, perhaps a Dodge, pulled up outside. The horn blared. Sardar emerged only to find a total stranger facing her. She didn't talk to him; nor did the stranger say anything to her. He parked the car some distance away and immediately walked into the house, as though he'd been coming here for years.

Sardar was bewildered. But Navab welcomed the man with a pleasing smile and led him courteously into the room with the palang. They had just sat down when Sardar—shrewd woman that she was—stepped in. It didn't take her long to assess that the man was from a wealthy family. He was also handsome and in good health. She greeted him deferentially and politely asked, 'Who has sent you our way?'

'She!' he said with a smile, lovingly poking Navab's cheek with his finger.

With a snap, Navab pulled away to one side and said with an air, 'Oh—but I've never met you before.'

The smile on the stranger's lips broadened. 'But we have, several times.'

'Where? When?' she asked. Her little mouth opened in utter amazement, enhancing the beauty of her face.

He grabbed her soft, plump hand and, looking at Sardar, said to the girl, 'You can't understand these things, at least not quite yet. Ask your mother.'

Naively, Navab asked her mother to explain where and when she had met him. Sardar instantly understood the matter. Someone among their regular clients must have mentioned Navab to him and given their direction. So she said, 'I will, I will,' and left the room. Then she plunked down on her cot, took out her small pillbox and, stretching out, put an opium pellet in her mouth. Her mind was perfectly at ease: The stranger looked like a nice man and she expected no trouble.

One cannot be sure, but most likely the stranger, Haibat Khan by name and a native of Hazara, was extremely wealthy. He was so taken with Navab's sprightly, coltish manners that, as he was leaving, he made it plain to Sardar that he didn't want anyone else to visit Navab any more. Clever Sardar told the man, 'Khan Sahib, how can that be? Are you sure you can afford to . . .'

Interrupting her, Haibat Khan dug into his pocket, drew out a wad of one-hundred-rupee banknotes and tossed it at Navab's feet. Next he removed his diamond ring, put it on the girl's finger and quickly vanished on the other side of the reeds.

Navab didn't even bother to give the money lying at her feet a cursory glance. She was busy contemplating her finger, adorned with a big diamond sparkling in the light. The car started up and sped away, spewing clouds of exhaust. Navab started and walked out to the reeds. All she could see was the dirt road and the trail of spiralling dust.

Meanwhile, Sardar had picked up the wad and counted the notes. One more and it would have been two thousand rupees, but the shortfall didn't bother her much. She deftly tucked the notes into the waistband of her billowing shalwar and headed for her cot. She took out a rather large opium pellet from its box, put it in her mouth and dozed off peacefully.

Navab was feeling very pleased. She couldn't stop looking at the diamond ring on her finger.

A few days later when one of the regular clients came, Sardar sent him away, saying that she had folded up her business because she was afraid of the police. The man was very rich and seemed genuinely disappointed. But Sardar had been much impressed by Haibat Khan. In her inebriated state, she thought it was infinitely better if she made as much money as before from only one client, and decided that she would send off all the old customers with the excuse that the police were after her and she didn't want to risk her reputation.

Haibat Khan showed up a week later. During this time Sardar had already turned away two old clients.

He came with the same pomp and pageantry as he had the first time. The moment he stepped in he pulled Navab to his chest and clasped her tightly. Sardar remained silent. Navab took him, or rather Haibat Khan took her, to the room with the palang. This time Sardar didn't interfere. She stayed on her cot, took her pellet, and started to doze off.

Haibat Khan enjoyed himself a lot. He was even more pleased by Navab's youthful coltishness. She was totally innocent of the wiles and antics of professional prostitutes, but also didn't show any trace of the domesticity of ordinary women. She had a quality that was entirely her own. She lay down with him like a child with its mother, running its hand over her breasts, sticking its fingers in her nose, pulling at her hair, and little by little falling asleep.

This was a wholly new experience for Haibat Khan. He found her to be an entirely new breed of woman: unique, interesting and delightful. He started coming twice a week. Navab had become an attraction he couldn't resist.

Sardar was happy that she was getting plenty of notes to tuck into her waistband. Navab, however, often wondered, in spite of her naivety and coltishness, why it was that Haibat Khan appeared to be afraid of something. Why did he start when a lorry or a car sped by on the dirt road beyond the reeds? Why did he withdraw his body from hers and hurry out stealthily to see who it might be?

One night, about twelve o'clock, when they were asleep in each other's arms, a lorry went by. A tremor shot through him and he abruptly sat up. Navab was in a light sleep and his tremor shook her like a seismic jolt. 'What happened?' she shrieked.

By now he'd gotten hold of himself a little. Making an effort to regain complete control over himself he said, 'Nothing . . . Perhaps I was frightened in my dream.'

In the stillness of the night the sound of the lorry could still be heard in the distance.

'No, Khan, it's something else,' she said. 'You react the same way every time a car or a lorry passes by.'

Navab had put her finger on his painful nerve. In a sharp tone, calculated to restore his male pride, he berated her, 'Don't talk nonsense! The sound of cars and lorries—huh, who's frightened of that?'

Her heart was much too fragile. His sharp tone cut her to the quick and she began to cry inconsolably. In his effort to calm her down he became aware of the most delicate pleasure of his life and his body drew even closer to hers.

Haibat Khan was a tall, handsome man with well-toned muscles. For the first time in her life Navab experienced the soothing warmth of his arms as he mentored her in the basics of sexual pleasure. She began to love him, or the meaning of whatever love was became known to her. Now when he disappeared for weeks she played doleful love songs on the gramophone, sang along . . . and sighed. But the puzzle of why he was so apprehensive of the sound of cars continued to agitate her mind.

Months went by. Her ability to give herself to him and her regard for him grew stronger. Now, though, another matter added to her confusion. He would visit her for only a few hours and then leave in a terribly agitated state. She understood that this was perhaps due to some reason beyond his control, otherwise he would have stayed with her longer.

She asked him about it several times, but he was evasive. One morning his Dodge pulled up beyond the reeds. Navab was still asleep. When he honked, she woke up and came out, rubbing her eyes. By then he had already parked the car and walked up to the house. Navab ran and wrapped herself around him. He picked her up and brought her into the room with the palang.

They talked for a long time, with words full of love. Heaven knows what came over Navab that she made her first ever request from him: 'Khan, buy me a pair of gold bracelets.'

He kissed her plump, rosy wrists several times and said, 'You'll have them by tomorrow. What are bracelets, I'll give you my life.'

With an air, but not without her peculiar coltish manner, she said, 'Never mind, Khan Sahib. It will eventually be I who gives up her life.'

Her words prompted him to offer his life as a sacrifice for her over and over again. He left after a delightful time in her company, promising to return the next day and clasp the bracelets around her wrists himself.

Navab was happy. That night she played cheerful songs on her gramophone and danced around the room with the palang well into the night. Sardar was happy as well. That night too she took a big opium pellet and fell asleep.

The next day Navab's happiness was even greater; she was going to get her gold bracelets and Haibat Khan would put them around her wrists himself. She waited all day. He didn't come. Perhaps his car broke down, she thought, perhaps he will come in the evening. She stayed awake the whole night, but he didn't show up. Her gentle heart was hurt badly. 'Look,' she repeatedly said to her mother, or whatever she was, 'the Khan hasn't returned. He went back on his promise.'

In the days that followed, she would lose herself in thought for a while and then wonder, cringing from some foreboding, 'Could something have happened to him?'

Many possibilities assailed her mind: car accident, sudden illness, attack by some highway robber. But her mind repeatedly went back to the sounds of cars and lorries that frightened him so. She thought about it for the longest time but couldn't comprehend why.

A whole week went by during which not one of her old clients visited, Sardar having already told them to stay away, although a few lorries and a couple of cars did go by, raising clouds of smoke on the dirt road. Every time one of them passed, the relentless desire to run after it and set it on fire overwhelmed Navab. She felt that these were the very things that were keeping Khan away. But after a while, she would wonder how such vehicles could be an impediment and laugh at her foolishness.

Why a strong man like Haibat Khan would cringe from fear at the sound of vehicles was beyond her understanding. That he cringed was a fact and no argument could change that. This made her very sad. On her gramophone she now played songs full of pain and anguish that made tears well up in her eyes.

A week later, after Navab and Sardar had finished their lunch one afternoon and were thinking of taking a nap, suddenly a car honked outside. They started because the horn didn't sound like Haibat Khan's Dodge. Sardar darted out to see who it was and send him away if it happened to be an old client. But as she got close to the reeds, she saw Haibat Khan sitting in a brand new car, with a well-dressed beautiful woman in the rear seat.

He parked the car some distance away and got out, so did the woman, and both approached the house. Sardar was confounded. Haibat Khan came here to have a woman, why has this well-dressed and beautiful young woman tagged along? What does she want?

She was still wondering about it when Haibat Khan stepped into the house with the woman, decked out in priceless jewels, in tow. Sardar followed them, but neither paid any attention to her.

When Sardar entered the room with the palang, she found Haibat Khan, Navab and the other woman sitting on it in a heavy silence—a strange silence. However, the bejewelled woman seemed to be a bit restless because one of her legs was shaking badly.

Sardar stopped at the door. The sound of her footsteps made Haibat Khan look up. She greeted him. He didn't respond. He looked terribly upset. But the woman stopped shaking her legs and spoke directly to Sardar, 'We're here; at least prepare something for us to eat.'

'Just say what you would like and it will be made ready,' Sardar replied hospitably.

The woman, whose very features and bearing screamed that she was used to being in control, said, 'Well then, let's go to the kitchen and get the fire going. You've got a big cooking pot, haven't you?'

'Yes,' Sardar affirmed, nodding her big head.

'Go and wash it. I'll be along shortly.' She got up from the bed and started watching the gramophone.

'I'm afraid there won't be any meat,' Sardar apologized.

'Don't worry, it'll be there,' the woman said, placing the stylus on the record. 'You just do as you're told. Make sure the fire is blazing hot.'

Sardar withdrew. The well-dressed woman now addressed Navab with a pleasant smile, 'Navab, we've brought you a pair of gold bracelets.'

She dug into her vanity bag and produced the bracelets wrapped in a thin, red paper. They looked quite heavy and gorgeous.

Navab was staring at Haibat Khan who sat next to her, sunk in deep silence. She glanced at the bracelets and asked him in a very soft but frightened voice, 'Khan, who is she?'

'Who am I?' said the woman, toying with the bracelets. 'I'm Haibat's sister.' She looked at him and he cringed at her answer. Then she again spoke to Navab, 'My name is Halakat.'

Navab was at a loss to understand. She was mortally afraid of the woman's eyes, which, though definitely beautiful, were dangerously widened. They seemed to be raining down plumes of fire.

The woman moved forward, grabbed Navab's wrists and put the bracelets on them. Suddenly she stopped, let go of the girl, and ordered the man, 'You make yourself scarce, Haibat Khan. I want to doll her up before presenting her to you.'

Haibat Khan was in a daze. When he didn't get up, the woman spoke sharply, 'You heard me, didn't you? Now go out!'

He left with his eyes fixed on Navab. He was feeling terribly agitated. He didn't know where to go or what to do.

On his way to the veranda, he passed by the makeshift kitchen with a gunnysack curtain and saw that Sardar already had the fire going. He walked out to the dirt road beyond the reeds without speaking to her. His condition was like that of a half-crazy person. Even the slightest sound made him jump.

A lorry was coming along in the distance. The urge to stop it, hop aboard and disappear gripped him. But when it drew near, it swirled up an atrocious cloud of dust that enveloped him completely. He tried to call out, but couldn't because of all the dust choking his throat.

When the dust settled he felt as though he was half dead. He wanted to go back to the house behind the reeds, the house where he had spent many days and nights of indescribable bliss by the side of that coltish girl, but he couldn't. His feet refused to budge.

Standing on the side of the dirt road for a long time, he wondered what was going on. His affair with the woman who had accompanied him here went back a long time. Her husband had been a close friend of his and he had first visited her to commiserate with her at her husband's death. As luck would have it, this turned into an affair. Barely two days after his friend's death he returned to her house. She ordered him inside as if he was her servant and offered herself to him.

Haibat Khan was a rank amateur where women were concerned. That Shahina had expressed her feelings for him, never mind her terribly commanding manner, was no small thing for him. No doubt she was extremely wealthy, but it was not her wealth—partly her own and partly her late husband's—that he cared about. His only interest in her was that she was the first woman in his life. If he had allowed himself to be cowed by her overbearing manner, it was because he was a complete novice.

Standing by the dirt road, he kept thinking for a long time. Finally, he couldn't hold back and walked over to the house. There, in the makeshift kitchen, he saw Sardar frying some meat. He continued towards the room with the palang but found the door closed. He rapped softly on it.

Some moments later the door opened. The first thing he saw was blood all over the floor. He trembled. Next he saw Shahina leaning against the door. 'There,' she said to him, 'I've dolled her up for you!'

With difficulty Haibat Khan moistened his parched throat with saliva and asked, 'Where is she?'

'Some of her is on the bed, but the best parts are in the kitchen.'

Haibat Khan didn't quite understand. All the same, terror engulfed him. He couldn't get a word out, and remained rooted to the spot by the door. It wasn't just the gore; he also spotted small pieces of flesh on the floor and . . . and a sharp kitchen knife. It looked as if someone was lying on the bed, covered in a blood-soaked sheet.

Shahina smiled and said, 'Shall I lift the sheet and show her to you . . . your bedecked and adorned Navab—why, I made her up myself. But first, you should eat. You must be starving. Sardar is making a delicious meat dish. I carved the meat myself.'

Haibat Khan began to shake. 'Shahina!' he screamed. 'What have you done?'

She smiled. 'Darling, this is not the first time. My husband, may God bless him with Paradise, was as unfaithful as you are. I butchered him and threw pieces of his flesh for the crows and buzzards to feast on. I love you, so, instead of you, I have . . .'

Without completing the sentence, she pulled the sheet off the heap on the bed. Haibat Khan choked on his scream and fell unconscious.

When he came to, Shahina was at the steering wheel and they were driving through an unfamiliar terrain.

Smell

It was a day during the rainy season—a day just like today. Outside the window, the leaves of the peepul tree stood drenched in the rain. A young woman from the hills, a *ghatan*, was lying curled up against Randheer on the spring mattress of the teak bed, which had now been moved away from the window a bit.

Beyond the window, the rain-washed leaves quivered like earrings in the milky darkness of the night, very much like the shivers the girl clinging to him sent coursing through his body.

Randheer had been reading an English-language newspaper the whole day and had been through not just every news item but practically all the ads as well. Towards evening he stepped out on to the balcony to amuse himself a bit and spotted the girl under a tamarind tree, shielding herself from the downpour. She probably worked in the neighbouring rope factory. He cleared his throat and coughed a couple of times to draw her attention and, after a while, he motioned to her to come up.

He'd been feeling quite despondent for the past several days. With the war going on, nearly all the Christian girls in Bombay, who could be had at a bargain price, had enlisted with the Auxiliary Force. Some had moved to the Fort area and set up dancing schools, which only gora soldiers were allowed to enter. Randheer was feeling quite miserable. One reason was that the Christian girls were no longer readily available. Another was the colour of his skin—although enviably suave and well mannered, educated, in good health and quite a bit more handsome than most young men, he was barred from practically all the brothels of the Fort area. After all, he was not a gora.

313

Before the war came along he had physical relationships with umpteen Christian girls around the Nagpara and Taj Hotel areas. He was far more adept in matters of the flesh than any of the Christian boys with whom those girls conducted fleeting affairs just to appear chic until eventually settling down with some fool or other.

He had called the ghatan over to get even with Hazel who had recently acquired this air of mannered haughtiness. Hazel lived in the flat below his. Every morning, outfitted in her army uniform, her khaki cap set at a rakish angle over her short-trimmed hair, she marched out of her place with such a swagger as if she expected everyone to roll themselves out as a carpet for her to walk on.

Why in the world did he feel so drawn to Christian girls?—he'd often wondered. Well, yes, they did show off all the seductive assets of their bodies to good effect, spoke unabashedly of their irregular periods and even their former love affairs, and swayed their legs the minute some dance tune or other drifted into their ears—but any woman could just as easily boast of these qualities, couldn't she?

When Randheer gestured to the ghatan to come up he had no thought whatsoever of getting her into bed with him. Noticing how thoroughly soaked she was, he feared the poor thing might catch pneumonia, so he said, 'Take off those wet clothes! You'll catch a cold.'

She thought she understood what was implied and blushed. When Randheer took out a fresh white dhoti and handed it to her, she hesitated for a moment and then undid her *kashta*, its grime made more visible by the rain. She pushed it aside and quickly wrapped the white dhoti around her hips and started to undo her snugly fitting choli, the two ends of which she had secured in a tight knot that had disappeared in the faint but grimy cleavage of her shapely breasts.

With her worn nails she struggled with the knot for quite a while but couldn't loosen what the rainwater had tightened so firmly. Eventually she gave up and muttered something to Randheer in Marathi which meant, 'What shall I do? It just won't open.'

Randheer sat down beside her to give it a try but he couldn't make the knot budge either. In exasperation he grabbed the two ends and tugged on them so vigorously that the knot came undone. His hands jerked from the force of the pull, baring two trembling breasts. For a moment he felt as though, with the dexterity of a master potter, his own hands had shaped a lump of soft, moist clay into a pair of exquisite cups on the girl's chest.

Her youthful breasts had the same rawness and allure, the same moist freshness and cooling warmth that oozes from vessels just fashioned by a potter. A strange glow was implicit in the earth tones of those pristine young breasts. A diaphanous layer of a sort of muted luminescence beneath their darkish colouring was giving off that strange glow, which was almost not a glow. The two mounds on her chest looked more like a pair of earthen lamps set afloat on the muddy waters of a pond.

Yes, it was a day during the rains—a day just like this one. The leaves of the peepul were trembling outside the window. The ghatan's dripping-wet, two-piece garment was lying on the floor in a messy heap, while she herself was wrapped around Randheer. The warmth of her naked, unwashed body evoked the same sensations in his own that he felt in the hot, filthy hammams of the barbers during blustery winters.

She had clung to his body all night long, as if their two bodies had melded together. They hadn't exchanged more than a couple of words. There had been no need to. Their breath, their lips, their hands conveyed all that needed to be communicated. With the tenderness of the gentlest breeze, his hands caressed her breasts all through the night—and however light the touch, her tiny nipples, in the middle of their large, dark, coarse areola, responded, sending a wave of tremulous pleasure through her body that never failed to arouse the same in his own.

Such tremors were not something Randheer hadn't experienced before. He had, many times, and he was familiar with the pleasure they gave. Hadn't he, after all, spent many nights with his chest pressed against the soft or firm breasts of some girl or other? And even spent time with such capricious girls that they had no qualms about sharing the kind of intimate stories about their families that are usually kept from strangers? He'd had sexual relations with women who took the initiative and did all the work themselves without encumbering him in any way. But this girl from the hills whom he'd beckoned up—she was something else altogether. So unbelievably different!

A strange smell wafting from her body flooded his senses all night—a smell at once pleasant and nauseating. It flowed from every part of her body: under her arms, around her breasts, her hair, her belly—it permeated every breath he took. All night long he wondered about this smell: without it creeping into every crevice of his mind, crowding out all his thoughts, new and old, would he have felt as close to this ghatan as he did now? Absolutely not!

This smell had fused them together for the night. They had taken possession of each other so totally, plunged into each other's depths so fully that they were carried away into pure human ecstasy—fleeting yet somehow immutable, in motion yet frozen, like a bird soaring so high in the sky's limitless azure that it appears perfectly still.

Even though he was familiar with the smell radiating from every pore of the girl's body, he couldn't quite describe what it was. It was like the smell of earth that had just been sprinkled with water. But not exactly. It was different somehow. And it didn't have the artificial aura of lavender or attar. It was something primal and timeless—like the relationship between man and woman.

Amazingly, though Randheer detested the odour of perspiration and routinely dusted his body with talcum powder and dabbed his underarms with deodorant after every bath, he found himself madly kissing the ghatan's hairy armpits over and over—yes, over and over—and feeling no revulsion; instead he found it strangely pleasurable. Damp with sweat, her soft, underarm hair was releasing a scent that was very conspicuous and yet completely unfathomable. He felt that he knew it, was familiar with it, and even understood what it signified, but couldn't explain it to anyone.

It was a day during the rains—just like today. He was looking out of the same window. The peepul leaves were trembling in the pouring rain, their rustling sound blending into the atmosphere. It was dark outside, but the darkness was suffused with a soft fluorescence, as though a little light had escaped from the stars and descended to the earth with the raindrops . . .

Yes, it was a day during the rains. His room had a single teakwood bed then; now it had two—the new arrival was placed next to its mate—and a brand new dressing table stood in one corner. It was the same season, the same weather, and a barely discernible light was coming down from the stars along with the raindrops, but now the atmosphere was filled with the overpowering scent of henna.

One bed was empty. On the other, Randheer lay face down, watching raindrops dancing on the fluttering leaves outside the window, and lying next to him was a fair-complexioned girl who seemed to have fallen asleep after her futile attempts to cover her nakedness. Her red silk shalwar lay bunched up on the empty bed, the tasselled end of its dark red waist-cord dangling down the side. Her other clothes were also on that bed. Her shirt with a golden floral pattern, her bra, underpants and dupatta were all of a deep red colour—a garish, dark red—and saturated with the strong scent of henna.

Flecks of glitter were scattered in her dark black hair like specks of dust, and glitter, together with a heavy layer of powder and rouge, gave an unbelievably strange colour to her face—pallid, as though all the life had been squeezed out of it. The dye from her bra had bled, leaving reddish stains on her fair chest.

Her breasts were milky-white with just a hint of blue and her underarms were shaved clean, leaving behind a grey shadow. Randheer glanced at her several times, and each time found himself thinking that he'd just pried open some crate and taken her out—as if she was a consignment of books or china. Her body had marks in several spots just like the marks and scratches left on books and china from packing and shipping.

When he undid the clasps of her tight-fitting bra Randheer noticed that it had creased her back and the soft flesh of her bosom. And the cord of her shalwar had been done up so tightly it left a mark around her waist. The sharp edges of her heavy, jewel-encrusted necklace had apparently grazed the delicate skin of her bosom in many places, as if unforgiving nails had scratched it.

Indeed, it was just like that other day. The rain was producing the same sound as it pelted down on the tender leaves of the peepul—the same pitter-patter that had filled his ears that other night long ago. The weather was divine. A cool breeze was blowing softly . . . but it was laden with the cloying scent of henna.

Of course his hands had roved over the girl's milky-white bosom for a long time, like the breath of a gentle breeze; he'd felt her body quiver in intermittent waves under his touch, felt the suppressed passions stirring within her. When he pressed his chest to hers every pore of his body heard the notes rising from her body—but where was that call: the call he had sensed in the strong odour emanating from the ghatan's body, more compelling than the cry of an infant thirsting for milk, the call that had gone beyond the limits of sound and needed no words to convey it.

Randheer was looking out through the grillwork of the window, somewhere far beyond the trembling leaves of the peepul, into the distance where he could make out an unusual subdued glow enmeshed in the dark grey of the clouds, the same glow he had seen radiate from the breasts of the ghatan, hidden like a secret, but discernible all the same.

He looked at the inert body of the girl stretched out beside him, as soft and white as flour kneaded with milk and butter, the scent of henna leaping from it now fading. He found it immensely revolting—this exhausted smell in the throes of death, somewhat tangy, oddly tangy, like the sour belches of indigestion. A pathetic, sickly smell!

He glanced at the girl lying next to him again. The femininity in her being seemed strangely compressed . . . the way white globs float listlessly in colourless liquid when the milk has gone bad. Actually, the smell that flowed from the ghatan so naturally, unbidden and without effort, still pervaded his senses. It was a smell infinitely more subtle and pervasive than the perfume of henna, not at all eager to be smelled, but flowing quietly into him to settle into place.

In one last attempt, Randheer ran his hand over the girl's milky-white body but felt no tremor. His new bride, the daughter of a distinguished magistrate, with a bachelor's degree, the heart-throb of countless boys at her college, failed to rouse her husband's passion.

From the dying scent of henna he desperately tried to retrieve the smell that had wafted from the ghatan's unwashed body and flooded his senses on just such a rainy day when the leaves of the peepul outside the window were bathed in a downpour.

Kingdom's End

The telephone rang. Manmohan, who was sitting beside it, picked up the receiver and spoke into it. 'Hello, this is 4457.'

A delicate female voice came from the other end. 'Sorry, wrong number.'

Manmohan hung up and returned to the book he was reading.

He had read this book nearly twenty times already, even though its last pages were moth-eaten; not because it was especially interesting, but because it was the only book in this barren office.

For the past week he had been the sole custodian of this office. Its owner, a friend of his, had gone away somewhere to arrange some credit. Since Manmohan had no place of his own, he had moved here temporarily from the streets. During this one week he had read the book nearly twenty times over.

Isolated here, he bided his time. He hated any kind of employment. Otherwise, had he wanted it, the job of director in any film company was his for the taking. But working for someone was slavery and he didn't want to be a slave. Since he was a sincere, harmless person, his friends saw to his daily needs, which were negligible: a cup of tea and a couple of pieces of toast in the morning, two *phulka*s and a little bit of gravy for lunch, and a pack of cigarettes that lasted the whole day—that's all.

Manmohan had no family or relatives. He liked solitude and was inured to hardship. He could go without food for days on end. His friends didn't know much about him, except that he had left home while still very young and had found himself an abode on the Bombay

319

pavements for quite some time now. He only yearned for one thing in life: the love of a woman. He would say, 'If I'm lucky enough to find a woman's love, my life will change completely.'

'Even then you won't work,' his friends would say.

'Work?' He would answer with a deep sigh, 'Oh, I'll become a workaholic. You'll see.'

'Well then, fall in love with someone.'

'No, I don't believe in love that is initiated by the man.'

It was almost time for lunch. Manmohan looked at the wall clock opposite him. Just then the phone rang. He picked up the receiver, 'Hello, this is 4457.'

A delicate voice asked, '4457?'

'Yes, 4457,' Manmohan confirmed.

'Who are you?' the female voice asked.

'I'm Manmohan. What can I do for you?'

When there was no answer, Manmohan asked, 'Whom do you want?'

'You,' said the voice.

'Me?' he asked, somewhat surprised.

'Yes, you. Do you have an objection?'

Manmohan was flummoxed. 'Oh no, none at all.'

The voice smiled, 'Did you say your name was Madan Mohan?'

'No. Manmohan.'

'Manmohan.'

Silence ensued. After some moments, he asked, 'You wanted to chat with me?'

'Yes,' the voice affirmed.

'Well then, chat.'

After a slight pause, the voice said, 'I don't know what to say. Why don't you start?'

'Okay,' Manmohan said, and thought for a while. 'I've already told you my name. I'm temporarily living in this office. Before, I used to sleep on the pavement, but now I sleep on the desk here.'

The voice smiled, 'Did you sleep in a canopied bed on the pavement?'

Manmohan laughed. 'Before I go on any further, let me make one thing clear. I've never lied. I've been sleeping on pavements for a long time. But, for about a week now, I've had this office all to myself, and I'm having the time of my life.'

'Doing what?'

'I found a book here. The pages at the back are missing. All the same, I've read it . . . oh, about twenty times. If I ever get hold of the whole book, I'll find out what became of the hero and heroine's love.'

The voice laughed. 'You're an interesting fellow.'

'Thank you,' he said with mannered formality.

After a pause, the voice asked, 'What's your occupation?'

'Occupation?'

'I mean your work. What do you do?'

'What do I do? Nothing, really. An idle man has no work to do. I loaf around all day and sleep at night.'

'Do you like your life?'

'Give me a few moments,' Manmohan started to think. 'The truth is, I've never thought about it. Now that you've put the question to me, I'm asking myself whether I do or not.'

'So did you get an answer?'

Manmohan took some time to reply, 'No, I didn't. But since I've been living it for so long, I suppose I must like it.'

The voice laughed.

Manmohan said, 'You laugh beautifully.'

'Thank you,' the voice intoned shyly and hung up.

Manmohan stood holding the receiver for some time, smiled and returned it to its cradle. He closed up the office and went out.

Next morning at about eight o'clock, while he was still asleep on the desk, the phone rang. He yawned and took the call, 'Hello, 4457.'

'Good morning, Manmohan Sahib.'

'Good morning,' he started. 'Oh, you! Good morning.'

'I guess you were sleeping,' said the voice.

'Yes, I was. Since I've come over here I've become spoiled. Settling back into life on the pavement will be difficult.'

'Why?'

'A person has to get up before five in the morning there.'

He heard a laugh and asked, 'Why did you cut off the call abruptly yesterday?'

'Why did you say I laughed beautifully?'

'What a question! If something is beautiful, shouldn't it be praised?'

'No, never.'

'You can't impose such conditions on me. I've never accepted any conditions. If you laugh, I'll certainly praise it.'

'I'll hang up.'

'You're free to do that.'

'You don't care about my displeasure?'

'First off, I don't want to displease myself. If you laugh and I don't say that it's beautiful, I'd be offending my own sense of beauty, which is very dear to me.'

There was a brief silence. Then the voice came back, 'Sorry, I was talking to the maid. So you were saying you care a lot about your sense of beauty. But tell me, is there anything you love to do?'

'What do you mean?'

'I mean . . . some hobby or work . . . or, how shall I put it, yes, is there anything you can do?'

Manmohan laughed. 'Nothing much, but I do like photography a bit.'

'That's a fine hobby.'

'Fine or not, I've never thought about it.'

'You must own an excellent camera, then?'

Manmohan laughed again. 'I don't own a camera; I borrow from friends every now and then and satisfy my urge. I have a camera in mind though. If I ever make any money, I'll buy it.'

'What camera is that?'

'Exacta. It's a reflex camera. I like it a lot.'

There was silence. Then the voice came back on, 'I was thinking about something.'

'What?'

'You haven't asked for my name or phone number.'

'I didn't feel it was necessary.'

'Why not?'

'What does it matter what your name is? And you already have my phone number. That's good enough. But if you want me to call you, then give me your name and number.'

'No, I won't.'

'That's another matter altogether! If I'm not asking you, the question of giving doesn't arise.'

'You're really a very strange man.'

There was a brief silence again.

'Thinking again?' Manmohan asked.

'Yes, but I seem to have hit a dead end.'

'Then why don't you hang up? Call some other time.'

The voice became sharp. 'You're very brusque. Please hang up, or better, I should hang up.'

Manmohan smiled and put the receiver down.

Half an hour later, after he had washed his face, changed and was about to go out, the phone rang again. He picked it up and said, '4457.'

'Is Mr Manmohan there?'

'Speaking. What can I do for you?'

'I just wanted to tell you that I'm not annoyed any more.'

'I'm happy to hear that,' he replied with good cheer.

'As I was eating breakfast it occurred to me that I shouldn't really be annoyed with you. Have you had your breakfast?'

'I was just going to go out to have some. But you called.'

'Then go and eat some.'

'I'm not in any hurry. Besides, I don't have money on me today. I think I'll skip breakfast.'

'Hearing you say all this . . . Why do you say such things? I mean, is it because something pains you?'

Manmohan thought for a bit. 'No. Whatever pains me, I've gotten used to it.'

'Shall I send you some money?'

'If you want to. You'll be one more person added to the list of my moneymen.'

'Then I won't.'

'As you wish.'

'I'm hanging up.'

'Fine.'

Manmohan put the receiver down and went out with a smile on his lips. He returned at about ten that night, changed, lay down on the desk and started to wonder who the woman who kept phoning him might be. Her voice betrayed that she was young and there was a trill, a singsong quality in the way she laughed. It was evident from her conversation that she was educated and refined. He kept thinking about her for a long time.

Just as the clock struck eleven, the phone rang. He answered it. 'Hello!'

'Mr Manmohan.'

'Speaking. What can I do for you?'

'I rang you up so many times during the day . . . Where did you disappear?'

'I may be jobless, but I still have things to do.'

'Like what?'

'Like loafing around.'

'When did you get back?'

'About ten.'

'What are you doing now?'

'I was lying on the desk, imagining what you must look like. But all I have to go on is your voice.'

'Did you succeed?'

'No.'

'Don't try. I'm very ugly.'

'Pardon me, please hang up if you are really ugly. I loathe ugliness.'

'In that case, let's say I'm beautiful. I don't want to foster hatred.'

Neither of them spoke for a while, then Manmohan asked, 'Were you thinking?'

The voice started, 'Well, no. But I was going to ask you . . .'

'Think hard before you ask.'

The sound of a refreshing laugh came on, and then, 'Shall I sing you a song?'

'Sure.'

'Give me a minute.'

He heard her clear her throat and then start to sing the ghazal by Ghalib which begins with the line, *'Nukta-cheen hai gham-e dil . . .'*

She sang it in the entirely new style of Saigal. Her voice was soft and full of pathos. When she finished, Manmohan commended her heartily, 'Very nice! Bravo!'

'Thanks,' the voice said shyly and hung up.

As he lay on the desk, the ghazal kept reverberating in Manmohan's mind throughout the night. He got up quite early the next morning and sat in the chair, waiting for the phone to ring for a good two and a half hours. He gave up, feeling a strange bitterness in his throat. He started to pace up and down the room restlessly. Then he stretched out on the desk feeling pretty annoyed. He picked up the solitary book and began reading it all over again. The phone rang in the evening.

'Who is it?' he asked in a stiff voice.

'It's me,' the voice replied.

'Where were you all this time?' he asked, still stiffly.

'Why?' the voice quaked.

'I've been rotting here since morning. Haven't had breakfast or lunch, even though I have money.'

'I only call you when I feel like it. You . . .'

'Look here,' he cut her off, 'stop being whimsical. Fix a time to call. I can't stand waiting all day long.'

'I apologize. Starting tomorrow, I will call you in the morning and again in the evening.'

'That'll do.'

'I didn't know you were so touchy.'

Manmohan smiled, 'I'm sorry. Waiting really irritates me, and when I feel irritated, I start punishing myself.'

'Oh? How?'

'You didn't call this morning. Logically, I should have gone out. But I stayed cooped up here, fretting away all day.'

'Oh, how I wish I hadn't made this mistake,' the voice was saturated with emotion. 'I didn't call on purpose.'

'And why is that?'

'Just to find out whether you would miss my call.'

'You're very naughty,' he laughed. 'Now hang up. I've got to go eat.'

'Fine. When will you be back?'

'Say, in half an hour.'

When he returned half an hour later, she called. They chatted for quite a while. She sang him another ghazal by Ghalib and he complimented her enthusiastically. They hung up.

She began to call him every morning and evening after that and he hurriedly leaped to take her call. Sometimes they talked for hours, but he never asked for her name or phone number. In the beginning he had tried to imagine her face from the sound of her voice. Now, though, he seemed to be contented with just her voice, which was everything—her face, her body, her soul.

'Mohan, why don't you ask me for my name?' she asked him one day.

He smiled, 'For me, your name is your voice.'

'Which is very musical.'

'No doubt about it.'

Another day she threw a very abstruse question at him, 'Mohan, have you ever been in love with a woman?'

'No.'

'Why not?'

A sudden despondency came over him. 'This is not a question I can answer in a few words. I'll have to sift through the entire rubble of my life. And if I still can't get an answer, it would irritate me very much.'

'Then let's drop it.'

Their telephonic contact had now endured for almost a month. She called him twice every day without fail. Meanwhile, a letter arrived from his friend, the owner of the office—he had managed to get the desired credit and would be back in Bombay in a week's time. A feeling of gloom washed over Manmohan.

When she next rang him up, Manmohan said, 'My kingdom is about to end.'

'Why?'

'My friend has succeeded in getting the loan. The office will become functional very soon.'

'But one of your friends must surely have a telephone?'

'Several of them do, but I can't give you their numbers.'

'Why not?'

'I don't want anyone to hear your beautiful voice.'

'But why?'

'I'm very jealous.'

She smiled and said, 'This is going to be a big fiasco.'

'Can't be helped.'

'Well then, on your kingdom's last day I'll give you my phone number.'

'That's better.'

That feeling of gloom disappeared in an instant and he started waiting anxiously for the day when his dominion over the office would end. He again tried to imagine what she must look like. He conjured up several images. None satisfied him. Well—he told himself—it's now only a matter of a few days. Since she was willing to give her phone number, he could be reasonably sure that he would also be able to see her in person. And that thought left his mind in a daze. What a day that would be when he would see her!

The next time she called him, he said to her, 'I'm dying to see you.'
'Why?'
'You said you'll give me your phone number on the last day of my dominion here.'
'Yes, I did.'
'It's reasonable to expect that you'll also give me your address and I'll be able to see you.'
'You can see me whenever you want. Even today.'
'No, no. Not today. I want to see you in proper clothes; I mean respectable clothes. I'll ask a friend; he'll order me a new suit.'
She laughed suddenly. 'You absolutely behave like a kid. Listen, I'll give you a present when we meet.'
Manmohan became emotional. 'There could be no greater present than meeting you!'
'I've bought an Exacta camera for you.'
'Oh!'
'I'll give it to you, but on one condition: that you'll take my picture.'
He smiled. 'I'll decide about that after we meet.'
They talked for a while longer. 'Listen,' she said, 'I won't be able to call you tomorrow or the day after.'
'Why?' he asked, feeling quite anxious.
'I'm going away with my relatives. Just for two days. You'll forgive me, won't you?'
He stayed inside the office for the rest of that day. When he woke up the next morning his body was unusually warm. Oh, it's nothing—just a slight depression brought on by the thought that she won't be calling today—he concluded. But by afternoon he was running a high temperature and his body was on fire. His eyes were burning. He lay back down on the desk. He felt terribly thirsty, which obliged him to get up repeatedly and drink from the faucet. By evening his chest felt as though it was thoroughly congested, and by the next day he was totally run down. His chest pains had become unbearable.

In his delirium he talked to his beloved's voice over the phone for hours. His condition had deteriorated badly by evening. He looked at the wall clock through blurry eyes. His ears were buzzing with strange sounds, as if countless phones were ringing all at once, and his chest was wheezing without letting up. He was engulfed in a sea of noises, so when the phone did ring, the sound failed to reach his ears. It kept ringing for a long time. He came to with a start and rushed to the phone. Holding himself steady against the wall he picked up the receiver with a trembling hand, ran his stiff tongue over his parched lips and said, 'Hello!'

'Hello, Mohan!' the woman spoke from the other end.

'Yes, it is Mohan,' his voice faltered.

'Speak a bit louder.'

He opened his mouth to say something but the words caught in his dried-up throat.

'I returned early,' she said. 'I've been calling you for quite a while. Where were you?'

His head started to spin.

'What's happening to you?'

With great difficulty he could only say, 'My kingdom ended—today.'

Blood spilled from his mouth and trickled down his neck, leaving a long, thin streak.

'Take down my number: 50314, repeat 50314. Call me tomorrow.' She hung up.

Manmohan fell over the phone face down. Bubbles of blood began to spurt from his mouth.

By the Roadside

It was the same season, the sky was as washed and clear a blue as his eyes, just like today. The sunlight had the comforting warmth of pleasant dreams. The smell of the earth was the same as it is now, crowding my senses. Lying down as I am today, I offered my throbbing soul to him.

'Believe me, my life was bereft of moments like the ones you've given me,' he said. 'All the empty spaces of my being that you've filled today are grateful to you. Had you not come into my life, perhaps it would have remained incomplete. I'm at a loss; what more can I say. I feel complete, indeed so complete that I don't think I need you any more.'

And he walked away, never to return.

My eyes shed tears and my heart cried. I begged him. I asked him over and over again: 'Why—why don't you need me any more, now when my need for you, with all its tumultuous passion, has only just begun . . . after those very moments which, as you say, filled the empty spaces of your being.'

'These moments have bestowed on me, one by one, whatever atoms of your being I needed to make myself whole,' he said. 'Now that my life's goal has been accomplished, our relationship naturally comes to an end.'

Oh the wounding cruelty of those words! I couldn't bear their onslaught. I screamed in pain, which left him unmoved. I told him, 'These atoms that perfected you were part of *my* being. Don't they bear some relationship to me? Could the rest of me ever disown them? Your fruition comes at the cost of leaving me severed in two. Did I make you my lord for this?'

'Bees suck the nectar of flowers and buds to make honey, but they're never so much as allowed to taste it, not even its dregs. God demands worship, but doesn't worship Himself. He spent a few moments in seclusion with Non-Being and brought forth Being. Where is Non-Being now? Does existence need it any more? It was the mother that died giving birth to Being.'

'All a woman can do is cry,' I said to him. 'She can't argue. Her most potent argument is the teardrop that falls from her eye. Look at me—I'm crying, shedding continuous tears. If you must leave me, at least gather a few of them in the shroud of your handkerchief. I'll be crying for the rest of my life, but at least I'll cherish the memory that you too participated in the funeral rites of a few of my tears . . . if only to make me happy.'

'I've already made you happy. I've made you experience the tangible happiness you saw only as a distant mirage. Can you not live by the memory of the bliss, the exhilaration of those moments? You say that my fruition has left you incomplete. Isn't this incompletion enough to keep your life dynamic? I'm a man. Today you've brought me fruition, tomorrow someone else will. My being is fashioned from such a substance that there will be many moments when I will experience this feeling of incompletion and many women like you will enter my life to fill the void created by those moments.'

I kept crying and agonizing.

These few moments, I thought, that I had within my grasp just now—no, I was within their grasp—why did I surrender myself to them? Why did I let my throbbing soul walk straight into the gaping opening of their cage? There was pleasure in it, exhilaration, even bliss—yes, there certainly was, but only in the mingling of our bodies. How is it that he remained whole, but I'm shattered to pieces? Why is it that he no longer needs me, but I long for him even more passionately? He came out of it stronger and I, feebler. Why is it that two patches of cloud come together in the sky only for one to rain down tears and the other to play with this rain like a flash of lightning, to just skip about and run away? What law is that? Who made it—the skies, the earth, or their Creator?

I kept shedding tears and trembling.

Two souls fusing into one and stretching out into an overpowering expanse—is this mere lyricism? No, two contracting souls surely come to that minuscule point which expands into the universe. But why is one soul sometimes left hurting and wounded in that universe—just because it helped its mate reach that minuscule point?

What kind of universe is that?

It was the same season, the sky was as washed and clear a blue as his eyes, just like today. The sunlight had the comforting warmth of pleasant dreams. Lying down as I am today, I offered my throbbing soul to him. He is no longer here. Only God knows the inconsolable anguish of what wisps of clouds he is playing around with like a flash of lightning. He attained his fruition and left . . . A snake that bit me and slithered away. But why is the spoor he left behind stirring inside my belly? Am I now receiving my completion?

No, no, this cannot be completion. It is ruination. But why are the empty spaces of my body filling up? What debris is packing the hollows of my body? What are these rustling sounds coursing through my veins? Why am I curling back upon myself in a desperate attempt to reach that minuscule spot within me? In what seas is my boat rising after sinking?

For what guest is milk being warmed on the fires blazing inside of me? For whom is my heart fluffing up my blood like carded cotton wool to fashion soft little comforters? And for whom is my mind stitching tiny clothes with the multicoloured threads of my thoughts?

For whom is my skin getting a wash of brilliance? Why are the sobs caught in every limb and pore of my body turning into sweet lullabies?

It was the same season, the sky was as washed and clear a blue as his eyes, just like today . . . but why has the sky tumbled down from its heights to stretch out inside of me? Why are its blue eyes scurrying through my veins?

Why is the roundness of my breasts assuming the holiness of the arches of mosques? No, no, this is no holiness. I'll pull down these arches. I'll extinguish the fires within me where a repast is being prepared for the uninvited guest. I'll toss the multicoloured threads of my thoughts into a jumbled mass.

It was the same season, the sky was as washed and clear a blue as his eyes, just like today. But why do I remember those days from which he has carried away every last trace of his footprints?

But whose footprint is this, flailing in the depths of my belly? Isn't it familiar?

I'll scrape it off . . . I'll erase it. It's cankerous, an ulcer of the most malignant kind.

But why does it feel like a ball of cotton wool? If it is cotton wool, what wound is it supposed to dress? The wound he inflicted on me before he went his way? No, no. It seems as though it is meant for the wound with which I was born. For a wound I'd never seen before, that lay dormant in my womb for who knows how long.

What is a womb but a useless pot of clay, a child's plaything? I'll smash it to pieces.

Who is this whispering in my ear, 'The world is a crossroads. Why do you wish to give out your secret to everyone here in the open? Mind you, fingers will be pointed at you.'

But why wouldn't the fingers point in the direction in which he went, went after completing his being? Don't the fingers know the way? But that day it was the fork in the road where he left me standing, either prong of which offered only gaping incompletion, and tears.

Whose teardrop is turning into a pearl inside my shell? Where will it be strung?

Fingers will be raised. Yes, they will be raised when the shell opens its mouth and drops its pearl in the middle of the crossroads, raised towards the shell and towards the pearl. The fingers will morph into a brood of vipers that will bite both of them and turn them blue with venom.

The sky was blue like his eyes, just like today. Why doesn't it fall? What invisible columns are keeping it aloft? Was the earthquake that day not enough to topple them from their bases? Why is the sky still stretched out over me as before?

My soul is drenched in sweat. Its every pore is open. A fire is blazing all around. Gold is melting in the vessel inside my body. The bellows are at work and flames are leaping up. Liquid gold is pouring out like lava from the volcano. Blue eyes are running through my veins gasping for breath. Bells are tinkling. Someone is approaching. Shut the doors! Shut them tightly!

The cauldron has been tipped over allowing the liquid gold to flow out. Bells are tinkling. It's coming. My eyes are beginning to close. The sky has turned murky and it's falling.

Whose cries are these? Make them stop! Its screams are falling on me like the blows of a hammer. Make it stop crying . . . stop crying . . . I'm turning into a lap. For heaven's sake, why?

My arms are spreading out. The milk is coming to a boil on the fires. My round breasts are becoming bowls. Bring it over, that lump of flesh, and lay it down on the soft swaddle of my carded blood.

Don't snatch it away. Don't separate it from me. For God's sake, don't!

Fingers . . . let them point. I don't care. This world is a crossroads. Let all my secrets be broadcast here.

My life will be ruined. Let it be. Give me back my flesh. Don't pluck this shard of my soul away. You have no idea how precious it is. It's a jewel, the gift of those few moments. Moments that selected some atoms of my being to make someone else whole and let me think I was left incomplete. But I've become whole today.

Believe me. Ask the void inside of me, ask my breasts filled with milk, ask the lullabies that are moving forward after calming all the sobs and hiccups in every part and every pore of my body, ask the rockers being placed in my arms. Ask the pallor of my face that has given all its ruddiness to the cheeks of that lump of flesh. Ask those breaths that have been stealthily delivering that lump its share.

Fingers . . . let the fingers point at me. I'll hack them off. If a hullaballoo breaks out, I'll plug my ears with those fingers. I'll become deaf and mute and blind. The piece of my flesh will have no trouble understanding my signs. And I'll feel it and know it's mine. Don't take it away from me, don't. It's the sindoor of the parting of my womb, the bindiya on the forehead of my motherly affection, the bitter fruit of my sin. Let people spit on it, I'll lick it clean with my tongue.

Look, I'm pleading with you with folded hands. I'm touching your feet with my forehead. Please don't overturn my milk-filled bowls. Don't set fire to the soft swaddling clothes made of my carded blood. Don't sever the cords of the swings of my arms. Don't deprive me of the songs I hear in his cries.

Don't snatch that lump of flesh away from me, don't separate it from me, for God's sake, don't . . .

Lahore, 21 January. The police found an abandoned newborn girl shivering from cold by the side of the road in Dhobi Mandi and took her under their protection. Some cruel person had tied a piece of cloth tightly around the baby's neck and wrapped her naked body in a wet cloth so that she would die quickly, but she was alive. She's a very beautiful baby with blue eyes. She has been admitted to the hospital.

Tassels

Behind the hedges of the spacious garden adjacent to the kothi, a cat had delivered a litter of kittens, all eaten up by the tomcat. Later, behind the same hedges, a bitch gave birth to a few puppies. They had now grown quite big and yelped all the time, inside the kothi and out, plus they deposited their terrible filth everywhere. Poison took care of them. They died one by one, their mother too. No one knew where the father had disappeared. But had he been around he would surely have met his end just as expeditiously.

Many years had passed since . . . The hedges of the garden adjacent to the kothi had been trimmed and pruned scores of times. Behind them, many more cats and bitches had brought forth their young ones and they had all gone down the same path to oblivion without leaving any trace of their existence. Her hens—by far the most ill-mannered ever seen—often used the same hedges for laying their eggs and she was obliged to collect them every morning and carry them into the house.

In the same garden some man had brutally murdered their maid . . . her red silk drawstring with tassels on the ends, bought for eight annas from an itinerant vendor only two days before, was coiled tightly around her neck. The killer had twisted the cord with such unforgiving force that her eyes had popped out.

The gruesome sight of the maid had so affected her that she fell victim to a raging fever and lost consciousness . . . and was perhaps still unconscious. But no, how could that be? Long after the murder, the hens had laid eggs, many cats had given birth to kittens, and a marriage ceremony had also taken place . . . a bitch with a red dupatta wrapped around her neck, her glittering kurta . . . of brocade with gold and silver threads woven into the fabric. But this bitch's eyes weren't bulging out of their sockets; they seemed, rather, to have sunk down into them.

A military band had performed in the garden . . . Soldiers in red uniforms had marched with those colourful skins tucked under their arms, spewing out a medley of strange sounds. When the decorative tassels attached to their outfits fell off, people rushed to pick them up and tie them to the ends of their drawstrings . . . but when morning came all of this had simply vanished without a trace . . . they'd all been poisoned.

God knows what got into the bride's head that she decided to give birth to a baby, just one baby, and not behind the hedges, but in her own bed . . . so roly-poly, a veritable red pom-pom . . . But the mother died . . . father too . . . both done in by the child . . . no one knew where the father was. Had he been there, his death was certain. Heaven knows where those band-wallahs in their tasselled uniforms had disappeared that they never came back. Tomcats roamed around the garden and gawked at her menacingly, taking her for a basketful of animal skin, membrane and pieces of tough meat, though her basket had only oranges.

One day she pulled out her two oranges and set them in front of the mirror. She backed up a little and looked at them, but she didn't see them . . . Because they're teeny-weeny, she reasoned . . . But they started to grow even as she was looking at them. She wrapped them in a silk cloth and put them away on the mantel above the fireplace.

Now the dogs went into action, barking their heads off . . . The oranges started to roll around on the floor. They bounced on every floor of the kothi, hopped into every room, and sprinted off nimbly to large, spacious gardens . . . The dogs played with them, and sparred with each other.

Strangely, two dogs in the pack died from ingesting poison. Her stout, middle-aged housemaid gobbled up the rest. She had been recruited to replace the young maid whom some man had murdered by tying her tasselled drawstring in a tight noose around her neck.

She did have a mother, six or seven years older than her stout, middle-aged housemaid, but not as stout or sturdy as her. She went out for a ride in the car every morning and evening, to lay eggs behind the hedges in faraway gardens like her bad-mannered hens. Neither she nor her driver picked them up.

She would fry omelettes, which left stains on her clothes. Eventually, after the stains had dried, she would throw the clothes away behind the hedges in the garden. Buzzards would swoop down to carry them away.

A girlfriend of hers came to see her one day—Pakistan Mail, Car No. 9612 PL. It was murderously hot. Daddy was in the hills, Mother on an outing . . . she was drenched in sweat. The minute she entered she took off her blouse, flung it aside and installed herself directly under the ceiling fan. Her boiling milk jugs cooled off gradually. Her own milk jugs were cold but slowly began to warm up. Finally, heaving away, both the hot jugs and the cold became lukewarm and morphed into a tart lassi.

The band played for that girlfriend, though the soldiers' uniforms had no fluttering tassels. Instead they had brass vessels, some small, some large, that produced sound, booming and soft . . . soft and booming, when pounded on.

When this girlfriend next met her, she said that she was noticing changes in herself. And in fact she had changed. Now she had two bellies: one old, one new, one riding over the top of its mate. Her boobs looked ravaged.

Then the band played for her brother . . . the middle-aged, stout housemaid cried inconsolably. Her brother tried his best to comfort her. Poor thing, she had remembered her own wedding.

Her brother and his wife quarrelled all night long, she crying, he laughing . . . In the morning, the stout, middle-aged servant took her brother away to comfort him. The bride was given her bath . . . her red, tasselled drawstring was threaded through the waistband of her shalwar . . . only heaven knows why it wasn't strung around her neck.

Her eyes were very large. If her throat was squeezed very hard, they would have popped out like the eyes of a slaughtered goat . . . and she would have come down with a high fever again. But she was still not free of that first one . . . Maybe it had subsided and this was a new fever from which she had now lost consciousness.

Her mother was learning to drive . . . her father had set himself up permanently in a hotel. He came now and then, visited with his son and left. The son called his wife home sometimes. Every two or three days, when an old memory revisited the stout, middle-aged servant, she broke into tears. He tried to calm her down, she tried to pat and caress him; the bride would go away.

Her sister-in-law—the bride—she . . . and yes, the girlfriend—
Pakistan Mail, Car No. 9612 PL—go for an outing and wander off
to Ajanta, where painting is taught. They gawk at the paintings and
are transformed into pictures themselves. A riot of colours—red,
yellow, green, blue—all screaming. Their creator—a good-looking
man with long hair who wears an overcoat in winter as well as
summer, uses wooden clogs whether inside or out—calms them
down. After he has muted his colours, he starts screaming himself
and is pacified by the three of them, who now begin to scream
themselves.

The three of them make hundreds of specimens of abstract art at
Ajanta. In the paintings of one, every woman is shown with two bellies,
in every imaginable colour; in those of another every woman is stout and
middle-aged; and in the work of still another everything is a profusion
of tassels. A jumbled mass of drawstrings.

Abstract paintings kept coming, but the boobs of all three kept
drying up and shrinking . . . It was really very hot, so hot that they
were bathing in sweat. Shortly after entering the room, its doors fitted
with *khus* frames, they peeled off their blouses and planted themselves
directly under the ceiling fan. The fan kept whirring away, but their
boobs failed to grow hot or cold.

Her mother was in the other room. The driver was wiping oil off
her body.

Daddy was at his hotel, where a lady stenographer was rubbing eau-
de-cologne on his forehead.

One day a band also played for her. The desolate garden sprang
into sudden boisterous life. None other than the owner of Ajanta Studio
decorated the flowerpots and the doors. Extremely dark lipsticks were
flummoxed by the riotous colours he had let loose, and one even darker
shade was so overcome that she instantly dropped down to his feet and
became his student.

He had also designed her wedding dress, giving it a motley of facets.
Looking directly at the front, she looked like bunches of many-coloured
drawstrings; a fruit basket from the side; a floral curtain draped over
the window when seen from a distance; from the back, a pile of crushed
watermelons . . . and a jar filled with tomato sauce from a different
angle. From above, a specimen of some quaint art; from down below,
the obscure poetry of Miraji.

The eyes of connoisseurs were so impressed that they burst into spontaneous praise for her . . . most of all the bridegroom, who firmly resolved to become an abstract painter the day after the wedding. So he went to Ajanta with his wife . . . where he found out that he was getting married and he has been shacked up at his wife-to-be's for the past several days.

His wife-to-be was the same one who wore her lipstick much darker than the other merely dark ones. At first, for a few months, the bridegroom's interest in her and abstract art endured. However, with the closing of Ajanta Studio and its owner's disappearance without a trace, the bridegroom went into the salt business, which yielded great profits.

In the course of carrying on his salt business, he met a young woman whose milk jugs hadn't run dry. He fell for them. No band played, but a wedding did come about. The first wife gathered her paintbrushes and went to live elsewhere.

The initial bitterness stemming from their differences eventually gave way to a strange sweetness. Her girlfriend who, after dumping her first husband for a new one and travelling across the whole of Europe, was now suffering from tuberculosis, portrayed this sweetness in cubic art: numberless clear and transparent cubes of sugar stacked one on top of the other amidst cacti in such a way that they gave the impression of two faces with honeybees sitting on them sucking nectar.

Her second girlfriend ended her life by swallowing poison. When she got this tragic news, she slipped into a coma. No one could tell whether this was a fresh assault of unconsciousness or the continuation of the same old one that had resulted from the initial raging fever.

Her father was in eau-de-cologne, where his hotel massaged his lady stenographer's scalp. Her mom had handed over the entire management of the household to the stout, middle-aged servant. She could drive now, but was taken seriously ill. Still she cared a lot about the driver's motherless pup and fed him her mobile oil.

The life of her sister-in-law and her brother was moving along on an even keel, becoming more mature and robust with the passage of time. They always met each other with great courtesy and love. Suddenly one night, when the maidservant and her brother were busy taking account of the household, her sister-in-law dropped by. She was alone, with neither a pen nor a brush in her hand, and yet she cleared the account of both in one fell swoop.

All that was seen in the morning were two blobs of coagulated gore, looking like two big pom-poms, which were then tied around the neck of her sister-in-law.

Only now did she emerge somewhat from her deep sleep. The differences with her husband, bitter at first, had been replaced by a strange sweetness. She made an attempt to daub it with a measure of bitterness. She took to alcohol. She failed because the amount imbibed was negligible . . . she increased it, indeed so much that she was swirling in it . . . people thought she would drown any minute, but each time she came up to the surface, wiping the residue from her lips and laughing hysterically.

When she got up in the morning she felt as if every fibre of her being had wept bitterly all night long. From the graves that could have been dug, all the babies that could have been born to her were wailing inconsolably for the milk that could have been theirs. But where was any milk to be found . . . It had been sucked dry by wild tomcats.

She started drinking more to drown in the bottomless sea, but her desire remained unfulfilled. She was intelligent, educated and talked matter-of-factly, without inhibition, on sexual matters. And she did not feel there was anything wrong in establishing sexual relations with men. Yet, sometimes in the stillness of the night, she longed to go behind the hedges like one of her bad-mannered hens and lay an egg.

People began to avoid her when they saw her drunk, a mere bag of bones . . . She understood everything and didn't run after them. She lived alone in the house, chain-smoking, drinking, lost in distant thoughts . . . She slept little and roamed around the kothi.

In the servant's quarter across from the kothi, the driver's motherless child kept up a litany of cries for the oil which had run dry in her mother. The driver had crashed the car. It was in the garage, her mother in the hospital, where one of her legs had already been amputated and the other was about to be.

Now and then when she peeked inside the quarter, she felt a vague tremor in the depths of her bosom, but that horrid tasting residue was too meagre to even wet the child's lips.

For some time now her brother had been living in a foreign country. Finally, in a letter from Switzerland, he informed her that he was there to seek medical treatment, that the nurse was exceedingly nice, and that he was planning to marry her as soon as he got out of the hospital.

The stout, middle-aged servant disappeared after stealing a bit of jewellery, some cash, and a lot of clothes belonging to her mom. Sometime later, following unsuccessful surgery, her mother died in the hospital.

Her father did make a token appearance at the funeral, and was never seen again.

She was all alone now. She had let go of all the servants, including the driver. She found an ayah for his baby. Every burden was now off her shoulders, except her own thoughts. If anyone ever showed up to see her, she screamed from inside the house, 'Go away . . . whoever you may be. Go away! I don't want to see anyone.'

She had found her mother's countless priceless jewels in the safe and had quite a few of her own for which she felt no attachment. In the evening she would sit in front of the mirror naked for many hours, decorate her body with all the jewellery, drink and croon obscene songs in her off-key voice. Since there was no other house in the vicinity, she had all the freedom she could hope for.

As it is, she had already bared her body in many ways. Now she aimed to bare her soul as well. But she felt the greatest difficulty in doing so. The only way she could think of to overcome her formidable diffidence was to drink, and drink with abandon, and make use of her naked body . . . but the supreme tragedy was that her body, stripped of its last shred of clothing, had actually become invisible.

She had tired of drawing pictures . . . her painting paraphernalia had been lying in a small box for quite a while now. One day she took out all the colours, mixed each one with water in a large bowl, cleaned her brushes and set them to one side, and installed herself stark naked before the mirror. She started painting her body with altogether new features, strange dimensions. This was her attempt at completely baring her being.

She could only paint the front of her body. She spent the entire day in this enterprise, without eating a morsel or taking a drink of water. She stood in front of the mirror and tried out different paints, tracing crooked lines. Her brushstrokes reflected perfect confidence and surety of touch . . . about midnight she drew away a little and observed herself closely, feeling satisfied. Then she proceeded to decorate her paint-smeared body with every one of her jewels and once again examined her body in the mirror. Just then she heard a sound suggestive of a presence.

She turned around abruptly . . . a masked man with a drawn dagger was standing before her, poised as if to attack. As soon as she turned around, a scream shot from the attacker's throat. The dagger fell from his hand. In utter confusion, he moved this way and that to find a way out . . . Finally he found an opening and bolted.

She ran after him, screaming, calling, 'Wait . . . wait, I won't say anything . . . wait!'

But the intruder paid no attention to her. He bounded over the perimeter wall and slipped clean away. Disappointed, she retreated inside. The intruder's dagger was lying on the threshold. She picked it up and went in . . . Suddenly her eyes fell on the mirror. Over her heart she had painted a leather-coloured sheath. She placed the dagger on it and looked. The sheath was a bit too small. She threw the dagger away, took four or five swigs straight from the wine bottle and started pacing back and forth, back and forth . . . She'd already been through several bottles and hadn't eaten at all.

After prolonged pacing she returned to the mirror. She saw that she was wearing a scarf around her neck which resembled a drawstring with fairly big tassels. She had painted it with her brush.

All of a sudden she felt the scarf begin to tighten, digging deeper, and still deeper into her neck . . . She stood quietly before the mirror, staring at her eyes which were popping out as the scarf was tightening . . . after a while the veins in her neck began to swell. She let out a big scream and fell face down on to the floor.

Hindi–Urdu

The Hindi–Urdu dispute has been raging for some time now. Maulvi Abdul Haq Sahib, Dr Tara Singh and Mahatma Gandhi know what there is to know about this dispute. For me, though, it has so far remained incomprehensible. Try as hard as I might, I just haven't been able to understand. Why are Hindus wasting their time supporting Hindi, and why are Muslims so beside themselves over the preservation of Urdu? A language is not made, it makes itself. And no amount of human effort can ever kill a language. When I tried to write something about this current hot issue, I ended up with the following conversation:

MUNSHI NARAIN PARSHAD: Iqbal Sahib, are you going to drink this soda water?

MIRZA MUHAMMAD IQBAL: Yes, I am.

MUNSHI: Why don't you drink lemon?

IQBAL: No particular reason. I just like soda water. At our house, everyone does.

MUNSHI: In other words, you hate lemon.

IQBAL: Oh, not at all. Why would I hate it, Munshi Narain Parshad? Since everyone at home drinks soda water, I've sort of grown accustomed to it. That's all. But if you ask me, actually lemon tastes better than plain soda.

MUNSHI: That's precisely why I was surprised that you would prefer something salty over something sweet. And lemon isn't just sweet, it has a nice flavour. What do you think?

IQBAL: You're absolutely right. But . . .

MUNSHI: But what?

IQBAL: Nothing. I was just going to say that I'd take soda.

MUNSHI: Same nonsense again. I'm not forcing you to drink poison, am I? Brother, what's the difference between the two? Both bottles are made in the same factory after all. The same machine has poured water into them. If you take the sweetness and flavour out of the lemon, what's left?

IQBAL: Just soda . . . a kind of salty water . . .

MUNSHI: Then, what's the harm in drinking the lemon?

IQBAL: No harm at all.

MUNSHI: Then drink!

IQBAL: And what will you drink?

MUNSHI: I'll send for another bottle.

IQBAL: Why would you send for another bottle? What's the harm in drinking plain soda?

MUNSHI: N . . . n . . . no harm.

IQBAL: Here, then, drink the soda water.

MUNSHI: And what will you drink?

IQBAL: I'll get another bottle.

MUNSHI: Why would you send for another bottle? What's the harm in drinking lemon?

IQBAL: N . . . n . . . no harm. And what's the harm in drinking soda?

MUNSHI: None at all.

IQBAL: The fact is that soda is rather good.

MUNSHI: But I think that lemon . . . is rather good.

IQBAL: Perhaps . . . If you say so. Although I've heard all along from my elders that soda is rather good.

MUNSHI: Now what's a person to make of this: I've heard all along from my elders that lemon is rather good.

IQBAL: But what's your own opinion?

MUNSHI: What's yours?

IQBAL: My opinion . . . hmm . . . my opinion. My opinion is just this . . . but why don't you tell me your opinion?

MUNSHI: My opinion . . . hmm . . . my opinion is just this . . . but why should I give it first.

IQBAL: I don't think we'll get anywhere this way. Look, just put a lid on your glass. I'll do the same. Then we'll discuss the matter leisurely.

MUNSHI: No, we can't do that. We've already popped the caps off the bottles. We'll just have to drink. Come on, make up your mind, before all the fizz is gone. These drinks are worthless without the fizz.

IQBAL: I agree. And at least you do agree that there's no real difference between lemon and soda.

MUNSHI: When did I ever say that? There's plenty of difference. They're as different as night and day. Lemon is sweet, flavourful, tart—three things more than soda. Soda only has fizz, which is so strong it just barges into the nose. By comparison, lemon is very tasty. One bottle and you feel fresh for hours. Generally soda water is for sick people. Besides, you just admitted yourself that lemon tends to be tastier than soda.

IQBAL: Well, that I did. But I never said that lemon is better than soda. Tasty doesn't mean that a thing is also beneficial. Take achaar, it's very tasty, but you already know about its harmful effects. The presence of sweetness and tartness doesn't prove that something is good. If you were to consult a doctor he would tell you the harm lemon does to the stomach. But soda, that's something else. It helps digestion.

MUNSHI: Look, we can settle the matter by mixing the two.

IQBAL: I have no objection to that.

MUNSHI: Well then, fill this glass halfway with soda.

IQBAL: Why don't you fill half the glass with your lemon? I'll pour my soda after that.

MUNSHI: Makes no sense. Why don't you pour your soda first?

IQBAL: Because I want to drink soda–lemon mixed.

MUNSHI: And I want lemon–soda mixed.

Upper, Lower, Middle

[My publisher refused to print this story, which made me squirm up, down and in the middle quite a bit. The thing was that a lawsuit had been brought against it in Karachi and I was fined twenty-five rupees. To find some amends, I wanted to squeeze another twenty-five rupees out of my publisher, but he didn't give in. I fidgeted around a lot and somehow scraped together some funds to have this story published so that it might reach you. Surely you'll welcome it because you're my reader, not my publisher.

Saadat Hasan Manto]

MIAN SAHIB: Ah, a chance to finally be together after quite a long time!

BEGUM SAHIBA: That's right.

MIAN SAHIB: Oh, these umpteen responsibilities the nation expects me to shoulder . . . For the sake of our people I can't shirk them . . . Oh, I can hardly breathe.

BEGUM SAHIBA: You know what your problem is—you're far too compassionate . . . just like me.

MIAN SAHIB: Yes, yes, I'm kept abreast of your social activities. If you can find a free moment, do send me copies of the speeches you made on different occasions recently. I want to read them in my spare time.

BEGUM SAHIBA: Well, all right, I will.

MIAN SAHIB: So, Begum, what about it . . . I mean . . . you know?

BEGUM SAHIBA: What about what?

MIAN SAHIB: Oh, maybe I didn't mention . . . By chance, I ended up in our middle son's room yesterday. Would you believe it, he was reading *Lady Chatterley's Lover*!

BEGUM SAHIBA: That wretched book!

MIAN SAHIB: Yes, Begum.

BEGUM SAHIBA: So what did you do?

MIAN SAHIB: I snatched the book from his hand and hid it.

BEGUM SAHIBA: You did the right thing.

MIAN SAHIB: Now I'm thinking of talking to the doctor and having him change our son's diet.

BEGUM SAHIBA: Exactly . . . the thing to do.

MIAN SAHIB: So how are you feeling these days?

BEGUM SAHIBA: I'm fine.

MIAN SAHIB: I was thinking . . . of asking you . . .

BEGUM SAHIBA: You're really becoming very naughty.

MIAN SAHIB: All your doing . . . your infinite charms.

BEGUM SAHIBA: But your health?

MIAN SAHIB: Health is good. Still I wouldn't do anything without consulting the doctor first. But I must also make sure you're fit as well.

BEGUM SAHIBA: I'll ask Miss Sildhana today.

MIAN SAHIB: And I'll ask Dr Jalal.

BEGUM SAHIBA: In principle, that's how it should be.

MIAN SAHIB: What if Dr Jalal says it's okay?

BEGUM SAHIBA: And what if Miss Sildhana says it's okay! . . . Anyway, you take care of yourself. Wrap the muffler securely around your neck. It's blistery cold outside.

MIAN SAHIB: Thanks.

*

DR JALAL: Did you give her the green light?

MISS SILDHANA: Yes.

DR JALAL: So did I . . . although to play with him a little bit, I didn't . . .

MISS SILDHANA: Me too . . . I felt like not letting her have the go-ahead . . . just for fun.

DR JALAL: I kind of felt sorry for him.

MISS SILDHANA: So did I.

DR JALAL: After holding back for a whole year he . . .

MISS SILDHANA: Yes, after a whole year.

DR JALAL: You know what? His pulse quickened as soon as I gave him the thumbs up.

MISS SILDHANA: So did hers.

DR JALAL: He was afraid. He asked me, 'Doctor, it seems as though my heart has weakened . . . Won't you take my electrocardiogram?'

MISS SILDHANA: She asked for it too!

DR JALAL: Instead, I gave him a shot.

MISS SILDHANA: So did I. A shot of only distilled water.

DR JALAL: Distilled water is perfect . . . the best.

MISS SILDHANA: Jalal, what if you were this Begum's husband?

DR JALAL: And you this man's wife?

MISS SILDHANA: It would have ruined my character.

DR JALAL: And it would have killed me.

MISS SILDHANA: People would also have taken it as a flaw in your character.

DR JALAL: So what's new . . . every time we visit these foolhardy socialites, we damage our character.

MISS SILDHANA: It will be damaged today no less.

DR JALAL: In fact, quite a bit.

MISS SILDHANA: But theirs take long intervals to spoil . . . and that's the problem.

*

BEGUM SAHIBA: This thing, *Lady's Chatterley's Lover*, why is it lying under your pillow?

MIAN SAHIB: I wanted to find out just how smutty it is.

BEGUM SAHIBA: Well then, I'll look at it along with you.

MIAN SAHIB: All right. I'll pick out passages at random and read them to you . . . you listen.

BEGUM SAHIBA: Suits me fine.

MIAN SAHIB: I've already changed our middle son's diet after consulting the doctor.

BEGUM SAHIBA: I was sure you wouldn't be negligent about the matter.

MIAN SAHIB: I never put off until tomorrow what I can do today.

BEGUM SAHIBA: I know that . . . especially the thing you have in mind for today.

MIAN SAHIB: You look very cheery today . . .

BEGUM SAHIBA: Your charm, what else.

MIAN SAHIB: Oh, I'm very amused . . . now, if I have your permission . . .

BEGUM SAHIBA: Wait. Have you brushed your teeth?

MIAN SAHIB: Yes, I have. I even rinsed my mouth with Dettol.

BEGUM SAHIBA: I did too.

MIAN SAHIB: The fact is: We're made just for each other.

BEGUM SAHIBA: No doubt about it.

MIAN SAHIB: So now, may I start reading from this wretched book at random?

BEGUM SAHIBA: Hold on. First check my pulse.

MIAN SAHIB: It's a bit fast . . . now check mine.

BEGUM SAHIBA: So is yours, a trifle fast.

MIAN SAHIB: I wonder why.

BEGUM SAHIBA: Your heart ailment . . . what else.

MIAN SAHIB: Makes sense. That must be it . . . but Dr Jalal said that it's nothing to worry about.

BEGUM SAHIBA: Miss Sildhana told me the same thing.

MIAN SAHIB: Did she give the go-ahead after a thorough examination?

BEGUM SAHIBA: Absolutely . . . after a very thorough examination.

MIAN SAHIB: In that case, I guess we can proceed.

BEGUM SAHIBA: You know best . . . Hope it won't have an adverse effect on your health . . .

MIAN SAHIB: Or on yours either.

BEGUM SAHIBA: One should take such a step only after long, hard deliberation . . .

MIAN SAHIB: Miss Sildhana has taken care of *that*, hasn't she?

BEGUM SAHIBA: Of what? Oh yes—yes, she has.

MIAN SAHIB: You mean, it's perfectly safe?

BEGUM SAHIBA: Yes, it is.

MIAN SAHIB: Okay, take my pulse again.

BEGUM SAHIBA: It's normal . . . Now check mine.

MIAN SAHIB: Yours is normal too.

BEGUM SAHIBA: Read now, some passage from this dirty book.

MIAN SAHIB: As you say. My pulse is jumping again.

BEGUM SAHIBA: So is mine.

MIAN SAHIB: Have you had the servants put the necessary stuff in the room?

BEGUM SAHIBA: Yes. Everything is here.

MIAN SAHIB: If you don't mind, please take my pulse again.

BEGUM SAHIBA: Can't you take it yourself . . . The stopwatch is handy.

MIAN SAHIB: Yes, we should note it down too.

BEGUM SAHIBA: Where are the smelling salts?

MIAN SAHIB: Got to be with the rest of the stuff.

BEGUM SAHIBA: Yes, they're there on the teapoy.

MIAN SAHIB: I think we should raise the temperature in the room a bit.

BEGUM SAHIBA: Yes, we should.

MIAN SAHIB: If you see me growing faint, please don't forget to give me medicine.

BEGUM SAHIBA: I will try if . . .

MIAN SAHIB: Yes, but otherwise, please don't bother.

BEGUM SAHIBA: Read, read this whole page.

MIAN SAHIB: Okay, listen . . .

BEGUM SAHIBA: What—you sneezed?

MIAN SAHIB: Don't know why.

BEGUM SAHIBA: I'm amazed.

MIAN SAHIB: I no less.

BEGUM SAHIBA: I know . . . I lowered the thermostat instead of raising it. Forgive me.

MIAN SAHIB: I think it was good that I sneezed. It alerted us in time.

BEGUM SAHIBA: I really am very sorry.

MIAN SAHIB: Oh, don't worry. Twelve drops of brandy will take care of it.

BEGUM SAHIBA: Stop! Let me pour them out. You always mess up the count.

MIAN SAHIB: Very true. You pour.

BEGUM SAHIBA: Drink slowly . . . very slowly.

MIAN SAHIB: This is slow enough.

BEGUM SAHIBA: So how do you feel now—better?

MIAN SAHIB: I'm getting there.

BEGUM SAHIBA: Maybe you should rest a little.

MIAN SAHIB: I was feeling the need for it myself.

*

MALE SERVANT: What's the matter. No sign of Begum Sahiba anywhere today.

MAID: She isn't feeling well.

MALE SERVANT: Mian Sahib isn't feeling well either.

MAID: We saw that coming—didn't we?

MALE SERVANT: Yes. But I'm at a loss to understand . . .

MAID: Understand what?

MALE SERVANT: These games Nature plays. We should have been on our deathbed* today instead.

MAID: What kind of talk is that? It's they who should be on their deathbeds.

MALE SERVANT: Now don't bring up their being on deathbeds . . . that would be a marvellous sight to see. I'd be seized by this overwhelming desire to gather her into my arms and carry her into my little room.

MAID: Where are you going?

MALE SERVANT: To look for a carpenter . . . that damned cot, it's about to crumble.

MAID: Yes, of course. Tell him to use very sturdy wood this time.

---

* Manto's use of the word is ironical. What is meant is the conjugal bed.

Green Sandals

'I don't think I can put up with you any more. Please divorce me.'

'For heaven's sake, what kind of talk is that? You know what, your biggest problem is that every now and then these strange fits take hold of you and you completely lose your senses.'

'And your senses—like they never leave you. When are you ever not drunk?'

'I do drink, I admit. But I never get drunk without drinking the way you do. And I don't spew out nonsense.'

'So I talk nonsense—is that it?'

'When did I say that? But stop and think, what's all this talk about a divorce?'

'I just want a divorce. A husband who couldn't care less about his wife . . . what else can she want but a divorce.'

'You can ask me for anything, but not a divorce.'

'As if you can really give me anything.'

'So now this is another accusation you're piling on me. What other woman could be as fortunate as you are. In the house . . .'

'Curses on such fortune.'

'Don't curse it. What could have displeased you so? I love you dearly, honest. Believe me.'

'God save me from such love.'

'Okay, stop making these caustic jibes. Tell me, have the girls gone to school?'

'Why should you care whether they go to school or to hell? Oh, how I pray that they'd die.'

'One of these days I might have to yank your tongue out with a pair of red-hot tongs. Uttering such nonsense about your own daughters . . . Aren't you ashamed of yourself?'

'I'm warning you: Don't use foul language with me! It's you who should be ashamed. You talk to your wife as though she's some street girl, rather than with respect and deference. It's all due to the bad company you keep.'

'And the kink you've got in your brain—what's the cause of that?'

'You. What else?'

'It's always me you have to dump on. God knows what's happened to you.'

'What's happened to me? Nothing. It's you who's gone mad. Always breathing down my neck. I've told you, I want a divorce.'

'Want to marry someone else, do you? Tired of me?'

'Shame on you. What kind of woman do you take me for?'

'So why do you want a divorce? What will you do?'

'I'll get the hell out of here. Go anywhere that I can find a room. I'll work, work hard to put food on the table for my children and myself.'

'You, working hard—ha! You get up at nine in the morning and go back to bed after breakfast. After lunch you take a three-hour nap. Hard work—huh! Don't deceive yourself.'

'Oh really! I'm the one who's sleeping all the time, and you, you're awake all day long! Just yesterday your office boy was here. He was saying that our *Afsar* Sahib is always dozing off with his head on his desk.'

'Who was that son-of-a-bitch?'

'Mind your tongue.'

'Oh, I'm just furious. When you're angry, it's hard to control your tongue.'

'I'm angry too . . . angry at you, but I haven't used such filthy language. One must never overstep the limits of propriety. You hang out with lowly people and now you've picked up their foul language.'

'Just who are these lowly people whom I hang out with?'

'That fellow who says he's a big cloth merchant . . . Have you ever seen the kind of clothes he wears: such crummy stuff, and grimy besides. Says he has a BA but his attitude, his manners, his conduct—God, they're revolting!'

'He's a *majzub*, god-enraptured.'

'What's that?'

'You wouldn't understand. I'd be wasting my time explaining it to you.'

'Oh, your time is so precious, is it? You can't afford to waste it explaining just one little thing?'

'What, exactly, are you trying to say?'

'Nothing. I said what I wanted to. Divorce me so that I'm finally rid of this daily squabbling that has made my life a living hell.'

'Even a word full of love makes your life hell—is there a cure for it?'

'Yes, there is. Divorce.'

'All right, then, send for a maulvi. If this is what you want, I won't stand in your way.'

'How am I going to send for one?'

'Aren't you the one who is asking for a divorce? If I wanted it, I would have summoned ten maulvis in one minute flat. Don't expect me to help you out in this. It's your business, you find a way.'

'You can't even do this much for me?'

'No. I can't.'

'Haven't you been telling me all this time that your love for me is limitless?'

'Yes, only to be together, not to break apart.'

'What am I to do then?'

'That's your business. And look, don't bother me any more now. Send for a maulvi, have him draft the papers and I'll sign them.'

'What about the *mehr*?'*

'What about it? You're initiating the divorce. The question of payment doesn't arise.'

'That's really something!'

'Your brother is a barrister. Ask him. He'll tell you that when a woman asks for a divorce, she forfeits her right to demand mehr.'

'In that case, you divorce me.'

'Why would I do such a foolish thing? I love you.'

'Spare me your wheedling. I don't like it. You wouldn't treat me so shabbily if you really loved me.'

'When have I treated you shabbily?'

---

* As required by Islamic law, the mandatory amount of money or possessions given at the time of marriage by the groom to the bride for her exclusive use.

'As if you don't know. Just yesterday or the day before you wiped your shoes on my brand-new sari.'

'*I did not!* I swear.'

'So maybe it was ghosts who did.'

'All I know is this: Your three daughters were wiping their shoes with your sari. I even scolded them.'

'They are not so ill-mannered.'

'Oh, but they are, quite a bit. And you know why—because you haven't bothered to teach them good manners. Ask them when they're back from school whether or not they were wiping their shoes on your sari.'

'I don't have to ask them anything.'

'What's gotten into your head today? If only I could crack it, I might be able to do something about it.'

'You keep thinking about that something. I know what I have to do. Let's make it short: Divorce me. There's no point in living with a husband who doesn't care about his wife.'

'I have always cared for you.'

'Do you know that tomorrow is Eid?'

'Of course I do. Just yesterday I bought new shoes for the girls and I gave you sixty rupees for their frocks a week ago.'

'As if that was a big favour to me, why, even to my father and his father.'

'No, it's not a question of doing a favour, to you or to anybody. Just tell me, what's bugging you.'

'All right, if you want to know. Sixty rupees weren't enough. The organdie cloth alone for three girls cost sixty rupees. The tailor charged seven rupees for each of the three frocks. You think this is a favour to the girls and me? Hardly.'

'So you made up the shortfall from your pocket?'

'If I didn't, who would have stitched their frocks?'

'Let me give you the difference, right now. Oh, I get it. So this is what was upsetting you.'

'Eid is tomorrow.'

'Yes, yes, I know. I'm ordering two chickens . . . sevaiyan, too. And you—what preparations have you made?'

'Nothing—how can I?'

'Why?'

'I wanted to wear a green sari tomorrow. I had ordered a pair of green sandals to go with it. I asked you so many times to find out from the Chinese shoe shop if they were ready, but why would you? When have I ever meant a thing to you?'

'For heaven's sake. Now I see. So all this bickering is over the green sandals. But I already brought them two days ago. The package is in your closet. You probably never opened it. You're always lazing around all day long.'

The Gold Ring

'Your hair looks like a rat's nest. Some new fashion or what? Can't understand.'

'Nothing of the sort. If you ever had to go through the hassle of getting a haircut, you would know the value of the peace that comes with letting your hair grow long.'

'Why would I want to get a haircut in the first place?'

'Women do. Thousands, indeed tens of thousands are getting their hair clipped short like men to keep up with the current rage.'

'A curse upon them.'

'Whose curse?'

'God's—who else's? Hair is a woman's ornament. It's mind-boggling that they should want to have it cropped short and parade about in pants like men. May they perish from the earth!'

'No matter how hard you pray, they're not about to perish from the earth. But I do agree with you about one thing: Women shouldn't wear pants, otherwise called slacks. And, yes, they shouldn't smoke either.'

'While you can go through a whole tin of cigarettes in a day.'

'That doesn't count—I'm a man. I'm allowed to.'

'Who allowed you? I'm rationing your cigarettes; you'll get only one pack a day from now on.'

'And your girlfriends, the ones who visit you all the time to snitch my cigarettes—where will they get their supply?'

'They . . . they don't smoke.'

'That's a blatant lie. Whenever one of them drops in, you grab my tin, why, even my matches, and disappear into the living room. Often I

357

have to call you to return it. And when I do get it back, it's always short half a dozen cigarettes.'

'Half a dozen—you're the one who's lying! My poor friends, they hardly smoke one cigarette.'

'What can be "hardly" about smoking one cigarette?'

'I don't want to argue with you about it. You love to argue; it's as though you have nothing else to do.'

'Why, I have a million things to do. Besides, it's not like you have a whole field to plough. You lie around in bed all day long.'

'And you stay awake around the clock drowned in some wazifa?'

'No, not wazifa, although I can say with confidence that I sleep only six hours at night.'

'And how many hours during the day?'

'None. I don't sleep; I just stretch out on my back for three, maybe four hours with my eyes closed. It's very relaxing. All the fatigue slowly washes away.'

'But where does your fatigue come from? You don't do any hard work like a labourer.'

'I get up at the crack of dawn, read newspapers, eat breakfast, take a shower, and then get ready to put up with your bitching. That's hard work.'

'You call it hard work? So tell me, how true is this accusation of bitching?'

'As true as it can be. In the early days, I mean for the first two years after our marriage, life was so pleasant and peaceful, and then suddenly, God knows what got into you, and you made it your routine to quarrel with me every day. I wonder what the reason is.'

'The reason always escapes you men. You never tried to understand.'

'When did you ever leave me in peace long enough to understand it? Every day you find one thing or another to bitch about. What was the matter today that you started making so much fuss over?'

'You haven't had a haircut for six months—you don't think that's reason enough to get upset? Just look at the collars of your achkans . . . how grimy they've become.'

'Shall I send them to be dry-cleaned?'

'It's your head that needs dry-cleaning. God, it's revolting to look at your hair, I swear. I feel like dousing it with kerosene and sticking a match into it.'

'To finish me off. But I don't have a problem if you want that. Bring some kerosene from the kitchen, pour it slowly over my head, and set it afire. The less rubbish in the world the better.'

'Do it yourself. If I tried, you'd say I don't know how to do anything properly.'

'Which is true. You don't. You don't know how to cook or sew, or even keep the house tidy. As for the children, you know nothing about raising them. God protect them.'

'Oh, that's right! It's you who's been raising them all this while. I'm a total moron, a good-for-nothing.'

'I don't want to say anything more about this matter. Stop this bickering for God's sake.'

'I'm not bickering. But to you every little thing is bickering.'

'Maybe they're little things to you. Now leave my hair alone. I've always had this much hair. You know well enough that I don't have a moment to breathe, much less to go to the barber.'

'When would you have time anyway, you're always up to your neck in your own enjoyment.'

'What enjoyment?'

'Do you work? Are you employed anywhere? Any salary? Anything that requires hard work, you shirk, labelling it the biggest calamity.'

'Don't I slog away? Just a few days ago I worked my butt off to supply bricks for a contract.'

'If anyone worked it was the donkeys who hauled the bricks; you were probably dozing.'

'Donkeys are passé. It's trucks, now, that I have to supervise. The contract was for ten crore bricks. I had to stay awake all night.'

'I can't believe you could stay awake even one night.'

'You've formed a wrong opinion of me and I can't get it out of your head. Even if I gave you a hundred proofs to the contrary, you're not likely to believe me.'

'I stopped believing you a long time ago. You're a liar, a first-rate liar.'

'You're second to no woman in making false accusations. I have never ever lied in my life.'

'Oh yeah. You told me the day before yesterday that you'd been at a friend's. Then you drank a little and it went to your head. Now you've told me that you had gone to meet some actress.'

'That actress is also a friend. She isn't an enemy; I mean she's the wife of one of my friends.'

'As a rule, all your friends' wives are generally either actresses or sluts.'

'It's not my fault if they are.'

'Then it must be my fault . . .'

'How so?'

'Because I married you. I'm neither an actress nor a slut.'

'I despise both . . . very much. I have no interest in them. Who says they're women? On the contrary, they're like writing slates. Anyone can scribble a few words or lengthy sentences on them and then just erase everything.'

'So why did you go to see her . . . that actress?'

'My friend invited me to come over and I obliged. He'd just married this actress who had been married four times before and he wanted to introduce us.'

'How did she look?'

'Considering her four previous marriages, she looked quite fit, unbelievably young. I'd even say in a lot better shape than ordinary unmarried girls.'

'What's the secret of these actresses for staying so young and fit?'

'I don't know much about it . . . except they take good care of their bodies.'

'I've heard that they have questionable morals . . . and they tend to be rather lewd.'

'God knows best. I know nothing about these things.'

'You always evade answering such things.'

'What answer can I give when I know next to nothing about a particular thing—your temperament for instance? What can I say about it with any degree of confidence when it keeps wavering between extremes.'

'Look, I don't want you to say anything about me . . . ever. You always put me down. I can't take it any more.'

'When have I ever put you down?'

'Isn't it putting me down to say that in fifteen years of being married you still haven't figured me out? What else does it mean except that I'm demented, half-crazy, a rank ignoramus, rough and coarse . . .'

'Well, at least you're none of those. All the same, it's difficult to figure you out. I still don't understand why you suddenly started talking about my hair, because when you do start talking about something suddenly, there's sure as hell always something else lurking behind it . . .'

'What could that something else be? All I wanted to say was that your hair has grown too long and you must get a haircut. The barbershop isn't very far, a hundred steps at most. Go get a haircut. Meanwhile, I'll get water heated for your bath.'

'I will, I will, but let me first smoke a cigarette.'

'No, you won't. You've—let me see the tin—my God, you've already smoked twenty cigarettes. Twenty!'

'That's not too many . . . it's getting on towards twelve o'clock . . .'

'Don't prattle on your way to the barber's . . . Get this extra baggage off your head.'

'I'm going, I'm going. Is there something you want done?'

'Nothing. Don't look for excuses to elude me.'

'Okay, I'm leaving.'

'Hold on.'

'Yes?'

'How much money do you have on you?'

'About five hundred rupees.'

'Well then, stop by Anarkali before going to the barber and buy a gold ring worth at least two hundred to two hundred and fifty rupees. It is my friend's birthday today.

'Why would I need a haircut after that? I'll go bald right there in Anarkali bazaar. I'm going, bye.'

Turnips

'Please have the servant bring my lunch. I'm starving.'

'It's three o'clock. Where will you get food at this hour?'

'So what if it's three o'clock—I live here. I need to eat. After all, I must have some rights in this house.'

'Oh yeah, what rights? How many?'

'Since when have you started keeping track of such things—questioning me like this?'

'If I didn't, this house wouldn't have lasted this long.'

'Oh, you're amazing! Now, will I get my lunch or not?'

'You can forget about lunch if you keep turning up at three in the afternoon day after day. Even in a restaurant you wouldn't get dal–roti at this hour. I absolutely don't like your habits.'

'What habits?'

'That you show up at three. The food gets cold while I'm languishing away, waiting for you, and only God knows where Your Majesty is loafing around.'

'Well, don't people have work to do? In any case, I was a little bit late just two days.'

'You call it a little bit late? Every husband has to come home by noon so that he's fed by one o'clock. And besides, he should be submissive to his wife.'

'Maybe he should just take a room in a hotel and live there? At least there the attendants would all be at his beck and call.'

'Wouldn't you love that? In fact, you're planning to take off any day, aren't you? Well, you can leave now, right this minute.'

'Without having my meal?'

'Eat it at your hotel.'

'But just now you said I wouldn't even get dal–roti in any restaurant at this hour? How quickly you forget!'

'You know why, because I'm going nuts, or rather, being driven nuts.'

'That's for sure. But who's driving you nuts?'

'You—who else? You've made my life a living hell. I have no peace, neither during the day nor at night.'

'Never mind the day, why don't you have peace at night? You sleep like a log, without a care in the world, or, as the saying goes, like one who's sold off all his horses.'

'Who can sleep after selling their horses? What a stupid saying.'

'All right, it is stupid. But just a few days ago you sold not only the horse but also the tonga along with it. And how soundly you slept afterwards, snoring all night long.'

'There was no need to keep the tonga after you'd bought me the car. And the accusation that I snore is total nonsense.'

'Your Majesty, how could you possibly know whether or not you were snoring when you were drowned in sleep? Your snores kept me awake the whole night, believe me.'

'Wrong, absolutely wrong. It's a vicious lie.'

'Okay, for your sake, let's say it's a lie. Now give me my food.'

'Not today. Go to a hotel . . . Why, you can live there for the rest of your life for all I care.'

'And you—what will you do?'

'Rest assured, I won't die without you.'

'God forbid that you should die. But tell me, how will you support yourself without me.'

'I'll sell the car.'

'And how much will you get for it?'

'Six, maybe seven thousand, at least.'

'How long will that feed you and your kids?'

'I don't splurge like you do. It will last me till the end of my days, and the children won't lack for anything either—you'll see.'

'Well then, teach me this secret. I'm sure you've hit upon some mantra that doubles money. You pull out some banknotes from your wallet, whisper the mantra over them, and presto, you have twice as much.'

'You ridicule me. Shame on you.'

'Let's put this aside and give me my lunch.'

'You won't get it.'

'For heaven's sake, why? What have I done wrong?'

'If I started to count your wrongs and misdeeds, I'd be counting till I'm dead.'

'Look, Begum, you've gone overboard. If you don't give me my meal, I'll burn down the house. For God's sake, here I am, dying of hunger, and there you are, rattling away this nonsense. I had some pressing work to take care of yesterday and today, that's why I was late. You're accusing me of coming home late every day. Give me my food, or else . . .'

'Don't you threaten me! You won't get food.'

'This is my house. I'm free to come and go as I please. Who are you to impose these unbearable conditions on me? I'm telling you, this attitude of yours won't get you anywhere.'

'As if your attitude has got me somewhere. This interminable vexation has reduced me to such a pitiable state.'

'Some state—you've gained twelve pounds while your crabby temperament has ruined my health.'

'What's wrong with your health?'

'Have you ever bothered to ask why I always look so tired? Or thought about why I huff and puff while climbing stairs? Have you ever felt it in your heart to give me a little massage when my head is about to explode from pain? You're a strange life-mate. Had I known I would end up with a wife like you, I'd never have come anywhere near you.'

'And I would have swallowed poison had I known I'd be saddled with a husband like you.'

'Poison—you can swallow it now. Shall I go get some?'

'Yes, please.'

'But first give me my lunch.'

'For the umpteenth time, you're not getting any today.'

'But surely I will tomorrow, and every day after tomorrow because by then you'll be in the next world. Anyway, I can't go out for your poison on an empty stomach. Who knows, I might pass out and drop dead while driving. Looks as if I'll have to do something on my own to get some food.'

'Like what?'

'I'll call the cook.'

'You will do no such thing!'

'Why?'

'Because I said so. You have no right to poke your nose into household matters.'

'This is the limit. I can't even call the cook. Well then, the servant. Where is he?'

'In hell.'

'Which is where I am now too. But I don't see him anywhere. Move aside, let me look for him. Who knows, maybe I'll find him.'

'What do you want to tell him?'

'Nothing—just that I'm letting him go and taking his place.'

'You, taking his place? Wouldn't that be the day?'

'Salaam, huzoor. Begum Sahib, the dish is ready. Shall I lay Sahib's food on the table?'

'Beat it.'

'But Begum Sahib, the turnips you cooked this morning burned because the flame was too high. Then you said Sahib would be coming late so I should quickly prepare some other dish. Well, I cooked two dishes in two hours. Now, if you like I can set the table. Both dishes are still on the stove; if left longer I fear they'll be charred like your turnips. I'm going. Just let me know when you want me to set the table.'

'Now I get it! That's what all the fuss was about!'

'What fuss? I roasted in the kitchen all that time . . . and this means nothing to you. You love turnips, so I decided to cook some myself especially for you. The cookbook was in my hands . . . I just dozed off for a minute and the damned turnips turned into charcoal. Where do you see my fault in all this?'

'No, of course not. No fault at all.'

'All right, then, get up now. Let's eat. Rats are gnawing at my stomach.'

'And there are alligators in mine.'

'Will you ever stop joking?'

'Joking or no joking, come over here. Let me have a look at your *turnips*. Let's hope they haven't turned into coals.'

'We'll see about that after eating.'

In this Maelstrom

(A Melodrama)

Characters:

BEGUM, the mother
AMJAD (a crippled young man) and
MAJEED (a stout, healthy young man), the Begum's sons
SAEEDA, Amjad's beautiful new wife
ASGHARI, a maid
KARIM and
GHULAM MUHAMMAD, servants
KAMAL, a chauffeur*

ACT I

A room in Nigar Villa. Its beautifully paned windows open on to hilly slopes that extend as far as the eye can see until they blend into the greyish-blue sky. The silk curtains on the windows are rustling in the gentle morning breeze. The room's furnishings give the impression that it is being converted into a bridal suite. A canopied teakwood bed is on the right near the windows. In a corner near

---

* Manto does not include him among the dramatis personae.

367

*the bed is a small glass-topped side table with a crystal decanter,
a goblet and an alarm clock on it. At the back, two servants are
arranging cushions on a sofa with beige-coloured taffeta covers.
A short distance away, a young, plain-looking maid is trying to
rearrange some items on the mantel above the fireplace. A virginal
silence, so delicate that it would lose its innocence at the slightest
touch, pervades the room. The sound of wood slowly tapping on
the tiles outside is heard. The three domestics react slightly and
then resume their respective duties. A dignified middle-aged
woman enters through the door, propelling herself on crutches. She
scrutinizes the room and evinces a feeling of satisfaction.*

BEGUM SAHIB (*hobbles about the room, making sure that everything is
in its proper place*): Looks fine! (*She removes one crutch from under
her arm, leans over to set it against the arm of the sofa in order to
sit down, but then changes her mind. In doing so, her hand leaves a
smudge on the shiny surface of the armrest. She uses one corner of
her dupatta to wipe it, then puts her crutch back under her arm and
addresses the maid*) Asghari!

ASGHARI (*facing her*): Yes?

BEGUM SAHIB (*suddenly realizing she has forgotten why she called
ASGHARI*): What was I going to say?

ASGHARI (*smiling*): That you aren't satisfied. I feel the same way,
Begum Sahib. Really. The bride is very beautiful. All of the room's
decorations will pale before her. (*She looks at the bride's portrait
hanging from silk cords in the centre of the wall above the fireplace.*)

BEGUM SAHIB (*smiling, slowly moves towards the fireplace and looks
closely at her daughter-in-law's portrait, beams but then suddenly
feels anxious*): Asghari!

ASGHARI: Yes?

BEGUM SAHIB: I've been feeling sort of uneasy since this morning.

ASGHARI: But of course. Amjad Mian is coming with his bride.

BEGUM SAHIB (*lost in thought*): Yes. He should be along soon. Kamal
has taken the car to the station.

ASGHARI: Next year get Majeed Mian married, too. The house will really
brighten up.

BEGUM SAHIB: God willing! God willing that will come off too, nicely.
(*Under her breath*) God willing!

ASGHARI (*looking at the bride's portrait, obviously impressed by her beauty*): May God protect her from the evil eye.

BEGUM SAHIB (*almost screaming, without meaning to*): Asghari!

ASGHARI (*startled*): Yes!

BEGUM SAHIB: Oh . . . oh nothing. When does the train arrive from Karachi?

ASGHARI: I don't know, Begum Sahib.

BEGUM SAHIB (*to a servant*): Karim, call the station and find out . . . but the train reached Rawalpindi yesterday . . . Majeed's telegram said so.

KARIM: Yes, it did.

BEGUM SAHIB: Oh, and I've sent Kamal to the station . . . (*confused*) God knows what's wrong with my head. Amjad was going to stay overnight in Rawalpindi with his friend Saeed . . . They must have left Rawalpindi by now. (*To another servant*) Ghulam Muhammad!

GHULAM MUHAMMAD: Yes?

BEGUM SAHIB: Go look for Kamal. Find out where he's taken the car.

GHULAM MUHAMMAD: Right away. (*Exits.*)

BEGUM SAHIB (*leaning over* ASGHARI's *shoulder for support*): I haven't been feeling well since morning. If I weren't an invalid . . . if that damn Dr Hidayatullah hadn't stopped me, I would have gone myself to bring the bride home. (*The faint ringing of a telephone is heard in the distance.*) Perhaps that's Amjad's friend calling to say that they've left. Run, Asghari, run! (ASGHARI *exits, running.*) (*To* KARIM, *to lessen her worry*) Well, Amjad Mian must be here soon.

KARIM: May God bring him back safely.

BEGUM SAHIB (*almost screaming*): What do you mean by that?

KARIM (*scared*): Just that, just that . . .

(ASGHARI *is heard screaming offstage,* "BEGUM SAHIB! BEGUM SAHIB!")

BEGUM SAHIB (*apprehensively*): What's happened?

(ASGHARI *enters, shaken.*)

ASGHARI: Begum Sahib! Begum Sahib!

BEGUM SAHIB (*tightly clutching her crutches*): What?

ASGHARI: Majeed Mian has called . . . to say that the train . . . the train was in an accident!

BEGUM SAHIB (*grasping the crutches even tighter*): And . . .

ASGHARI: Amjad Mian and his bride were injured. They're in the hospital!

BEGUM SAHIB (*Her grip loosens and the crutches fall from under her arms. For a moment she stands there frozen, then a small tremor runs through her and she moves towards the door.*): Tell Kamal to get the car out. We're driving to Rawalpindi.
(THE BEGUM *is walking towards the door while* GHULAM MUHAMMAD *and* ASGHARI *watch her, stunned.* ASGHARI *screams and* THE BEGUM *whirls around to look at her.*)

BEGUM SAHIB: What is it?

ASGHARI: You're . . . you're walking! You can walk!

BEGUM SAHIB: Me . . . (*Noticing she is no longer on her crutches*) How? How can I be walking? (*All at once she collapses on the floor, unconscious.*)

ASGHARI (*to* GHULAM MUHAMMAD *as she walks over to* THE BEGUM): Go telephone the doctor.
(GHULAM MUHAMMAD *exits.* ASGHARI *tries to revive* THE BEGUM.)

ACT II

The same room as in Act I. The furniture appears dull and devoid of its earlier sheen. Now everything looks well used. It is morning. The silk curtains on the windows are fluttering gently in the light morning breeze. SAEEDA, *the bride, lies covered with a blanket on the teakwood bed to the right. On the side table the alarm clock showing nine o'clock begins to ring. There is some movement under the blanket.* SAEEDA *rolls over and opens her eyes. She looks over at the clock and smiles. In doing so, her thick lashes flutter on her beautiful face. She flips back over, props herself up on the pillows and looks out with childlike glee at the alluring view of the hills spreading out endlessly before her. Then, suddenly, she kicks off the blanket, jumps out of bed, draws the curtains and looks outside. She hears a bird's musical trilling and becomes lost in her thoughts. She is young. Although the silk nightgown hanging loosely on her body is attractive in itself, it nonetheless shows to good effect the curves beneath it. She is ravishing, and aware of it. Suddenly* ASGHARI'S *raucous voice rises in the background,*

contrasting sharply with the sweet sound of the singing bird.
SAEEDA *starts. When* ASGHARI *is visible she gives her a look as though asking, 'What was that?'*
ASGHARI (*entering*): Majeed Mian has just returned from the hospital. He said to see if you were up yet.
SAEEDA: What news does he bring?
ASGHARI: I'll send him in.

(ASGHARI *exits.* SAEEDA *withdraws from the window, goes over to the dressing table and looks at herself for a moment, then casually smoothing her mussed hair with her hands, she slowly moves towards the canopied bed, removes her white georgette dupatta hanging from it and very inattentively throws it around her shoulders. The creaking sound of heavy leather boots is heard coming from outside. With slight hesitation she looks over towards the door through which enters* MAJEED, *a robust young man of medium height with a light almond complexion, his features showing a maturity far beyond his years.*)

MAJEED: Salaam, Bhabhijan.
SAEEDA: Salaam.
MAJEED (*going over to the sofa*): How are you feeling?
SAEEDA (*listlessly*): All right, I guess. (*Sits down on the sofa.*) Tell me, what's the news from Rawalpindi?
MAJEED (*coming up close in front of* SAEEDA): Nothing much. (*Lets out a half-sigh.*) Well, they're bringing him home.
SAEEDA: Why?
MAJEED: He's tired of languishing in the hospital. (*Pulls over a wicker chair and sits down.*) Had I been in his place . . . I would have probably killed myself.
SAEEDA (*getting up and walking to the window*): Who would have imagined this would be my fate . . . So many people died . . . Why didn't I die with them?
MAJEED: That was not God's will.
SAEEDA (*looking at the hilly scene outside*): Yes, it wasn't God's will. Rather, God's will was that I escape with just a minor scratch on my leg but my whole life be crippled. (*Tears well up in her eyes which she delicately dries with her white dupatta.*) God's will was to cut short my days of bridal happiness and let me float in

the wind for the rest of my life like a kite severed from its string. (*Sobs.*)

MAJEED (*rising*): Have some courage, Bhabhijan. Who knows, he might still get well.

SAEEDA (*reproachfully*): Majeed, you of all people trying to deceive me! He's been lying glued to a hospital bed for six months. I know very well what the doctors say his prognosis is. He'll never get well . . . both of his legs are utterly useless now . . . but . . . but I'll grant you that he's a very courageous man. Whenever I go to see him, he makes me sit close to him and tells me, 'Saeeda, don't you worry. I'm going to get well soon—very soon. Then I'll take you out for a walk in those hills I've told you about so often in Karachi. I love those hills so much that if I talk about them any more you might get jealous.' And then he attempts to boost my sagging spirits by saying, 'Saeeda, what is life but a series of accidents? I thank God that I didn't die or else . . . or else . . .' But what he says next gives me the creeps.

MAJEED: Like what?

SAEEDA (*staring off into space with moist eyes*): Like 'You will come to love someone else and marry him.' (*Suddenly trembles.*) Why does he think of such things, why, Majeed?

MAJEED: I don't know.

SAEEDA: You should know. (*Walks slowly over to the sofa and sits down. Her dupatta slides down; her heaving bosom presses against her silk nightgown, transferring to it all its velvety rise and fall.*) You're a man . . . you're his brother . . . What if you had such an accident?

MAJEED: I would never have thought of the things that cross Amjad Bhai's mind.

SAEEDA: Why?

MAJEED: We're both men, we're even brothers—but we *feel* and *think* differently.

SAEEDA (*mumbling*): Feel and think . . .

ASGHARI (*entering*): Majeed Mian, Begum Sahib wishes to see you.

MAJEED: Go on, I'll be there.

ASGHARI: She said to come right away.

MAJEED: All right. (*Looking at* SAEEDA) I'll be right back. (*Exits.*)

(ASGHARI *sits down on the rug at* SAEEDA's *feet; she's about to massage them.*)

SAEEDA (*pulling her feet away*): Don't bother, Asghari.

ASGHARI (*nearly wrapping herself around* SAEEDA's *feet*): It's no bother, Dulhan Begum. (*Begins to press her toes.*) What news did Majeed Mian bring?

SAEEDA: He said Amjad wants to come back home.

ASGHARI: Good news.

SAEEDA (*with a stab of pain*): Yes.

ASGHARI: Begum Sahib was quite annoyed that Majeed Mian stayed so long.

SAEEDA: Where?

ASGHARI: Here . . . with you.

SAEEDA: With me? What exactly did Begum Sahib say?

ASGHARI: Nothing much. She's become very irritable these days. Nothing, absolutely nothing pleases her . . . She feels a lot sorrier for you than she does for Amjad Mian. She's always thinking about you . . . So, has Amjad Mian gotten better?

SAEEDA (*pulling her feet away in a huff and standing up*): Yes, he's gotten better. (THE BEGUM *enters the room;* ASGHARI *springs up.*) Salaam, Khalajan.

BEGUM SAHIB: Salaam, child. (*Comes over and affectionately strokes* SAEEDA's *head.*) Majeed's told you—hasn't he?

SAEEDA: Yes.

BEGUM SAHIB: He really grew to hate it there in the hospital. (*Looks over at* ASGHARI) Asghari, you can go now. (ASGHARI *exits.*) He wants . . . he wants to be with you. He told me, 'If I must die, then let my Saeeda be before my eyes.' (SAEEDA's *eyes brim over with tears and she throws herself in* THE BEGUM's *arms.*) He . . . (*tears trickling down her face*) he loves you so very much, but . . . he told me to make sure you wouldn't mind his returning home.

SAEEDA: Mind . . .

BEGUM SAHIB: Yes, child. It could make you feel even worse. You know . . . it's possible.

SAEEDA: Why must he think that way, Khalajan, why?

BEGUM SAHIB: Child, he's just that sort of person . . . always concerned about others.

SAEEDA: He should come, why shouldn't he come? (*Her voice sounding almost like a groan.*) He mustn't think like that!

BEGUM SAHIB: The doctors say that if he stays happy, then, God willing, he should be able to get around on crutches in a month or two. (*Suddenly begins to cry inconsolably.*) Crutches . . . I got rid of them after I heard about the train wreck. Had I known they were about to enter his life, I'd have held on to them tightly. But, child, the strongest boat gets sucked down into the whirlpool we call life while a mere straw takes one safely to shore. (*After a pause*) Saeeda, child, Amjad wanted me to ask you one more thing.

SAEEDA: What is it, Khalajan?

BEGUM SAHIB: Will you still love him?

SAEEDA (*stunned*): Love him . . .

BEGUM SAHIB (*stroking* SAEEDA's *head*): I don't want to trouble you any more. (*Exits.*)

SAEEDA (*delicately wiping away her tears with her dupatta, mutters*): Love . . . Love his . . . heart, his mind? (*Walks slowly over to her portrait above the fireplace and addresses it.*) Tell me, will you love him?

(*The sound of teacups clattering on a tray is heard.* ASGHARI *enters with a teacart, wheels it over to the sofa and lays out the breakfast neatly on it.*)

ASGHARI: If Dulhan Begum won't love Amjad Mian, what other woman will?

SAEEDA (*startled*): What was that?

ASGHARI: Oh, nothing . . . just talking to myself. Please have some breakfast.

SAEEDA: Please leave me.

ASGHARI: Yes, ma'am. (*Glances at* SAEEDA *and then at her portrait as she exits.*)

(SAEEDA, *deep in thought, walks slowly towards the sofa, but then goes and lies down on the bed*).

SAEEDA (*staring at the ceiling and mumbling*): If Dulhan Begum won't love Amjad Mian, what other woman will? Dulhan Begum—if she won't love Amjad Mian, then what other woman will? (*In a louder voice*) Who will? Who else can?

(*Curtain*)

ACT III

The garden adjacent to Nigar Villa. In the centre of some neatly trimmed low shrubbery, a fountain spits out short spurts of water. The sun is bright, the sky without a wisp of cloud, the atmosphere is pristine, uninhibited in its glorious prime. Every element waits expectantly to be beheld and appreciated. The breeze wafting through the garden appears to have momentarily stopped: to allow the vines to straighten their tresses, the flowers to freshen up their bright faces, and the bees, who had been yearning to kiss the blossoms, to do so fearlessly. Chairs are laid out on the smooth carpet of grass. SAEEDA, *in a pink dress, is sitting in one, looking as perfect as one of her own portraits. The bright warm sun sets her rosy cheeks still more aglow. In another chair sits* MAJEED, *serene, puffing a cigarette and blowing bluish smoke rings. In front of both is* AMJAD, *wearing a look of trapped immobility—very much like the wheelchair in which he sits—pale, but his eyes agleam, fired by* SAEEDA's *beauty.*

AMJAD (*looking around*): Absolutely gorgeous weather!

SAEEDA (*turning instantly to face him*): Yes, indeed, gorgeous.

AMJAD: Go on, Majeed. Take Saeeda for a walk. Show her these hills. (*Makes an effort to turn and look behind him but fails.*) It's a shame I can't turn around. Majeed, get up and turn my wheelchair. I must have this scene in front of me—always.

(MAJEED *rises but* SAEEDA *has in the meantime got up and turned* AMJAD's *chair around. All three are now facing the hills, washed by a brilliant sun to the horizon's end.*)

AMJAD (*taking in the scene before him*): Saeeda, these are the hills I love. I love them so much that I can't put it into words. (*To* MAJEED) Go on! Take Saeeda with you for a stroll. (*To* SAEEDA) Saeeda, when you start panting during your climb and feel as though you'll never be able to catch your breath, you'll know there's no pleasure in the world greater than this. I really used to force Majeed into coming along, but he'd give up after just one slope, saying, 'Bhaijan, I must say I don't find this hobby of yours the least bit amusing—that a man should huff and puff and pass out—there's no sense to it.' (*Laughs.*) He never will understand the lure of the hills and the desire to conquer them. Right, Saeeda?

SAEEDA (*smiling*): Yes.

AMJAD (*to* MAJEED): Go on, yaar. Take Saeeda out. Do some work for a change.

MAJEED (*to* SAEEDA): Let's go, Bhabhijan. (*To* AMJAD) But I bet that after today she'll never go into the hills again.

SAEEDA: No, no! How can you say that?

AMJAD: Because he has that sort of personality.

SAEEDA: That sort of personality? What in the world is that sort of personality?

MAJEED: You'll find that out halfway up the first slope.

AMJAD (*laughs*): Rubbish! Saeeda's life has a mountain blocking its path. If she should be unnerved by a simple ordinary hill . . .

SAEEDA: Let's go now, Majeed Mian.

MAJEED: Let's go.

(*Both exit.* AMJAD *smiles.* ASGHARI *enters holding a plate of peeled and sliced apples. Throwing a meaningful look at the exiting* MAJEED *and* SAEEDA, *she comes over to* AMJAD *and addresses him.*)

ASGHARI: Here, have some apple.

AMJAD (*absorbed in watching* SAEEDA *and* MAJEED *go down the slope*): All right.

ASGHARI (*also looking at the two*): How lovely Dulhan Begum looks today.

AMJAD (*suddenly turning to face* ASGHARI): Looks?

ASGHARI (*a trifle discomfited*): Yes, yes.

AMJAD (*looking back at the two receding figures*): She is lovely! She doesn't just look lovely. ASGHARI, there's a vast difference between being lovely and just looking lovely.

ASGHARI: Yes, so it is.

AMJAD: Give me some apple.

ASGHARI (*offering the plate*): Here. But . . . but they've been peeled.

AMJAD: Are you trying to say something?

ASGHARI: What's peeled can deceive anyone. (*Laughs.*) Its blushing red cheeks have been peeled off.

AMJAD (*laughing*): Asghari! You're fast turning into a real devil.

ASGHARI (*becoming suddenly serious*): Devil? Amjad Mian, didn't you once tell me that the Devil was God's foremost Angel and refused to bow to Adam—a mere clay doll?

AMJAD: So I did.

ASGHARI: And this ringleader of the angels was punished for it?

AMJAD: Right.

ASGHARI: Then this is right, too.

AMJAD: What?

ASGHARI: Oh, nothing. After all, what's right? Something you think is right or try to think is right. Or a mistake you make once, confident that it will right itself in due time. Or something that is right but you turn it into a mistake and hope you can make it right later. But this is all nonsense. I'm a dense woman, Amjad Mian.

AMJAD: Why are you talking like this today?

ASGHARI: I said I was dense, but a woman nonetheless, Amjad Mian.

AMJAD: I still don't get you.

ASGHARI (*picking up a wedge of apple and holding it in front of* AMJAD's *mouth*): Here, you eat some apple.

AMJAD (*taking the wedge of apple in his teeth*): You've never talked like this before.

ASGHARI: It must be the weather. It's so breathtakingly lovely!

AMJAD: Isn't it, though?

ASGHARI (*picking up another wedge*): Here, have another piece. (*Puts it into* AMJAD's *open mouth.*)

AMJAD (*pauses as he chews the apple slice*): Asghari!

ASGHARI (*wrapped up in the mountain scene, jumps*): Yes?

AMJAD: Shouldn't we get you married?

ASGHARI: Married?

AMJAD: Yes. It's about time you got married.

ASGHARI: But why, Amjad Mian?

AMJAD: Marriage is a really great thing. Everything in the world should get married. There is no greater joy in life than being married, I'll tell Ammijan to get you married right away.

ASGHARI: No, Amjad Mian, no!

AMJAD: Why not?

ASGHARI: I'm afraid.

AMJAD: Of what?

ASGHARI (*sitting down on the lawn, and speaking in a voice full of dark forebodings*): Of marriage.

AMJAD (*laughing*): You're crazy.

ASGHARI: No. I really am scared. Besides, the marriage of a maidservant isn't such a big deal. Whether she marries or remains single, what's the difference? But if marry she must and, by chance, the train derails and . . .

AMJAD (*anguished*): Asghari!

ASGHARI (*continues*) . . . and Asghari barely escapes being made into mincemeat: she loses one leg, one arm, and one eye—half of Asghari disappears and half survives. No, Amjad Mian, don't even mention marriage. Marriage is something whole, something complete. Something one-half or one-fourth can't be marriage.

AMJAD (*brooding*): Asghari?

ASGHARI (*in a choked voice*): Yes?

AMJAD: You know, you're right. (*In an extremely pained voice*) But don't make me feel sad. I want to stay happy, in spite of my crippled legs. Please don't torment me. It hurts.

ASGHARI (*throwing herself on* AMJAD's *feet and grabbing them solicitously*): Forgive me—please, Amjad Mian. (*Her eyes fill with tears.*) I don't know what I was raving about. You stay happy! God keep you happy!

AMJAD (*acting brave*): Don't bring God into it. If He had wanted me to be happy, He wouldn't have done this to me. And if He had done this, He would have killed me right off. Don't even mention God; it's all over between Him and me. If I'm to stay happy, it will have to be with what's left of me. I'll have to gather twigs and build myself a nest of happiness on these broken branches.

ASGHARI: Happy . . . for your sake alone?

AMJAD (*in an extremely pained voice*): Asghari! Please, don't be so cruel! For God's sake if you must speak, does it have to hurt me? Help me, I beg you. Help an invalid put the broken pieces of his life together to spend his last few remaining days in peace.

ASGHARI: Please don't beg me, Amjad Mian. It breaks my heart. You're my master. You can order me. My whole life's at your bidding.

(ASGHARI *cries; big drops of tears stream down from her eyes onto* AMJAD's *slippers. She gets up and rushes away.* AMJAD *bends over and looks at his slippers, wet with* ASGHARI's *tears, and then, straightening himself up, at* ASGHARI's *receding figure.* THE BEGUM *appears from the Villa. She's wearing a shawl and carrying some jewellery boxes. She comes over to* AMJAD.)

BEGUM SAHIB: Amjad, my boy.

AMJAD (*quickly hiding his feet under his blanket*): Yes?

BEGUM SAHIB: The jewellery you picked out for Saeeda has just been delivered. Here . . . (*Puts the boxes in* AMJAD's *lap.*)

AMJAD (*opens each box with childlike curiosity and looks at every single piece of jewellery, beaming with joy*): They're really very nice . . . excellent . . . gorgeous . . . but not as much as Saeeda. Asghari! Asghari! Come over here! (ASGHARI, *who is leaning against a cypress tree, comes back to* AMJAD *who shows her the entire collection of jewellery.*) What do you think?

ASGHARI: You've said it for me: they're beautiful, but not as beautiful as Dulhan Begum.

AMJAD (*to* THE BEGUM): Ammijan, when will the dresses come?

ASGHARI: They'll be delivered tomorrow.

AMJAD: And the movie projector—why hasn't it arrived yet?

BEGUM SAHIB: Son, Majeed's already put in an order for it. It'll be here in a couple of days.

AMJAD: All right. (*After a pause*) Mother?

BEGUM SAHIB: Yes, son?

AMJAD: We ought to get something more for Saeeda. I can't bear to see her sad, even for an instant. We really must have something new for her every day.

BEGUM SAHIB: Everything is within your power. Order anything you like, whenever you like.

AMJAD: Within my power? (*Pauses*) Well then, Mother . . .

BEGUM SAHIB: Yes?

AMJAD: Please send Kamal to the sports shop to buy whatever games he can. Saeeda and Majeed will play. And I can watch. And, yes, please tell him to also buy the sort of stuff that I can play with her too.

BEGUM SAHIB (*overcome by a surge of motherly affection holds* AMJAD's *head in her hands*): Yes, my son.

(AMJAD *bursts into sobs.* ASGHARI, *unable to restrain herself, screams and runs off to one side. Silent tears drip down from* THE BEGUM's *eyes.*)

(*Curtain*)

ACT IV

The same room as in Acts I and II. It is evening. A breathless silence pervades the room. SAEEDA *is sprawled out awkwardly on the bed, her head propped up on a bunch of pillows. While she appears to be reading a book, her eyes are focused, instead, on her heaving bosom, whose alluring contours are outlined by the blanket covering her body. To the left is a steel hospital bed, beside which* AMJAD *is sitting in his wheelchair holding a book in his hand as though it were some glass object. Again and again, his restless, anxious eyes leave the book and travel to* SAEEDA, *settling on her hands and sometimes on her head of golden hair buried in the pillows. Unable to hold back any longer, he closes the book, puts it in his lap.*

AMJAD (*in a low, gentle voice*): Saeeda!

SAEEDA (*with a start*): Yes?

AMJAD: I think you ought to go to bed now.

SAEEDA (*turning over to look at him*): If you want to go to sleep, I'll call Ghulam Muhammad and Karim and they'll put you to bed.

AMJAD (*in a hollow voice*): Put me to bed ... no, Saeeda ... I'm tired of lying down ... Tonight I'll sleep right here in my chair ... If it isn't too much trouble, could you get up and switch off the lamp and turn on the green nightlight?

SAEEDA (*rising*): Why do you keep talking about my trouble?

AMJAD: Because I'm troubled. I know what it means.

SAEEDA (*irritated*): I'm well aware of that, Amjad Sahib. But please tell me, what more can I do for you ... I'm willing to do anything within my power ... but the trouble is, you're always worried about troubling me. I'm not troubled at all.

AMJAD: Saeeda, you're so good!

SAEEDA (*turns off the lamp; for a few moments the room remains plunged in complete darkness, then a dim green light slowly begins to illuminate everything*): I wish I were good . . . that I could be good. (*She sits down on the couch. Her restlessness is evident from her heaving bosom.*)

AMJAD: You're already too good! How could you be any better, Saeeda?

SAEEDA (*sharply*): No! Little do you know . . .

AMJAD (*very gently*): Forgive me if I've offended you in some way.

SAEEDA (*looks at* AMJAD, *rises from the couch and smiles as she runs her long fingers through his hair*): The fact is, Amjad Sahib, I'm not good enough for you.

AMJAD (*grabbing her hand*): That shows just how good you really are. It's the purity of your heart that makes you say so.

SAEEDA (*continuing to run her fingers through his hair*): Go to sleep. You've been up so many nights already. In fact, you haven't slept a wink since you came back home.

AMJAD: I just can't seem to fall asleep, Saeeda.

SAEEDA: Why?

AMJAD: I don't know why . . . It feels as though I've never slept and never will. Now, I can't even recall the nights when I could sleep.

SAEEDA: How I wish I could give you my sleep.

AMJAD: No, Saeeda . . . I wouldn't want to rob you of such a precious thing. It's meant for your eyes, which become more beautiful during sleep. Go, sleep now.

SAEEDA: Poor, miserable me. I'll sleep, of course.

AMJAD: Don't call yourself miserable . . . May God make you fortunate . . . Go to sleep now.

SAEEDA (*irritated*): Why do you always treat me so kindly? It . . . Amjad Sahib, it really bothers me . . . By God, your gentleness, forbearance and humility—they'll drive me to insanity some day. (*In frustration she rushes to the bed and flings herself on to it.*)

AMJAD: I feel as if everything coming out of my mouth is just as crippled as I am.

(SAEEDA *remains silent. She turns over in bed to face the other direction.* AMJAD *picks up the book from his lap and starts flipping its pages. A deathly quiet, made brittle in the dim eerie green light, pervades the room. A long time passes in wearisome silence. The*

pale green light on AMJAD's *face looks like the jade-green covering on
a grave. His eyes repeatedly rise from the book, travel over to* SAEEDA,
then furtively return. He looks very restless now.)

AMJAD: Saeeda!

SAEEDA: Yes?

AMJAD: I . . . I have a favour to ask you.

SAEEDA (*without bothering to turn over*): What?

AMJAD: Could . . . could this be our wedding night . . . (*She trembles in
her bed.*) The night we never had. (*After a pause during which she
remains silent*) Saeeda.

SAEEDA: Yes.

AMJAD: Would you consider my wish?

SAEEDA (*flips over to face him, a wounded desire to give herself completely
floating in her eyes*): How, Amjad Sahib?

AMJAD: Pretend . . . just for my sake . . . pretend that I'm lying next to
you . . . And I'll pretend that you're lying with me. I'll say those
things to you that I wanted to say on our first night . . . and you
answer as you would have . . . Please, Saeeda, for my sake . . . could
you play this make-believe game for me?

SAEEDA (*tears of pity replacing the earlier wounded desire to give herself
in her eyes*): I'm ready, Amjad Sahib.

AMJAD: Thank you! (*After a long pause*) Tonight is our first night, Saeeda
. . . the night when youth takes its first step into earthly paradise
. . . the night into whose spaciousness two beings plunge to become
one . . . Don't be shy . . . For this is the night when all concealed
truths restlessly await their inevitable unveiling; when just a soft
whisper, a gentle sigh, a light caress, the slightest puff of escaping
breath is enough to blow their veils aside . . . so gently that one barely
hears a rustle and yet is instantly face-to-face with Vision in all its
resplendent glory; when eyes collide setting off a cascade of dazzling
stardust that falls on the foreheads of two who have become one. This
is the night . . . the first, the very first night . . . when Eve was formed
from Adam's rib . . . this is the night that poets pray will never end
. . . this is the night the young often wish for . . . this is the night when
Nature itself unties the knots of modesty . . . this is the night when all
of Creation's workshops concentrate on producing just one item . . .
the cog that gives motion and life to the whole Universe . . . this is the
night when all sounds subside into their points of origin to let the

one sound that resonates with the command 'BE!' be heard clearly
... This is the night whose every veil is woven with silvery threads
of light ... this is the night in whose presence all subsequent nights
stand in reverential attendance ... this is the night in which every
pore of the body speaks out without inhibition and listens raptly to
the great untold secrets ... the great unsung melodies ... (*Abruptly
screams*) Cover it! Cover it ... cover your body, Saeeda ... It's biting
me like a snake ... It's slashing my crippled desires like a razor's edge
... Cover it ... for God's sake cover your body!

SAEEDA (*lying like a dead body made of tender blades of grass in the green
light, with every part of her body trembling*): Yes.

AMJAD (*crying uncontrollably*): Cover your body!

(SAEEDA *pulls the blanket over her tremulous body while* AMJAD, *his
hand over his face, continues to cry.*)

(*Curtain*)

ACT V

*The garden adjacent to Nigar Villa. Evening. Water gurgling
in the fountain. The shadows have lengthened. The grey hills in
the background look even more sombre in the ebbing light. The
sky is ashen. A solid silence has settled over the lush green lawn.
The lawn chairs are unoccupied, the whole atmosphere vacant,
like an empty picture frame waiting to be filled. The sound of
* MAJEED's *and* SAEEDA's *laughter intrudes. Moments later they
both walk in laughing, exhausted.* SAEEDA *slumps over in a chair
while* MAJEED *stands by her.*

SAEEDA (*pounding her thighs with her fists*): Ooooh!

MAJEED (*laughing*): Tired? Shall I give you a rubdown? Let me ...

SAEEDA (*flustered*): Oh no! Please, no! Just send for Asghari. Right now
I couldn't move two steps.

MAJEED (*smiling*): As you say. (*Steps forward and pushes aside a loose
curl snaking over* SAEEDA's *face.*)

SAEEDA (*even more flustered*): I think I'll go inside now. (*Begins to rise.*)

MAJEED (*looking off to one side*): Look, here comes Asghari on her own. Over here, Asghari! Give Bhabhijan's feet a massage.
(ASGHARI enters. The ends of her mouth quiver as though impatient to say something. She comes closer.)
ASGHARI (*to* SAEEDA): Tired, Dulhan Begum?
SAEEDA (*drumming her thighs with her fists*): Very!
ASGHARI (*sits down on the grass and begins to massage one of* SAEEDA's *calves vigorously, but her words are intended for* MAJEED): This is all Majeed Mian's fault. Such a long hike and so fast at that (*sharply*) . . . one ought to proceed slowly (*rubbing slowly down* SAEEDA's *leg*) like this . . . slowly. (*Addressing* SAEEDA) Feel any better, Dulhan Begum?
SAEEDA (*her free leg quivering nervously*): Yes, yes, much better.
ASGHARI (*to* MAJEED): Majeed Mian, you should go wash up. Your face is so dusty it looks like an unwashed potato.
MAJEED (*snaps*): You've really become quite cheeky. All this . . .
ASGHARI (*interrupting him*): Blame Dulhan Begum, she's spoiled me. (*Looks at* SAEEDA) And what a lovely face she has.
(MAJEED *exits, his eyes radiating suppressed anger.*)
ASGHARI (*laughing*): By God's grace Majeed Mian has a nice handsome face, but it looks so grotesque when he's angry. What do you think?
SAEEDA: Don't say such things to me. (*Tries to get up but is thwarted by* ASGHARI's *iron grip.*) Let me go!
ASGHARI (*continues to massage*): I don't want to deprive myself of the pleasure of serving you. (*Removes the sandals from* SAEEDA's *feet.*) Majeed Mian said that I've become cheeky. Have I, Dulhan Begum?
SAEEDA: Absolutely.
ASGHARI (*unperturbed, cracking* SAEEDA's *toes*): This is horrible. A servant should never be cheeky. You should box my ears.
SAEEDA: Be quiet!
ASGHARI: That's not fair! Preventing someone from speaking is downright tyrannical, Dulhan Begum. What have I said that offends you so?
SAEEDA (*agitated*): Everything you say offends me.
ASGHARI: What can poor Asghari do now? (*After a pause*) I thought I'd learned all there was to learn serving an educated mistress like

yourself for a whole year. Now I see I was wrong . . . I haven't learned a thing . . . but whose fault is that—the pupil's or the teacher's?

SAEEDA (*pulling her legs away and speaking in a clear, decisive tone of voice*): What is it that you really want to say?

ASGHARI (*with feigned surprise*): Me?

SAEEDA: Yes, you. What do you really want to say?

ASGHARI (*thinking*): Oh, there's a whole lot I want to say . . .

SAEEDA (*rising and walking barefoot on the grass*): Then spit it out! I don't particularly enjoy your daily needling. I'm ready to hear you out.

ASGHARI: You really are brave, Dulhan Begum.

SAEEDA: Brave or cowardly—leave that out of it. Get whatever you want to say out of your system.

ASGHARI: Spit it out? All right. But it will nauseate both of us.

SAEEDA: Don't bother about me. I'll manage.

ASGHARI (*thinking*): I used to think you'd cower when I bared my fangs. But I see you're past worrying about being wounded . . . It's you who frightens me now.

SAEEDA (*pacing nervously to and fro*): Asghari!

ASGHARI (*startled*): Yes?

SAEEDA: Just tell me this: what would I have done if Amjad Mian had died in the train wreck?

ASGHARI: You? I don't know what you would have done.

SAEEDA: I'm young. I'm beautiful . . . numberless desires surge inside of me. For seventeen long years I've nurtured them with the nectar of my dreams. How can I stifle them? I've tried, God knows I've tried, Asghari . . . but I couldn't bring myself to strangle them. Call me weak . . . cowardly . . . immoral . . . whatever you like . . . And although you're just a maid, nonetheless I confess before you that I cannot ravage the garden of my youth, where the vein of every leaf and flower throbs with the hot blood of my unfulfilled desires . . . No, not with my own hands . . . though I wouldn't mind someone else closing my eyes . . . numbing up all my senses and lowering me into the deepest pit of widowhood or old age . . . or with just one push hurling me off this quaking cliff of desire where I've stood to this day huddled against the cold, gusting wind . . . I'd even allow you to do that.

ASGHARI (*rising, feeling battered*): Enough, Dulhan Begum, enough!

SAEEDA: I stand at a crossroads where the ground quakes under my feet. Whichever way I turn, it turns away from me . . . Whatever I plan slips from my grasp; I rush after it pell-mell, and when I've caught it, it crumbles in my hand like sand . . . Asghari, you don't know how long I've been rolling around on this bed of live coals. When I douse them with water, the rising steam carries me to the highest point in space, only to hurl me down—ravaged, battered and mauled . . . Every single bone in my body has been crushed. It would've been much better, Asghari, if *I* had been crippled instead of Amjad Sahib. (*After a long pause, during which* ASGHARI *stands frozen, while* SAEEDA *paces to and fro extremely agitated*) Tell me, what should I do?

ASGHARI (*roused from her thoughts*): What should you do? . . . You should . . . you should wait until Amjad Mian dies.

SAEEDA (*after a moment's thought*): Call me heartless if you will . . . but I have to ask . . . When will he die?

ASGHARI: When God wills. (*Mumbles*) But Amjad Mian has cut off relations with Him.

SAEEDA: What? What did you say?

ASGHARI: Nothing. (*Taking hesitant steps, she exits.*)

(SAEEDA *continues to pace fretfully on the cool, comforting grass.*)

(*Curtain*)

ACT VI

A large, spacious living room in Nigar Villa decorated with old-style furnishings that exude an aura of heaviness and durability. Oil paintings of various family members hang on the walls. One is of THE BEGUM *from the time when she was young. She is sitting directly beneath it on the sofa. The gaiety and the carefree look of the painting contrast sharply with her present care-ridden face, ravaged by dark anxiety and sorrow. She's knitting something out of wool, but it seems more like she's untangling her confused thoughts that tangle up again like the yarn.* ASGHARI *enters.*

BEGUM SAHIB: Did you find Majeed Mian?

ASGHARI: Yes.

BEGUM SAHIB: Where was he?

ASGHARI: In the garden.

BEGUM SAHIB: What was he doing?

ASGHARI: He . . . (*faltering*) he was sitting there, all by himself.

BEGUM SAHIB (*looking at* ASGHARI *and then lowering her gaze*): Is he coming?

ASGHARI: Yes, he is.

BEGUM SAHIB: You may go now.

    (ASGHARI *leaves just as* MAJEED *enters, looking at her.*)

MAJEED: What is it, Mother?

BEGUM SAHIB: Oh, nothing. Sit down.

MAJEED (*sitting in the chair near the couch*): It's chilly in here.

BEGUM SAHIB: Yes, quite chilly.

MAJEED (*after a pause; uneasily*): I have the distinct feeling that you've called me here because you have something to say.

BEGUM SAHIB: Yes . . .

MAJEED: Well? I'm listening.

BEGUM SAHIB: I want to send you away from here.

MAJEED (*rising suddenly*): Me? Where?

BEGUM SAHIB: Sit down.

MAJEED (*sitting*): Okay.

BEGUM SAHIB: I haven't told Amjad yet.

MAJEED (*rises again*): About what?

BEGUM SAHIB: That I'm sending you away.

MAJEED: But why? I mean . . . is it some important business or . . .?

BEGUM SAHIB: Sit down.

MAJEED (*sitting down again*): Is it?

BEGUM SAHIB: No.

MAJEED: Then why, may I ask, do you feel it necessary to send me away?

BEGUM SAHIB: Because I think it's better this way.

MAJEED: Better? Better for whom?

BEGUM SAHIB: For all of us . . . for the family.

MAJEED (*gets up again*): You're talking in riddles, Mother.

BEGUM SAHIB: Majeed, you're my son and I'm your mother . . . Nothing should happen between us that would stain this sacred relationship

... I want you to leave for Karachi today and stay there for as long as I say.

MAJEED: But, Mother ...

BEGUM SAHIB (*cutting him short*): You have plenty of friends there. I'm sure that with their help, or just on your own, you'll get your boat safely ashore through this maelstrom we call life.

MAJEED (*wants to say something, but fails and sits back down*): Okay ... I'll go.

BEGUM SAHIB: Your decision ... (*Drops into silence as she notices* AMJAD *enter the room in his wheelchair pushed by* KARIM.)

AMJAD: You're a strange fellow, Majeed ... All this time I was waiting for you in my room so we could decide what to get Saeeda for her birthday ... Instead, I find you lounging around here. (*To* THE BEGUM) Ammijan ... so have you thought of something for a present? What kind should it be? ... I'm going crazy thinking about it.

BEGUM SAHIB: Why don't you ask Saeeda?

AMJAD (*laughs*): Listen to that. You're the limit, Mother dear ... If I ask her it wouldn't be a surprise, no fun. (*To* MAJEED) Well, Majeed? (MAJEED *remains silent*) Speak up!

MAJEED (*rising*): Ask Ammijan. As for me ... well, I'm leaving.

AMJAD (*surprised*): Leaving? Wherever for?

MAJEED: Karachi.

AMJAD: Have you gone mad? Karachi ... What for?

MAJEED: What for? ... (*With a faint smile*) To get my boat out of a maelstrom.

AMJAD (*to* THE BEGUM): What's happened to him? (*To* MAJEED) Sit down, yaar ... The day after tomorrow is her birthday ... we should make a decision right now.

MAJEED: The decision has been made.

AMJAD: What?

MAJEED: That I'm going to Karachi for good.

AMJAD: What are you babbling about? (*To* THE BEGUM) Mother, what is all this?

BEGUM SAHIB: Nothing ... just a little mother–son quarrel.

AMJAD: Over what?

BEGUM SAHIB: That you can't ask.

AMJAD: I may be overstepping myself . . . but Majeed is my brother. If there's been a misunderstanding between the two of you then it's my duty to clear it up . . . I know Majeed better than you do . . . He couldn't possibly do something that would cause such a problem. (*To* MAJEED) Hey, come over here.

MAJEED: Bhaijan, I've got to pack now.

AMJAD: For heaven's sake . . . what's going on? (*To* THE BEGUM) Ammijan, for God's sake, stop him! If not for me, then for Saeeda's sake. He's the only one here who keeps her spirits from sagging. He does so much for me. If you were to let him go, God knows what'll become of me, Ammijan. Whenever he takes Saeeda out for a stroll, I imagine I'm the one who's walking with her; whenever he plays some game with her, I feel the great void in my life created by Fate's cruel hands beginning to fill. I often say to myself, 'Amjad, what would your life be without Majeed for a brother? The debris of your life wouldn't even be fit for the garbage dump.' Please stop him. Why are you separating us? Don't play God, Ammijan. (*Breaks into sobs.*)

MAJEED: Ammijan, I'm leaving.

BEGUM SAHIB: Wait!

(MAJEED *stops.*)

BEGUM SAHIB (*gets up and begins to stroke* AMJAD's *head affectionately*): Son, don't cry . . . Majeed's not going anywhere . . . everything will stay right where it belongs, for that's the will of God. (*To* MAJEED) You sit down with your brother and think about Saeeda's birthday gift. (*Exits.*)

MAJEED (*after thinking for a while moves towards* AMJAD's *wheelchair and speaks in a hushed voice*): Bhaijan, please let me go.

AMJAD (*lifting his head up*): Let you go? Go where? Don't be crazy!

MAJEED: You don't understand.

AMJAD: I understand everything. Take out your handkerchief and wipe my tears, come on. (*After some hesitation* MAJEED *takes out his handkerchief and begins to wipe away* AMJAD's *tears rather hastily.*) What are you doing, yaar? Not like that! You don't even know how to wipe tears . . . (*Smiles*) It's really such a simple thing, you know.

MAJEED: Not as simple as you think, Bhaijan.

AMJAD (*still smiling*): All right, then, it isn't. It's a formidable task . . . Anyway, come and sit beside me. We've got to think about Saeeda's birthday gift. Sit!

MAJEED (*sitting down in a chair beside* AMJAD): So think!

AMJAD (*sighing*): I'm thinking, I'm thinking! What else is there to do? But you have to think, too. (*Both of them lapse into deep thought.*)

(*Curtain*)

ACT VII

The garden adjacent to Nigar Villa. Evening. The water coming out of the fountain has stopped, as though it has bubbled itself out. In the background, the sombre grey hills are trying to hide their formidable height in the evening mist. The grass appears to be heavily trampled. To the right, away from the fountain and behind the dense shrubbery, sits AMJAD *in his wheelchair.* ASGHARI *is standing behind him holding the handles of the chair. Presently she begins to push it.*

AMJAD: No, Asghari, wait a bit.

ASGHARI (*stops*): But Amjad Mian . . .

AMJAD: I want to receive the last wound of my life tonight.

ASGHARI: If receive it you must, why not in your imagination? But . . . but haven't you been dealt that wound already? Why must you insist on reopening it?

AMJAD (*attempting to smile*): There's no limit to the stupidity of a man in my condition . . . He rips open the stitches of his wounds to probe inside; feels the stab of pain and considers himself the greatest martyr there ever was. (*Laughs*) Asghari, you've never had something of yours destroyed. How can you ever know the misery of people who having sunk into the depths of despair try to mould anew the debris, the rubble of their destruction into tall, imposing structures.

ASGHARI (*smiling*): I've gone beyond even that, Amjad Mian . . . I've built those tall, gigantic structures and then torn them down with my own hands . . . and in the process, calluses have formed in my heart.

AMJAD (*shudders*): Asghari, you frighten me. Yes, you really do.

ASGHARI (*laughs*): I'm a wasteland. Every wasteland is frightening, though it shouldn't be. It doesn't have the time to mourn itself, much less frighten others. It just cowers . . . timidly.

AMJAD: Have you also had some misfortune or other in your life then?

ASGHARI: NO! What misfortune can possibly befall a person who is herself a misfortune!

AMJAD: You sound as though you've been singed.

ASGHARI: Only because now you can sense the burning.

AMJAD: You mean this sense was asleep before?

ASGHARI: Yes . . . sound asleep.

AMJAD: What woke it up?

ASGHARI: The train that went off the track.

AMJAD (*muttering*): The train . . . that went off the track . . . (*A little louder*) Will it derail again?

ASGHARI: Whatever God wishes will come to pass.

AMJAD: Don't mention God . . . He and I are no longer friends.

ASGHARI: No, Amjad Mian. Miserable as we are, our bond with Him is never severed . . . However much and however often we may break it, it just mends itself again.

AMJAD: That's nonsense.

(*Suddenly they are startled by the sound of approaching feet.* MAJEED *and* SAEEDA *appear, both out of breath.* SAEEDA, *who looks extremely fatigued, sits down on the rim of the fountain while* MAJEED *remains standing.*)

SAEEDA: I really am tired today.

MAJEED: Even though we didn't walk very far.

SAEEDA: That's true.

MAJEED (*after a pause*): It would've been infinitely better if I had left for Karachi.

SAEEDA: I guess so.

MAJEED: I'm caught in a strange dilemma. I could have gone to Karachi . . . but the question is: Would I have succeeded in bringing my boat ashore through this maelstrom? . . . No, I would never have made it.

SAEEDA: I know.

MAJEED: You know . . . and I know . . . Just about everyone but Bhaijan knows. And that's the most agonizing part of the story.

SAEEDA: I've often thought of telling him, but (*rising abruptly*) I'm afraid the shock will kill him.

MAJEED: Exactly. That's what I fear most, too. The doctors are unanimous that he has, at the most, a year to live . . . It would be downright cruel to snatch even this bit from the poor man.
(*Behind the cover of the shrubbery* AMJAD *suddenly clenches his teeth.* ASGHARI *firmly grasps his shoulder.*)

SAEEDA: We must try to keep him happy as long as he lives. His feelings are sensitive to the lightest touch. We have to be careful.

MAJEED: What if one of our own blisters bursts in the process . . .

SAEEDA (*almost screaming*): That would be disastrous!

MAJEED: All the more reason why I should go away . . . Until Bhaijan . . .

SAEEDA (*cutting him short*): Don't talk like that, Majeed . . . don't be so cruel.
(AMJAD *trembles in his wheelchair.* ASGHARI *clutches his other shoulder firmly as well.*)

MAJEED: Love is always cruel and selfish, Saeeda. It's not even ashamed of dancing for joy on another man's grave.

SAEEDA: We mustn't think such things.

MAJEED: You're right, but what if such thoughts drift in on their own?

SAEEDA: What can we do? . . . Let's go in.
(SAEEDA *starts off towards the villa.* MAJEED *follows with a soft, slow stride. Behind the bushes* AMJAD *sits in his wheelchair with his head hung low.* ASGHARI *stands directly behind him, immobile like a statue.*)

ASGHARI: Should we go in now?

AMJAD (*his head still hung low*): No, not now . . . I'm thinking.

ASGHARI: About what?

AMJAD: I don't know. Maybe I'm thinking about what I should be thinking.

ASGHARI: That's useless thinking.

AMJAD (*lifting his head*): Don't I know that? What else can I do? (*After a pause*) You're even more cruel than they are. You won't even let me think. You're really cruel, Asghari.

ASGHARI (*smiles*): Love is cruel and selfish, Amjad Mian. It doesn't even hesitate to dance at its own death.

AMJAD: Come in front of me. (ASGHARI *goes over in front of* AMJAD, *who looks into her eyes, thinks of something, and then mutters*) Where was this book all this time?

ASGHARI: Somewhere in the wastebasket . . . where it properly belongs.

AMJAD: Let's go. Take me inside.

(ASGHARI *begins to push the wheelchair towards the house.*)

(*Curtain*)

ACT VIII

The same room as in Acts I, II and IV. It is night. An emerald-green light filters down from the ceiling giving everything in the room a sickly hue. The bed is empty—as if it had never been occupied. ASGHARI *wheels* AMJAD *into the room.*

ASGHARI: What made Dulhan Begum move out into Begum Sahib's room?

AMJAD: She was afraid.

ASGHARI: Of you?

AMJAD (*smiling ruefully*): Who'd be afraid of me? . . . She was afraid of herself.

ASGHARI: She isn't all that vulnerable, Amjad Mian.

AMJAD: Time eats even the biggest mountains hollow. She's just a young woman.

ASGHARI (*after a pause*): Do you want to sleep now?

AMJAD: Sleep? (*Laughs*) Don't mock me, Asghari. Don't disgrace my misery . . . my burning wounds.

ASGHARI (*after another pause*): Do you love Saeeda?

AMJAD: NO!

ASGHARI: Then why the burning wounds?

AMJAD: Let me think . . . Will you let me think?

ASGHARI: Go right ahead.

AMJAD (*after a protracted pause during which he remains totally immersed in thought*): I don't love Saeeda . . . I certainly don't. Just as one picks the nicest thing from the market, I picked Saeeda from among countless other women to be my wife. I was proud of my choice and rightly so. She is beautiful beyond all comparison. The only right I have over her is that I chose her and made her my mate for life . . . the same life which now lies in a crumpled heap in this wheelchair and can't move without someone's help . . . The doctors have given me a year to live at most . . . I can't understand why I want to keep her shackled in chains whose every link is as uncertain as my life . . . I don't understand it at all . . . (*He thinks for a while.*) There can only be one reason for it: her youth and beauty (*with a start*), of course! This has to be the only reason! (*Feeling a stab of pain*) Oh! Oh! That vision . . . I can never forget it . . . She . . . beauty itself . . . lying in this canopied bed, in all her breathtaking youth, her ardour, her tenderness . . . putting the choicest silks of the world to shame . . . this vision clings to me . . . No, rather, I have clung to it . . . (*After a pause*) Asghari!

ASGHARI (*startled*): Yes.

AMJAD: Could there be a way to expel this vision from my thoughts?

ASGHARI: Every problem carries its solution within it.

AMJAD: Then we must look for the solution. But . . . but why do I feel so diffident?

ASGHARI: I don't know. This is your problem. Certainly there would be no shame if you were to look for the solution yourself.

AMJAD: I know. I know . . . I'm well aware of all the base desires that inflame this passion. But this matter will be decided tonight.

ASGHARI: What matter?

AMJAD: Come in front of me. (*She does so.*) Go and lie on the bed!

ASGHARI (*hesitates*): Amjad Mian? I don't have the youthful beauty that puts the world's choicest silks to shame. My poor youth—all it needs is a piece of coarse burlap.

AMJAD: Go lie on the bed, Asghari!

ASGHARI (*tears streaming down her eyes*): No, Amjad Mian, it'll be unkind to the bed . . . it's become used to Dulhan Begum's soft, delicate body.

AMJAD: That's an order!

ASGHARI (*lowering her head in submission*): You're the master. (*Lies down on the bed, her eyes fixed on the ceiling.*)

AMJAD: Do you know what night this is? . . . This is the night when a crushed, warped, and worthless youth is about to become whole. This is the night of resurrection, of annihilation. Under its dark cloak Existence will melt in the fires of Non-Existence to assume a new, immortal form . . . No other night will follow this night. Its blind eyes will come wearing such collyrium that its blindness will be transformed into interminable, clear vision. This is the night when the last drops of Life itself will trickle out, terrified, from the mangled udders of Death. The night when grand palaces, their turrets reaching to the heavens, will rise from the womb of destruction and the waters of Zamzam and crawl back into the farthest reaches of the earth, replaced by clouds of dust with which the pure souls will cleanse themselves; and the Author of Fate will overturn His inkpot and wistfully weep in some lonely corner of the sky. Tonight Amjad divorces, in an irrevocable divorce, all the Beauty of this world and marries in its place Ugliness (*suddenly screams*), Asghari . . . Asghari . . .!

(*In the meantime* ASGHARI *has risen from the bed, gone over to the window and opened it. She is poised on the windowsill, looking down intently into the depths below.*)

AMJAD (*screaming*): What are you doing, Asghari?

ASGHARI (*turns around on the windowsill and looks at* AMJAD): Proposal and consent are necessary . . . my master. (*Flings herself out.*)

AMJAD (*covering his eyes with both hands*): Asghari! (*Removes his hands and stares for a few moments at the open window that yawns like a dark wound on the green wall.*) Proposal and consent (*murmurs*) proposal and consent—yes, indeed! (*Pushes his wheelchair forward with both of his hands and manages to reach the window with great effort.*) I knew . . . I knew this was the way to solve my problem . . . but perhaps I needed someone to hold my hand. (*Grasps the windowsill and with great difficulty heaves his crippled body on to it and lets it hang over the other side.*) My hills! My dear hills! My dear Asghari! (*His body slips over and then instantly his entire being is lost in the darkness.*)

(*Curtain*)

Co-translated with Wayne R. Husted and Azam Dadi

The Fifth Trial*

[Translator's Note: The magistrate who appears in the second part of this piece was Mehdi Ali Siddiqi. In a social meeting, which took place in a coffee house the day after the trial, Manto asked him why he had fined him if he admired him and considered him a great writer, to which Mr Siddiqi replied, 'I'll give you my answer after a year.' He did give his answer in a piece, 'Mantō aur Maiñ' (Manto and I), which appeared a few months after the writer's death. At the time, Mr Siddiqi did not know that Manto had already written the second part of 'The Fifth Trial' as it did not appear in print until two years after the publication of his own piece. The two accounts of their meeting are somewhat, perhaps even significantly, different and vividly portray some aspects of Manto's personality.]

One

I have been dragged into court four times concerning my short stories and now, recently, a fifth time. I want to talk about what transpired during this last trial.

My first four stories to be tried were 'Kālī Shalwār' [The Black Shalwar], 'Dhuvāñ' [Smoke], 'Bū' [Smell], and 'Thandā Gosht' [Cold Meat]. The fifth one was 'Ūpar, Nīche, aur Darmiyān' [Upper, Lower, and Middle].

I was acquitted on the first three stories. I had to travel two or three times to Lahore from Delhi to be present at the hearing for 'Kālī Shalwār'.

* 'Pāñchvāñ Muqaddama', from *Dastāvez* (June 1982), pp. 174–84.

However, 'Dhuvāñ' and 'Bū' turned out to be a real pain because I had to come all the way from Bombay.

But it was the court case on 'Thandā Gosht' that proved to be the most vexing. It really left me completely exhausted.

Although the proceedings of the case took place right here in Pakistan, they involved such convolutions that a person with my sensitive disposition could hardly withstand it. Here, you're subjected to every kind of indignity and humiliation. May you never have to go to the weird place called 'court', the likes of which I've never seen anywhere.

I hate the police, for they've always accorded me the treatment reserved only for the meanest criminals.

Recently, when the Karachi periodical *Payām-e Mashriq* reprinted without permission my short story 'Ūpar, Nīche, aur Darmiyān' from the Lahore-based newspaper *Ehsān*, the Karachi administration lost no time in issuing a warrant for my arrest.

Two sub-inspectors of police, along with four constables, came to my house and surrounded it. I was not at home. My wife told them so, adding that, if they wanted, she could send for me. But they insisted that I was hiding inside and she was lying.

Actually, at the time I was at Chaudhry Nazeer Ahmad's publishing establishment Nayā Idāra, which also doubled as the office of the literary journal *Saverā*, writing a short story. I had barely written a dozen lines or so when Chaudhry Nazeer Ahmad's brother Chaudhry Rashid Ahmad, the owner of the Maktaba-e Jadīd publishing house, walked in. After a few minutes silence he asked, 'What are you writing?'

'A short story . . . a rather long one.'

'I've come to give you some very bad news,' he said in a terribly anxious tone.

You can well imagine how I reacted to that. What could the bad news be? I wondered for a few moments. Many possibilities came to mind. I wavered among them but couldn't figure it out. Finally I asked Chaudhry Rashid, 'Brother, what's the matter?'

'The police have surrounded your house. They're adamant that you're hiding inside and they're trying to break in.'

Hearing this, Ahmad Rahi and Hameed Akhtar, who were sitting beside me, became very upset. They decided to accompany me. We hopped into a tonga and headed for my home. When we got there, we saw the police standing outside the door of my flat. My sister's son

(Hamid Jalal) and my brother-in-law (Zaheeruddin) were standing by their cars, busily talking to the policemen. 'You're welcome to search the house if you want, but believe us, Manto is not inside.'

Just then Ahmad Rahi, Hameed Akhtar and I arrived. We had already instructed Chaudhry Rashid Sahib to phone the newspapers so that they would publish an account of whatever happened to me in the next day's issue.

We also saw Abdullah Malik engrossed in talking to the police officers outside the door. Abdullah Malik is a communist and whatever he writes is unabashedly and quite overtly 'red', but, strangely, I've never spotted a trace of true 'redness' in him.

So there he was, talking to the sub-inspectors and the constables, who had threatened my wife that if she didn't let them in to search the house they would attempt to force their way in.

I'm sure my arrival must have caused them sufficient embarrassment. I invited them politely to step inside the house, which they *graciously* accepted. They were a pair of pretty rude and headstrong police officers. I asked them the purpose of their visit. They said they had come from Karachi and had a warrant to search my house. I was hugely surprised. I am not someone who deals secretly in contraband, or sells opium or illegal wines and liquors, not even a pinch of cocaine. Why did they want to search my house? In any case, the first question they asked me was: Where is your library?

What could I have told them? Here in Pakistan my entire 'library' consisted of only a few books, of which three were dictionaries. So I said, 'Whatever books I owned were left behind in Bombay. If you're looking for a particular magazine or piece of paper, I'm afraid you'll have to go to Bombay. Here is the address.'

They failed to appreciate my witty response, so bereft were they of any sense of humour, and started rummaging through my house. My house is not some bar or tavern, though I did have half a dozen empty bottles of beer which they didn't bother to glance at. There were a few porcelain bowls in a cupboard and some papers in a small box on the tea table. They went through the box methodically and looked at every single scrap of paper. They found some newspaper clippings, which they promptly confiscated.

I politely asked them to show me the search warrant they had brought from Karachi but they refused. The one who had it in his hand simply waved it at me from a distance saying, 'This, here.'

'What is it?' I asked.

'The thing that has brought us here.'

When I made it plain that I was not about to let them continue without seeing the warrant, one of them, holding on to it firmly, opened it and said, 'Here, you can read it.'

On reading it I discovered that the warrant wasn't only for a house search but also for my arrest.

So now there was the question of bail. The officers were so headstrong that they wouldn't accept it from anyone, not even my nephew or my brother-in-law who are both gazetted officers. The police officers told them: 'But you're government employees, what if you were let go from your jobs tomorrow?'

Thereafter, I twice wrote to the Karachi court to be excused from being present at the hearing on account of illness and attached the relevant medical certificates with my request. But, of course, that was only a temporary solution. I couldn't hope to be lucky all the time. Eventually, I had to go to Karachi.

An interesting joke: There was no one in the house to arrange for bail when the warrant for my arrest finally arrived. I went looking for friends but, as luck would have it, found none. Finally, I went to see Muhammad Tufail Sahib. He is a very decent man. He went with me willy-nilly, or maybe willy-willy, and posted the bail. How? Well, he runs a literary establishment (he is both the editor and the owner of the journal *Nuqūsh*) and the balance of the books in his shop is guarantee enough that he can put up a bail for five thousand rupees.

And, here is another joke. Listen. Tufail Sahib did post the bail, but now he feared that I might not show up on the date of the hearing.

As God is my witness, I was absolutely penniless. I didn't even have money to buy a drop of poison, as the saying goes. Tufail Sahib materialized at my door at five in the morning, with two second-class train tickets in his pocket. He also gave me the fare for the tonga, accompanied me to the station and hung around with me until the train started moving. He had asked one of my friends, Naseer Anwar, to go with me, perhaps to forestall any possibility of my not reaching Karachi and jumping bail.

What I went through in Karachi I'll tell you some other time. Right now, I'm too terribly ill to continue.

Two

I had started writing an article entitled 'The Fifth Trial' in one of the issues of *Nuqūsh* (nos. 29–30; Feb.–Mar., 1953) but was unable to finish it on account of my severe illness. I'm still unwell, and it seems I will remain so forever. 'Your illness,' some friends quip, 'is all you've got.' By 'all' they perhaps mean my short story and non-fiction writing.

Tufail Sahib, the editor and owner of the literary magazine *Nuqūsh*, has also written an article about me, entitled 'Manto Sahib'. Brother Ahmad Nadeem Qasimi, who has, unfortunately, been appointed the stand-in editor of *Imroz*, has penned the following review of this article under the name of 'Critic':

> Muhammad Tufail's article 'Manto Sahib' is personal and, to a large extent, overly intimate. In our opinion he should have kept those secret matters bearing on his and Manto's mutual relationship a secret. Were the relations of publisher/editor and writer to be revealed in the open so unabashedly, there would be no place left for either of them to hide. Who doesn't have flaws and weaknesses, but to expose them in print like this! At least in our opinion, it is overstepping the bounds of moderation. It is true that unveiling the little flaws of writers and artists does help to bring out their personalities more fully, but such unveiling that it disgraces! However, the article does leave the impression that Tufail Sahib means well. He seems to have been carried away by emotion and has said certain things that would have been better left unsaid, or at least not in the way he has said them.

I had already sent the following letter to Tufail Sahib before Qasimi Sahib's review appeared in print:

> My brother, *as-salāmu alaikum!*

> Last night Safia* told me that you have written an article about me in *Nuqūsh*. I couldn't read it properly at the time as I'd had too much to drink. Since Safia liked it, I asked her to read it to me. She read some

---

* Manto's wife.

random parts, which I absolutely didn't like; I even cursed you up and down. Then I fell asleep.

Reading it myself the next morning, I liked it a lot. I don't disagree at all with whatever you have chosen to say about me. Regardless of my flaws, I'm very happy that your account of them is blissfully free of any trace of hesitation. Whatever I am, it is there in your article, and in abundance. It mentions certain things about me that I had in me all along; it's just that I was not aware of them.

Humbly, Saadat Hasan Manto

I don't wish to say anything more about that article. I'd be the last person to stand in the way of truth. If I drink, why should I deny it? Equally, if I have borrowed money from someone, I shouldn't deny that either. If the world wants to put me down for this reason, let it. If I worried about what the world has to say, I wouldn't have written in excess of one hundred short stories. Mr Critic* comments: 'It is true that unveiling the little flaws of writers and artists does help to bring out their personalities more fully, but such an unveiling that it disgraces!' I don't know whether I've been disgraced since Tufail Sahib's article. Time will tell.

I do want to say one thing, though, about that article. If what really moved Tufail Sahib to put off his brother's medical treatment and come to my aid was his sudden recollection of his elders' saying, 'One should never provide a guarantee on behalf of someone,' then I truly regret it. Had I only known of his weakness, I'd never have appeared in the court. He would have been arrested and would have looked for someone to bail him out. I would then have said to him: Mister, time to remember the advice of your elders which you threw overboard out of politeness. Forget about the bail, and come with me to the slammer . . .

As you've probably read in the first part of this article, it is an account of my fifth trial.

So my friend Naseer Anwar and I arrived at the railway station. Tufail Sahib had already bought our tickets. Our problem now was how

* Ahmad Nadeem Qasimi.

to find room in a carriage. Then again, we had carried a supply of beer bottles, and there was no room to be found for them either. Suddenly I remembered that one of my classmates, Yaqub Taufeeq, was assistant stationmaster at the Lahore station. By chance, he was on duty at the time. I talked to him and he quickly arranged seats for us. And so we set out for Karachi.

A maulvi sahib was also travelling in the same carriage. He was rolling his prayer beads on his fingers. Darn it, what a fiasco, I said to myself. Then I thought of a way. 'Come on, open a bottle,' I said to Naseer Anwar. He quickly pulled out a beer from under our seats, uncapped it, and handed it to me. The maulvi sahib exited the carriage at the next station, his fingers still rolling the beads.

I remember another amusing anecdote. A man entered our carriage at Lahore with his wife in tow. We could have put up with the man somehow, but his wife, that was impossible—well, actually, it was she who could not have put up with us. So when the couple got in, I told the man plainly, 'Look, sir, we're both hard drinkers and we're carrying some fifteen bottles of beer. When we're drunk, we have no control over what comes out of our mouths. You're a respectable gentleman and travelling, perhaps, with your wife. It would be better if you found room in some other carriage.'

As I'm writing this piece, Tufail Sahib tells me that this man who was with his burqa-clad wife went straight to the stationmaster and complained that two rogues were ensconced in such and such carriage where they had been allotted seats. The stationmaster showed great surprise and said, 'Oh, but it's Saadat Hasan Manto, a thorough gentleman, who's travelling in that carriage.' The man wouldn't buy it and insisted, 'No, he himself told me that he's one hell of a drunkard.'

Anyway, they were finally off our backs. They were assigned seats in a different carriage and we felt relieved.

The trip to Karachi was absolutely ghastly. Even the second-class carriage was miserably full of dust. But, thanks to the beer, we somehow overcame the discomfort of the journey. At Karachi I wanted to stay in a hotel but couldn't afford it. Finally I decided to stay at Khwaja Naseeruddin's, but only because my wife had insisted, 'Look, you must stay with my brother . . .' One can ignore the whole world, but not the brother of one's wife—no, sir! So I put the whole world

aside and went to stay with my brother-in-law, who is a thorough
gentleman. He has a good job, makes a decent salary, and lives in a
spacious flat. He took excellent care of us. By chance, the flat next to
his was unoccupied, and he got it for us. I felt no desire to prolong my
stay in Karachi. The city failed to excite me, a bummer, especially after
my fifteen years in Bombay.

The next day we appeared before the Additional Magistrate Sahib.
His office was in a small room in a very unexceptional building. As I
had been through several lawsuits at Lahore, I was quite familiar with the
manners of its court; familiar, that is, with a place that was singularly
devoid of manners. I stood before the Magistrate Sahib, transmogrified
into the perfect image of submission. He looked at me and asked, 'What do
you want?' The polite tone of his voice took me by surprise. I submitted,
'Sir, my name is Saadat Hasan Manto. You've summoned me under
Section 292 of the Obscenity Law concerning my piece "Ūpar, Nīche,
aur Darmiyān".' He looked at me closely and then said, 'Please sit down.'

I thought he was asking someone else to sit down as such courtesy
was alien to the Lahore courts with which I was familiar. So I remained
standing.

Finding me still standing, he said again, 'Please sit down, Manto
Sahib.'

I took a seat on the bench close to his desk. After some time he
turned to me. 'Why did you take so long to come?'

'Sir, I was ill.'

'You should have sent a medical certificate.'

'I was too ill to even think about sending it,' I lied.

He heard my lie, remained silent, and then said, 'What do you
want?'

What do I want? I began to wonder. I only wanted to be out of this
mess, and I wanted to be out of it pretty damn quick. The thought of
Tufail Sahib repeatedly drifted into my mind. He had bailed me out and,
being well acquainted with my devil-may-care nature, had later even
come to my home early in the morning with two second-class tickets
to ensure I made it to Karachi. I thought for a while and said to the
Magistrate Sahib, 'Please wrap up my case; I want to return home as
soon as possible.'

'Not so fast. I'm afraid it will take some time. I still haven't read your
story. God willing, I'll read it today and give my decision tomorrow.'

Both Naseer Anwar and I bid him goodbye, piled into an autorickshaw and went looking for a bar to drink a few beers in. I found the autorickshaw quite fascinating. It speeds along making *phut-phut* sounds, traversing long distances in a matter of minutes, and doesn't cost much to ride.

The next day when we showed up at the court the Magistrate Sahib returned my salaam and asked me to sit down. I did. He pulled out a small piece of paper and said, 'I've written out my judgement.' He then looked at the reader and asked, 'What's the date today?' The man promptly replied, 'The twenty-fifth.'

I'm a bit hard of hearing. It's been some time that my ears don't hear well. I thought he had fined me twenty-five rupees. 'Sir, a fine of twenty-five rupees?' I asked.

A twenty-five-rupee fine foreclosed any possibility of appeal, and my sentence would have remained. The Magistrate had probably decided on a fine of five hundred rupees, but when he heard me say twenty-five, he smiled, picked up his pen, struck out the original amount and changed it to twenty-five.

Naseer Anwar quickly took twenty-five rupees from his pocket and paid the fine, saying to me, 'You got out of it with a negligible fine. You didn't want to get into the headache of appeals and constant knocking about the courts, did you? Don't you remember what all happened during the trial for "Thandā Gosht"?'

I remembered it and shuddered.

I thanked God for getting me out of this mess so quickly.

I was about to say goodbye to the Magistrate and leave when he asked me, 'When are you going back to Lahore?'

'Today, if I can.'

'Please don't go today. I want to chat with you.'

I was hugely surprised. Why did he want to meet me? I wondered. 'Okay,' I said, 'I'll put it off until tomorrow.'

'Where can I see you tomorrow at four in the afternoon?'

I rattled off to him all the bars I had been to for beer. He was a pious man. So we finally settled on a coffee house.

Although the time that had been decided for the meeting was four o'clock, we arrived fifteen minutes late. He was already there. After we talked formally for a while, he said, 'Manto Sahib, I consider you a great short story writer of our time. The reason I wanted to meet with you was that I didn't wish you to go back thinking that I am not an admirer.'

I was flabbergasted. 'If you're an admirer, sir, then why did you fine me?'

He smiled. 'Why? I'll give you my answer after a year.'

Several months have gone by. Only a few remain. Let's see what kind of rabbit the Magistrate Sahib, who looked like someone who keeps his word, pulls out of his sleeve.

Manto and I[*]

Mehdi Ali Siddiqi

It was the beginning of 1953.

I was busy with work. The courtroom was filled with litigants. My deputy came and told me, 'This gentleman would like to have his case taken up expeditiously.'

I looked up. A good-looking man of medium height, somewhat indisposed and quite anxious, with the top few buttons of his sherwani undone and a muffler thrown around his neck, was saying in a shaky, rather choking voice, 'I am Saadat Hasan Manto. I have come from Lahore. I am very ill. I accept my offence. Please, decide my case as soon as you can.'

There was another man with him, standing behind him as though he had Manto in his custody. He was his guarantor, or one sent by the guarantor to see him through the trial.

I said, 'Please, have a seat.'

'What!'

'Please sit down,' I repeated.

Manto sat down hesitantly on a bench behind my deputy. I picked up his file and started studying it.

Manto had been charged for writing and publishing his short story 'Ūpar, Nīche, aur Darmiyān'. I had known about his case for some time now and had prepared myself for it. I had never given up my fondness

---

[*] 'Manto aur Maiñ' appeared as 'Pāñchvāñ Muqaddama—Tīn', in *Dastāvez* (June 1982), pp. 184–88.

for literature, but at the time I wasn't abreast of fictional, especially Urdu fictional, literature. So, for a few months I read only short stories. I read closely through however many collections of Manto's stories I could lay my hands on, but not the story in question nor any critical commentary on it, lest I end up with preconceived notions about the matter. You can imagine what I must have felt when Manto used the admission of his guilt as a cover.

Meanwhile, I tried to look at him stealthily but he had disappeared from the bench and was pacing nervously on the veranda outside the courtroom.

He came inside again and said, 'Please wind up my case.'

'All right, but do sit down, please,' I said and started to fill in the register of cases.

Manto resumed his position on the bench, but kept shifting continually from side to side in his place. When I was finished, I recorded, as per procedure, his confession. Everyone thought that I would fine him a large sum. But when I said, 'Manto Sahib, I'll give my judgement tomorrow,' he, more than anyone else, felt terribly disappointed.

He insisted that I settle the matter then and there. To him, this was like rendering obsolete the very purpose of an admission of guilt and the existence of magistrates. And here was I, wanting to read the story in question and think long and hard about it to establish whether it met the strictly legal definition of obscenity. Believe me, true justice requires as much genuine reflection as action; arbitrariness and mere adherence to rules go against the spirit of justice. It is a strange aspect of our times, however, that essence is always sacrificed to accident.

In short, however unwillingly, Manto had to consent to wait for a day.

The next day, after the court began its session, I wrote my brief judgement. Manto had come with his companion to hear the judgement in the same agitated state as was apparent on him the day before. 'Manto Sahib,' I asked, 'how is your financial condition?'

'Very bad.'

'What is the date today?' I asked.

'Twenty-fifth,' someone else answered.

'Manto Sahib, I'm fining you twenty-five rupees.'

At first he didn't understand and said to his companion, 'Is he asking for the date or giving his judgement?'

His guarantor was more vigorous. He quickly went to pay the fine, and Manto again started to pace on the veranda.

A little later I saw them both in the courtroom. 'Yes?' I asked. Whereupon Manto's companion said, 'We've come to bother you . . .'

I accepted their invitation without hesitation. During court proceedings one has little opportunity to talk freely, least of all informally, and I myself wanted an informal meeting with Manto because, as far as I was concerned, he was the greatest Urdu short story writer after Munshi Premchand.

After work I proceeded straight away to the Zelin Coffee House. Since it was filled to capacity, I waited on the staircase. When Manto and his companion materialized, I noticed that Manto looked tipsy but in full control of his senses. He paused now and then as he spoke, but it betrayed no interruption of thought. In the middle of addressing me he would sometimes make some pointed comments about me to his companion, every word of which sounded utterly sincere and unpretentious. His mind, his thoughts were free of any reservations or misconceptions, and his speech betrayed not the slightest desire to impress his addressee or be impressed by him. Fearlessly and boldly he called what was good, good, and bad, bad, though the standard by which he judged these was entirely his own and unconventional—a standard which was unshakeable, unlikely to change with the times. In short, it was then that I saw, for the first time in my life, what a true realist, a candid, fearless, great artist looked like. That image is still vivid in my mind and will remain with me forever.

Our conversation was long but interesting. 'You don't drink?' he asked.
'No.'
'A mullah, eh?'
'No . . . just a Muslim.'

He started laughing. His companion ordered a coffee for me.

I learned that they had come to the coffee house just for my sake, abandoning a very lively meeting in some bar. 'Actually, it is I who should have played the host,' I apologized. 'After all, I'm the local . . .'

'No, not at all, you look like a *muhajir*,'* Manto remarked.

---

*Used for Indian Muslims who migrated to Pakistan during Partition. The word also has the connotation of a refugee who is destitute and in need of assistance. Whether Manto intended this subtle meaning is hard to say. Most likely, he did.

'Even so, I live in Karachi.'

He then asked, 'Why did you ask me to sit down during the proceedings? No magistrate has ever treated me with such courtesy.'

'I do not consider rudeness a part of court manners.'

He immediately started laughing and said to his companion, 'He seems like a decent enough fellow.'

A while later he asked, 'I haven't read your judgement. What have you written in it?'

I handed him a copy of my judgement. He read it carefully, and then he turned to his companion and said, as if I wasn't there, 'Seems like an educated man . . . very educated,' and then, looking at me, 'All right, tell me, how far have you studied?'

I told him about my educational qualifications and certificates. He started laughing again. 'Didn't I say he was a very educated man? And he writes good English, such good English . . . Well then, why did you sentence me?'

Precisely at that moment the realization hit me in all its intensity that this man was a true artist. Manto didn't have the foggiest idea that he had written anything obscene; he had merely written a short story.

He told me that the story in question was to a large extent based on real events. So if it was obscene, there was little he could do about it. Contemporary society was itself obscene. He merely portrayed what he saw; naturally the image bad people see in the mirror doesn't please them. They become enraged. He hadn't used a single obscene word in the story, which is absolutely true.

I wasn't ready at all to respond to him with his enthusiasm and clarity, so, to get him off my back, I merely said, 'Obscene words are not the only touchstone of obscenity.'

'Then what is—that one should hide the reality? You punish and fine me for speaking the truth.'

Although, at the time, I didn't think it provident to give him a clear and frank answer, I still believed that there has to be some difference between reality and its expression, which must be maintained. Otherwise, what would be the justification for covering one's nakedness? Why does one look for privacy for the performance of the sexual act? Why are subtle allusion and suggestion considered literary qualities? A writer is not a photographer; he's a painter. And even photographers don't wander around snapping pictures of genitalia and scenes of cohabitation.

I evaded him again, 'I'll tell you some other time why I've fined you.'

'Promise?' he asked.

'I promise . . .'

I was unable to fulfil my promise during Manto's life. However, I'm doing so today:

The Law doesn't wish to get in the way of literature fulfilling its demands and purpose. It only wishes that such demands and purpose be beneficial for man. If the purpose is not salutary and lies only in arousing the libido, or even does not aim to do that but the subject and words are such that they drive weak, sick or immature minds to seek erotic pleasure, then the Law establishes that such writing is harmful and obscene. 'Ūpar, Nīche, aur Darmiyān' describes the preliminaries and the background of the sexual act, and how they differ in all three strata of society. The Law doesn't find such a subject useful, even though the events described may be based on reality. The Law also recognizes that ordinary people would use them to indulge in sexual arousal and pleasure, rather than observing in them the engaging portrayal of the differences obtaining in the three layers of society. This apprehension and determination of the Law isn't all that misguided. It is possible, in fact it is certain, that writers will not agree with my assessment. I cannot elucidate the legal definition of obscenity with any more clarity than this, and neither can I provide a sounder justification for this definition.

The fact is, even from a literary point of view, I considered this story obscene, but it was not pertinent to expound upon it at the time.

Anyway, our meeting in the coffee house lasted a good hour and a half or maybe two. Just as Manto had extracted a promise from me, he also made a promise to me, which he too didn't get the time to fulfil.

So this was my first and last encounter with Manto. Afterwards, he wrote a couple of letters to me from Lahore. I did my best to do as he asked. But none of these favours were meant for him personally. He loved his friends and valued their friendship, and his letters sought help only for them. His last letter to me, dated 17 January 1955, was written only a day before he died. I received it after he was no more.

But the dearest memento of our brief but entirely selfless relationship is something quite different. He had started writing the account of the trial regarding 'Ūpar, Nīche, aur Darmiyān' as 'The Fifth Trial' in *Nuqūsh*. Only its first instalment, which covers up to the events of his arrival at the court, has been published. God knows whether he was able to complete it. I'm sure he would have expressed his opinion of me in the next instalment. I read the first instalment and was eagerly waiting for the second, but the waiting prolonged.

At the tail end of 1954 I came to know that Manto had published a fresh collection of his work called Ūpar, Nīche, aur Darmiyān. I felt both surprised and happy when people told me that Manto had dedicated it to me. Try as hard as one might, it is not possible to find a greater expression of Manto's sincere affection and trust than this. I'm not a well-known person. I'm happy this will perhaps give my name a few moments of life as a literary curio.

'Iṣmat-Farōshī (Prostitution)*

Selling one's virtue ('iṣmat-farōshī)† is not something that goes against reason or infringes any law. It is a profession; women who engage in it meet certain societal needs. If something is available in the market and customers exist for it, this should not surprise us. And neither should we object to the means by which women earn a living, even if one of those means happens to be selling their bodies, for their customers are found in every city.

Virtue-selling is considered a grave sin. Maybe it is a grave sin. But, I do not wish to pursue it from a religious point of view here. By plunging into the maze of sin and reward, crime and recompense one can hardly expect to reflect on this issue with a cool head. Religion is a formidable problem in itself. If I were to probe the issue from a religious perspective, I would get nowhere. So I will put religion aside and proceed.

What, precisely, is virtue-selling? Well, it is to sell the jewel believed to be a woman's most precious ornament. What further boosts its value is our experience of how a woman loses her respect in society once she has lost this jewel. This jewel is lost in many ways: after marriage, thanks to her husband; sometimes a man takes it from her forcibly; sometimes out of wedlock, when she surrenders it willingly to the man she loves;

---

* 'Iṣmat-Farōshī', from the author's collection *Manto ke Mazāmīn* (Lahore: Idāra-e Adabīyāt-e Nau, 1966), pp. 155–72.

† Literally, 'iṣmat' means 'innocence', the preservation of 'chastity', 'modesty', 'purity'; figuratively, 'virginity', which is intended here. Manto is aware of the inherent contradiction of the compound noun 'iṣmat-farōshī' and deals with it later on in this piece.

sometimes she sells it when circumstances compel her and sometimes she trades in it.

Here, I want to talk about the last category: women who sell their bodies as a profession. Although it is evident that this priceless jewel can be lost or sold only once, not over and over again, nevertheless, inasmuch as prostitution is commonly designated as 'virtue-selling', we will also use this appellation.

Throughout the ages a prostitute has been considered the most shameful of creatures. But have we ever given a thought to the fact that it is this same degraded individual whose doors we often knock at. Don't we ever think that this makes us equally shameful?

Regrettably, men never give it a moment's thought. They will always attribute every last stain on their good names to the darkness that fills the heart of the prostitute. The reality, though, is the exact opposite. Prostitute or not, ninety-nine per cent of women without their virtue are likely to have, in spite of their ungodly trade, hearts that are much more radiant than those of dissolute men. Whether a prostitute or a lady with her virtue well preserved, women have always taken a back seat to men, because men control the present system and are free to think of women as they will.

Have we not heard often of the rich profligate who, having burned his last penny himself in the crucible of his flaming passion, blames such-and-such slut or courtesan for his ruination? This is mind-boggling. I wish someone would unravel this mystery for me.

A *fille de joie*, who runs her sex business strictly according to the rules of her profession, will, inevitably, attempt to extract the maximum possible cash from everyone who comes to her as a customer. Now, whether she sells her commodity at a reasonable rate or an exceptionally exorbitant price, why moan about it? It is her business after all. A provisions seller does the same . . . by adjusting the weight of the item you have come to buy. Some shops charge less, others considerably more.

The confusing point is this: We hear all the time that prostitutes are veritable snakes; there is no remedy for their bite. Why then do we willingly allow ourselves to be bitten by them and fuss over it after? A prostitute does not pillage a man's wealth consciously or out of some feeling of revenge. She strikes a deal and earns her living. Men pay her for their sexual gratification. That's all.

It is possible that a prostitute might sometimes love a man. But everyone who crosses her threshold with a specific purpose in mind begins to entertain the notion that she should also love him truly—how is that possible? We go to buy a rupee's worth of flour—wouldn't it be ridiculous if we expected the shopkeeper to invite us to his home and offer us a certain cure for baldness?

A man who demands love from a prostitute merely forces her to fake a posture of true love. This will make her customer happy. But she cannot feel within the depths of her heart any stirrings of pure love for every man who gets drunk and starts swaying his head at her kotha full of the desire to induct her into a world of glamorous romance.

One only looks at a prostitute from the outside. Her comportment, her airs, her gorgeous outfit, the decor, the furnishings of her parlour—all these create the impression of her being well situated and affluent. Nothing could be farther from the truth. It does not take exceptional intelligence to appreciate the true situation of a woman whose doors are open for anyone with cash in his pockets, cobbler or sweeper, lame or disabled, handsome or repulsive. An ugly man, blowing stinking puffs of breath from a mouth wasted by periodontitis comes to her place because he has enough money to buy the use of her body for a specific period of time. Even if she finds him utterly revolting, she can't turn him away. So she holds back her revulsion and entertains him, putting up with his ugliness, his fetid breath. She is smart enough to know that not all of her clients will be the living image of Apollo.

Nobody gawks at a female typist with consternation, or at midwives with hatred, or at sweeper women carrying baskets of refuse on their heads with belittlement. But, strangely, women who sell their bodies, whether in a delicate or crude manner, are looked upon with all three: consternation, hatred, and belittlement.

Gentlemen, prostitution is indispensable. You see gorgeous, ritzy cars in the street—don't you? Such classy vehicles aren't meant to transport garbage. There are vehicles for that purpose, but you see them less often. And when you do see them, you quickly cover your nose. Well, just as we can't do without garbage trucks, neither can we do without prostitutes. They are absolutely necessary; they carry away our dirt, our filth. Had they not existed, our streets and pathways would have been filled with the most unseemly, the most vulgar acts of men.

These women are like dreary, desolate gardens; open sewers running by garbage piles. They live in the middle of this filth. How can everyone live a lush and exuberant life?

Just think about it: tucked away in a corner of the city is the room of a woman who sells her flesh; in the darkness of the evening, a man with a heart even darker than the night, barges in to assuage the leaping flames of his passion. She knows how evil this man is, that his very existence is a danger to humanity's peace, over which it blazes like an ugly stain. She knows he is a frightening specimen of a creature from the age of barbarity, but she cannot slam the door shut in his face—can she? The door that one is compelled to open out of sheer economic necessity and want can't simply be shut, not without the greatest difficulty.

This woman—a bawd first, a woman second—gives her body over to a man in exchange for a few coins, but it is a body bereft of her soul in those moments. Listen to what one such bawd has to say:

> Men take me out into the fields. I just lie there, immobile, without a sound—dead, inert. Only my eyes are open, gazing far, far into the distance, where some she-goats are going at one another under the shade of the trees. Oh, what an idyllic scene! I start counting the she-goats, or the ravens on the branches—nineteen, twenty, twenty-one, twenty-two . . . Meanwhile the man has finished, withdrawn, and is panting heavily some distance from me. But I'm not aware of any of this.

Observation tells us that *vaishiyas* tend to be God-fearing. At every Hindu vaishiya's place you will invariably find small idols or, at the very least, a picture of Lord Krishna or Lord Ganesha in one room or another. She worships it with the same reverence and purity of heart as any virtuous woman would. Likewise, if she happens to be Muslim, she will fast unfailingly during the month of Ramzan, close her business and wear black for the duration of Muharram, help the needy, and, on special occasions, bow to God in utmost humility and submission.

On the face of it, such attachment by prostitutes to religion might seem fake. When, in fact, it portrays that there is a part of their soul which they have kept well protected from the corrosive effects of society.

This holds equally true for prostitutes of other faiths. You will find them as devoted to their religion as any. A Christian vaishiya will not fail to attend mass in church or light an earthen lamp before the picture of the Virgin Mary. In this commerce of the flesh, a vaishiya trades her body, not her soul. It is not necessary for a seller of charas and bhang to be addicted to these substances himself. By the same token, not every pandit or maulvi is pious as a rule.

The body can be stained, not the soul.

What with her gloomy business, a prostitute can have a radiant soul. She can be merciless in collecting her earnings, but she can also help numberless poor. Her richest clients may not succeed in winning her love, but she wouldn't think twice about giving it to a drifter who only has the sidewalks to sleep on at night.

Yes, she craves money. But does that mean she cannot crave love?

The answer to this question calls for a detailed discussion. There is a big difference between a hereditary prostitute and one who is new to the profession. Then there are also those women or girls who are driven to sell their flesh to support their poor parents or to take care of their fatherless children, but their case is entirely different from the two main types mentioned above.

A hereditary prostitute is one who is born to a prostitute and grows up in her household, in other words, a woman who is instructed in the ways of prostitution according to the principles of her occupation. Women who grow up in such an environment generally consider love a coin that has no purchase in their trade. This makes sense; for if they were to give their hearts away to every client who visits them for a few hours, they wouldn't be able to run their business successfully.

Such women, as commonly observed, rarely feel the stirrings of love in their hearts. Said differently, in comparison to other women, they are very circumspect. Indeed, they can be quite stingy about falling in love. Their interaction with men generates indescribable feelings of bitterness in their hearts for them, whom they begin to consider worse than animals. That's why they become, to a degree, 'disbelievers' in love. Which, of course, doesn't mean that their hearts are entirely bereft of the delicate, tender feelings of love.

Just as a sweeper's daughter would probably not feel any revulsion towards carrying her first basket of filth on her head, similarly prostitutes would likely feel no hesitation or shame upon their debut in the profession. Bashfulness, hesitation and their complementary sentiments gradually wear off to the point of non-existence. How can tender feelings of love find their way into the hearts of prostitutes whose doors are open for lustful men?

Just as decent, virtuous women gaze at vaishiyas with bafflement
and shocked disbelief, so do the latter gaze at the former. While the eyes
of virtuous women are filled with the question, 'Could a woman sink so
low?' the virtue-less woman wonders, 'What are these chaste women?
Who are they?'

A vaishiya whose mother, whose grandmother, and so on were all
vaishiyas, who has suckled at a vaishiya's breasts after being born in the
midst of the oldest profession in the world, who grew up in its milieu and
started selling her flesh there—how can she ever understand virtue or
virtuous women?

Out of every one hundred girls born into prostitutes' families, perhaps
only one or two ever feel revulsion at their environment and firmly commit
to surrendering themselves to only one man. The rest follow the path of
their mothers.

A shopkeeper's son desires to open his own shop and expresses this
desire in a variety of ways. It is no different with the teenage daughters of
prostitutes. They also long to set up their own business, which is what leads
them to display the attributes of their bodies, their charms, their beauty in
ever-newer, eye-catching ways. And when they launch into the business,
their debut follows the enactment of specific initiation ceremonies. This is
no different from the protocol for beginning any new business.

This being the case, obviously, it is hard for love to sprout in the
hearts of these hereditary prostitutes. By love, I mean the kind that our
society has been witness to over the ages—the proverbial love of Heer
and Ranjha, Sassi and Punnu.

But these seasoned, hardened prostitutes also love, though in a
radically different way. They can't replicate the love of Laila and Majnun
or Heer and Ranjha for the all-too-obvious adverse effect it would have
on their business. If a vaishiya were to set apart a few moments during
her work hours for a man from whom she doesn't care to receive money,
well, we would say that she has feelings for this fellow. But as a rule, she
is greedy only for a man's wealth. She would be breaking a rule if she
cared for him and not his money, and would also be making it obvious
that her heart is at work behind this care, not any desire to cash in on his
riches. And where the heart is involved, feelings of love must inevitably
find their way.

Ordinarily, love springs from the unalloyed desire for sexual
gratification. So, here too, we will consider sex the operative agent of what

is called love. But many other considerations can also set love in motion. For instance, a woman who sells sex for money and is used to lording it over men might also tire of being endlessly wheedled and indulged in her whims by her clients. Yes, she likes to be the boss, but there may be times when she would like nothing better than being subservient herself. Surely, fulfilment of every request is hugely profitable, but rejection, too, has a flavour all its own. Raking in piles of money as a routine inevitably makes her want, sometimes, to spend it on someone else. If everyone plays up to her, she too might want to flatter someone. If she is adamant with someone, someone must also be adamant with her. She always spurns and snubs others; someone should snub her, tease her, treat her badly. All these latent desires compel her to choose a particular man for herself. And so she chooses.

Selection is an exceedingly delicate, indeed, unpredictable matter. It is entirely conceivable that she might open the doors of her heart to the scion of some rich man, or end up throwing herself at the feet of the filthy, charas-addicted miraasi who fills the hookah-bowls at her kotha—she, for a kiss of whose curls distinguished kings and princes would shower thousands of gold pieces without thinking twice. Nor should we feel surprise when that filthy man kicks her away with contempt. One often observes and hears about such incidents.

A famous *tawaif*, whom a nawab sahib was madly in love with, had given her heart to a very ordinary man. She would ridicule the nawab's love, while people derided her for hers. The nawab earned disgrace for loving a tawaif, and she lost esteem in the eyes of the people for loving a nobody.

A vaishiya's love, compared to that of ordinary women, is more intense. Her association with men introduces her to unfamiliar emotions of loving, and when she herself falls in love, those emotions affect her with greater force.

Stories abound in bazaars where prostitutes conduct their business, especially stories about the pleasure-loving rich whose bags of money open up at prostitutes' kothas. And there are those who love to tell those stories with great gusto. Sarangi-players, drummers and others who regularly come and go at kothas will tell you many such spicy tales.

Among those stories, we can cite by way of example the one about a particular prostitute who literally bathed in money, but had lost her heart to a labourer in tatters and who trampled it mercilessly under his calloused feet every day. She collected piles of money from her admirers every night, but remained miles away from the grimy embrace of the labourer. She hopelessly tried to find her way into his heart, and failed. Far too often she, with a body as delicate as a flower, slept on the bare cobblestone sidewalk to win the affection of her labourer!

Such paradox, the colour of true love, does appear quite outlandish and mysteriously romantic in the milieu of brothels. But it is the backdrop that accentuates and highlights the objects that occupy the foreground. Since we normally think that all a prostitute ever cares about is money, that she is altogether bereft of feelings of love, a story such as the one just told always seems incredible and bizarre; hence, our heightened interest in listening to it—rather than the love affairs of ordinary men and women—as if it was an account of something highly improbable, although, in point of fact, the heart and its stirrings have nothing to do with the selling of one's virtue or keeping it unstained. A virtuous woman can have a heart that does not throb for love; conversely, the meanest bawd of a brothel can possess a heart fully responsive to such promptings.

One should never forget that not every woman is a vaishiya, but that every vaishiya is a woman.

There's something special about a vaishiya's love that is worth mentioning. It is that her love never gets in the way of her business. One rarely finds a vaishiya who permanently folded up her business for the sake of her love (any more than a respectable shopkeeper closes down his business because of his love for an honourable girl). Normally, a vaishiya will continue her business even though she loves someone. One could say that a businessman's appetite for money becomes part of her psyche. Making new customers and selling her flesh turns into something like a habit, which eventually becomes her nature, with absolutely no effect on other areas of her life. Just as a servant, after speedily making his master's bed, turns to his own comfort, in like manner, these women return to their own happiness and comfort just as soon as they have entertained the last customer of the evening.

The heart is not something one can portion off, and women tend to be comparatively less promiscuous than men. Inasmuch as a vaishiya is a woman, she can't give her heart to all of her clients. A woman loves only one man in her life, or so the saying goes. I tend to think that this is largely true. She will open her heart only to the man for whom she feels love; she can't give it to everyone who crosses her threshold.

How often is the complaint not heard that prostitutes are generally very cruel and tyrannical. Perhaps the thinnest sliver in a population of hundreds can be characterized this way, but not all; they cannot be. One must never compare a prostitute to a woman who preserves her modesty. Indeed such a comparison is grossly misleading. A vaishiya works for her living; the modest woman has many to provide for her needs.

The words of a vaishiya, which reflect the depths of her feelings, are still echoing in my ears. Listen:

> A vaishiya is a helpless woman with no one to watch over her. A whole host of men visit her every evening—for only one purpose. She feels alone even in the company of her lovers—all alone. She is a train that travels in the darkness of night, drops off her passengers at their destinations, and then stands empty under the metal roof of a shed—all alone, abandoned, forlorn, covered with dust and smoke. People call us bad. Heaven only knows why. The very clients who buy us for their comfort in the darkness of night, disparage, belittle and hate us in the light of day. We sell our bodies openly; we don't hide it as a secret. Men come to us to buy sex, and then keep this transaction a secret . . . one wonders why.

Think of the prostitute who has no one in the world to call her own—no brother, no sister, no parents, not even a friend. When the last customer of the evening has gone away, she is left all alone in her room. Try to imagine the state of her mind and heart then—a void made a hundredfold more frightening than the darkness of her night.

Imagine the condition of a porter who has no means to relax after a day's gruelling work, neither a wife to talk with to amuse himself, nor a mother who will put an affectionate hand gently on his shoulder and take away all his misery, soak up all his fatigue. Have you any idea what such a man must feel like? Materially, a vaishiya's situation is not much different from his. But why, then, does she look so full of vivacity and exuberance?

For the answer we must dig deep into our hearts. The fault lies in the way we look at a prostitute; hence, we must commune with our inner self in order to discover the reasons for our short-sightedness. What I have been able to work out, after much hard thinking, is this:

The minute the word vaishiya is uttered, the image of a woman sails before our eyes—a woman who can gratify a man's desire for sex in whatever manner and whenever he feels the need for it. But we forget that a prostitute and a woman are two different entities, so when we think about the former, what we inevitably see is a woman and her profession rolled into one. Now it's true that one's profession and milieu do considerably affect a person, but there are times when this person is simply a human being, apart from whatever else she may be. Likewise, there can be times when a vaishiya sheds the accoutrements of her calling and becomes just a woman. But alas, we are used to only looking at her and her profession as one and the same thing. Thus we see her as a woman and as one who gives pleasure, the pleasure being ordinarily pure sexual gratification.

What is sexual pleasure?

It is that ephemeral physical experience, lasting barely a few moments, which comes from joining together with one's wife or with any other woman. Why, then, does a married man leave his wife and go to a prostitute to get it? Why does he knock about everywhere outside when this desire can be satisfied just as easily inside his home?

The answer is fairly simple. You must have seen numberless people who dine in restaurants when they can eat more sumptuous and savoury dishes at home. This is because they become addicted to restaurant food. Surely it is less nourishing, but it has something which attracts them immensely. We might call this something 'the peculiar ambience of the restaurant'— admittedly a vice which becomes a virtue, in other words, an attraction—a fabricated attraction in which the restaurateur plays no small part.

Additionally, the exuberance, the gaiety of the restaurant is not something he can replicate at home. By nature man likes variety. His desire for a change in his daily routine need not surprise us. Surely the restaurant diet is not as good and healthy as home-made food, and far more expensive. But this is what these people love, what draws them to a restaurant. Call it folly or stupidity if you will, but they like it.

The case of married men who seek pleasure in the embrace of a prostitute is no different. Do they succeed in finding it?—you might ask. Certainly, I would say. The women they visit are adept at providing maximum gratification. After all, this is what they sell; it is their profession—to give a pleasure all its own, utterly different from what a housewife can provide. How else will their business flourish?

Let me reiterate what I said at the beginning of this piece: prostitution is not at all irrational.

The Short Story Writer and Matters of Sex[*]

Regardless of how insignificant a thing may be, it never fails to create problems. A mosquito finds its way inside a mosquito net and stirs up a whole host of difficulties: how to expel the offender, what proper safeguards might prevent this culprit and other offenders of its ilk from entering the netting ever again. However, the biggest problem, the grandfather of problems, came about in the world when Adam felt the pangs of hunger. A somewhat less pressing, nonetheless interesting, problem surfaced when the first man on earth encountered the first woman on earth.

Both problems, as you well know, stem from two basic kinds of hunger. They are intimately connected—precisely why we see them at work in the back of all of our contemporary problems, be they societal, social, political or military.

But hunger, never mind what kind it is, is an extremely dangerous thing. If only chains are offered to those who hanker after freedom, revolution will inevitably occur. If the starving are forced to fast day after day, desperation will drive them to snatch food from the mouths of others. If man is denied the sight of the female body, he will perhaps look for its image among his own sex and animals.

Hunger is the font of every conceivable ill. It sends you out to beg, entices you to commit crimes, to sell your body and it teaches extremism. Its assault is unforgiving, its blow unfailing, its wound very deep. Hunger breeds madmen; madness doesn't create hunger.

[*] 'Afsāna-Nigār aur Jinsī Masā'il', from the author's collection *Mantōnāma* (Lahore: Sang-e-Meel Publications, 1990), pp. 684–87.

No matter where a writer is situated on Earth, whether he is progressive or conservative, young or old, all he sees is a plethora of problems afflicting the world. He picks from them and writes about them—once in favour of a problem, once against some other.

Today's writer is not much different from his counterpart from five hundred years ago. It is Time, not man, that tags everything as new or old. Today we are called 'new' writers. Tomorrow we will be labelled 'old' and put away in some cupboard. This doesn't mean we lived for nothing, that our lives were a waste, that we toiled in vain. When a clock's hand crawls to two, it doesn't render the previous digit useless, because the hand goes through its cycle and comes back to one. This is the law that governs a clock, just as it governs the world.

Today's problems are not fundamentally different from those of yesterday. The seeds for all the ills that plague us today were sown yesterday. Likewise, sexual problems that confront us now also challenged earlier writers. They wrote about them in their own way, as do we.

I don't know why I'm questioned so often about the sex in my stories. Could it be because some people consider me a progressive, or because I've written some stories on sexual themes? Or perhaps because by calling some new writers 'sex-crazy' some people want to banish them from literature, religion and society in a single blow? Whatever the reason, here is how I look at things:

Bread and stomach, man and woman—these are correlations that go back to the beginning of time. Eternal. Which of the two is more important—bread or stomach, woman or man—I can't say with any certainty. Why? Because my stomach demands bread, but does wheat also crave my stomach equally? This I absolutely do not know.

Occasionally, the thought drifts through my mind that if the earth has produced wheat it can't be without a purpose—which suggests to me that all those golden stalks of wheat swaying in the vast, open fields are meant just for my stomach. Immediately, on the heels of that thought, comes another: Perhaps my stomach came first, the ears of wheat some time later.

Whatever. It is as evident as daylight that all of world literature is the product of just these two relationships. Even revelations, a kind of heavenly literature, don't fail to touch on bread and stomach, man and woman.

The question then arises: If these issues are so primeval that even sacred books mention them, why are contemporary writers still harping on them? Why is the relationship between woman and man never left alone and, as someone has said, obscenity bruited about. The answer is simple. If the world could give up lying and thieving through a single act of exhortation, just one Prophet would have sufficed, but, as you know, the list is rather long.

We writers are not prophets. We look at problems from different perspectives in different circumstances and present them according to what and how we perceive them. But we never foist anything upon anyone.

We're not lawgivers, not even inquisitors. Framing laws and keeping track of people's morals is for others. Of course, we take the government to task, but we never aspire to become rulers ourselves. Yes, we draft plans for buildings, but we aren't builders; we diagnose ailments, but don't run hospitals.

We don't write about sex per se. If anyone thinks otherwise, they are mistaken. Rather, we write about the circumstances of particular men and women. If a husband hates his wife for her simplicity and her preference for white clothing in our story, other women should not take it as an incontrovertible norm. However, if you want to know what circumstances caused this hatred and why, you will definitely find the answer in the story.

Those who read our stories to find ways to titillate their senses will certainly be disappointed. We are not wrestlers who can teach you proven holds and manoeuvres to knock down your opponent. But if we see someone flat on his back in the arena, we can speculate and explain to you what might have caused his defeat.

We are optimists who never fail to see a silver lining even in the darkest cloud. If a prostitute spits out the paan spittle from her mouth, aiming it at the passer-by under her balcony, we neither laugh at the passer-by nor curse the whore. We just pause, let our gaze tear through her revealing clothes down to her dark, sinful body, deep into her heart and grope around inside, morphing, in our imagination, into that self-same filthy, revolting whore, and strive to describe not just the incident in all its vivid detail, but also to find its true motivation.

If a beautiful, healthy young girl from a respectable family runs away with an ugly, scrawny, penniless young man, we don't call her a wretch. Surely others will drag her past, her present and her future before a moral tribunal. Conversely, we will do nothing of the sort; we will instead try to undo the tiny knot that had numbed her sense of judgement.

Humans are not very different from one another. One person can commit the same mistake another has. If one woman can open shop in the bazaar to sell her body, so can every other woman. Man is not culpable; his circumstances are—circumstances that lead him to commit his mistakes and live through their consequences.

I Too Have Something To Say[*]

In 1942, my short story 'Kālī Shalwār' [The Black Shalwar] appeared in the special annual number of the monthly literary magazine *Adab-e Latīf* (Lahore). Some people consider it obscene. I'm writing this article to disabuse them of their mistaken notion.

Writing short stories is my profession. I know all the ins and outs of this art. I have written many others on this subject before the story in question. None of them are smutty, nor will the many more which I will write on this subject in the future be so.

Storytelling goes all the way back to the fall of Adam, and will continue, I believe, till doomsday, though it will go through many incarnations. However, man will persist in communicating his feelings to the ears of other men. A lot has already been written about prostitutes; a lot more will be written. What one sees will always provoke discussion and writing. Prostitutes are not a recent phenomenon; they have existed in our midst for thousands of years. They figure even in sacred books. Now that there is no longer any scope for a fresh heavenly book or a new prophet, you won't read about them in the sacred lines of revelations, but rather in newspapers, magazines, or books, which you can pore over, unencumbered by the need to surround yourself in the spiralling haze of aloes-wood and frankincense smoke, and, when done, toss in the trash bin.

Well, I'm someone who writes in such magazines and books. I write because I feel I have something to say. I share with others the way I

[*] 'Mujhē Bhī Kuchh Kahnā Hai', from the author's collection *Mantōnumā* (Lahore: Sang-e-Meel Publications, 1991), pp. 732–42.

see things, and the angle from which I see them. If writers are lunatics, please consider me a lunatic as well.

The backdrop of 'Kālī Shalwār' is a prostitute's lodging. It isn't as astonishing as the nest of a weaverbird, about which we hear all kinds of wonderful things. In Delhi, they have set up an area exclusively for such women and built numberless residential units to house them. My Sultāna also lives in one such unit. She hasn't constructed it herself like the weaverbird, nor does she catch fireflies to light it in the evening like that bird. For light, there was electricity, and since she couldn't get that for free, any more than she could the unit in which she lived, she had to work. Had she been married, all this would have come to her free. But she wasn't married and she was a woman. When a woman is obliged to pay for lodgings and electricity and is saddled with a good-for-nothing layabout like Khuda Bakhsh, who trusts in God and runs after fakirs and holy men, it's obvious that she can't be the kind of woman we see in our respectable homes.

My Sultāna is a brothel woman. She does precisely what women do in a brothel; it is her profession. Who doesn't know these women? Nearly every city and town has its red-light district. Who isn't aware of running gutters—nearly every city and town has them, and they're there to carry away the filth.

If we can talk about our marbled bathrooms, about soaps and lavenders, why can't we talk about these drains and gutters that carry away the filth of our bodies? If we can talk about temples and mosques, why not about whorehouses visited by some people on their way back from those temples and mosques? If we can talk about opium, bhang, charas and wine contracts, why not about brothels where this stuff is consumed liberally?

We treat *bhangi*s as untouchable. Whenever one of them passes by carrying the basket of our filth, we instantly cover our noses with handkerchiefs. Surely we find it all revolting, but just as surely we can't deny their existence, any more than we can deny the faeces we discharge daily from our bowels. Medications for treating constipation and diarrhoea exist because it is necessary to purge noxious matter from our bodies. New ways to flush out the filth are being thought up continually because it piles up daily. If by some miracle our bodies could be transformed and its functions undergo a radical change, we wouldn't be caught dead talking about constipation and diarrhoea. Likewise, if some mechanical methods could be invented to dispose of our filth, sweepers would go out of business.

If the talk is about sweepers, garbage and filth will inevitably figure in it. Just as inevitably, what prostitutes do will feature in the conversation when we talk about them.

We don't visit a prostitute's chamber to offer ritual prayer or shower blessings upon the Prophet. Why, we go there because . . . Well, it's obvious. We go there because we can, and buy freely and without objection what we've come for. Now, if we're allowed to go there without restriction, if any woman can decide to become a prostitute of her own free will, get a licence and start selling her body, if such a transaction is sanctioned by law, then why can't we talk about her?

If talking about her is obscene, her existence is no less obscene. If taking about her is forbidden, her business too should be forbidden. Remove the prostitute and we'll cease talking about her without any prompting.

We talk openly about lawyers, barbers, laundrymen, innkeepers and kunjars; relate stories about thieves, shoplifters, thugs and highwaymen; fabricate tall tales about fairies and genies; make preposterous claims such as the Earth is balanced on the two horns of a bull; author *Dāstān-e Amīr Hamza* and the tale of *Totā-Mainā*; praise the mace of Landhūr the wrestler; talk about 'Amr the Trickster's magical cap and bag; and recite stories of parrots and mynahs who can speak in any language. We can talk about wizards and their incantations and how to neutralize the effects of their spells, and discuss whatever our fancy demands about spells cast by spirits, and about the practice of alchemy. We can quarrel about the length of beards and trousers and hair. We can think up new recipes for cooking rogan josh, pilaf and korma and wonder what kind and colour of buttons would go well with a green fabric. Then why can't we think about prostitutes and talk about their profession or comment on their clients?

We can make a girl and boy fall in love and set up their first rendezvous at the tomb-sanctuary of Dātā Ganjbakhsh and drag along an old hag as their go-between so the two restless souls can meet often. We can squash their romance in the end or make them take poison and arrange for their coffins to be borne out from their respective neighbourhoods at the same time, and have the lovers buried, by some miracle, in adjoining graves, and, if need be, arrange for angels to shower flowers over them . . .

Why, then, can't we talk about the life of a prostitute, who needs no angels or flowers? When she dies no one from neighbourhoods other than her own joins the funeral procession and no grave ever wants to be next to hers. Her existence itself is a coffin which society is carrying aloft on its shoulders. Unless she is interred for good, there will be talk about her.

Even if this corpse is in a state of decomposition, is stinking, is grotesque and revolting, what is so wrong in seeing its face? Does she have no connection to us? Is she not one of our own? We will remove the shroud from her face now and then to look at it and show it to others.

That's precisely what I've done in my 'Kālī Shalwār': shown the face of just such a corpse. Have a look.

A warehouse stretched from one corner to the other on that side of the street. To the right, huge bales and piles of different goods lay under a metal roof. To the left was an open space with innumerable intersecting railway tracks. Whenever the iron tracks flashed in the sun, Sultana's eyes fell on her hands where the protruding blue veins looked very much like those tracks. Engines and carriages were moving all the time in the open space, this way and that, creating a veritable din with their chug-chug and clatter. On the days when Sultana woke up early in the morning and went out to the balcony, a strange sight greeted her: engines in the misty dawn spewing out thick smoke that climbed slowly towards the murky sky like plump, beefy men. Clouds of steam rose noisily from the tracks and quickly dissolved in the air. Now and then the sight of a shunted carriage left to run on its own along a track reminded her of herself: She too had been pushed out to run on her own along the track of her life. Others simply changed the switches and she kept moving forward—to God knew where; one day, when the momentum had slowly spent itself, she would come to a halt, at some place unknown to her.

Could there be more revealing hints than these for an intelligent reader? Here I've made a successful attempt to present the true conditions of Sultāna's life. When the Delhi municipal authorities were setting up a special, separate area for prostitutes they could not have imagined how tellingly the warehouse would come to represent Sultāna's life. The juxtaposition of those special housing units and the warehouse would provoke the sagacious to write several stories like 'Kālī Shalwār'.

I have pulled away the shroud from over the corpse's face in yet another story. I begin my famous story 'Hatak' [Spurned] thus:

> Drained from the day's gruelling work, Saugandhi had fallen asleep almost as soon as she hit the bed. Minutes ago, the city's sanitary inspector—she called him 'Seth'—had gone home to his wife, dead drunk, after a prolonged session of stormy sex which had left even her bones aching. He would have stayed for the night but for the regard he had for his wife who loved him dearly.
>
> The money that she had received from the inspector for her services was still stuffed in her tight-fitting bra, now stained with the man's drool. Ever so often the silver coins clinked a bit with the rise and fall of her breathing, the sound blending with the irregular rhythm of her heart. It was as if the molten silver of the coins was dripping into her bloodstream. Her chest was on fire, partly from the half-bottle of brandy the inspector had brought along and partly from the raw country liquor they had downed with plain water when the soda ran out.
>
> She was lying face down on the large teakwood bed, her bare arms splayed out like the bow-shaped rib of a kite that has come loose from its dew-drenched paper. The grainy flesh visible in her right armpit had acquired a bluish tint from frequent shaving and looked like a graft from the skin of a freshly plucked chicken.

This then is the portrait of Saugandhi, a sister of Sultāna. I end the story thus:

> When the dog returned, wagging his stumpy tail, and sat at her feet flapping his ears, Saugandhi was startled. She felt a terrifying stillness around her, a stillness she had never experienced before. A strange emptiness engulfed everything, and she couldn't help thinking of a train standing all alone in its metal shed after disgorging every last one of its passengers. This feeling of emptiness which had suddenly arisen weighed heavily on her. She made repeated attempts to fill the void but failed. She was trying to stuff her brain with countless

thoughts all at once, but it was like a sieve. As fast as she filled it, everything filtered out.

She sat in the chair for the longest time. When she couldn't find anything to distract her mind with even after a long and desperate search, she picked up her mangy dog, put him down beside her in the spacious teakwood bed, and went to sleep.

If you read 'Kālī Shalwār' closely, you will conclude the following:

1. Sultāna is an ordinary prostitute. She ran her business at first in Ambala and later moved to Delhi at her lover Khuda Bakhsh's suggestion.

2. Khuda Bakhsh was a man who had put his trust in God and believed in the saintly graces—karāmāt—of fakirs.

3. Sultāna was consumed by despair when her business failed to pick up in Delhi. Her despair progressively grew worse when Khuda Bakhsh started chasing after fakirs and holy men.

4. Muharram was just around the corner. Sultāna's girlfriends had already got their black outfits made; Sultāna couldn't, because she had no money.

5. Just at that point Shankar drops in from the blue. A footloose and fancy-free man, he too has nothing other than his sharp intelligence, quick wit and eloquence. In exchange for these assets he demands from her the commodity she sells for a given price. Sultāna doesn't accept this deal.

6. The second time, it is not Shankar who comes up to her; it is she who beckons to him, accepting him merely as a casual event in the stagnant waters of her life. She cheers up on seeing him, but can't get the thought out of her mind that she doesn't have a black shalwar to commemorate Muharram. She tells him: 'Muharram is coming and I don't have enough money for a black shalwar. You've already heard from me all about my woes. I've given my shirt and dupatta to be dyed just this morning.'

7. On the first of Muharram Shankar returns to her with a black shalwar . . . Khuda Bakhsh's God and his belief in holy men don't help much. What does help is Shankar's sharp intelligence. If this is the impression you get after reading the story, well then, it is not a story that offends one's sense of morality. If that is the case, it is certainly not a song that people might sing, and sing repeatedly, to titillate themselves. No gramophone company would put it on a record because it is bereft of stirring dadras and thumris.

8. Stories like 'Kālī Shalwār' are not written for amusement. Upon reading them you don't start drooling with a surfeit of sensual passion. I haven't committed an immoral act by writing it. In fact, I'm proud that I wrote it, and thank God that I didn't write a *masnavī* with such lines as these in it:

> Out of breath while scuffling
> Covering while taking liberties
> Your forcing your lips against mine
> Your pushing your tongue against mine
> Your taking me in your love's embrace
> Your clinging to me in your passion
> Your calling out my name in moans
> Your gently swatting me with sagging hands
> Your faltering whispers while supine
> Your watching me with glazed eyes
> Your asking me to let you be in God's name
> That you are tired and sleepy; to not shake you
> Your helpless body becoming languid all at once
> Then rising suddenly and your calling out, 'Enough!'
> All desire is now spent.
> Like the day night's dark has spent.
> Will your lust ever reach its climax?
> Or will this go on the whole night?
> There is nothing left in me of desire.
> And it is now morn, no longer is it night.
> Enough or I might now hit you,
> Or call out to someone to help
> When every limb has been knocked out of shape,
> Pray, why wouldn't one scream.
> If you remained unbent still
> None would hold up with you in this game.
>   (Extract from the *Masnavī* of Mīr Dard)*

And thanks also that I haven't written such blazing poetry as this to slake my thirst and inflame my starving sensual desires:

* Musharraf Ali Farooqi has especially translated this and the following extract.

Keeping your lips pressed to mine
But not letting your head rest on my arm
Teasing me by lying on my chest
And becoming cross when I speak of my desire
The pleasures of your tongue in my mouth
The manifest hint of your desire in your acts
And when I wish for something more
When I desire a greater intimacy
You place your hand and furiously refuse
My unfastening your trousers
Your shaking off my hand with each advance
Your pushing me back against the pillow
Your kicking me languidly
And refusing me each time with a new excuse
Your pulling your hand away forcibly
And biting me in frustration
Your moving under me furiously
And breaking free from my hold
Your tearing up in such helplessness
And calling out with suppressed anger,
'Night and day you amuse yourself thus,
In a play not to my liking,
Never are you satisfied,
Never do you call it quits.'

(From *Kullīyāt-e Mōmin*, 'Masnavī 2')

If one writes about the sexual relationship between man and woman in the above manner, I would consider it opprobrious because every grown person knows that when a man and a woman get into bed for sex, they engage in some such animal exercises, although they are never so pretty as the poetry above makes them out to be. They have been just overlaid with poetry, screened behind it. This, of course, is the poet's mischief, which is censurable.

If these ghastly acrobatics were made into a film and shown on screen, I'm sure all sensible people would turn their faces away in revulsion. The poetry above, however, presents a very misleading picture of those animal exercises.

I call such poetry 'mental masturbation'—reproachable as much for
the writer as for the reader. My 'Kālī Shalwār' is blissfully free of any
such reproach. Nowhere in it have I depicted the sexual act in titillating
language. What kind of sexual pleasure could one expect from my
Sultāna who used to hurl obscenities at her gora customers in her own
tongue and considered them 'silly fools'? She was a businesswoman to
the hilt, pure and simple. After all, when we go to a wine shop, we don't
expect the man behind the counter to be Umar Khayyam or have Hafiz's
entire poetic corpus at the tip of his tongue. Wine merchants sell wine, not
the quatrains of Umar Khayyam and the poetry of Hafiz Shirazi.

My Sultāna is a prostitute first, a woman second. Prostitute first
because the most important thing for man during his life is his stomach.
Shankar says to her, 'Surely, you must do something?'

'I waste my time,' she replies. She doesn't say, 'I sell wheat, or deal
in gold and silver.' She knows what she does for a living. If you asked a
typist, 'What do you do?' the answer would be, 'I type.' Naturally. There
isn't a whole lot of difference between my Sultāna and a typist.

Afterword*

Fārigh mujhē na jān ke mānind-e subh-o-mehr
Hai dāgh-e ishq zīnat-e jaib-e kafan hanūz
—GHALIB

I feel like talking to you, my readers, informally today, not in the stiff language of forewords or legalese. Actually, even things which reside in some deeper recess of a person's mind and are meant for his exclusive use often find their way into my short stories, plays and semi-fictional articles, but since they're framed as fiction you take them for fiction.

I feel blue today, strangely weary. I felt the same gloom and weariness of the spirit some four or four and a half years ago when I said goodbye to Bombay, my second home. I was sorry to leave the place where I had spent the most arduous days of my life, the place that had found room for even a tramp like me, a person spurned by his family. That place had whispered to me: Look, you can be happy here whether you make two paisas a day or ten thousand rupees, but if you want to, you can also live here as the unhappiest man on earth. Whatever you do, rest assured, no one here will run you down. There won't be anyone to counsel you either. You'll have to do all the hard work yourself. As far as I'm concerned, it makes no difference whether you sleep on the sidewalk or in some gorgeous mansion, whether you stay or leave. I am where I am, and I plan to stay there.

---

* 'Jaib-e Kafan' appeared in the author's collection *Mantonāma* (Lahore: Sang-e-Meel Publications, 1990), pp. 221–42.

Thanks to my twelve years in Bombay and all that I learned there, I'm now able to survive in Pakistan, and wherever else I might end up next. I'm Bombay on wheels, alive and kicking. I will create a world of my own no matter where I go.

A feeling of dejection swept over me after leaving Bombay. I had friends there whose friendship I'm proud of. I was married there. My first child was born there, as was my second. I earned from as little as a few rupees to tens of thousands there, and spent them. I loved Bombay. I still do. For years I wasn't able to react to the cataclysmic upheavals following the partition of the country in any way other than the most rebellious. Later, I accepted this horrific reality, but I didn't allow hopelessness to come anywhere near me.

I plunged into the bloody sea that one human had created by spilling the blood of another and emerged with a few priceless pearls—pearls of the toil and shame man exerted in spilling the last drop of his brother's blood, of the tears some eyes had shed in their irritation at not being able to extinguish humanity entirely. I have presented these pearls in my book *Siyāh Hāshiye* [Black Margins].

I'm a human, but one who violated humanity, who made extinction the inevitable fate of everyone, who sold human flesh like any other commodity in their shops with ever more garish displays. I'm the same human who rose to the station of prophets and the same human who stained his hands with their blood. I have all the vices and virtues that others have. But believe me, I was pained, greatly pained, when some of my contemporaries laughed at my effort. They called me a joker, a liar, eccentric, unreasonable and reactionary. A dear friend went so far as to accuse me of rummaging through the pockets of corpses and robbing them of their cigarettes, their rings and other such items. This dear fellow even published an open letter to me, which he could just as easily have given to me in person. In it he openly spilled his guts against my *Siyāh Hāshiye*.

I'm a human. I lost my cool. I accumulated filth far greater than his, filth that might have stuck to the faces of my so-called critics for a long time. But reason prevailed; I realized this would be a mistake. Yes, it is human nature to respond with a heavier stone when you've been hit by a rock. No doubt about it. But the better part of wisdom is to conceal your feelings. It is a sign of man's forbearance, his fortitude.

I was angry, not because X had misunderstood me, but because he had doubted my intentions—motivated by nothing more than a desire to appear chic and using a standard that only recognized everything red as pure gold. He had done this at the bidding of a bankrupt and hollow movement that was receiving its marching orders from outside the country.

I was angry at what had happened to these people. What kind of Progressives were these people who were heading straight down the reactionary path? Why did the 'red' they so loved always hasten towards the dark and the macabre? What kind of love of the peasantry was this that impelled them to incite the farmer to demand his wages before he'd even shed one drop of sweat? Why were they so eager to arm themselves with capital while pretending to be fighting against capitalism, to hand over their cherished weapons of sickle and hammer to their opponents? What kind of literary revolution were they planning by devising schemes to transform machines into ghazals and vice versa?

I was angry at their frequent manifestos, long-winded resolutions and effusive statements—the substance of which came straight from the Russian Kremlin to the Bombay Khetwadi and then on to McLeod Road. Such and such Russian poet has said that . . . such and such Russian short story writer has stated . . . such and such Russian intellectual has . . . I was furious. Why don't they ever talk about the land whose air they breathe? If we can no longer produce our own intellectuals, can this state of barrenness be remedied by just spreading red seeds imported from the Soviet Union?

I was angry because no one deigned to listen to me. A confused state of laissez-faire took hold of the country following Partition. People weren't hankering after just evacuee properties—residential houses and mills and what not—but also high positions. They didn't stop to think for a minute that after such a seismic upheaval the situation wasn't likely to remain the same as before. No one could predict with any degree of confidence whether the existing narrow trails would expand into spacious highways or vanish altogether. Nor could a clear idea of the difference between the rule of the Other and the rule of one's own be formed in the ensuing chaos. What kind of atmosphere would it be and how would thoughts and feelings be nurtured in it? What would be the nature of the relationship of the individual and the community with the government? These questions required deep thought and much deliberation, not slavish adherence to foreign prescriptions and precepts. Lamentably, our so-called intellectuals acted very hastily. In their eagerness for leadership they ignored whatever talent they had and left it to rot unutilized.

Initially these progressive custodians of literature decided to prohibit writers of their group from working for or publishing in government publications. I opposed their proposition and reasoned with them, showing how such a decision was manifestly wrong—not just wrong but entirely ridiculous.

It was wrong because it betrayed the fear of the Progressive Writers' Association that their members lacked, or might lack, steadfastness. Then again, such a decision should have been made more appropriately by their opponents, which too I would have considered absurd because no government would choose to do something which ran counter to its own interests.

Our government did resort to the same ridiculous absurdity, but a bit later, after the Progressives had already openly touted their resolution of non-cooperation. The government banned the inclusion of any Progressive thought in their publications and on national radio. Later on, the provisions of the Amrat Dhara Act were invoked to put some Progressives in prison. Government, after all, is another name for foolishness. So I have no wish to comment on the series of stupid moves they made to silence the Progressives.

I feel sorry that Ahmad Nadim Qasimi and Zaheer Kashmiri, two of the most harmless souls one ever saw, whose mental and physical constitutions are incapable of comprehending the true meaning of the word 'conspiracy', were imprisoned uselessly. One of them is fond of making 'brothers', the other 'sisters'. It is mind-boggling how the government managed to detect the odour of some subversive element in this innocent pastime.

Anyway, beside itself with anger, the government thoughtlessly threw them behind bars, handing them over to the barber who would surely disfigure them beyond recognition, so that when they emerged from prison after some time no one could say what sort of creatures they were: bald from head to toe or hairy all over like a chimpanzee. Would they be called 'ghazi' or 'shaheed'? Would they become leaders, or snake-oil pedlars pushing their concoctions with hype and brio to the crowds gathered around them? Would they give up writing poetry and fiction? Or drape their tentacles around literature like the old man of Sinbad's voyages. I'm not mocking them at all. If I were sent to prison,

I would have said the same, or perhaps worse, about myself because I'm much too sensitive.

Well, the government and the band of Progressive writers both fell prey to their own sense of inferiority. I felt sorry about it and still do, though I felt sorrier for the Progressives. They had butted into the government's affairs without rhyme or reason. These amateur pharmacists were blending a remedy for head colds with portions of literature and politics according to a recipe supplied by the Kremlin, but they paid no attention to the patient's temperament or pulse. Well, you know the result. Isn't everyone talking about this stagnation in literature?

I feel terribly gloomy today about how the representative periodicals of the Progressives had to somersault every which way, along with their leaders; how they were obliged to scrape away every last word of their wise counsel, statements and resolutions; and how they had to cook up fresh excuses and apologies to win back the cooperation of the same writers they had earlier blacklisted and condemned.

I feel very gloomy today seeing those who had firmly withheld their cooperation from the government now revising their decision. Why didn't they see that man's struggle to earn a livelihood is central among the fairly expansive orbit of his earthly struggles? Of course our manly courage can scale up to the heights of the Almighty, and we can ensnare even Gabriel in the wastelands of our madness. However, there are times when the only course we have before us is to sing the praises of some stupid nawab for the sake of our stomachs. Of course this is man's greatest tragedy, but this tragedy is another name for being human.

And now all my anger has turned into a gloom of the spirit. I feel distraught, weighed down by anguish and sadness. What I've seen and continue to see only deepens this feeling. I'm exhausted. My life today is rife with difficulties. Even after a grinding day of work, I'm barely able to earn enough for my daily needs. The painful thought that if I were to die suddenly there would be no one to look after my wife and my three little girls gnaws at my heart night and day. Call me whatever you like: a pornographer, terrorist, eccentric, comedian, or even a reactionary, but I'm also a husband and a father. If my wife or one of my daughters were taken ill and I was forced to go door to door begging in order to pay for their proper treatment, it would certainly make my hackles rise. And I also have friends who are in more strained circumstances than I am. It hurts me terribly if I can't help them when I'm most needed. Believe me, I'm anguished to see anyone's, or even my own, head lowered from need. How would I feel if the libraries and the radio opened their doors to my writing after my death, or if my short stories were given the same status the late Iqbal's poetry is being accorded now? Oh, that would put my very soul on edge and make it terribly restless. When I think about that restlessness, I feel infinitely more contented with the way I've been treated so far. May God save me from the termites that will gnaw at my desiccated bones in the grave!

I feel very low today hearing the know-it-all pundits around me declare that literature has stagnated, that it is in decline, that it is in suspension. This sort of talk is the twin of the absurd claim that Islam is in danger. Literature, like Islam, is a self-existent entity. Energy never declines, and is never swept away by stagnation or suspension. The atom's power existed before its discovery and will continue to exist even after. Its disuse or misuse doesn't imply a decline in its power, or its being near death, or having already died.

Literature is as alive and exuberant today as it was before it was discovered. The question of its stagnation or suspension doesn't arise. It is our own stagnation and suspension that we foist upon it.

As to the reasons for this crisis we should try looking not so much in literature as in our own minds. This is not a difficult thing to do. If we ourselves wander off the straight path of literature, we shouldn't say that the path has moved away from us.

Politics has its own place. It's not fair to use literature to get to it. Likewise, it is wrong to use the labyrinthine by-lanes of politics to arrive at a literature worthy of its name.

No matter how much one touts the greatness of Soviet Russian literature, the fact is, it is plain hypocritical. It isn't literature—no, it is not. It is something else. Just look at anything written by a contemporary Russian author.

Literature cannot be monopolized, now or ever. It cannot be made to order by handing out contracts. 'Literature is stagnant' is a sham, just as 'Islam is in danger' is a sham. It is nothing more than a slogan yelled from the top of the minaret until a few months ago by the very same people who proclaimed after Partition that it is the Progressive writers who have saved the honour of literature. The poor were dying but the Progressive writers revived them through the gift of their own blood. Why, then, so soon after the incarceration of a handful of members, has the life of literature been thrown into jeopardy? Isn't it amazing!

I'm very down-spirited today. I was accepted as a Progressive at first; then suddenly I was turned into a reactionary. Now again these muftis are thinking to anoint me a Progressive. And the government, so fond of its counter-fatwas, considers me a die-hard Progressive—a pinko, a communist. And now and then, in extreme irritation, it accuses me of writing smut and drags me to the court. On the other hand, the same government openly advertises in its publications that Saadat Hasan Manto is a great short story writer of our country and that his pen remained active even during the recent cataclysmic period. My sad heart trembles at the thought that this whimsical government might not refrain from pinning some medal on my shroud, which would be the greatest insult to my scarred love.

Since Partition I have presented to you the following books, in quick succession. They will help you understand unequivocally the state of my mind:

1. *Talkh, Tursh, aur Shīrīñ*
2. *Lazzat-e Sañg*
3. *Siyāh Hāshiye*
4. *Khālī Bōtlēñ, Khāli Dibbē*
5. *Ṭhaṇḍā Gōsht*
6. *Namrūd kī Khudā'ī*
7. *Bādshāhat kā Khātima*

And now this, my latest collection. Only two short stories in it, 'Yazīd' and 'San 1919 kī Ēk Bāt', have been published earlier; the rest are entirely new. How long it took to be completed and published can easily be gauged from a perusal of the relevant dates. I had just started on 'Mummy', the last story of the collection, when, on 16 October, the news of the assassination of Khan Liaquat Ali Khan, the prime minister of Pakistan, arrived and greatly upset me. Soon thereafter my second daughter Jajia came down with a terrible case of typhoid. This also kept me agitated for several days, with the result that the completion of the work was delayed.

Foreword*

The first edition of this book [*Chughad*] was published in Bombay. After Partition I handed over the manuscript to Book Publishers Limited and left for Pakistan. From here I wrote to Ali Sardar Jafri, who was then employed at Book Publishers, saying that the only way to hasten the publication of the book was for him to write the foreword and that I would accept whatever he said. He replied:

> Of course, I'll write it with pleasure. However, the book doesn't need a foreword, much less one by me. You are well aware that our literary views are far apart. That aside, I regard you very highly and expect great things from you.

'In that case,' I wrote to Jafri Sahib, 'let the book go without a foreword.' But by then, as became clear from his subsequent letter, he had already written a brief foreword and included it in the book. Regardless of its contents, it is there in the first edition of *Chughad*. However, I've excised it from the present edition, not because I have, God forbid, developed a sudden enmity towards Jafri Sahib or started hating him, but in view of the absurd furore the so-called Progressives of Bombay have raised about my work lately, I didn't think it was proper to have their most active member become an appendix to my 'reactionary' work.

---

* 'Dībācha' appeared in the author's collection *Mantonāma* (Lahore: Sang-e-Meel Publications, 1990), pp. 344–47.

I was still in Bombay when 'Bābū Gōpīnāth', one of the stories of this collection, appeared in the literary magazine *Adab-e Latīf*. All the Progressives praised it to high heaven, even anointing it as the best short story of that year. Ali Sardar Jafri, Ismat Chughtai and Krishan Chandar especially applauded it. Krishan Chandar even gave it a prominent place in 'Hal kē Sā'ē'. Then, all of a sudden—God knows what got into their heads—every single Progressive turned against the story's greatness. First they faulted it in hushed voices and condemned it in whispers. But now every Progressive of India and Pakistan has begun running it down, openly and loudly, as reactionary, immoral, sordid and depraved.

The same treatment was meted out to another of my stories, 'Mērā Nām Rādhā Hai' [My Name is Radha], though when it was first published the Progressives could not stop applauding it, beside themselves with enthusiasm and exhilaration. Anyway, when Ali Sardar Jafri penned his foreword as an offering to 'progressivism', he wrote to me:

> I would like to know your opinion of my foreword. I've written it with much sincerity and love, and I'm now thinking of writing a longish article about your short stories. So far, run-of-the mill people have only reviled you. It is useless to expect anything better from them.

Don't these lines cry out to have every single word in them thrown in the face of all Progressives and let 'reactionism' smile quietly? In the same letter, Ali Sardar went on to say: 'I consider your short story 'Khol-do' [Open It!] a masterpiece of this period.'

The tragedy that befell the Progressives, or perhaps this story, was its publication in *Nuqūsh* (Lahore), under the editorship of His Honour Ahmad Nadim Qasimi—the guru of Pakistani Progressives and the architect of the pithy '*zindagī-āmoz-o-zindagī-āmez adab*'—otherwise it too would have been consigned to the dustbin of 'non-literature,' leaving me gawking at 'progressivism's' red face.

The only reason my book *Siyāh Hāshiye* didn't go down well with the Progressives was that Muhammad Hasan Askari, whom they'd already put on their blacklist, had written its foreword. And so, with his characteristic sincerity and love, Ali Sardar Jafri again wrote to me:

What is this I hear from Lahore that Muhammad Hasan Askari is writing the foreword to some new book of yours? How on earth the two of you could hit it off baffles me. I don't consider Hasan Askari a sincere person at all.

One really must hand it to the Progressives for mounting such an efficient and speedy system of communication. News from here travels in the blink of an eye to Khetwadi's Kremlin with total accuracy. What Ali Sardar Jafri had heard was absolutely correct. The end result was that *Siyāh Hāshiye* had hardly been out before it was condemned and trashed as a bunch of 'reactionary' writing. It is amazing, though, that as Ali Sardar Jafri was drafting his preface for my *Chughad*, it never dawned on him that he and Manto were two mutually exclusive entities and that our literary views were, according to him, far apart. Alas, my Progressive friends are averse to thinking! They consider it a negative act.

Let me present an example of this aversion. The magazine *Saverā*, a publication of Nayā Idāra, which is owned by Nazeer Ahmad Chaudhry, is the 'Mouthpiece of the Progressive Literary Movement'. It has blacklisted me. In its pages I'm routinely dubbed as reactionary, opportunistic, individualistic, hedonistic and escapist. And yet Nayā Idāra advertises one of my books in the following words:

> Saadat Hasan Manto is the standard-bearer of truth. He is armed with the double-edged sword of truth, which he brandishes fearlessly in the thick forests of the government and society, tearing asunder all their veils of hypocrisy and affectation. Abuse is heaped on him, but he smiles. He marches down a path that he alone can travel, impervious to any thought of reward or punishment.

Did I smile on reading this advertisement in the pages of *Saverā*? No, I laughed my head off. Forget the subliminal message, 'it will greatly help the readers', rather think: Aren't the Progressives and their equally progressive publishers travelling along a path which they alone can travel, without caring a fig about their consciences? During the recent Bhopal Conference, Ismat Shahid Latif* valiantly, and at one go, openly disowned any of her stories that didn't measure up to the standard

---

* Ismat Chughtai.

of 'progressivism'. Why don't these progressive publishers take their cue from Ismat's forthrightness? They should burn all the books by 'blacklisted reactionaries'. And if they were to do so, I would surely kiss their hands.

How I Write Stories*

Honourable ladies and gentlemen!

I've been asked to explain how I write stories.

This 'how' is problematic. What can I tell you about how I write stories? It is a very convoluted matter. With this 'how' before me I could say I sit on the sofa in my room, take out paper and pen, utter *bismillah*, and start writing, while all three of my daughters keep making a lot of noise around me. I talk to them as I write, settle their quarrels, make salad for myself, and, if someone drops by for a visit, I offer him hospitality. During all this, I don't stop writing my story.

If I must answer how I write, I would say my manner of writing is no different from my manner of eating, taking a bath, smoking cigarettes, or wasting time.

Now, if one asked *why* I write short stories, well, I have an answer for that. Here it goes:

I write because I'm addicted to writing, just as I'm addicted to wine. For if I don't write a story, I feel as if I'm not wearing any clothes, I haven't bathed, or I haven't had my wine.

The fact is, I don't write stories; stories write me. I'm a man of modest education. And although I have written more than twenty books, there are times when I wonder about this fellow who has written such fine stories—stories that frequently land me in the courts of law.

---

* 'Main Afsāna Kyunkar Likhtā Hūn', from the author's collection *Ūpar, Nīche, aur Darmiyān* (Lahore: Gosha-e Adab, 1990), pp. 237–40.

Without my pen, I'm merely Saadat Hasan, who knows neither Urdu, nor Persian, nor English nor French.

Stories don't reside in my mind; they reside in my pocket, totally unbeknownst to me. Try as hard as I might to strain my mind, hoping for some story to pop out, trying equally hard to be a short story writer, smoke cigarette after cigarette, but my mind fails to produce a story. Exhausted, I lie down like a woman who cannot conceive a baby.

As I've already collected the remuneration in advance for a promised but still unwritten story, I feel quite vexed. I keep turning over restlessly in bed, get up to feed my birds, push my daughters on their swing, collect trash from the house, pick up little shoes scattered throughout the house and put them neatly in one place—but the blasted short story taking it easy in my pocket refuses to travel to my mind, which makes me very edgy and agitated.

When my agitation peaks, I dash to the toilet. That doesn't help either. It is said that every great man does all his thinking in the toilet. Experience has convinced me that I'm no great man, because I can't think even inside a toilet. Still, I'm a great short story writer of Pakistan and Hindustan—amazing, isn't it?

Well, all I can say is that either my critics have a grossly inflated opinion of me, or else I'm blinding them in the clear light of day, or casting a spell over them.

Forgive me, I went to the toilet . . . The plain fact is, and I say this in the presence of my Lord, I haven't the foggiest idea how I write stories.

Often when my wife finds me feeling totally lost and out of my wits, she says, 'Don't think, just pick up your pen and start writing.'

So I follow her advice, pick up my pen and start writing, my mind totally blank but my pocket crammed full of stories. And all of a sudden a story pops out on its own.

This being the case, I'm forced to think of myself as not so much a writer of stories but more as a pickpocket who picks his own pocket and then hands over its contents to you. You can travel the whole world but you won't find a greater idiot than me.

Marginotions[*]

Muhammad Hasan Askari

A new literary movement has added some priceless gems to Urdu fiction in the past ten years. However, incontrovertibly, much of the new short story seems to be inspired not so much by the writer's inner creative passion as by external conditions and events, regardless of whether they had relevance for the writer personally or his milieu. Perhaps it was the result of the then prevalent belief that man's inner life could by changed simply by changing his outside conditions. So this is how it has been generally. Whenever our writers have slumped creatively, they have not blamed themselves for it or worried about rekindling their creative fires by internal effort; rather, they have sat back smugly, attributing their lack of creativity to the absence of external events requiring expression in literary creation. Some six or seven years ago I heard an Urdu short story writer, who had gained considerable popularity by writing stories about poverty, slavery and Kashmir, say that spring tide would break over literature should the Japanese invade India and cause a lot of commotion.

God has an uncanny way of making wishes come true—the Japanese did not attack India but famine did. One became rich by selling rice on the black market, another amassed heaps of popularity by churning out story after story about the calamity. Nothing wrong about it: whatever happens in the world happens for the good of man.

---

[*] 'Haashiya-aaraa'i', his preface to *Siyāh Hāshiye* (Black Margins), in Saadat Hasan Manto, *Mantonuma* (Lahore: Sang-e-Meel Publications, 1991), pp. 745–52.

Famine, in those days, became such a hot and hallowed subject that even students dropped writing about their sexual experiences in favour of the starving humanity, arrogantly confident that no editor of a literary periodical would dare turn down their work, and if he did, he would be chastised for being stony-hearted and utterly insensitive. In short, our writers had a field day thanks to the Bengal famine. Story after story popped out—events, emotions, everything was there for the taking, so why toil over it.

The fury of famine had barely subsided when the seamen's strike broke out; elsewhere a riot erupted during victory celebrations. Well, one thing or the other kept the business going. And when 1947 rolled along, it was like an unbidden windfall from God Almighty. You could write a tragic story, a comic essay, grate your teeth over man's life, or expose the machinations of the colonial powers—anything and everything was game. If you had had enough of these, well, generate some heat by stories of the violation of women's bodies, peppering the accounts now and then with a dash of uncommon incidents of human kindness and compassion in the midst of crass brutality, only to wonder at the end with utter naivety: Have Hindus and Muslims banished their reason? Brothers until yesterday, why are they so hell-bent on spilling each other's blood today? As for the danger that you may be taking sides, that's no problem at all. If five Hindus were butchered in the beginning of the story, make sure that you even out the number of the slain on either side—kill off five Muslims towards the end of the story. The blame for the atrocities should be distributed equally. The crux is this: you should prove your love for humanity, pure heartedness, impartiality and desire for peace, without offending the sensibilities of anyone.

If someone is a skilled tightrope walker, doesn't he have a claim on our admiration? Shouldn't we praise him? After all, expressing one's noble sentiments and thereby stirring up the noble sentiments of others, too, is a way of serving the cause of humanity. The trouble with noble sentiments, though, is that they can't create literature. I don't have some imaginary and inoperable criterion before me as I say this. The fact is literature on *fasādāt* (riots) has failed to abide by the very conditions it has imposed upon itself, the primary condition being that writers will speak the truth, nothing but the truth. At the same time, they are worried about offending Hindus and Muslims. Impartiality is taken to mean that neither party be portrayed as more culpable than the other. This literature wants to condemn *zulm* (inequity), cruelty and brutality, but shies away from calling inequity what it is. No, it doesn't want to assume that responsibility. We do not demand this kind of truth–falsehood from literature as we do from books on history, sociology or politics. Our demand from a writer is not that he should speak truth about an ideology or the external world but that he should speak truth about himself. Writers on riots may have written truthfully about the whole world, but they certainly haven't about themselves. They go to great lengths to hide their natural inclinations and partiality, although it is a biological necessity for such feelings to surge during traumatic upheavals such as Partition. If these writers truly want to make their stories meaningful in human terms, it is imperative that they admit their own human weaknesses before all else. One can't create true literature by looking away from truths and falsehoods within oneself. Such looking-away can produce only popular literature because the common reader too only wants to assure himself that his noble sentiments haven't deserted him.

Actually, literature isn't at all concerned with who is oppressing and who is not. Its main concern is to observe the inner and external attitude of the oppressor and the oppressed when an act of outrage is being committed. External acts of aggression and their equally aggressive complements are entirely meaningless insofar as literature is concerned. Our writers look only at the social aspect of tyranny, turning a blind eye to its effect on the inner lives of the oppressed and the oppressor. Guns and swords abound in their stories, but never the living hand that pulls the trigger or the equally alive chest that receives the bullet or the wound. God forbid, it is not my intention to question their sincerity. Certainly some are truly good-hearted and good-intentioned. However, ordinary good heartedness and good intention perform no useful function in literature. They wish to incite emotions of intense abhorrence towards aggression among readers, by portraying external acts of inequity. But unless we know the human background of an act, its mere external demonstration is unlikely to produce any long-lasting, palpable and deeply meaningful reaction in us. We can love or hate humans, not oppressors and the oppressed.

One method used by our writers on riots to excite revulsion against tyranny is to create dread among readers by enacting graphic scenes of horror before them. But the carnage of 1947 is so fresh in our mind, its devastation so vivid in the memory of those who witnessed or heard about it from their close friends, that the mere recital of an inventory of atrocious acts leaves them cold. Their nerves are no longer frayed when they read about the rape of a few women or the slaughter of some children. This period is so extraordinary that singular acts of oppression have become commonplace. Exceptional events no longer register with people or even arouse their curiosity, let alone their moral sense. So those riot stories weren't literature, but the pity is they didn't fulfil their social purpose in a fitting manner either: what they offered didn't even amount to news.

Manto, too, has written on communal riots: comic vignettes and short fictional pieces. A gross error on my part to say 'on communal riots.' His stories are not about communal riots; they are about the human beings who appear in them in different forms, as prostitutes, as spectators, and so on. But they are basically humans—the only difference being that they have been portrayed as either oppressors or oppressed—and communal riots in particular circumstances. Manto hasn't bothered about a social purpose at all. If man could be reformed by exhortation alone, Mr Gandhi wouldn't have lost his life. Manto nurtures no grandiose notions about the efficacy of short stories to reform nor has he saddled himself with such a responsibility. True, he narrates some incidents, but is careful to steer away from judging them as good or bad. He doesn't curse the oppressor nor does he shed tears for his victim, or label the oppressor as necessarily evil and the oppressed as a good person. The communal riots that have taken place on the Indian subcontinent are an exceedingly complex phenomenon, enmeshed as they inextricably are in not just a history that goes back quite a few centuries but also an equally-long future. The nearness of the events doesn't allow one to label them good or evil so flippantly. A sensible writer at least cannot stoop to the level of politicians and issue indictments about such harrowing incidents. Manto has done what any honest—honest not in its political meaning— writer who is writing in the immediate aftermath of those harrowing conditions and events ought to do. Manto has entirely flung the question of good and evil out of the discussion. His perspective is neither political, nor sociological nor moral. If anything it is literary and creative. He has only tried to see the relation of an act of oppression with the different demands of the personality of the oppressor and his victim. What other impulses, besides the desire to tyrannize impels an oppressor? How much space does inequity claim for itself in the oppressor's cerebrum? Does he lose interest in other activities of life or does he participate in them? Manto excites neither emotions of compassion nor of anger or hate. He only invites the reader to reflect in a literary and creative manner on man's psyche, his character and his personality. If he does wish to excite an emotion, it is the one that behooves a true artist, viz., a feeling of infinite wonder and curiosity about life. In the entire corpus on communal riots the only thing that merits to be called a human document are these stories.*

And yet, inasmuch as Manto's stories are genuine literary creations, they also do not fail to affect us morally, though this was not Manto's primary purpose. Creating was all he was after. What surprises us during unusual circumstances is not the extraordinary character of events and acts but, rather, very ordinary and everyday things. Perhaps it is neither surprising nor unexpected that after killing two hundred women and children a killer would string their skulls to wear as a trophy around his neck. When killing becomes commonplace it fails to terrify, but when we watch the killer's anxiety over dirtying the train compartment with the blood and gore of his victims, we feel a disquieting chill run down our spine. Murderers' uninterrupted killing does not create horror; what does create horror is that such sticklers for cleanliness could kill with impunity. Ultimately, it is the juxtaposition of opposites, of paradoxes, of contradictions that confers upon a piece its ultimate meaningfulness. The most extraordinary acts during extraordinary conditions tell us only that those conditions can reduce man to the state of animal. But his preoccupation with very ordinary things as he commits an exceptional act gives us a deeper and a more fundamental insight about him: he is both human and animal at the same time, all the time. The frightening aspect here is how he could bear being animal in spite of his humanity, which is not without its comforting aspect: with all his bestiality man can never entirely rid himself of his humanity.

Both aspects—the frightening and comfort-giving—exist side by side in Manto. Man in these jocular vignettes appears in all his helplessness, folly, refinement and purity. Manto's laughter is dipped in vitriol; nonetheless it consoles us too. It is no small achievement to

* Those in Manto's *Siyāh Hāshiye* (Black Margins) and other works.

say out loud that even during extraordinary conditions man's interest in very ordinary things and his equally mundane inclinations simply couldn't be suppressed. Manto neither portrays man as oppressor nor as oppressed. He only points out that man is a strange creature, a compound of discordant elements, and then he keeps quiet.

This, in a manner of speaking, does create quite a poignant feeling of despair. However, if you look at man's contradictory nature closely, it will not fail to inspire a feeling of true optimism either. Had he been only entirely good or entirely bad, he would be extremely dangerous. What gives us hope is that one can't be sure about man—he can be good, but then again he can be bad. Additionally, he is caught within the bonds of his humanity; he can't become an angel, any more than Satan can. However much he may strive to become exceptional, the demands of everyday life will drag him back to his limits. The power of ordinary quotidian life is such that if he cannot become an exceedingly good man, neither can he be an extraordinarily bad one. This ordinary life will always straighten out his crookedness and knock him back into shape.

The most prominent merit of these stories is the acknowledgment of precisely this power and greatness of quotidian existence. Other writers endeavour to shepherd Hindus and Muslims back to the Straight Path by shaming them. However, after we are done reading their short stories, we are never sure whether their exhortation will bear fruit or not. Manto, on the other hand, wishes to shame no one nor drag anyone to the Straight Path. He tells mankind, with a highly ironical smile, that try as hard as you may to wander off the Straight Path, you are unlikely to go very far. In that sense, Manto displays an unfailing confidence in the nature of man, while others insist on seeing man only in a particular light. Before accepting him they foist some conditions on him. Manto accepts him in his true colours, regardless of what they may be. He has seen that man's humanity is so strong that his barbarity simply cannot extinguish it. It was this humanity in which he had placed his trust.

These tiny droll vignettes of Manto are the most harrowing and most optimistic piece of writing to emerge in the entire corpus on communal riots. His horror and optimism have nothing to do with the horror and optimism of politicians or the pure-hearted servants of humanity. They are the horror and optimism of a writer. Disputation and reflection play no part in them. If anything does, it is a solid creative experience. Which is Manto's singular distinction.

Communal Riots and Our Literature[*]

Muhammad Hasan Askari

The communal riots of 1947 constitute an enormous national tragedy for Muslims. They have touched every one of us, some more than others, but nobody has escaped their effect. Perhaps such an event is unprecedented in world history. Because of the proximity of the incident, many authors wrote about the riots as a duty, others as a harrowing personal experience. In any case, in the space of the past ten or eleven months a goodly number of short stories and poems have appeared on the subject. Some readers find them satisfactory, others complain that our writers have ignored the Muslim point of view, and still others feel that it is best that writers steer clear of adopting an unambiguous point of view and just concentrate on the hope for a glorious future for mankind.

Well, there are opinions and opinions—always. However, the questions that needed to be asked have not been asked: Can such events, in and of themselves and purely as events, ever be the subject of literature, quite apart from their importance in the history of mankind or of a nation? What effect might they have in shaping life several centuries hence? What stimulation might they provide for someone to reflect on human nature or other major questions? And, how might they help a philosopher reaching a theoretical conclusion?

Even though it may be hard, we must put our personal and collective afflictions aside when looking for answers to such questions. After all,

[*] Muhammad Hasan Askarī, 'Fasādāt aur Hamārā Adab', (Aligarh: Educational Book House, 1976), pp.139–49. Dates of authors added by the translator.

writers are a hard-hearted lot. Human history goes back a few million years. God alone knows what all has happened and what may yet come to pass. If literature should show deference, how many individuals or groups should it show deference to—is there no end? If we want to find a truly satisfactory answer to the question, we need to put aside our sense of victimhood, at least for a while.

We can make our exploration somewhat easier by picking a similar cataclysmic event and looking at the literary responses to it. The First World War produced a lot of literature. How much of it is alive today? W.B. Yeats (1865–1939), with the ruthlessness and granite objectivity of a true writer in regard to The First World War, unequivocally stated that he had not included a single poem about the war in his new collection because passive sympathy is not a subject of literature. It is worth remembering here that another poet who wrote about the war stated in no uncertain terms that the balance of his poetry sprang from its pain.

The point is this: literature articulates emotional experiences and passivity is not an experience, though it may be called a 'feeling'. If riots mean murder and mayhem and carnage, physical pain and misery, the inescapable conclusion is that they cannot be viable subjects of literature, regardless of all the anguish we may feel on account of our emotional attachment. The most significant literature about national catastrophes and the physical suffering of an entire group of people is found in some parts of the Old Testament. But what makes it literature is not their account of the slaughter and plunder of countless Jews, the rape of their women, or the banishment of a whole nation. What makes it literature is something quite different. Jews believed that they were God's chosen ones and the object of His love and favour, and yet they had to endure all this. The telling contradiction between belief and reality caused immense spiritual torment for the Jews and their inner selves were ravaged by the conflict between doubt and certainty, hope and hopelessness, fear and boldness, rebellion and loyalty. It was this complex spiritual experience of the Jewish people that conferred upon the lament of their Hebrew prophets the status of the loftiest literature. Hence, the subject of these sections of the Old Testament is not the trials and tribulations of a group but its collective experience.

Of course this does not mean that writers shouldn't write about such events even though they fall outside the thematic parameters of literature. Writers are not producing literature all the time. They have two kinds of responsibilities: as writers and as members of a group. No doubt the first of these is a writer's primary responsibility. However, there are times when a writer is obliged to attend to his second responsibility, which does not necessarily contradict the primary at all.

To understand this better let's consider the attitude of writers of different nationalities during the Second World War. In Russia, writers took to their secondary responsibility with such gusto and verve that they quite forgot their primary responsibility; indeed they started calling the product of their secondary responsibility pure literature. During the war years the duty of a Russian writer was defined as praising the nation, the armed forces, the character of their soldiers and presenting the Germans in a negative light in all respects. While it is true that the Russian nation faced a massive catastrophe and whatever help its writers offered was perfectly understandable, it is unbecoming of a writer to ignore his primary allegiance and become a slave to a secondary purpose, regardless of how noble that purpose might be. Even if we want Pakistani literature to reflect the highest ideals of Islam, this Russian attitude is hardly the one to light the way. Muslims are exhorted not to hesitate to testify against themselves if the situation calls for it, so even from an Islamic point of view, literature that praises Muslims cannot be acceptable. The Russian paradigm is not just bankrupt as a model, it is downright misleading.

British writers provide our second example. Since military duty had become incumbent during the war, writers were also conscripted. One had to fly bombers; the other had to join the fire brigade. It is entirely possible that they acquitted themselves willingly and with an unflinching sense of duty, but, as far as I am aware, none of them, at least no sensible writer among them, tried to serve their nation through their pen. One might say that this was perhaps due to the fact that the Germans were unable to set foot in England and the population was spared the humiliation which became the lot of some Russian regions and France. Had this been England's lot too, they would likely have written something in defence of their country. At any rate, the war affected their lives by filling it with a sense of vacuity and desolation. The birds, the flowers were all gone; dear ones were lost and scattered; and incredible restrictions were placed on personal freedom. The loss of mental and personal comforts tormented them, such that they began to moan in memory of the old life that was so exuberant and full of gaiety. In short, the attitude of British writers was quite passive. Such passivity cannot create a vibrant literature. Mere feelings of annoyance, dissatisfaction and malaise cannot serve literature for long. Even crazy, intense hatred is more productive than such passivity. So while one can praise British writers for keeping their true writerly status intact even as they actively served the nation, one must also admit that the kind of intellectual and emotional experience they went through was not terribly worthwhile from a strictly literary point of view. Even as they helped the nation, their minds were never free from the fear of further restrictions that the country might impose on their freedom in the days to come. This attitude betrays a lack of confidence in their status as writers. The thought of what kind of treatment the country might subject them to in the future should not have bothered them while they were serving it. They should have resolved instead that if, after the war, the nation did impose restrictions on its writers, they would fight *against* the nation just as energetically and relentlessly. British writers, at least, should have considered literature important enough to defend it without any fear of the consequences, but they admitted defeat without putting up a fight. They just assumed that if the nation treated them severely, they would find themselves entirely defenceless.

In contrast, French writers adopted a very balanced and dignified attitude. They did not sacrifice either of their responsibilities. This is because they never confused the two responsibilities or lost sight of the difference between them. It is true that, just as the war started, one or two major writers left France thinking they had no country, they were neither for France nor for Germany. But serious writers did not call their intentions into question, nor think of them as cowards or traitors; on the contrary, they continued to respect them. Apart from this smattering, the rest of the writers opposed the Germans in every way possible, even inciting people to rebel. In short, they did not flinch from rendering whatever assistance they could in their nation's hour of need. At least the major writers, in spite of their passion for their country, did not allow themselves to betray for a moment the ideals and values they had professed all along, or consider themselves free from their obligation to literature after they had served the nation, or regard as literature something they had only written to arouse a feeling of freedom among the people. The following minor incident is revealing of the mental equilibrium of the French writers. To resist the Germans and to continue their literary activity during this cataclysmic period, some writers started producing a series of underground books with the title *Les* Éditions *de Minuit*. When France became free, these writers were given a major literary award but they declined to accept it saying that everything they had written was simply to serve the nation. It was not literature, nor had they intended it as literature, so how could they accept a literary award? During the war even French writers who were far removed from politics and considered devotees of 'pure literature' wrote propaganda. André Gide (1869–1951), who never shied away from speaking the truth, not even when it would have been prudent and expedient to do so, and who always preferred a reclusive life over fanfare and hullabaloo, was so overcome by freedom that he burst forth from his quiet corner, though he still kept praising the Germans. French writers participated wholeheartedly in their country's fight for freedom, but dissociated themselves from politics and returned to their writing as soon as the war ended. While the country was struggling to stay alive, they did not allow literature to get in the way of their national duty, but when that deathly moment had passed they did not allow any kind of politics to strangle literature either. Today, when writers everywhere are wondering what to write and what not to write—and who knows whether an atomic bomb might just do away with the world tomorrow—French writers continue their creative work with supreme indifference, as though they are immortal.

Studying these three attitudes vis-à-vis death and destruction closely, I seem to like that of the French writers best. And really, what other attitude could there be for a true writer in the face of national catastrophe. When the country's life is threatened, a writer reacts no differently than a taxi driver. The country can enlist both, and neither should hesitate to render assistance. But once that perilous moment has passed, it is time for a writer to become indifferent to the country. In ordinary circumstances, a writer belongs only to his literary vocation. Even the mightiest power cannot demand his loyalty. In short, a writer must know precisely how to act at a given time—as a citizen or as a writer.

Unfortunately this difference is not clearly understood in Urdu. Our criticism keeps confusing the two roles of the writer. When it is demanded of the writer to write about the riots, it is never made clear in which of his two capacities he is expected to approach the subject—as an ordinary citizen or as a writer. As a writer he cannot write about the riots, simply because riots are not a viable literary subject, but as an ordinary citizen he can, though in that case he will be writing from a particular point of view, which will be entirely unliterary. He will be adopting some political or social point of view and promoting it in his writing. This is not such a bad thing. I have already accepted that there are times when a writer should not shy away from offering non-literary assistance. The trouble arises when our writers who have produced fiction about the riots insist on holding on to a literary point of view. If some noble sentiment has compelled them to adopt a particular position, they should not be ashamed of owning up to that position.

Let's now look at Urdu short stories that deal with the riots to see what kind of political or social outlook they espouse. Our evaluative standard will be to explore whether a writer has distorted reality in adopting his specific point of view. Does he believe what he says? For even when someone writes for a non-literary purpose, he cannot be absolved of the responsibility to speak the truth. A writer does not serve the nation by supporting it with lies; rather he serves it through writing that inspires certainty and confidence in the populace when the nation is facing a critical moment, and he believes his nation is in the right. Regardless of which point of view is adopted, a writer has to speak the truth in all circumstances. We shall employ this touchstone in our analysis of Urdu short stories on the riots. So far, the bulk of such stories more or less support a few specific ideas. The basic theme is that the barbarity witnessed during the riots was terribly heinous. The purport of such stories is to create aversion towards that barbarity and, along with it, explore its cause. Generally such barbarism is not found among humans; it was a product of the political conditions and the hatred for which the British were responsible. They had created it to promote their own political interests. The partition of India was one of their machinations. Had there been no partition, there would have been no rioting. Hindus and Muslims would have lived together as brothers. It is hoped that this hatred will soon evaporate and brothers will again embrace each other. Actually, some writers believe that India and Pakistan will again become one country. In such stories the writer makes every effort not to assign blame to either of the two protagonists and pegs it, instead, on the English. The result is that atrocities are shown in equal measure on both sides, without the least regard for what transpired in East Punjab—one would search a dictionary in vain to find the right words to describe it.

Well then, this is more or less the intellectual background of these short stories. Their conceptual webbing is so weak that the writer himself would hardly believe it. Only a sly or artless person would believe that the hatred was merely an offshoot of British politics. Even if we suppose the writer's intention is pure, the fact that he himself does not believe what he is recording, and that he knows he is deluding himself, let alone others, still remains. This kind of writing, all of it, lacks honesty. It is lifeless and hollow, devoid even of a modicum of rhetorical eloquence because the entire conceptual framework is a fabrication. These stories are not only false; they have a dangerous aspect to them. They are bubbling with vitriolic propaganda against Muslims and Pakistan. It is possible all of this is unintentional and quite innocent, but the cumulative effect does go against Muslims. For one thing, Muslims are blamed disproportionately for causing the riots; for another, Partition is identified as the root cause of unrest and anomie, while the fact is that Partition, that is, the establishment of Pakistan, has been the most cherished political ideal of Muslims. These stories attempt to create scepticism among Muslims with regard to the basic principles behind the creation of Pakistan.

Our writers (that is, those who support Pakistan) have made no reasonable attempt to counter this 'literary' onslaught. After all, we might also try, at least now and then, to serve the nation a bit, but this does not mean that we should malign India and spread intolerance towards it. Let others indulge in name-calling. We should mind our own business. All we want from our writers is for them to tell us what we have experienced and why. We do not need elegies and laments about the hundreds of thousands of Muslims who were massacred. In and of itself, even the death of lakhs of people does not mean much. Indeed, if even fifty lakh of our men die as self-respecting human beings battling tyrants, this is something to celebrate. It would, however, be a tragedy if even five of our men fled the battlefield to save themselves. We only want our writers to subject our characters to a relentless scrutiny and tell us what our tragedy has been. Tell us: Does our character measure up to our traditions? We do expect at least this bit of national service from our writers. Not a critique of others but of our own nation.

Alas, thus far our writers have not acquitted themselves of this responsibility. Just one little book, recently published, is all there is to show, Qudratullāh Shahāb's (1917–86) *Yaā Khudaā!* [Oh, God!]. This is an invaluable work of short fiction, and I am inclined to go so far as to recommend it to every single literate Pakistani as a *must-read.* It begins with a preface by Mumtaaz Shirin (1924–73) in which she has analysed literature focusing on the riots. She has demonstrated how writers, swept away by the wrong kind of humanity and justice, have tended to lie even to themselves and have deliberately avoided presenting the reality they experienced and observed, thus harming both literature and Pakistan, because some people are spreading propaganda against Pakistan in the guise of literature. Shirin Sahiba must be complimented for her frankness and intellectual honesty. Shahāb Sahib does not depict an act of human compassion in his story. He has not called the atrocities and cruelty committed by others to account as much as he has the perverseness of Pakistanis themselves. If his book is against anyone, it is the Pakistanis. The tragic story of its female protagonist Dilshād is not drawn from the barbarity of the Sikhs alone, her real tragedy lies in finding Pakistanis so terribly different from what she had imagined them to be. Shahāb Sahib has portrayed this tragic aspect of her life with rare artistic finesse. Whatever vitriol he could pack into his irony is expended on himself, not on others. The book is not devoid of a certain measure of 'sentimentality', but since we are examining it from the perspective of 'goal-oriented literature', such an objection would be out of place here. Shahāb Sahib has been both daring and honest in his criticism of the moral character of Pakistanis. If Pakistani writers continue with the same fearlessness and honesty with which Pakistani literature is beginning, I see a great future for literature in Pakistan.

A second sign for Pakistan's possibly great literary future comes from the short stories of Saadat Hasan Manto (1912–1955) that are written against the backdrop of the communal riots. In truth, they are not about the riots at all; if anything, they are about 'man'—man in particular circumstances. I feel a sense of pride in discovering that it is a Pakistani writer who has risen above the others in treating the experiences of the riots in a befitting literary manner, diverting his mind from creating senstionalism to produce a true literary work. Rising above all manner of interests, Mano has only sought human meaning and truth—which is precisely what literature is all about.

Recounting Irregular Verbs and Counting She-Goats: Manto and His Alleged Obscenity

Muhammad Umar Memon

Saadat Hasan Manto's non-fictional piece "Iṣmat-Farōshī"—selling of virtue: prostitution—is an impassioned defence of women who practice the world's oldest profession. He goes into great detail arguing vigorously for prostitution's similarity to every other profession, and hence, deserving of respect. We do not look down on a typist, or even a sweeper woman, why should we ride roughshod over a bawd? All three do what they do in order to earn a living.[*]

No exceptional intelligence is required to detect in the back of this almost pathological engagement with prostitutes, Manto's defence of himself against frequent charges of obscenity. (I say pathological for good reason: Manto not only wrote a goodly number of stories in which the vaishiya occupies centre stage, he also revisited her in quite a few of his articles, as if he was obsessed with, indeed fixated on this much maligned being.) The Karachi judge Mehdi Ali Siddiqi, in whose court Manto was tried for 'Upar, Neeche, aur Darmiyan' (Upper, Lower, Middle), considered him 'the greatest Urdu short story writer after Munshi Premchand'[†] but nevertheless fined him twenty-five rupees

[*] Saadat Hasan Manto, *Manto ke Mazāmeen* (Lahore: Idāra-e Adabiyāt-e Nau, 1966), pp. 155–72.

[†] Mehdi Ali Siddiqi, 'Manto aur Maiñ', in *Dastāvez* (June 1982), p. 185.

for the offence, which infuriated Manto. Later, in a friendly meeting, Manto asked the judge how the fine reconciled with 'greatest writer, etc.' The judge replied that he would give him the reason at a later time. And he did. By then Manto was dead, perhaps being repeatedly grilled by the inquisitors Munkar and Nakeer of the Divine Supreme Court.

Where Ghulam Abbas could get away by writing his masterly suggestive 'Aanandi' without stepping on the toes of the ever-vigilant law, Manto was dragged to the court on a charge of obscenity for a number of his stories. But, even if one subjected Manto's so-called 'obscene' stories to the harshest scrutiny, one would come away terribly disappointed, unable to find anything remotely smutty. (In Judge Siddiqi's words, 'He hadn't used a single obscene word in the story ['Upar, Neeche, aur Darmiyan'], which is absolutely true' (187)). Such stories do not dwell on the sex act and its titillating details, but simply use lovemaking to underscore some aspect of the character's mind and personality. Not a whiff of a desire to excite or inflame the reader's passion is noticeable in those of Manto's stories characterized as obscene. Take, for instance, 'Thanda Gosht' (literally, cold meat). The language of the back-and-forth between Kalwant Kaur and Eshar Singh might appear to contradict what I have said, but only if the end of the story is thrown overboard. However, the power of the story's denouement, which does not derive from sex, breaks upon the reader's senses with such overwhelming force that he can't even think of anything else. Besides, the language of the couple swings perfectly with the personality of the characters. It is the very idea of promiscuity that raises the hackles of 'righteous' people. And relations between the lawfully married—though they can be as stormy and gratifying as anything with a prostitute—are not something you talk about. You just do it, in the privacy of your bedroom, or wherever else its indomitable force overtakes you. Chances are, God will even reward you for it. (Marry and be fruitful, something like that—remember?)

While a goodly number visited prostitutes, and no power was ever able to root out this 'vice' from society, words such as *tawaif, vaishiya, kasbi, randi, rakhel* and what have you, were taboo in polite society. Now, it was a different matter if in a different city while on a debating contest tour, students of the team didn't fail to scout out its red-light district.

Manto's problem, if it was a problem at all, was his straight thinking, and even more, his straight-talking. He didn't care about such taboos.

If people made love, then there was nothing wrong in talking about it, especially when the subject of his stories was not the act but what lay behind it in the protagonist's psyche. According to the aforementioned judge, '[Manto] told me that the story in question was to a large extent based on real events. So if it was obscene, there was little he could do about it. Contemporary society was itself obscene. He merely portrays what he sees . . .' (187). Which made the judge conclude, 'Precisely at that moment the realization hit me in all its intensity that this man was a true artist. Manto didn't have the foggiest idea that he had written anything obscene; he had merely written a short story' (186).

A few years ago I read Tahar Ben Jelloun's novel *Corruption*.* The subject of this fictional piece is familiar to South Asians, who daily witness the myriad forms of this abominable practice in their national life. The novel contains numerous graphic descriptions of the love life of a lawfully wedded couple. How graphic? To give you a foretaste of what you will find there, here are a few lines of the intimacy of this lawfully wedded couple:

Was it love? My shyness, my hang-ups, and my seriousness were handicaps to knowing the truth. Now, I know that I desired her physically. At the beginning of our marriage we spent a lot of time making love. What was surprising was that she went wild in bed. She made love with her entire body. One day, from underneath the bed, she pulled out the book of Sheikh Nafzaouvi, a manual of Muslim erotology, and decided that for one month we were going to execute every position described by the sheikh, twenty-nine in all. It was funny: we made love with a manual in front of us. She knew this book by heart and recited entire passages to me. I memorized a few names of positions I found comical, like 'black-smith's copulation,' 'the camel's hump,' 'Archimedes' vice,' and so on. Why the black-smith? At a certain moment, while the woman is on her back, 'her knees raised toward her chest so that her vulva is exposed, the man executes the movements of copulation, then removes his member and slides it between the woman's thighs, like the black-smith removing the red-hot iron from the fire . . .' (p. 10).

* Translated from the French by Carol Volk (New York: The New Press, 1995).

Far be it from Manto to use such graphic language, or even the language used by Mir Dard and Momin Khan Momin in their masnavīs, which Manto has cited elsewhere* as telling specimens of what is called 'obscenity'. But even in *Corruption*, this minor detail, like so many others, tells the reader something about the inner workings of the protagonist's mind—a simple, upright man who would not accept a bribe, in any form or fashion, because such practices went against his conscience, his innate sense of moral fairness. By the time we finish the novel, the minuscule details of his married life are entirely forgotten, submerged, as it were, in the trials and tribulations which Mourad, a decent, honest man, must go through in order to live a decent, honest life. Then again, reference to conjugal intimacy is not thrown into the novel merely wilfully, nor for titillation. Mourad has come to doubt whether it was he who wanted to marry his wife or she who had trapped him using cunning and wile. The doubt has surfaced because she, a competitive, ambitious woman, pining to live a luxurious life and keep up with the Joneses, never fails to hold him responsible for their modest style of living, insinuating in so many ways that he ought to adopt the ways of the world, of his colleagues—i.e., start accepting bribes.

Which, of course, is not the case with Aziz Ahmad's short story 'Pagdandī' (literally, foot trail),† where it is hard to see Azad, the protagonist who is studying in Paris, as anything other than a sex maniac, forever chasing after young women. Although in his later years Aziz Ahmad did quite a bit to redeem himself by writing on Muslim intellectual history, it is hard to miss an undercurrent of sexuality qua sexuality in some of his earlier fictional work. Anyway, faking love, Azad finally gets what he wanted. He takes Yvonne for an outing to a small village on the banks of the Seine, some twenty miles from Paris. As they are walking on a foot trail, Yvonne censures him for being an incorrigible materialist.

'Revolutionaries are materialists too,' he said and kissed her again.
This time she melted completely. He thought that perhaps no one

---

* See, 'Mujhe Bhi Kuchh Kahnā Hai' in the author's collection *Mantonumā* (Lahore: Sang-e Meel Publications, 1991), 732–42.

† Translated as 'The Foot Trail' by Muhammad Umar Memon in *The Annual of Urdu Studies* 25 (2010), 194–204.

had kissed her so passionately before, no one had taken such liberties with her body. He knew that at this moment her mind was completely incapable of dealing with the complexities of revolution, materialism, communism, love, and emotions. What was evident, though, was that her warm, young flesh was trembling with excitement. He didn't let the opportunity slip. He lifted her in his arms, quickly found a spot in the thicket, gently laid her down and started to unbutton her pale yellow jacket. He caressed her breasts, which resembled pink blossoms among the lush green trees. Then he covered her whole body with his like a stretch of cloud spreading itself over a clump of flourishing trees.

Later, when he helped her get up from the bed of grass he felt a strange feeling of satisfaction wash over him. This girl was not a virgin, and he was not the first man in her life. Some other comrade, some other revolutionary and materialist had kissed her before, taken liberties with her body and accepted her virginity as a tribute (p. 202).

Lyricism aside, 'comrade', 'revolutionary', 'materialism', 'communism'—the familiar Progressive jargon is all here, and serves no useful purpose, except *samañ-bandī* (atmospherics), if that can be a purpose, or simply an act to use Yvonne for his own pleasure. The story doesn't move beyond lovemaking, minus the love. Yvonne, too, is a terribly immature, indecisive, naïve and confused girl, with no ability to fathom the impulses of her body. Then again, perhaps she is none of these and this is only how the narrator chooses to see her; after all, he too is an Indian. The story tells us precious little about the ideological underpinnings of this self-conceited, self-obsessed protagonist. What it does tell us, though, is something we can well do without, for if we reflect a bit more, a none-too-wholesome window will burst open to reveal the preoccupations of a flamboyant scion blowing his parents' money in Europe not on study but on 'skirt-chasing'. The only image of the protagonist that is formed in our minds after we are finished reading the story is that of a young Indian man desperately trying to bed down with a white European woman, with the belief, rampant among the élite of the South Asian subcontinent back in pre-Partition days (and maybe even now), that European women are promiscuous and easy to get. Now, this is what Manto would unhesitatingly call 'obscene'.

After this brief excursus, here interposed to explain Manto's preoccupation with sex providers, I cite a delightfully revealing passage from the article 'Iṣmat-farōshī'.

> This woman—a bawd first, a woman second—gives her body over to the man in lieu of a few coins, but a body bereft of her soul in those moments. Listen to what one such woman has to say: 'Men take me out into the fields. I just lie there, immobile, without a sound—dead inert, only my eyes are open, gazing far, far into the distance, where some she-goats are going at one another under the shade of the trees. Oh, what an idyllic scene! I start counting the she-goats, or the ravens on the branches—nineteen, twenty, twenty-one, twenty-two . . . Meanwhile the man is finished, withdrawn, and is panting heavily some distance from me. But I'm not aware of any of this' (p. 160).

This reminds me of the scene from Milan Kundera's novel *The Book of Laughter and Forgetting*,* where Tamina has surrendered her body to this 'nice guy' Hugo, not because she is after sex, but because he has promised to bring back to her the diaries she left behind in Prague when she and her now deceased husband had escaped from Czechoslovakia. They contain her memories of their life together, all those yearly vacations they took. 'But when she was fully naked, Hugo [. . .] was stupefied to discover that Tamina's genitals were dry' (p. 108). And when he goes into action, Tamina

> quickly shut her eyes. Once again she began going through the vacations, like irregular verbs: first the vacation at the lake, then Yugoslavia, the lake, and the spa—or was it the spa, Yugoslavia, and the lake?—then the Tatras, then Bulgaria, then things got hazy, then Prague, the spa, and finally Italy (pp. 110–11)†.

Why has Tamina succumbed to Hugo—Tamina, who loved her husband dearly, and is described by the narrator touchingly as: 'I picture

---

* Translated from the Czech by Michael Henry Heim (New York: Penguin, 1984).

† Earlier, when undergoing a minor surgery without anesthesia, Tamina had 'forced herself to conjugate English irregular verbs' through the procedure to kill the ensuing pain (ibid., p. 109).

the world growing up around Tamina like a circular wall, and I picture
her as a small patch of grass down below. The only rose growing on that
patch of grass is the memory of her husband'(p. 83).

Doesn't this sound like a cruel paradox?

All seven parts of Kundera's novel defy our conventional notions
about the form of the novel, as they are held together polyphonically
by two dominant themes, 'laughter' and 'forgetting', returning to them
in umpteen variations. Eroticism, though liberally spattered, is not a
dominant theme of this novel, but, as Kundera explained to Philip Roth,
'I have the feeling that a scene of physical love generates an extremely
sharp light which suddenly reveals the essence of characters and sums
up their life situation' (p. 236).

So what we have in 'Iṣmat-farōshī' and *Laughter and Forgetting*
are experiences of two different women: one a prostitute, the other a
but widowed woman. What is common between the two experiences
is the subjects' total state of apathy during lovemaking. Even as they go
through the motions—one, because her livelihood depends on it, and
the other because she sees no other way to get hold of her diaries so
redolent of the memory of her dead husband—each denies herself any
pleasure from the act by subtly turning off her sense of touch, her ability
to feel and reciprocate, in what one might describe as a self-induced
semi-comatose state. Instead, each subverts the whole meaning of the
act, one by counting she-goats, the other by going through all those
many vacations taken with a husband who is no more.

In short, neither heart nor soul is involved in the act being performed
on their bodies. On his first diplomatic assignment in Rangoon (now
Burma), Pablo Neruda—according to the reconstructed fictionalized
biography of the poet by Roberto Ampuero*—used to round up a bunch
of whores for something like an orgy. The whores went wild with sexual
pleasure inside the undulating mosquito net, but the poet was never sure
about their response and found it terribly frustrating. 'It sounds exciting,'
the poet said, 'but in truth it's not so much in the end. I only entered
their bodies, never their souls. Understand? I always succumbed like an
exhausted castaway before the unconquerable walls of those graceful,
mysterious women' (p. 51). In other words, the soul was missing, with

---

* *The Neruda Case*, translated by Carolina de Robertis (New York: Riverhead Books,
2012), 51.

the noticeable difference that while the Burmese whores seemed to enjoy what they were doing, Manto's vaishiya and Kundera's Tamina did not.

Paradoxically, but no less poignantly, it is 'love' that has determined their identical response of apathy, their sensual paralysis. For one, it is a love longed-for, shimmering somewhere in some hopefully not-too-distant future when the right man comes her way. For the other, it is a love which circumstances have chosen to snatch away from her—it is not as though the ability to love, and to enjoy lovemaking with the man she loves, never existed. Tamina knows that the demands of her body will make it impossible to go on without a mate, whom she may grow to love some day. The vaishiya also knows that she will find a man with whom what she now does for a living will assume a different meaning, an utterly satisfying flavour.

I see Manto in the court, with all his disarming innocence and perplexity, asking the judge: 'Your Honour, where is there any obscenity in all this?'